Towards a Sustainable Economy

The Sustainable Development Goals (SDGs) were introduced by the United Nations (UN) for all member nations with a total of 17 goals and 169 targets to be achieved between 2016 and 2030. The recent pandemic has presented more challenges to achieving the UN's SDGs. This book examines Bangladesh's ascendancy in socio-economic terms and the prospects of Bangladesh overcoming the challenges to become a higher-middle-income nation by 2030.

This book traces the transformation of Bangladesh from 1996 through 2020 and examines various factors contributing to its success from rural economy, external support, manufacturing, and structural transformation to energy consumption. This book also looks at the challenges and opportunities for Bangladesh as the Fourth Industrial Revolution unfolds and as climate change, to which Bangladesh is highly vulnerable, escalates.

This book will be a useful reference document for those who are interested in gaining more insights into inclusive growth and sustainable development from the case study of Bangladesh.

Moazzem Hossain has taught at Griffith University, Australia, since 1990 and he holds an adjunct associate professorial position presently in the Department of Business Strategy and Innovation (BSI), Griffith Business School at Griffith University, Australia. He was the inaugural Sheikh Mujibur Rahman (SMR) Professorial Fellow at University of Hull, UK, in 2000. Currently he is the chairman of the Board of Trustees of the University of Skill Enrichment and Technology (USET), Narayangonj, Bangladesh.

Qazi Kholiquzzaman Ahmad is widely known at home and abroad as a renowned economist. He was the founding chairman of Bangladesh Unnayan Parishad (BUP). He is currently the chairman of the Palli Karma-Sahayak Foundation (PKSF) and the Dhaka School of Economics (DScE). He was the elected president of the Bangladesh Economic Association (BEA) for three consecutive terms (2002–2010).

Mazharul M Islam has been working at the Department of Chemistry of Cardiff University UK since 2021.

Routledge Studies in Development Economics

Human Capital and Gender Inequality in Middle-Income Countries
Schooling, Learning and Socioemotional Skills in the Labour Market
Elizabeth M. King and Dileni Gunewardena

Digital Financial Inclusion and Regulation
Ogochukwu Monye

Household Demand for Consumer Goods in Developing Countries
A Comparative Perspective with Developed Countries
Eliyathamby A. Selvanathan, Saroja Selvanathan, and Maneka Jayasinghe

Unlocking Private Investment in Sustainable Infrastructure in Asia
Edited by Bhajan Grewal, Nella Hendriyetty, Iskandar Abdullaev, Chul Ju Kim, Naoyuki Yoshino, and Eisa Khan Ayoob Ayoob

The Political Economy of Bilateral Aid
Implications for Global Development
Peter Blunt with Cecilia Escobar and Vlassis Missos

Development and Economic Growth in India
Drivers for Indian States
Biswa Swarup Misra

Towards a Sustainable Economy
The Case of Bangladesh
Edited by Moazzem Hossain, Qazi Kholiquzzaman Ahmad and Mazharul M Islam

Development as Swaraj
Towards a Sustainable and Equitable Future
Sumanas Koulagi

For more information about this series, please visit: www.routledge.com/Routledge-Studies-in-Development-Economics/book-series/SE0266

Towards a Sustainable Economy

The Case of Bangladesh

Edited by Moazzem Hossain, Qazi Kholiquzzaman Ahmad, and Mazharul M Islam

Routledge
Taylor & Francis Group
LONDON AND NEW YORK

First published 2023
by Routledge
4 Park Square, Milton Park, Abingdon, Oxon OX14 4RN

and by Routledge
605 Third Avenue, New York, NY 10158

Routledge is an imprint of the Taylor & Francis Group, an informa business

British Library Cataloguing-in-Publication Data
A catalogue record for this book is available from the British Library

ISBN: 978-1-032-14006-3 (hbk)
ISBN: 978-1-032-14007-0 (pbk)
ISBN: 978-1-003-23191-2 (ebk)

DOI: 10.4324/9781003231912

Typeset in Galliard
by MPS Limited, Dehradun

Bangabandhu Sheikh Mujibur Rahman

Father of Bangladesh Nation

On His 100th Birth Anniversary, 2020

Contents

Figures

Images

Tables

Contributors

Dr. Moazzem Hossain taught environmental economics, development and trade in the Department of Business Strategy and Innovation (BSI), Griffith Business School (GBS) at Griffith University over 1990 and 2016 and retired as an associate professor. He is in an adjunct position until June 2023. With his Griffith position, he supervised 12 PhD scholars and numerous master's and honors students. His major research includes climate change issues in the Asia-Pacific, including the Bay of Bengal delta and Sundarbans region. He was a visiting fellow in various European and US academic institutions including the University of London; University of Sussex; University of Hull; Institute of Social Studies, The Hague; University of Heidelberg; and Boston University since 1991. Dr. Hossain has produced 15 authored and edited volumes about South Asian economic development, economic reforms, telecommunications reform, climate change and growth in Asia, climate change, and the realization of Asian century. South-South migration and Pathways to a sustainable economy published by the prestigious Routledge, Edward Elgar and Springer Nature over the last 25 years. Additionally, Dr. Hossain published two volumes on the *Political Economy of Bangladesh: Bangladesh's Development Agenda and Vision 2021* and *Democracy's Roller Coaster Ride in Bangladesh.* Both volumes were published by the Dhaka based the University Press Limited (UPL) in 2003 and 2009, respectively. Dr. Hossain published in several world-class journals such as the *Journal of Applied Economics, South Asia Research, Disaster Management Journal, Singapore Economic Review, South Asian Journal of the South Asian Studies Association of Australia, International Journal of Environment, Australian Economic Papers*, and *World Association of Sustainable Development (WASD)* journals. Dr. Hossain was awarded the Sheikh Mujibur Rahman (SMR) Professorial Fellowship, out of an open search worldwide, by the University Hull, UK, in 2000. He is the founding chairman of the Trustee Board of the University of Skill Enrichment and Technology (USET), in Narayangonj, approved by the Bangladesh government and University Grants Commission (UGC) in August 2019. Dr. Hossain was nominated by the Australian Government as an expert reviewer of the IPCC's Sixth Assessment Report (AR 6) and related materials. He graduated from Bangladesh Agricultural

University (BAU), Mymensingh in agricultural economics (Hons.) in 1972. He was awarded first class in his post-graduate degree program in agricultural marketing in 1973 from BAU. He has completed a master's in agricultural development economics (MADE) degree from the Australian National University (ANU) with distinction, Canberra in 1978 and a PhD in agricultural economics at the University of Western Australia (UWA), Perth in 1986.

Dr. Qazi Kholiquzzaman Ahmad is widely known at home and abroad as a renowned economist. He was the founder chairman of Bangladesh Unnayan Parishad (BUP). He is currently the chairman of Palli Karma-Sahayak Foundation (PKSF) and Dhaka School of Economics (DScE). He was elected president of the Bangladesh Economic Association (BEA) for three consecutive terms (2002–2010). He has served on the Syndicate, Senate and/ or Academic Council of University of Dhaka, Bangladesh University of Engineering and Technology (BUET), Jahangirnagar University, and Shahjalal University of Science and Technology. Dr. Ahmad is also known for his expertise in global climate change affairs. He was a lead/coordinating lead author of the Inter-governmental Panel on Climate Change (IPCC) for the Third and Fourth Assessments (completed in 2001 and 2007, respectively) and also a member of the UNFCCC Clean Development Mechanism (CDM) Executive Board (2009–2014). He has represented Bangladesh in many international fora and conferences on climate change and other issues. Dr. Ahmad has been relentlessly working on both theory and practice of sustainable development. He has to his credit, 39 books and over 250 articles as author, co-author, editor, or co-editor, published at home and abroad, both in English and Bengali languages. Dr. Ahmad is a freedom fighter; he participated in the Bangladesh War of Liberation in 1971. He is the recipient of the Highest Bangladesh National Civilian Award 'Swadhinota Puroshkar' (Independence Award).

Dr. Mazharul M Islam has been working as a senior researcher at the Department of Chemistry of the University of Cardiff, UK, since July 2021. He has completed his BSc (Hons) and MSc in chemistry from Dhaka University, Bangladesh in 1999 and 2001, respectively. He has receivedhis PhD in theoretical chemistry from the University of Hannover, Germany in July 2005 with the 'George-Christoph-Lichtenberg' Scholarship of the Land Niedersachsen. As of 2022, Dr. Islam has over 17 years of experience as a research associate and senior research fellow in computational chemistry. Prior to joining Cardiff, Dr. Islam has worked as a senior researcher at the University of Bath between 2018–2021, as senior research fellow between 2010–2018 at the Mulliken Center for Theoretical Chemistry of the University of Bonn, as postdoc at ENSCP, CNRS, Paris between 2007–2010, as a visiting researcher at the University of Milano in 2009, and as a research associate at the University of South Australia between 2005–2007. Over the years, he has gained vast experience in the computational simulation of a wide variety of materials having practical applications in daily lives through interdisciplinary research areas including (i) energy materials such as batteries and solar energy; (ii) investigation of photocatalytic activities of TiO_2; (iii) materials for construction, transportation, power generation etc.; and (iv) catalyst materials based on mesoporous oxides. He has the expertise to teach many courses in chemistry and materials science including theoretical and computational chemistry, inorganic chemistry, materials science, solid-state chemistry, and energy materials for undergraduate and postgraduate levels. Dr. Islam has been active for the initiation of the Theoretical and Computational Chemistry Department at Dhaka University since 2016. He has designed the following courses: Introduction to Computational Chemistry, Quantum Mechanics, Solid-State Chemistry, Chemistry of Surfaces and Interfaces, Fundamentals of Nanomaterials, Energy (production, storage and conversion), Green Catalysis, and Modern Computational Organic Chemistry. He has taught a course on computational chemistry for MSc students there in 2016–17. To date, Dr. Islam has achieved over 55 publications in internationally reputed peer-reviewed journals, published and edited 6 books, and written 5 book chapters.

Dr. Syed Ali Abbas is a lecturer in economics in the School of Management at Cardiff Metropolitan University, Wales, United Kingdom. He studied MSc economics and finance and later MS economics from Lahore School of Economics, Pakistan. He then earned an MPhil degree in economics from Bond University, Australia and later received a doctoral degree in economics from Griffith University, Australia. He has worked as a research and teaching associate at Lahore School of Economics and at the Forman Christian College (A Chartered University), Pakistan.

Dr. Samsul Alam is a leading expert with experience in creating real-world impact around his research areas: carbon economics, economic development, sustainable tourism development, and business sustainability. One of his recent research papers titled: "Does board gender diversity affect renewable energy consumption" has become sensational and is highlighted in more than 50 international news outlets around the world, including *Forbes, Yahoo News!, The Guardian,* and *The Telegraph.* More importantly, he had published top journals in his research areas, including *Journal of Corporate Finance, Annals of Travel Research, Energy Economics Journal of Business Ethics,* and *International Financial Review.* Besides academic research, he has extensive experience of practical research with practitioners and policymakers.

Rubaiyat Shaimom Chowdhury is an assistant professor of finance at Bangladesh University, Dhaka, Bangladesh, and a PhD fellow at the Faculty of Applied and Human Sciences, University Malaysia Perlis (UniMAP), Malaysia. He has his bachelor's (BBA) and MBA degree in finance from the University of Dhaka and earned his MSc in economics with a major in econometrics from North South University. Rubaiyat is a capital market researcher and investment expert in Bangladesh. With a diverse research interest in finance, he has published articles in different renowned peer-reviewed journals. Currently, his research field is Fintech.

Dr. Paul Howard was previously the program director for the bachelor of Asian studies and is a lecturer within the Department of Business Strategy and Innovation at Griffith University (Nathan Campus – Brisbane, Australia). Dr. Howard is a member of the Griffith Asia Institute. His research broadly focuses on policy and development in Asia. More specifically, his current research focuses on the political economy of sanitation in Asia, with a specific focus on India and Cambodia. The interplay between formal policy and actual outcomes for citizens is an area of interest. Dr. Howard also has research interests in specific aspects of political economy and development in the region. This focus has included research on China's climate policy, the development of renewable energy in the region, and worker migration and development in the Mekong sub-region.

Dr. M Mozammel Huq: a graduate of the Universities of Rajshahi (BA Hons and MA) and Glasgow (MLitt and PhD), he has taught for over 40 years at the University of Strathclyde and part-time for several years at the University of Glasgow. His career also includes some early teaching involvements in Bangladesh and, on a visiting capacity, some short teaching periods in Ghana (University of Cape Coast), Nigeria (University of Nigeria), Tanzania (Institute of Finance Management), India (Raiganj University), Pakistan (Government College University Lahore), and Nepal (Nepal Academy of Science and Technology). Currently, he is also a visiting professor of economics at Uttar Bangla University College (Northern Bangladesh). On a UN Consultancy, during the late 1980s and the early 1990s, at Bangladesh Institute of Development Studies (Dhaka), he directed a major research project on technology transfer and evaluation, closely surveying three industry sectors of Bangladesh: leather, fertilizer, and machinery manufacturing. He also served as a consultant to several national and international organizations including the Bangladesh Planning Commission, Commonwealth Secretariat, DFID, EU, and ILO. He is the author of several books including *The Economy of Ghana: 50 Years of Economic Development* (Palgrave Macmillan, London, 2018, 2nd edition, with M Tribe as an associate author); *The Social Safety-Net and the Attack on Extreme Poverty* (Routledge, London 2014, co-author A Clunies-Ross); *Development Economics* (McGraw-Hill, London, 2009, co-authors A Clunies-Ross and D Forsyth); *The Economy of Ghana: The First 25 Years since Independence* (Macmillan, London, 1989); three books on industry studies focusing on technology issues published in the early 1990s (University Press Ltd, Dhaka); and several edited volumes including *Science, Technology and Development: North-South Cooperation* (Frank Cass, London, 1991); *Strategies for Industrialization: The Case of Bangladesh* (UPL, Dhaka, 2000); *Technology and Development in the New Millennium* (Karachi

University Press, Karachi); and *Building Technological Capability: Issues and Prospects* (UPL, Dhaka, 2003). Other works have also appeared in journals such as *World Development, Journal of International Development, Bangladesh Development Studies, Science Technology and Development, Bangladesh Journal of Agricultural Economics,* and *Pakistan Development Review.*

Dr. A M Muazzam Husain possesses an extensive experience as a university professor in agricultural economics, and as a pioneering researcher and activist in the fields of rural development, policy research, poverty reduction, and as an environment worker in Bangladesh. He received a PhD from Texas A & M University (USA), 1964 and B.A. (Hon) and M.A. in economics, from Dhaka University, in 1957 and 1958, respectively. Professor Husain commenced working at Bangladesh Agricultural University (BAU) in 1964 as a senior lecturer in the Faculty of Agricultural Economics and Rural Sociology. He served as dean of this faculty for two terms and as director of planning and development over his long career with this university. He was a research specialist and then research director for BRAC and finally worked as a chairperson in the Department of Economics and Social Sciences at BRAC University. He participated in a large number of consultancy services for both national organizations including the planning commission and other ministries of the government, and international organizations such as the DFID, UNDP, WFP, World Bank, FAO, Ford Foundation, ILO, GTZ, Oxfam GB, CARE, WorldFISH, Concern, and IRRI. He has worked as an expert member in a good number of national-level committees on development planning, rural development, poverty alleviation, and small farmer development. Professor Husain was awarded a post-doctoral fellowship in 1979 for one year by the Agricultural Development Council, Inc (Winrock International) to work at Wye College, UK. Professor Husain's major publications include: Husain AMM. *Some reflections on the impact of micro-finance in Bangladesh.* CDF Newsletter 2000 Mar–Jun; 8:6–9; Husain AMM. *Study on poultry vaccination and artificial insemination: an example of Government-NGO collaboration.* Access 2000, Jan; 33:14–5; Hossain M, Janaiah A, Husain AMM, and Naher F. *The Rice Seed Delivery System in Bangladesh: Institutional and Policy Issues,* Bangladesh Dev Studies. 2001, Dec xxvii (4): 1–40; Husain AMM, Hossain M, and Janaiah A. *Socio-economic assessment of hybrid rice adoption by farmers in Bangladesh.* AGREN Newsletter 2001 Jul; 44:2; Husain AMM. *Agricultural development in Bangladesh and the role and effectiveness of NGOs: the case of BRAC.* Farm Economy (The Journal of the Bangladesh Agricultural Economists Association). n.d. 11:27–42; Husain AMM. *Bangladesh agriculture in 2020: review of trends and potentials for growth.* In: Hossain M, Nabi AKMN, Islam I. Bangladesh's development agenda and vision 2020. Dhaka: The University Press Limited, 2003:77-90; Husain, A.M. Muazzam. *A Sustainable Method of Rice Cultivation for Bangladesh: The System of Rice Intensification (SRI).* Bangladesh Journal of Political Economy,

Vol. 24, Nos. 1 and 2. Dhaka: December 2008: Pp. 643–661; Mushtaque Chowdhury, Muazzam Husain, Md. A. Saleque, Hugh Brammer. *From the Ground Up: BRAC's Innovations in the Development of Agriculture in Bangladesh and Beyond*. The University Press Ltd. Dhaka: December 2019.

Dr. Shafiqul Islam is an academic and a well-known practitioner around the areas of climate change adaptation, disaster risk reduction, sustainable environment, public policy, and local government. He holds a doctor of philosophy in environmental science, awarded by Griffith University in 2020; his thesis dissertation was "The Challenges and Opportunities in Integrating Disaster Risk Reduction and Climate Change Adaptation in Bangladesh from a Political Economy Perspective". During his PhD, he published six research articles in a few reputed international journals. He has demonstrated his ability to teach and train employees in the Ministry of Finance, Government of Bangladesh. He is a high-ranked government official and has been working in various important leading role in the Ministry of Finance, the Ministry of Public Administration, the Ministry of Local Government, and the Ministry of Disaster Management in Bangladesh.

Dr. Maneka Jayasinghe is the head of business discipline and senior lecturer in economics at the Asia Pacific College of Business and Law at Charles Darwin University, Darwin, Australia. She has also taught previously at Griffith University (Australia). She was educated at the Griffith University (Australia), National University of Singapore, and University of Colombo (Sri Lanka). She is an applied economist, and her research interests include poverty and wellbeing, consumer demand analysis, energy economics, and tourism analysis. She has published two research monographs and numerous articles in leading international refereed journals such as *Energy Economics, Journal of Travel Research, Applied Economics, Economic Record, Social Indicators Research, International Journal of Tourism Research,* and a number book chapters with leading publishers.

Dr. Ripon Kumar Mondal is an associate professor in the Department of Agricultural Economics, Sher-e-Bangla Agricultural University, Dhaka, Bangladesh. He also worked as an economist at the Food and Agriculture Organization of the United Nations. He received his PhD in economics from the Griffith Business School, Griffith University, Australia, and Master of Economics from Kobe University, Japan. His interested research areas covered agricultural economics, applied economics, food security, agriculture transformation, and economic development focusing on developing countries.

Dr. M K Mujeri received a PhD in economics from McMaster University in Canada in 1978 after his graduation from Rajshahi University, Bangladesh in 1970. Currently, he is the executive director of the Institute for Inclusive Finance and Development in Dhaka. During his professional career, Dr. Mujeri has worked in different institutions including director general of

Bangladesh Institute of Development Studies (BIDS) in Dhaka, chief economist of Bangladesh Bank (central bank), Poverty Monitoring and Analysis Advisor of UNDP in Cambodia, project leader of IDRC's Programme of Micro Impact of Macroeconomic and Adjustment Policies (MIMAP) in Bangladesh, director of research at the Centre on Integrated Rural Development for Asia and the Pacific (CIRDAP), visiting faculty at Department of Economics, University of Queensland, Brisbane, national expert in Bangladesh Planning Commission, and associate professor of economics, Rajshahi University. He has wide-ranging experience in research on development issues and has published widely in professional journals. His recently published books include *Bangladesh's Quest for Inclusive Development: Challenges and Pathways* (Routledge, 2022), *Structural Transformation of Bangladesh Economy: A South Asian Perspective* (Springer, 2021), and *Bangladesh at Fifty: Moving beyond Development Traps* (Palgrave Macmillan, 2020).

Dr. Saroja Selvanathan is a professor of econometrics at Griffith University, Queensland, Australia. She has also taught previously at the University of Jaffna (Sri Lanka), Murdoch University (Australia), and The University of Western Australia. She was educated at the University of Jaffna, Murdoch University and The University of Western Australia. She is the co-editor in chief of the *Journal of the Asia Pacific Economy.* Her research interests include consumer demand, time series analysis, energy economics, tourism economics, and applied econometrics. She has published six research monographs and over 75 journal articles. Her publications have appeared in internationally refereed journals, such as *Review of Economics and Statistics, Energy Economics, Resource Economics, Economic Modelling, Journal of Travel Research, Tourism Analysis,* and *Tourism Economics.* She is a co-author of the Australian best-selling textbook, *Business Statistics,* published by Cengage.

Dr. Eliyathamby A Selvanathan is the director of the Economics Policy Analysis Program (EPAP) and professor of econometrics at Griffith University, Queensland, Australia. He has also taught previously at the University of Jaffna (Sri Lanka), Murdoch University (Australia), and The University of Western Australia. He was educated at the University of Jaffna, Bucharest University (Romania), Murdoch University, and The University of Western Australia. He is one of the authors of the best-selling textbook *Business Statistics* published by Cengage. His research interests include applied econometrics, tourism economics, energy economics, consumer demand models, and stochastic index numbers. He has published nine research monographs and well over 125 articles in leading journals such as *Review of Economic Studies, Journal of Econometrics, Journal of Business and Economic Statistics, Review of Economics and Statistics, Energy Economics, Journal of Travel Research,* and *Tourism Economics.*

Dr. S. M. Sohrab Uddin is a professor at the Department of Finance, Faculty of Business Administration, University of Chittagong, Bangladesh. He obtained a BBA and MBA from the University of Chittagong, and MBA and PhD from Ritsumeikan Asia Pacific University, Oita, Japan. His research areas focus on financial market, institutions, and instruments with particular emphasis on banking sector development including Islamic finance in developing countries.

Preface

At the beginning of the 21st century the United Nations introduced the Millennium Development Goals (MDGs) initiative for its developing and less developed member nations to attain eight goals related to poverty eradication, education, health, growth, and development during 2000–2015. Given mixed achievements related to MDGs and in view of worsening disparity nationally and across nations and intensifying climate change, the United Nations adopted a second plan of action in 2015, called 2030 Agenda for Sustainable Development or, in short, SDGs for all member nations with 17 goals to be implemented from 2016 and 2030.

As the implementation of the SDGs was shaping up around the world, suddenly the world was turned upside down by the COVID-19 global pandemic starting in early 2020. Consequently, economies of all nations were shattered. Only a handful of countries, including two in Asia, Bangladesh and China, posted fairly respectable positive GDP growth rates in the wake of the devastations caused by the pandemic.

In this edited volume, there are some analyses on how socio-economic and other aspects of development of Bangladesh progressed in the era of MDGs under various domestic and international uncertainties with a high population (currently about 170 million) and how the country has been shaping up since, weathering the new challenges given by the COVID-19 pandemic.

It may be noted that just as four years of the implementation of the SDGs programme was completed, COVID-19 struck in March 2020. It is not certain when will this pandemic end. The impacts of COVID-19 on the economies of the developing world are hard to predict since the rolling out of vaccines in the different developing regions remains slow. Bangladesh is, in fact, one of the exceptions in this regard. However, the coming years face uncertainties for all the countries of the world, even more so now because of the Ukraine war.

The overall aim of this volume is to look back on how Bangladesh has performed over the past two decades or so, particularly since 2000, and how the prospects look like in the next decade and beyond. Why a study on Bangladesh? This is the only nation in this region that has been posting positive economic growth rates over the last two years, despite the adverse effects of the COVID-19 pandemic. According to the IMF, Bangladesh achieved a GDP growth rate of

4.3 per cent in fiscal 2020. Of course, Bangladesh has suffered a decline, too, as the GDP growth rate declined by 3.85 percentage points in fiscal 2020 from 8.15 per cent in fiscal 2019.

All three editors of this volume have been publishing on Bangladesh's development issues over many years, both domestically and internationally. Dr. Moazzem Hossain published 15 authored and edited volumes with top international publishing houses including Routledge over the last 30 years. He commenced publishing with Routledge with back-to-back volumes in the mid-1990s. The first project was an edited volume with a law colleague about privatization with reference to selected nations titled, *Who Benefits from Privatization?* in 1998. The second project was an authored volume with two colleagues in development studies called *South Asian Economic Development (SAED)*; the first edition was published in 1999. The second edition of *SAED* with the invitation of Routledge was published in 2010. The fourth, an edited volume published by Routledge entitled *South-South Migration* was published with two colleagues from social sciences in 2017. The rest of the volumes were joint works published by Edward Elgar, Nova Science, and Springer Nature over 2000 and 2018. Dr. Qazi Kholiquzzaman Ahmad has so far published (authored/co-authored/edited) 43 books and over 250 articles on diverse subjects, in Bangladesh and internationally (e.g., NOVA, Springer, Taylor & Francis and Pearson Education).

With this brief background of our journey in publishing with Routledge and other reputed international publishers, it is our intention to explore how the countries of this region have been performing over the period of the MDGs and moving on to the implementation of the SDGs. More importantly, it is now confirmed from various sources in the region that the COVID-19 pandemic has severely destabilized the regional economies; except that Bangladesh is making a rather solid recovery in an overall sense. In fact, even while Bangladesh is recovering in an appreciable manner, the nation has a good deal to make up to be back on a pre-pandemic track in terms of even economic growth. Social sectors are lagging with education facing major challenges in overcoming the setbacks.

M.H, Q.K.A and M.M.I
Dhaka, June 22

Acknowledgements

The present volume has come out of an international conference held in Dhaka in October 2018 to commemorate the 100th birth anniversary of the Father of Bangladesh Nation, Bangabandhu (Friend of Bengal) Sheikh Mujibur Rahman. This is the third volume that has been prepared as was planned at the conference. The first was published in early 2020 by Nova Publishing, NY, and the second by Springer Nature, Switzerland, in late 2020. These are: *Climate Adaptation for a Sustainable Economy: Lessons from Bangladesh, an Emerging Tiger of Asia*, pp. 310 and *Science and Technology Innovation for a Sustainable Economy*, pp. 197. The present and third volume contains 13 chapters under five parts.

These are: PART I presents an overview of Bangladesh's development in retrospect and prospect, particularly since the beginning of the MDGs programme in 2000: an introduction and chapter 1. PART II contains chapters 2 to 6 on the transformation of the economy over the period, 2000–2020. These chapters have analyzed how Bangladesh has been transforming over the last two decades in economic and social terms, including a piece presenting the impact of COVID-19 on the ready-made garments industry. PART III deals with issues of innovation and opportunities created before the pandemic hit the world in early 2020, chapters 7–9. PART IV identifies the challenges the economy would face as it moves towards 2030. The challenges to prosperity due to the impact of sudden global catastrophe (the COVID-19 pandemic) have been presented in chapters 10–12. Finally, PART V contains chapter 13, which presents conclusions.

As mentioned earlier, this volume is one of three volumes that has come out of an international conference on "Pathways to a Sustainable Economy: Vision 2041 Agenda for Bangladesh" held in Dhaka, Bangladesh in October 2018. The conference was supported by an organizing committee formed and represented by Palli Karma-Sahayak Foundation (PKSF), Dhaka; University Grants Commission (UGC); Jagannath University (JU); Bangladesh Foundation for Development Research (BFDR), Dhaka; Griffith University, Brisbane, Australia; Bonn University, Bonn; and Bremen University, Bremen, Germany. There were 21 papers presented at the conference over two days, including inaugural and concluding sessions.

We wish to record our sincere appreciation to PKSF for playing a major role and to its staff who worked tirelessly to ensure that more than 150 delegates from different parts of Bangladesh and 10 international speakers from Australia, the United Kingdom, the United States, and Germany enjoyed two packed days of parallel and discussion sessions with productive interaction between presenters and audiences.

We acknowledge the personal support and encouragement of Dr. Jashim Uddin, deputy general manager of the PKSF, and Mr Monaem Sarker, director general of the BFDR. Both PKSF and BFDR shared logistic support for running the conference smoothly.

We must also acknowledge the chairs of the several scientific sessions. They are Professor Mijanur Rahman (former VC, JU); Professor Mesbahuddin Ahmed, Dhaka University; Professor Haseena Khan, Dhaka University; and Professor Giasuddin Miah (VC, BSMRAU). Panel discussant for the Science and Technology Panel was Eng A K M Hameed (President IDEB) and for Social Science and Business Panel was Professor Atiqul Islam (VC, North South University).

Finally, we wish to sincerely thank Professors Selva Selvanathan and Saroja Selvanathan of Griffith University, Australia, for extending editorial support to selected chapters based on quantitative modelling. Professor Shafi Ahmed of PKSF has extended English editorial support in preparing the conference materials. Mr. Jyotirmay Debnath, executive secretary to chairman, Dhaka School of Economics (DScE) provided secretarial assistance over 2018 and 2022 with his excellent skill in managing the manuscript.

M.H, Q.K.A and M.M.I
Dhaka, June 2022

Part I
Overview

Introduction

Moazzem Hossain

1 Introduction

At the beginning of the 21st century, the United Nations introduced a development initiative called Millennium Development Goals (MDGs) which contained eight targets for the less developed member nations to be able to enjoy better livelihoods in the future. This program was commenced in 2000 and the eight targets expected to be achieved by 2015 (UNESCAP, 2019). The targets were, in short:

1 Eradicate extreme poverty and hunger: Halve, by 2015 from 1990 level.
2 Achieve universal primary education: Ensure that, by 2015, children everywhere, boys and girls, will be able to complete a full course of primary schooling.
3 Promote gender equity and empower women: Eliminating gender disparity in primary and secondary education, preferable by 2005 and in all levels of education no later than 2015.
4 Reduce child mortality: Reduce by two-thirds, from 1990 level, the under 5 mortality rate.
5 Improved maternal health: Reduce by three-fourths, between 1990 and 2015, the maternal mortality rate.
6 Combat HIV/AIDS, malaria, and other diseases: Have halted by 2015, and began to reverse, the spread of HIV/AIDS.
7 Ensure environmental sustainability: Halve, by 2015, the proportion of people without sustainable access to safe drinking water. Have achieved, by 2020, a significant improvement in the lives of at least 100 million slum dwellers.
8 Develop a global partnership for development. (see detail in Hossain, 2007; Baird and Shetty, 2003).

Given the mixed achievement in attaining the eight targets at the conclusion of the MDGs in 2015, the United Nations adopted a second plan of action in September 2015 called Sustainable Development Goals (SDGs), for all member nations with 17 goals to be achieved between 2016 and 2030. These are also

DOI: 10.4324/9781003231912-2

known as the 2030 Agenda (UN, 2015). In the middle of implementing the SDGs, suddenly the world was turned upside down by the COVID-19 pandemic in early 2020, likened to a once-in-a-century human-to-human transmitted virus. The World Health Organization (WHO), the lead global health sector agency of the United Nations, declared COVID-19 a pandemic on 11 March 2020 (WHO, 2021). Presently, the pandemic is out of control and has spread all over the world with confirmed cases of infection close to 112 million, out of which 2.4 million deaths have been recorded on 23rd February 2021 (WHO, 2021). The pandemic has contributed to a majority of individual country economies going into recession; the exceptions being nine nations, including two nations of Asia: China and Bangladesh.

In view of the above, this monograph aims at investigating Bangladesh's ascendancy in socio-economic terms, keeping in mind the performances under MDGs and SDGs from 2000 to 2019. Given this nation's solid progress over the last ten years (2009–2019) under the cover of "Vision 2021" and now in the middle of a pandemic, this volume examines the prospects of keeping prosperity sustained until Bangladesh's goal of becoming a middle-income nation by 2030, the concluding year of the SDGs. It must be remembered that the SDGs program was commenced in 2016 and having only nine more years to go to 2030. The million-dollar question is, when will the pandemic end? The impacts of COVID-19 on Bangladesh's economy are hard to predict since the rolling out of vaccines in this region remains relatively slow.

In view of the above, the overall aim of this volume is to make a medium to long-term assessment of the ascendancy of Bangladesh. Why Bangladesh? This is the only nation in South Asia, since the declaration of the pandemic, that has been posting economic growth. According to the IMF, this nation has achieved a GDP growth of 4.3 per cent in fiscal 2020. Of course, Bangladesh has suffered a decline, too. For example, the GDP declined by 3.4 per cent in fiscal 2020 from a strong growth of 8.2 per cent in fiscal 2019 (PC, 2020).

It is now confirmed from various sources like the International Monetary Fund (IMF) and the World Bank (WB) that, due to the 2020 pandemic, the South Asia region has taken a deep downturn economically except for Bangladesh. It occurs to the editors of this volume that the pandemic has thrown the region into an alarming position economically and health-wise. Moreover, the future remains uncertain in the short to medium term. Despite being one of the most populous nations in the region, and while reporting a reduction of almost half the prior year's economic growth in fiscal 2020 (8.2 in 2019, 4.3 in 2020), Bangladesh is the only nation in South Asia that has reported growth in fiscal 2020. Moreover, Bangladesh achieved significant economic progress in terms of GDP growth and per capita income over 2009–2019. The GDP growth was continuously at over 6 per cent per annum up to fiscal 2015, over 7 per cent in the following three years, and over 8 per cent in fiscal 2019. Per capita income increased from USD 781 in 2010 to USD 1,909 in 2019 and hit USD 2,236 in 2020. Significant improvements have been made in key social indicators, including poverty and extreme poverty ratios; infant, child, and maternal mortality rates; life expectancy at birth; and literacy rate.

The pandemic, however, has impacted the nation strongly. It would be interesting to assess the recovery and the growth trajectory in the short to medium term in years to come. Given that Bangladesh's growth has ranged from 6 to more than 8 per cent between 2009 and 2019, it certainly warrants a close look at the nation's hidden capacities to grow further in the post-pandemic period. The editors are of the view that, given Bangladesh's ascendancy over the last one and a half decades, this country certainly provides a developmental role model for South Asia. Bangladesh's developmental capability has recently been noted by its long-term political arch-rival Pakistan, which referred to the country with following words, "Fifty Years of Bangladesh: The Rising Sun! … . an inspiration and a challenge for policy makers, the story of Bangladesh is an unmatched development. The country's economic performance and all-round achievements are unprecedented in the region and worth emulating" (South Asia, March 2021).

It is indeed a prime time now to investigate the secrets of Bangladesh's miracle and lessons learned by other South Asian economies and beyond. Most recently, in the middle of a pandemic, Bangladesh celebrated its 50th year of independence (1971–2021). It appears that over the last 50 years the nation attracted friends and foreign investors from all over the world. More than 27 nations, including leaders from the United States, Canada, United Kingdom, Japan, South Korea, EU, Russia, and China made commitments in their messages to the leader of Bangladesh that they will keep investing for Bangladesh's prosperity to next 50 years. Moreover, leaders of India, Nepal, Maldives, and Bhutan have visited Bangladesh as state guests have established 100 industrial development parks all over the nation and invited the foreign businesses to take part with Bangladeshi counterparts engaged in international trade. This nation also is in the middle of building infrastructure with mega projects like the more than six kilometers long Padma Bridge, Karnafuli river tunnel, deep seaport, and metro rail projects in Dhaka. All these mega projects are scheduled to open for business by 2025 and 2030. All the leaders of these nations visited Bangladesh between 17 and 26 March 2021 in the middle of the COVID-19 pandemic and made commitments to become part of Bangladesh's ascendancy. There were 54 big businesses and foreign investors joined with their respective nations and committed with their counterparts in Bangladesh in international business collaboration in the future.

It is now universally accepted that sustainability is the game changer for both developing and more developed nations in the 21st century. A volume published by Princeton University Press entitled *Pursuing Sustainability* presents some thought-provoking issues about sustainability. The book made it clear that it will help support teaching and research which "deals with sustainability in particular sectors such as energy, food, water, and cities, or in particular regions of the world" (Matson, Clark, and Anderson, 2016). Among other things, the volume helps in working collaboratively in governance processes to influence how society takes actions to promote sustainability. Two issues are important in this respect: one, unlocking sustainable good governance process of a nation and two, society's actions toward promoting sustainability. Perhaps in these regards the interdisciplinary nature of sustainable development would play a major part to prosperity or wealth creation of nations (Matson, Clark, and Anderson, 2016).

In Bangladesh's context, the nation has been thrown into a transition process since 2009 in many respects: development (sustainable or not), transformation of society, sustainable good governance (both national and local) and so on. The major issue now is, the way changes are taking place at present, indeed, a transition to get rich or the nation is in the verge of having relative prosperity but seems kept the issue of equity or equality at bay. In the era of economic globalization over the last half a century, the equity issue has been certainly put on the back burner. The wealth distribution has been kept out of the growth equation in the sense that lets allow the cake (GDP) to grow, the distribution would look after itself. Unfortunately, this has not materialized anywhere in the past, even in China when unprecedented growth this nation witnessed over the last 40 years.

Having said that, let us come to the point of today's subject: sustainable growth and prosperity. Sustainable growth is important in the transition period of prosperity of a nation. Bangladesh is no exception. What is transition? It means we leave our past behind, enjoying a relative prosperity now and looking forward to a prosperous future (UN, 2019). All nations on earth went through such a process since the time of first Industrial Revolution, more than 200 years ago. According to many development experts, China, India, and other large nations, including former states of the Soviet Union, are in transition too.

All these countries have been looking forward to attaining prosperity in this era of globalization and information revolution (regardless the COVID-19 pandemic since 2020). One cannot deny the fact that sustainability has become the major issue for all transition states including Bangladesh. The most important issue under transition to prosperity is responsible and good governance, scientific innovations, and effective use of them to create wealth in a shortest possible time. In Bangladesh it is well known between 1975 and 1990, in both political and economic terms, the nation lost direction or those were one and a half lost decades. However, over the last quarter of a century or more, the political governments ruled, except between 2006 and 2008. There is no doubt that over the last decade, the democratic governance brought prosperity in several sectors such as food, transport, health and sanitation, education, macroeconomic stability, and so on. It is, however, hard to find many reforms that took place over this period with sustainability or to pursue sustainable growth and development.

In terms of the society's actions towards promoting sustainability and sustainable development, let us define sustainable development first. There are many ways sustainable development can be defined, the most used one was from the Report for World Commission on Environment and Development in 1987. "Sustainable development is development that meets the needs of the present without compromising the ability of future generations to meet their own needs" (Brundtland Report, 1987). This early version definition contains two important concepts: first is the concept of needs, which underlines that the world should prioritize the needs of the poor; second is the idea of limitations, which reminds the world that it should use resources available in the environment with technology and social organization in a responsible manner. As we know, after all those years, the United Nations, from Jan. 2016, introduced a global program called "Sustainable Development Goals (SDGs)" to 2030.

The global higher education development in modern times is the most important elements of any society, not only in giving or transferring knowledge, but this is also core centre for learning of all societies and its progress with applying scientific knowledge to the new ventures, keeping in mind the costs and benefits to the society and the nation at large. To estimate both social and economic costs and benefits of new innovations and discovery, sciences, social sciences, and other relevant disciplines play a major role (Brundtland Report, 1987; UN, 2019).

Bangladesh's specialized universities (agriculture, physical sciences, and technologies) immediately come to mind. Certainly, in agricultural sciences, the achievements over the last three decades have been overwhelming, keeping sustainability in crops and horticultural production. The time is right now to catch up by allowing science and technology-based institutions to make a breakthrough in attaining sustainable growth for prosperity (see more in Chapter 8 on agriculture).

Having said that, there is no denying the fact that the present government has been looking, over the last two terms, the makethe nation prepared for long-term prosperity. The Hon Prime Minister Sheikh Hasina has been talking about Vision 2041, which she thought, when Bangladesh has the potential to reach the ultimate dream of the Father of the Nation, Bangabandhu Sheikh Mujibur Rahman, to make the country a truly Sonar Bangla (Golden Bengal), a sustainable prosperous Bangladesh would be materialized. While to some it is tall talk, the PM is right to claim this, given the backdrop of making her Vision 2021 a reality, 2000–2021 (Hossain et al. 2003; Hossain et al. 2020; Islam et al. 2020). This agenda over the last 20 years surpassed all the records of the major socio-economic criteria articulated in Vision 2021, ahead of time. Given such a record under the belt, the government is convinced and highly positive about the outcome in the year 2041, given mega infrastructural projects currently being established, such as more than six-kilometre-long Padma Multipurpose Bridge, Dhaka Metro Rail, Karnafuli (under the River Tunnel), and so on. It has been predicted that the Padma Bridge alone would add almost additional 2 per cent per annum to GDP.

In view of the above, due to the present authors' professional interest, this volume would closely investigate sustainability issues of Bangladesh's future development. In one sentence, as we gathered, Bangladesh in 2041 would enter a golden age. Indeed, the momentum the nation gathered over the last ten years in both social and economic terms, the opportunities certainly have opened towards a prosperous 2041. This was also documented and predicted by many development scholars and agencies in recent years. For example, in 2017, a study by PriceWaterhouseCoopers suggested that Bangladesh is likely to become a $3 trillion economy, graduated from current 32nd to 23rd largest economy of the world by 2050. In other words, at par with Canadian economy and would become larger than the Australian economy. The prediction is, in the year 2050, the national income of Bangladesh would hit $3 trillion, Canada 3.1 trillion, and Australia less than 3 trillion (PriceWaterCoopers, 2017).

It is well known that Nobel Prize in economics in 2018 was won by two economists for their lifetime work on sustainable growth and impact of climate change on everyone's wellbeing. According to Paul Romer: research, education and skills are behind increased productivity which contributes to economic growth. Fellow Nobel Prize Winner William Nordhaus has suggested that nations,

> aimed mostly at obtaining a certain growth rate and ignoring the fact that many economic goods, such as natural resources and clean air, are hard to reproduce. Climate change and its effect in everyone's well-being is not a part of national accounts, while profits and GDP are.
>
> (see more in Popov, 2018)

In summary, both Nordhaus and Romer have contributed to the economics profession in the same way over long time. They recognized that economic growth should not be driven solely by putting more people into factories and getting more out of them. In other words, they pushed the ball to the court of political leaders and scientists to work out which way they should go now, whether to achieve speed of growth, or grow sustainably (Popov, 2018). In Bangladesh's case, the nation's carbon footprint is too low to register on the world radar at this moment, but it needs to develop the ever-expanding energy sector by opting for renewable energy. Sundram (2018), former assistant secretary general of the United Nations, has said, day by day, the cost of solar energy production is going down, and Bangladesh is in a better position than most to take this advantage now, connecting SMEs with solar power. One should emphasize that the SMEs would be the engines of growth over the next quarter of a century to 2041.

References

Ahluwalia, M.S. (1976). 'Inequality, Poverty and Development', *Journal of Development Economics*, 3: 307–342.

Alam, G. M. M., Alam, K., and Mushtaq, S. (2018). 'Drivers of Food Security of Vulnerable Rural Households in Bangladesh', *South Asia Economic Journal*, 19(1): 43–63.

Alam, M.S., Islam, M.S., Jawad, M., and Shazia, B. (2020). 'Rapid Rise of Life Expectancy in Bangladesh: Does Financial Development Matter?', *International Journal of Finance and Economics* (Undated).

Alam, S. and Planning Commission (2021). Eighth FYP: Crop, Livestock, Fisheries, Forest, Water Resource Management, Safe Food and Nutrition Security, presentation at BAEA virtual seminar, 3 July, Dhaka.

Anand, R., Mishra, S., and Peiris, J. S. (2013). *Inclusive Growth: Measurement and Determinants*, IMF Working Paper No. 13/135, International Monetary Fund, Washington D.C.

Baird and Shetty (2003). *Getting There: How to Accelerate Progress Toward the Millennium Development Goals*, IMF eLibrary, Washington DC.

Barro, A (2000). 'Inequality and Growth in a Panel of Countries', *Journal of Economic Growth*, 5: 5–32.

Brundtland Report (1987). *Our Common Future*, United Nations, Oxford University Press, Oxford and New York.

Cobham, A. and Sumner, A. (2013). *Putting the Gini Back in the Bottle? 'The Palma' as a Policy-Relevant Measure of Inequality*, King's College, London.

Commission on Growth and Development (2008). *Growth Report: Strategies for Sustained Growth and Inclusive Development*, World Bank, Washington D.C.

Cross, R. and Strachan, D. (2001). 'Three Pillars of Conventional Wisdom', *Review of Political Economy*, 13(2): 181–200.

Deininger, K. and Squire, L. (1998). 'New Ways of Looking at Old Issues: Inequality and Growth', *Journal of Development Economics*, 57: 259–287.

Dollar, D., Kleineberg, T., and Kraay, A. (2013). *Growth is Still Good for the Poor*, World Bank Policy Research Working Paper No. 6568, World Bank, Washington D.C.

Dollar, D. and Kraay, A. (2002). 'Growth is Good for the Poor', *Journal of Economic Growth*, 7(3): 195–225.

Fields, G. S. (1980). *Poverty, Inequality, and Development*, Cambridge University Press, New York.

Forbes, K. (2000). 'A Reassessment of the Relationship between Inequality and Growth', *American Economic Review*, 90: 869–897.

Foster, J., Greer, J., and Thorbecke, E. (1984). 'A Class of Decomposable Poverty Measures', *Econometrica*, 3. 52 (3): 761–766.

Gaventa, J. and Martorano, B. (2016). 'Inequality, Power and Participation – Revisiting the Links'. *IDS Bulletin*, 47, (5).

Hossain, M., Ahmad, Q. K., and Islam, M. (2020). *Climate Adaptation for a Sustainable Economy: Lessons from Bangladesh, an Emerging Tiger of Asia*, Nova Science Publishing, NY.

Hossain, M. (2007). "Human development and poverty alleviation in South East and East Asia: A post crisis account" in C. Tisdell (ed.), *Poverty, Poverty Alleviation and Social Disadvantage: Analysis, Case Studies and Policies*, Serials Publications, New Delhi, India.

Hossain, M., Nabi, N., and Islam, I. (2003). *Bangladesh's Vision 2021: Rhetoric or Reality*, University Press Limited, Dhaka, Bangladesh.

Huq, M. (2003). "Bangladesh Industrialisation for Sustained Output Growth, Employment Generation and Export Expansion: Implications of Performance since Independence" in M. Hossain, N. Nabi, and I. Islam (eds), *Bangladesh's Development Agenda and Vision 2020*, UPL, Dhaka 2003.

Huq, M. (2020). "Liberalised Trade Policy with State Commitment to Growth: The Case of Bangladesh" in M. Tribe (ed), *Economic Neoliberalism and International Development*, Routledge, London and New York, pp. 125–145.

Independent Group of Scientists Appointed by the Secretary-General, UN (2019). *Global Sustainable Development Report 2019: The Future is Now: Science for achieving sustainable development*, United Nation HQ, New York.

Islam, M. and Hossain, M. (2020). *Science and Technology Innovation for Sustainable Economy*, Springer Nature, Switzerland.

Khan, A. R. (2015). *The Economy of Bangladesh: A Quarter Century of Development*, Palgrave Macmillan, London.

Love, J. (1995). "Adoption of the Export-Led Growth Strategy in Bangladesh: Some Thoughts" in R. H. Grieve and M. Huq (eds.), *Bangladesh: Strategies for Development*, University Press Ltd, Dhaka.

Maston, P., Clark, W. C., and Anderson, K. (2016). *Pursuing Sustainability: A guide to science and practice*, Princeton University Press, Princeton and Oxford.

Planning Commission (2020). *Growth Performance of Agriculture Sub-Sector during the 7th FYP (2015–2019)*, Planning Commission, GOB.

Popov, S. (2018). October 9, Australian Edition, pp 1-4. https://the conversation.com/paul-romer-and-william-nordhaus-why-they-won-the-2018-economics-nobel-104588

PriceWaterCooper (2017). *Report on Bangladesh in 2050*, PriceWaterCooper, London, UK.

Robinson, E. A. G. (1973). *Economic Prospects of Bangladesh*, ODI, London. Retrieved from: https://www.odi.org/sites/odi.org.uk/files/odi-assets/publications-opinion-files/8026.pdf (Accessed: 18 February 2020).

South Asia (2021). *Fifty Years of Bangladesh: The Rising Sun!*, South Asia Magazine, March.

Sundram, J. (2018). Annual Speech of the Centre for Policy Dialogue (CPD), Dhaka.

Tisdell, C. (2007). "Bangladesh's performance and the Millennium Development Goals: A sketch of progress" in C. Tisdell (ed.), *Poverty, Poverty Alleviation and Social Disadvantage: Analysis, Case Studies and Policies*, Serials Publications, New Delhi, India.

UN (2015). https://sdgs.un.org/goals, 2030 Agenda for Sustainable Development, New York.

UNESCAP (2019). *Survey 2019, Ambitions Beyond Growth*, United Nations Economic and Social Commission for Asia and the Pacific, 5 April, Bangkok.

WHO (2021). https://who.int/publications/m/item/weekly-epidemiological-update, 23 February, Geneva.

1 Socio-Economics of Bangladesh: Present Status and Future Trajectory

Qazi Kholiquzzaman Ahmad

Introduction

There are two major challenges that Bangladesh faces, which are its geographical and climatic vulnerabilities and extremely high population density. Geographically, it is a deltaic country, located at the bottom of 3 (three) mighty river systems – the Ganges, the Brahmaputra, and the Meghna (GBM) – and the Bay of Bengal makes up the southern border. About two-thirds of the country is less than 13 feet above sea level. The country is criss-crossed by a large number of rivers and has about a 710 kilometres long coastal belt. About 80 per cent of the country is flood-prone and certain low-lying areas are often affected by flash floods. Again, certain parts of the country are drought-prone. Over 92 per cent of the total annual run-off that the country experiences comes from outside and only 8 per cent is generated within. There are 57 transboundary rivers that flow through Bangladesh, all coming down from upper catchments, 54 from India and 3 from Myanmar. As a result, Bangladesh is highly climate vulnerable.

The area of the country is 147,500 sq. km., with a population of about 166.5 million (2019), eighth largest in the world. The population density in Bangladesh is the highest in the world, except for certain city and tiny states, at 1,125 per sq. km, as of 2019.[1] Just to put this in perspective, population density in certain other countries may be mentioned here. As of 2020, it is 464 in India, 203 in Nepal, 287 in Pakistan, 137 in Thailand, 314 in Vietnam, 150 in China, 87 in Kenya, 49 in South Arica, 278 in the United Kingdom, 36 in the USA, and 9 in Russia.[2]

Bangladesh has had to negotiate these formidable challenges, along with other constraints such as resource limitations, human capability gaps, and so on, to make a headway in relation to socio-economic development. In fact, the country has achieved enviable progress, particularly over the past decade or so. Generally, data used in this paper relate to 2019, the last pre-COVID-19 year. Occasionally, when relevant and available, certain data relating to more recent times, which are surely COVID-19 affected, have been used.

Socio-Economic Progress Since 2010

Let us first consider economic growth. Bangladesh started its journey as an independent sovereign nation on 16 December 1971, with a war-ravaged

DOI: 10.4324/9781003231912-3

economy, non-functional governance and financial institutions and administrative machinery, zero foreign exchange reserve, devastated transportation networks, an education system in disarray, deeply disrupted productive sectors including agriculture, industries and international and domestic trade and commerce and a poverty ratio of 80 per cent or so. However, during the first three years and a half when Bangabandhu Sheikh Mujibur Rahman was at the helm of the affairs of the newly independent state, he was able to lay the basics for recovery and rejuvenation in relation to all the above mentioned and other economic and social sectors and also infrastructures and environment. His political and philosophical position on development was human-centricity, focusing on effective inclusion of the poor and disadvantaged in particular.

The country has achieved, since 2010, in constant prices of 2005–2006, an annual GDP growth rate of over 6 per cent every year from fiscal 2011 to fiscal 2015, over 7 per cent from fiscal 2016 to 2018, and 8.15 per cent in 2019, the year just preceding the coronavirus pandemic. In the past, there was no such achievement in the country in terms both the level and consistency of growth rate over a decade or so. The per capita income was USD781 in 2010, which increased to 2,064 in 2019–20 and 2,554 in 2021. Moreover, in terms of per capita income, Bangladesh reached the lower-middle-income status by 2015 and the goal is to move on to higher-middle-income status by 2031.

In foodgrain production, Bangladesh is now almost self-sufficient. Rice production has increased to 36.39 million metric tons (MTs) in 2018–19 from 26.5 million MTs in 2005–06. Overall, foodgrain production including wheat rose from 27.79 million MTs in 2005–06 to 42.11 million MTs in 2018–19. Besides, the production of greens, potato, fish, poultry, and livestock has increased significantly. However, in terms of production of balanced food for all, there is still a deficit at the national level. But, during the coronavirus pandemic, the agriculture sector has done well and, as a result, Bangladesh has not faced a food crisis at the national level.

At household and individual levels, the poor and disadvantaged (including people with disabilities, day labourers, women-headed poor families, and various other marginalized groups) people face occasional food insecurity, particularly in relation to a balanced diet. But, for these people, the government of Bangladesh implements a substantial social safety net programme every year, which provides succur to them either on a regular basis through various allowances as well as during agricultural off-seasons when employment opportunities decline sharply. During the coronavirus pandemic, coverage of such activities has been expanded to support, in addition, the people who fell into economic turmoil due to lookdowns and other medically required restrictions during the COVID-19 pandemic resulting in loss of income earning opportunities. It may be mentioned, the budget allocation for safety net programmes was 14.11 per cent in 2020–21, accounting for 2.58 per cent of GDP.

The money is disbursed through various projects to the target groups. The social safety net programme has, over the years, notably contributed to poverty reduction. Given the contribution of this programme, access to food is almost universal in Bangladesh. However, there is still a problem of access to balanced diet for adequate nutrition, faced by many. In fact, about 36 per cent of people of the country suffer from nutritional deficits of various levels. However, this is not only a problem of access to food, but also of a lack of knowledge among not only illiterate and poor people but also among economically and socially better placed people regarding choice of food basket that can provide adequate nutrition.

Thus, while it is important that policy and practical support is provided for raising the incomes of the marginalized people for them to be able to buy adequate amounts of foods required from nutritional adequacy point of view, it is also essential for spread of nutrition-related education widely. There are certain foods (e.g., vegetables, fruits, and eggs) which the rural people in particular can produce using their own agricultural land, even in homesteads and consume for improving their nutritional status. Indeed, there are ongoing efforts on both counts at both governmental and non-governmental levels, which could be strengthened for better results. Civil society is also active in this regard. 'Right to Food Bangladesh', a network of individuals and institutions, established in 2015, has been collecting and analyzing data and information in these regards and presenting the findings and conclusions to the government. It has been advocating for 'Right to Food (and Nutrition) Act', which will enable people to legally demand assurance of nutritionally sound foods, if deprived due to adverse circumstances. Prime Minister Sheikh Hasina agreed to this recommendation in her address as chief guest at the South Asia Right to Food Conference held in Dhaka in 2015. Although there has been some progress towards enacting such an Act, it is still not a reality.

Regarding food issue, Bangladesh has made tremendous progress, particularly over the past decade or so. Even during the coronavirus pandemic, the country faced no food crisis at the national level. But, nutritional deficits exist, as noted above, among certain segments of population. This issue is now being addressed more purposefully by the government and other stakeholders.

Export earnings rose to US$40.5 billion in 2018–19, which was only US $10.5 billion in 2005–06. However, export sector is very narrowly based. Only ready-made garments and knit wear account for about 80 per cent of all exports earnings. Other mentionable exports include pharmaceutical products, agricultural products (e.g., raw jute), refrigerated foods including fish, shoe, and jute goods. Diversification of exports has been a longstanding policy goal, but not much progress has yet been achieved.

Inward remittance has increased fast over the past decade or so. In 2005–06, it was only US$4.8 billion. By 2019–20, it was up to US$18.2 billion. It further increased during the coronavirus pandemic and stood at US$24.77 billion in 2020–21.[3]

A significant expansion of digitalization has also been achieved at all levels of society including at the union level (the lowest administrative level). This is facilitating faster communication and transmission of funds. It is, in fact, helping increase productivity and transparency in various sectors.

In the generation and distribution of electricity, a noteworthy progress has been achieved over the past decade. By now, the whole country has been brought under electrification, although not everywhere is it uninterrupted yet. That may take a few more years. But, the achievement so far is highly praiseworthy. As of 25 May 2022, electricity generation capacity rose to 25,566 MW, while the actual highest daily generation was 14,782 MW (on 16 April 2022). In 2009–10, the electricity generation capacity and actual generation were, respectively, 5,823 and 4,046 MW.[4]

Over the past 12 years, electricity generation capacity increased almost five times and actual generation about three and a half times. This widespread access to electricity is playing a significant role in relation to consolidation and acceleration of production in agriculture, industry, and other productive sectors as well as in education, health, communication, digitalization, commerce, habitation, and other socio-economic sectors. In view of the importance given to electricity by the government, its further expansion as appropriate can be expected to happen.

Not only in economic, electricity, and digital sectors, but also in the case of different social indicators, Bangladesh has achieved unprecedented improvement. Poverty ratio declined to 20.5 per cent in 2019 from 40 per cent in 2005 and extreme poverty ratio to 10.5 per cent in 2019 from 25 per cent in 2005. Life expectation at birth rose to 73 years recently, while it was about 65 years in 2005. Infant (less than one year of age) and child (less than five years of age) mortality (number per thousand live births) came down sharply to 21 and 28 as of 2019 from 50 and 54, respectively, in 2005. Maternal mortality (per cent of live births) declined to 1.65 per cent in 2019 from 3.48 per cent in 2005.

A significant improvement has also been achieved in educational expansion. The literacy rate among population above seven years of age went up to 74.4 per cent in 2019 (women: 74 percent; men 76.5 per cent). These numbers were 57.6 per cent (54.8 per cent; 61.1 per cent) even in 2014. In 2019, enrolment rate at the primary level was close to 100 per cent. Improvements achieved in education relate to both women and men. It is noteworthy that the proportion of females at both primary and secondary levels is higher compared to males. A major reason behind this progress of female education is widespread stipends provided by the government to female students all across the country.

The dropout at the level of primary education has sharply declined since 2010—from 39.8 per cent at that time to 17.9 per cent in 2019. There has also been improvement in this regard in the case of secondary education. Higher secondary has also spread a great deal in the country. There are now colleges not only in small towns, but also in villages around the country.

The number of public and private universities has increased to 49 and 105, respectively, as of 2019 – to a total of 153. However, in higher education, the proportion of female students is much lower, at around 40 per cent, than male students. A major reason for this is rooted in social norms and practices such as early marriage. Once married, female students, by and large, drop out. However, female participation in higher education is now increasing.

Overall and in particular among female students, there appears to be some reluctance to studying science subjects. Reasons seem to include the following.

Science education is relatively more costly and science graduates and master's degreeholders face rather limited job opportunities. This is indeed a matter of concern, given the importance of science and technology in the context of knowledge-based development that is clearly going help shape the future trajectory of humanity's forward march. Approaches need to be worked out to encourage science and technology education in the country.

However, there has been reasonable improvement in recent years with respect to vocational and technical education. There was little interest among students in this kind of education even 10 or 12 years ago. The reasons included a limitation of institutional facilities and a lack of social recognition and dignity associated with jobs open to people with this kind of education and training. In both respects there has been notable improvements in recent years, i.e., institutional facilities for imparting these skills are increasing and an attitudinal change is taking place in society in relation to according of due respect to human beings regardless of what kinds of jobs they are engaged in. Moreover, technical and vocational skills enable people to find jobs relatively easily which encourages the young people belonging to poor, low-income, and lower-middle-income households to undertake these training courses. Thus, while the admission rate from among the people qualified to undertake these skill training courses was only about 1 per cent in 2010, it rose to 16 per cent in 2019.

However, there is a question mark relating to the quality of education at all levels. This issue is well known and is often discussed. But, progress in removing the bottlenecks and improving facilitation remains rather limited. The problem has been accentuated during the coronavirus pandemic. Dropout has also increased, particularly at primary and secondary levels in the countrysides. In the case of female students, a major cause of dropping out is child marriage, which has increased significantly during the coronavirus pandemic. Many boys belonging to poor, low, and even lower-middle-income families have dropped out to take up income-earning activities to support their families devastated by the coronavirus pandemic.

Inclusive education is a major weapon that is needed to support forward movement along inclusive sustainable development pathways. Therefore, it is crucial that for recovery and rejuvenation of education at all levels of society, well thought-out programmes are formulated and effectively implemented. The government of Bangladesh is consciously working in this context. One hopes for the best possible results, but how things shape up will be known in the course of time.

Regarding empowerment of women, Bangladesh is ahead of all other South Asian countries. In addition, Bangladesh is ahead of Pakistan and India in respect to various important socio-economic indicators.

Advancements achieved, largely over the past decade or so, by Bangladesh in various socio-economic respects highlighted above, have earned the country a high reputation internationally. The people of Bangladesh are inspired to move ahead further and achieve the goals of reaching a higher-middle-income country by 2031, while at the same time, achieving inclusive sustainable development goals, particularly the prioritized targets by 2030.

A question may be raised as to how all this could be achieved in a short time of just about a decade. In my judgement, it has been mainly due to two basic reasons.

First, the government of Bangladesh, led by Prime Minister Sheikh Hasina, has provided an appropriate policy regime creating a conducive environment and, within that framework, farmers, farm workers, other workers, entrepreneurs at various scales (tiny, small, medium, and large), and others engaged in various economic and social sectors have worked hard and achieved remarkable successes. Being hopeful about a brighter future, they are generally putting in all possible efforts to move ahead further.

If the country's high levels of geographical and climatic vulnerabilities and very high population density, noted earlier, are taken into consideration, the significance of the advancements realized are surely even more pronounced than meets the eye. Let us now turn to these vulnerability issues and the responses being implemented towards further achievements in the coming years.

Certain Major Vulnerabilities and Responses

The long coastal belt is subject to storm surges and salinity ingress. Both are increasing as the sea level is rising due to climate change. The haors (large lowly areas) are affected by flash floods on account of heavy rains upstream in India in particular and the resulting waters belting down to Bangladesh. The northwest parts of the country are drought-prone. Frequently occurring river erosions in different parts of the country are displacing large numbers of people. These and other natural disasters such as cyclones, floods, and heat waves certainly occurred in the past, but due to worsening climate change, these are now occurring more frequently and more devastatingly. Although reliable data are not available, there is no doubt that the GDP of the country is adversely affected, which will worsen further as climate change keeps intensifying and more and more natural disasters hit. Economic sectors and infrastructures suffer much at the advent of a major natural disaster.

To address the issues outlined above and other impacts of natural disasters, the government of Bangladesh has been actively making policy and action responses. Mention may be made of the Bangladesh Climate Change Strategy and Action Plan (BCCSAP) 2009 (reconstructed in 2020), National Environment Policy 1992, Bangladesh Environmental Conservation Act 1995, Bangladesh Climate Trust (BCCT) 2010, National Water Policy 1999, and National Water Act 2013.

Bangladesh is also playing an important role in the international arena in relation to formulation of policy making and action programming. Climate change is a global issue, brought about by the now-developed countries by emitting greenhouse gasses (GHGs) since the beginning of the first Industrial Revolution. Other countries have now joined in emitting GHGs more and more. The concentration of GHGs in the atmosphere now is the highest in 2 million years according to the Intergovernmental Panel on Climate Change (IPCC) 6th Assessment Working Group (WG)-1 report. This report also indicates that the goal of the Paris

Agreement (2015) on climate change of keeping global warming limited to a 1.5°C increase from pre-first Industrial Revolution levels by the end of this century will be reached between 2030 and 2040. The WG-2 report of the same IPCC assessment provides facts and analyses on the impacts and vulnerabilities caused by climate change around the world, which indicate that there is not much time left before the situation may get out of hand. Maybe there is a window of about ten years or less to reduce GHGs drastically and fast in order to keep global warming on track for the Paris goal to be realized. But, global leaders, particularly of the developed countries, remain basically unresponsive in this context. Bangladesh, being highly climate vulnerable, is one of the worst suffering countries in the world due to climate change, to which it has made no contribution.

Bangladesh is very vocal in demanding to the world, particularly the developed countries and other fast industrializing large developing counties, to reduce their GHG emissions drastically over the next ten years or so to keep the Paris goal alive and in calling upon the developed countries to provide climate finance and necessary technologies to developing countries, especially to more vulnerable and resource-short countries to enable them to address climate change impacts.

While vocal in the international arena, Bangladesh has also been implementing projects in the country, largely for climate change adaptation purposes with own funding. Annual budgetary allocation is made to BCCT, which is used to fund relevant projects across the country and across sectors. Up to 2019–20, a total of 396 projects (239 by various agencies of the government and 57 by non-governmental organizations) were implemented with funding from this fund.[5] Besides, various ministries of the government also implement action programmes relating to various aspects of climate change impacts within the ambit of their mandate. In fiscal 2020, a total of the equivalent of US$5 billion (about 1.5 per cent of GDP) was allocated to these ministries.[6]

Not much climate finance has been received by Bangladesh from international sources. In fact, much climate finance is not provided by the international community to the developing world, often disregarding the promises made. Since the Green Climate Fund (GCF) became operative, Bangladesh has received about US$100 million as grant and US$250 million as loans. Some more funds were received from various multilateral and bilateral sources through projects concerned with climate change and its impacts and other projects with climate change–related components. Although an estimate is not available on how much was received through such projects, cursory information indicates that the total annual amount received is not of much significance compared to Bangladesh's expenditure from its own sources. It must be noted that funds available from the government and international sources are together quite small in relation to funds required to properly address the increasing adverse impacts of the worsening climate change.

In fact, despite limited abilities (financial and expertise), Bangladesh is admirably active in relation to addressing climate change and its impacts in both national and international arenas. In fact, all stakeholders in Bangladesh including government, civil society, and NGOs, actively participate in this process.

Government of Bangladesh is also very active in trying to recoup and rejuvenate much degraded environment and much depleted biodiversity but without much avail so far. Also, water and air pollution and encroachment on rivers and forests are widespread in the country. There are action programmes to alleviate these, which must be pursued more effectively for making an appreciable headway. Moreover, the polluters, as relevant, must be brought to justice.

Another important sector is water. Per capita availability of water, in Bangladesh, on an annual basis is substantially more than is required at 7,568 cubic metres.[7] In India, it is 1,586 cubic metres (as of 2011),[8] and, in Pakistan, 1,017 cubic metres.[9] But, Bangladesh is in a dilemma because of highly uneven spatial and seasonal distribution of water availability: abundance of water in the rainy season and its scarcity in the dry season (01 January to 31 May, particularly March and April). Major floods in the rainy reason now occur more frequently and devastatingly than before due to intensifying climate change and cause widespread losses and damages, give rise to health hazards, and may also cause deaths. However, normal floods inundating 20–30 per cent of the country occur every year, which the people of Bangladesh have learnt to live with. Such floods also play a positive role in relation to recovery of land fertility and productivity. In the dry season, production is affected in agriculture and other productive sectors, resulting in certain degrees of hardships and health issues for the people concerned. Coastal people suffer a great deal due to storm surges and widespread intrusion of salinity.

The issue of rehabilitation of flood, cyclone, and drought-devastated people and large numbers of people displaced by river erosions and salinity ingress is becoming increasingly challenging, requiring more and more elaborate action programmes involving more funds and human power. This is certainly putting pressure on the limited availability of those resources. Other issues to be addressed are waster scarcity and salinity toward ensuring quality water to the affected areas and people – not an easy task. All of these constitute a major challenge, but that needs to be met for the sake of the affected human beings as well as devastated economic activities, for which international cooperation is necessary.

One other major issue in the context of water management in Bangladesh is the regional aspect. India has constructed dams on most of the 54 transboundary rivers involving Bangladesh and India, and diverts water, more than its legitimate share, in the dry season so that Bangladesh faces severe water shortages in the catchments of these rivers in Bangladesh. Negotiations for fair distribution of the waters of these rivers between India and Bangladesh has been going on since the independence of Bangladesh. But, little progress has taken place. There is, though, a water-sharing agreement between India and Bangladesh in the case of the Ganges. But, this will also expire in 2026. I know of no negotiations taking place for the Ganges sharing beyond 2026. No agreement has been signed in respect of any other river. The government of Bangladesh has always been keen on a water-sharing arrangement with India in respect of all major transboundary rivers. Being upper riparian India has little real interest, but does often make non-committal diplomatic gestures. But, in the Ganges Treaty, it is stated that appropriate water-sharing arrangements would be put in place for other common rivers as well. Bangladesh is continuing to argue the case for legitimate shares of the transboundary rivers, but so far to no avail except for the Ganges.

Bangladesh adopted a National Water Policy in 1999 and a Water Act in 2013. These two together constitute a framework for an effective and more inclusive water regime to be instituted in Bangladesh. But, there are implementation deficits with respect to both. What is required is to adopt, by keeping the perspectives and directions provided by the aforementioned policy and act in focus, prioritized action programmes and activities involving the people concerned at all stages from planning to implementation. This will, I believe, bring about desirable improvements regarding human-centric and needs-based availability, utilization, and distribution of water.

Other Challenges and Responses

It has been clarified that Bangladesh has, overall, achieved remarkable socio-economic development that is widely recognized at home and abroad. Of course, when a nation or society makes forward strides, there may still remain certain persisting problems or certain others may arise. Some of them may be regional (e.g., sharing of transboundary rivers) and global (e.g., climate change), which a particular country such as Bangladesh cannot solve alone. But, Bangladesh should be and, indeed, is in active pursuit of resolving these issues in cooperation with other countries – often not to much avail. This is so because success can be achieved only when all parties come together to find the solutions, which is often not an easy thing to happen. As noted earlier, certain problems faced by Bangladesh are due to its geographical realities, some of which have been overcome but others cannot be addressed properly due to non-availability of appropriate technologies and shortage of financial and other resources. Some of these have been mentioned above. Yet Bangladesh has made tremendous socio-economic headway regardless; and, at the same time, is seeking to address those issues.

In addition, there are some other major issues which need to be resolved in order to effectively consolidate the achievements so far and accelerating the process of moving forward, keeping in perspective the pursuit of sustainable development, which is necessarily inclusive as, in this process, nobody is to be left behind, i.e., everybody has to be genuinely included.

One of the two major goals set to be achieved over the remaining years of this decade is the prioritized targets under the 17 SDGs. In fact, the government has prioritized 39 targets with the tenet of inclusion of everybody to be ensured in all cases. The ministries and other agencies that will lead and those that will play a supporting role in respect of different prioritized targets have also been identified and intimated accordingly. The other goal is to achieve a higher-middle-income status by 2031. It remains to be seen how effectively the implementation of SDGs and other programmes are carried out. Obviously, the coronavirus pandemic and its aftermath have given rise to major constraints compounded by the Ukraine war, which need to be overcome to reestablish the pace and pattern of forward movement not only in the case of the pursuit of SDGs but also in respect of all other aspects of the economy and society.

However, it is noteworthy that Bangladesh has achieved enviable economic outcomes even during the coronavirus pandemic. A small number of countries around the world posted respectable positive GDP growth rates; Bangladesh is among them. In fact, Bangladesh is among the top performers. Bangladesh's GDP grew by 3.5 per cent and 6.4 per cent, respectively, in 2019–20 and 2020–2021.

As Bangladesh, along with other countries around the world, started its recovery phase from the devastations caused by the coronavirus pandemic, the country posted an estimated GDP growth rate of 7.25 per cent in 2021–22, less than 1 per cent short of the high rate of 8.15 per cent in the latest pre-coronavirus year (2018–19).

But, now the globally disruptive Ukraine war is raging. Production of commodities and international movement of goods and services face disruptions and prices of commodities (including petroleum products, natural gas, edible oil, wheat and wheat flour, rice, and so on) have gone up sharply in international markets. Consequently, the inflation rate has sharply increased and the rising trend will continue if the war lasts longer. In the USA, Europe, India, and elsewhere, the inflation rate is already around 8 per cent as of April 2022 and increasing. In Bangladesh, as of April 2022, it is somewhat less at 6.29 per cent. But, given the intensifying global economic turmoil and rising inflation, Bangladesh is going to face further imported inflationary pressure, but also there are domestic reasons for inflation rate to rise, which include production and distribution disruptions and market machinations. So, the most important challenge Bangladesh faces at least in fiscal 2023 and, perhaps, beyond is to manage a very likely surging inflation. Both appropriate monetary and fiscal measures will need to be applied in response to the evolving national and international market realities.

Concluding Remarks

As the country moves forward, weathering the adverse consequences of the coronavirus pandemic and Ukraine war as well as other persisting bottlenecks discussed in this paper, with regard to consolidation and acceleration of moving forward, there are other important challenges which also need to be addressed toward ensuring an upward-moving development trajectory characterized by inclusiveness and sustainability. These challenges include increasing socio-economic disparity, widespread corruption, centralized governance, and widespread un- and under-employment, particularly among the youths who make up about a third of the total population of the country.

As Bangladesh has made enviable socio-economic progress in the 2010s, overcoming or minimizing or bypassing various formidable challenges, the nation should be confident enough to repeat the feat in the 2020s and achieve the above-mentioned goals as this decade comes to an end. This is what one hopes for confidently at this time, but how things will actually turn out internationally and domestically as the decade wears on and how best those are negotiated by Bangladesh will determine the actual outcomes.

Notes

1 Bangladesh Bureau of Statistics (BBS), Ministry of Planning, Government of Bangladesh, *Statistical Yearbook Bangladesh 2020*, May 2021.
2 The World Bank Data – Population Density per sq. km. of land area (FAO and World Bank Population Estimates), 2020 https://data.worldbank.org/indicator/EN.POP.DHST?locations=en
3 Bangladesh Wage Earner Remittance Inflow, Bangladesh Bank https://www.bb.org.bd/en/index.php/econdata/wageremitance
4 Power Cell, Government of Bangladesh, Summary Statistics regarding electricity sector <powercell.gov.bd>
5 *Bangladesh Economic Review* 2010, 2014, and 2020, Ministry of Finance, GoB (for all data and information relation to various economic and social indicators and electricity).
6 Ministry of Environment, Forest and Climate Change, Government of Bangladesh (GoB).
7 *Sustainable Water Regime in Bangladesh: Availability, Management, Access.*
8 'Per Capita Availability of Water'; Ministry of Jal Shakti, Government of India (Posted on 25 March 2021: https://pib.gov.in/PressReleaseIframePage.aspx?PRID=1707522).
9 Water Crisis: Why is Pakistan Running Dry", Posted in June 2019: https://www.dw.com/en/water-crisis-why-is-pakistan-running-dry/a-44110280

References

Bangladesh Bureau of Statistics (BBS) (2021). Ministry of Planning, Government of Bangladesh, *Statistical Yearbook Bangladesh 2020.*

Bangladesh Economic Review (2010, 2014 and 2020). Ministry of Finance, GoB (for all data and information relation to various economic and social indicators and electricity).

BCCT (2019). Annual Report, 2019–20, Bangladesh Climate Change Trust (BCCT), Ministry of Environment, Forest and Climate Change, (Bangla Version).

Ministry of Shakti (2021). "Per Capita Availability of Water'; Ministry of Jal Shakti, Government of India (Posted on 25 March 2021: https://pib.gov.in/PressReleaseIframePage.aspx?PRID=1707522).

Posted in June (2019). https://www.dw.com/en/water-crisis-why-is-pakistan-running-dry/a-44110280. "Water Crisis: Why is Pakistan Running Dry"?

Q. K. Ahmad (2022). "The Troubled Global Economy and Bangladesh" (in Bangla), Presented as an Invited Speaker at the Bangladesh Academy for Securities Markets (Academic Wing of Bangladesh Securities Exchange Commission), Dhaka, 29 May (unpublished).

Q. K. Ahmad, *et al.* (2021). *Ganges-Brahmaputra-Meghna Region: A Framework for Sustainable Development*, The University Press Limited (UPL), Dhaka.

Q. K. Ahmad (2017). *Sustainable Water Regime in Bangladesh: Availability, Management, Access, Outcome of National Water Convention 2016*, organised by Palli Karma-Sahayak Foundation (PKSF) in association with Bangladesh Unnayan Parisad (BUP) and NGO Forum, published by PKSF, Dhaka.

Q. K. Ahmad, *et al.* (1994). *Converting Water into Wealth - Regional Cooperation in Harnessing the Eastern Himalayan Rivers*, Bangladesh Unnayan Parishad (BUP)/Academic Publishers Dhaka.

Part II

Transformation Over 1996 to 2020

The second part of this volume presents an analysis of how Bangladesh has transformed over the last decades in economic and social terms.

DOI: 10.4324/9781003231912-4

2 Manufacturing Growth and Structural Transformation: The Case of Bangladesh[1]

M Mozammel Huq

2.1 Introduction

The push for industrialization has brought a major transformation in the macroeconomic structure of Bangladesh. Agriculture, which used to dominate the economic life of the country for centuries, is no longer the key sector. It is also particularly remarkable that in manufacturing, Bangladesh has moved out from its old days with dependence on goods such as jute and jute products (considered as providing static comparative advantage) to the production and exports of goods such as ready-made garments and pharmaceutical products with features of dynamic comparative advantage. Thus, it is of special interest to analyze the huge transformation that has taken place in a low-income developing country such as Bangladesh on which, at its birth in 1971, several people had expressed serious reservations (see, e.g., Robinson, 1973; Faaland and Parkinson, 1976). However, it appears that currently the sector is failing to attract the close research attention that it deserves, although there is evidence of some solid investigation that was carried out in the late 1980s and during the 1990s, undertaken especially on behalf of the Bangladesh Institute of Development Studies (BIDS). Indeed, a major issue of the *Bangladesh Development Studies* (the journal of BIDS: March–June 1991) was devoted to "Industrial Policies and Industrialization in Bangladesh", edited by Dr. Zaid Bakht in his capacity as the research director of the Industry Division of BIDS. (Bakht, 1991). Again, at BIDS during the late 1980s and the early 1990s, an investigative study was carried out to examine the technology selection and development issues based on primary research focusing on three major industries, leather, fertilizer, and machinery manufacturing (Huq and Islam, 1991 and 1992, and Huq, et al., 1993). Also at this premier research institute, as an outcome of an Industrialization Link Programme between BIDS and the University of Strathclyde in Glasgow, which was conducted in the mid-1990s, there took place some solid research, the findings of which were presented in a series of workshops held at BIDS, culminating in an international seminar on "Export Competitiveness of Bangladesh Industries: Achievements and Policy Agenda" (held at the Bangladesh Planning Commission in 1996), which was addressed, among others, by the then Finance Minister Shah ASM Kibria of the Government of Bangladesh (Huq and Love, 2000). It is true that some extensive evaluations are there

DOI: 10.4324/9781003231912-5

especially in the Five Year Plans (see, for example, the 6th Five-Year Plan 2010–15 (GoB, 2011, Part 2: 50–125); the 7th Five-Year Plan (GoB, 2015: 181–226); and the 8th Five-Year Plan July 2020-June 2025 (GoB, 2020b: 197–203) and also some occasional studies at the individual level [see, for example, Nath (2012) and Amin and Sonobe (2013)], but at the institutional level, there does not appear to be any major research work being carried out in recent years on Bangladesh manufacturing.

A note is also perhaps in order about the data sources. As will be found, we have depended heavily on data from official sources especially the publications by the various departments of the Government of Bangladesh including those by the Bangladesh Bureau of Statistics, the Ministry of Finance and Export Promotion Bureau. In particular, the earlier Census of Manufacturing Industries (CMIs) as carried out for several years until 1995–96 and then the Survey of Manufacturing Industries (SMIs) as conducted in 2005–06, 2012 and 2019 provide some highly valuable data. However, it needs to be mentioned that according to Khan (2015, p. 68), the figures of the share of manufacturing in GDP as found in the Survey of Manufacturing Industries 2012 and the Cottage Industries Survey 2011, "the share of manufacturing in GDP at current prices in 2010/11 would have been 22.4 percent instead of 17.8 percent", i.e. as he has estimated (for total manufacturing covering small, medium, and large enterprises).

The order of discussion is as follows. The next section presents the structural transformation that has taken place in the Bangladesh economy since the independence of the country. Section 2.3 focuses on the strategies of development which have been directed towards the growth of manufacturing, followed by a section each on output and employment growth (Section 2.4), export growth (Section 2.5), and ownership distribution (Section 2.6). In Section 2.7, various concerns and challenges faced are briefly presented. Finally, in Section 2.8, some brief concluding remarks are made.

2.2 Bangladesh Economy: Growth and Structure

In Bangladesh, for centuries agriculture used to dominate the economic life of the country but this is no longer the key sector. As may be seen from Table 2.1, the share of agriculture in GDP has declined from around 50 per cent of GDP during 1972/73 to less than 15 per cent in the late 2010s, while that of the industrial sector has more than doubled over this period; the corresponding values are 13.78 per cent and 34.78 per cent, and within the industry sector the share of the manufacturing sub-sector increased from less than 10 per cent in the early 1970s to around 24 per cent in the late 2010s. Table 2.1 also shows that the share of the services sector has significantly increased over this period: from 36.47 per cent to over 50 per cent of GDP.

Another major development is the increase in the employment share by the industry sector In general and, in particular, the manufacturing sub-sector (which is a

Table 2.1 Sectoral Shares in the Bangladesh Economy, 1972/73 to 2019/20 (% of GDP)

Sectors	*1972/73**	*1979/80***	*1989/90***	*1999/00***	*2009/10*	*2015/16*	*2018/19*
Agriculture	49.76	33.2	29.5	25.6	20.3	15.31	13.65
Industry	13.78	17.1	20.8	25.7	29.9	31.54	35.00
(Manuf.)	(9.00)	(8.0)	(8.9)	(11.0)	(12.7)	(21.74)	(24.08)
Services	36.47	49.7	49.7	48.7	49.8	53.12	51.35
Total	100	100	100	100	100	100	100

Data for 2009/10, 2015/16 and 2018/19 are at 2005–06 prices.
Sources: Huq and Love (2000: 4) for 1972/73; Khan (2015, p.12) for 1979/80, 1989/90, 1999/2000, and 2009/10; and GoB (2021: 278) for 2015/16 and 2018/19.

Notes
* 1972/73 prices.
** 1995/96 prices.

Table 2.2 Share of the Broad Economic Sectors in Employment (%): Selected Years

Sectors	*1999/00*	*2005/06*	*2009/2010**	*2015/16*	*2016/17*
Agriculture	51.3	48.0	47.3	42.6	40.6
Male	52.2	41.8	40.1	34.0	32.2
Female	47.6	68.1	64.8	63.1	59.7
Industry	13.1	14.5	17.6	20.5	20.4
(of which Manufacturing)	(9.5)	(11.0)	(12.4)	(14.4)	(14.4)
Male	11.3	15.1	19.6	22.3	22.0
	(7.4)	(10.8)	(12.7)	(14.2)	(14.0)
Female	20.0	12.5	13.3	16.1	16.8
	(17.9)	(11.5)	(11.7)	(14.9)	(15.4)
Services	35.6	37.5	35.1	36.9	39.0
Male	36.4	43.0	41.1	43.7	45.8
Female	32.2	19.3	21.8	20.8	23.5
Total	100	100	100	100	100

Source: BBS (2011, 2015, and 2018).

Note
* Data for 2010.

part of the industry sector). As may be seen from Table 2.2, while the share of employment in agriculture has declined (from 51.3 per cent in 1999/00 to 40.6 per cent in 2016/17), the corresponding shares for the industry sector are 13.1 per cent and 20.4 per cent, and for manufacturing 9.5 and 14.4 per cent. Indeed, as per the 7th Five-Year Plan, the employment share in manufacturing was expected to increase from 15.4 per cent of the total employment in 2015 to 20.0 per cent in 2020 (GoB, 2015: 26) (Table 2.2).

2.3 Strategies for Manufacturing Growth

Bangladesh started its economic life with an aim to move to socialism as its basis of resource allocation, with significant state controls especially in the manufacturing sector, perhaps due to the poor state of the private sector that prevailed at the time of independence in 1971, and also partly due to a semi-socialist type of development strategy as believed by the political party that was then in power. Indeed, the ISI strategy, which it inherited from the Pakistan days, was strongly pursued, especially with an overvalued exchange rate, high nominal and effective rates of protection, and direct controls, thus providing incentives for the domestic producers for the local market. However, in the early 1980s, a shift began taking place in government policy away from government controls and regulations and towards greater dependence on market forces. (GoB, 1982). Indeed, the liberalization process that was started in the early 1980s became more pronounced in the mid-1980s, as reiterated in the Revised Industrial Policy (GoB, 1986) with its emphasis on stimulating industrial development through private-sector growth. Later denationalization of a large number of public-sector industries took place.

The pursuit of market-based strategies was reflected in the various industrial policies that have been subsequently advanced, and this was particularly evident in the Industrial Policy 2009 which strongly emphasized the government's commitment to the private sector-led industrialization strategy. However, the industralization target of the country has also been strongly emphasized. Thus, the Industrial Policy 1999 aimed to achieve, within a decade, a sizable industrial sector where manufacturing would account for at least 25 per cent of GDP and 20 per cent of the employed workforce. (GoB, 1999). The aim was re-emphasized in the Industrial Policy 2005 which envisaged that the "industrial sector is likely to grow rapidly over the next decade raising its contribution to the country's GDP to 30 to 35 per cent, and the workforce in this sector is expected to increase to 35 per cent of national employment" (GoB, 2005a: 3). In the spirit of this key development objective, the manufacturers have been provided with a range of incentives (Huq, 2021).

The strong importance attached to industralization is also clearly demonstrated in the aims and objectives of development, as emphasized in the various planning documents of the country. As observed in the Perspective Plan of Bangladesh 2010–21 (GoB, 2012: 4): "Accelerated pace of industrialization will be necessary to address the increasingly diminishing capacity of agriculture to absorb the incremental labour force, strengthen backward and forward linkages with agriculture and services sectors, cater to the growing domestic demand for industrial goods, and take advantage of emerging opportunities in the global market". It further goes on to add that the "industrialization process must play a central role in accelerating growth and achieving real GDP growth of 10 per cent by 2021. This means that in an era of increasing globalization, the only *mantra* for survival and progress is to facilitate the competitive strength of our industrial sector. In terms of a broader goal, the industrial sector will continue to account for a much larger share of GDP – reaching 37 per cent in 2021. This dominant performance of the industrial sector is necessary for it to address the increasingly diminishing capacity of agriculture to absorb the incremental labour force. … . Within industry, the manufacturing sector is to display superior double digit performance for the period 2011–21" (Ibid: 98).

Since the independence of the country in 1971, a number of policy documents have been advanced aiming to achieve manufacturing growth. The ones adopted immediately after independence were biased towards management and establishment of public-sector industries. But gradually the country started liberalizing its economy with encouragement of private-sector investment and management.

Along with the various Industrial Policy documents as advanced over the years (a total of eight Industrial Policy documents), the Government of Bangladesh has also followed it up with a number of other policies including the Industrial Investment Policy 1973 and the Revised Industrial Investment Policy 1975. While the former argued for the nationalization of various medium and large scale industrial enterprises, the latter focused on private sector–led growth and, accordingly, some large-scale denationalization of industrial enterprises took place, also private-sector investment began to pick up following liberal credit policies and generous lending by commercial banks and Development Financing Institutions (DFIs).

One particular policy advanced in the early 1980s perhaps needs a special mention, and this was the National Drug Policy (1982) which has played a major role in the development of the pharmaceutical industry of Bangladesh (Islam, 1999). In the course of Bangladesh's industrial development and, in particular, its pharmaceutical industry, this policy has received strong praise from various circles. Indeed, this policy has turned out to be highly instrumental in the rapid development of the pharmaceutical industry of the country, particularly strongly promoting the local entrepreneurs. For the country which used to depend heavily on imported drugs, thanks to the National Drug Policy (1982), the situation had completely changed, as is apparent from the following observation: "Just before the National Drug Policy was launched in 1982, Bangladesh had 166 approved drug firms, of which approximately 80 were in operation. Many of them were micro-enterprises producing folk medicine, and others were small-scale subcontractors for multinational firms. Although the number of firms in operation was large, the total production of drugs in the country, even including the output of the local subsidiaries of the multinationals, met only 35 percent of the domestic demand for drugs. The situation is different now. There are more than 250 approved domestic firms, of which more than 170 are in operation. They meet 97 percent of the domestic demand for drugs" (Amin and Sonobe, 2013: 5).

2.4 Manufacturing: Output and Employment Growth

The growth in manufacturing that has taken place in Bangladesh clearly reflects the aspirations of the policy makers to move towards industralization, see Table 2.3. It is true that in the early years, especially up to 1990, the actual growth rates in both GDP and manufacturing, were significantly lower than the target growth rates. However, one observation is particularly worthy of note: the policy makers of Bangladesh have kept a clear target of achieving manufacturing growth faster than the GDP growth. Furthermore, in both GDP and manufacturing growth, overall the actual average annual growth rate has been increasing especially since the late 1990s.

As shown in Table 2.1, in the early years, the share in GDP of the manufacturing sector was significantly lower, only 9 per cent in 1972/73. Since then, the figure has generally been increasing with the latest showing 23.59 per cent of GDP in 2019/20, slightly lower than in 2018/19 (24.08 per cent). However, in the early years, the sector was dominated by cottage industries and small-scale manufacturers (i.e. enterprises employing 10 persons or less; see Table 2.5). The share of cottage and small-scale manufacturing was about 70 per cent of the total manufacturing sector in 1972/73, but since then a significant increase in large-scale manufacturing has taken place, so in recent years its share is much higher, over 80 per cent in 2014/15 (82.30 per cent in 2019/20) (Table 2.4).

Table 2.6 shows the growth of the value added from manufacturing during 1970 to 2018. Although in the early years generally there was low growth (even a negative rate in 1975), overall the sector has continued to grow and the positive trend has been particularly strong since 2000, with recent years showing double-digit increases.

Table 2.3 GDP and Manufacturing Growth in Various Medium-term Plan Periods, 1973–2020

Plan period	*Annual average growth rate (%)*			
	Target (GDP growth)	*Actual GDP Growth*	*Target Mfg Growth*	*Mfg Growth (Actual)*
1st Five-Year Plan (FY73-FY78)	5.5	4.0	7.35	2.5
Two-Year Plan (FY78-FY80)	5.6	3.5	7.3	6.3
2nd Five-Year Plan (FY80-FY85)	5.4	3.8	8.4	4.7
3rd Five-Year Plan (FY85-FY90)	5.4	3.8	10.1	4.02
4th Five-Year Plan (FY90-FY95)	5.0	4.2	9.02	7.05
5th Five-Year Plan (FY97-FY02)	7.1	5.1	13.94	5.78
6th Five-Year Plan (FY11-FY15)	7.3	6.3	10.4	9.88
7th Five-Year Plan (FY16-FY20)	7.4	7.13	11.48	11.44

Sources: GoB (1978: 36–37); GoB (1997: 55 and 57); GoB (2015: 2, 55, and 201); GoB (2020b: 2 and 56).

Table 2.4 Manufacturing Output: Relative Share of Small- and Large-Scale Manufacturing, 1972/73–2019–20: Selected Years (Taka Mil.: Current Prices)

Year	*Small-Scale Manufacturing*		*Large-Scale Manufacturing*		*Total Manufacturing*	
	Tk. Mil.	*% of Total*	*Tk. Mil.*	*% of Total*	*Tk. Mil.*	*% of GDP*
1972/73	2,740	69.51	1,202	30.49	3,942	7.91
1974/75	4,983	55.76	3,954	44.24	8,937	7.19
1979/80	11,238	29.69	26,612	70.31	37,850	13.48
1984/85	22,579	29.06	55,128	70.94	77,707	13.83
1989/90	37,475	29.31	90,376	70.69	127,851	12.74
1994/95	64,222	28.60	160,338	71.40	224,560	14.72
1999/00	98,984	28.41	249,387	71.59	348,371	14.69
2004/05	172,602	29.36	415,350	70.64	587,952	15.86
2009/10	352,090	29.31	848,991	70.69	1,201,081	17.30
2014/15	484,911	19.05	2,059,920	80.95	2,544,831	16.79
2018/19	851,831	17.70	3,961,758	82.30	4,813,589	19.89

Sources: BBS (2019: 416–17); GoB (2011: 7–12); GoB (2017: 271–72); GoB (2019: 277–78); GoB (2021: 272).

Notes:
Small-scale manufacturing includes production by cottage industries.

The distinction between large- and small-scale sectors is based on the definition used by BBS. The small-scale sub-sectors cover all manufacturing establishments employing ten people or less and includes cottage industries. Establishments employing ten or more people are classified as the large-scale sub-sector.

Table 2.5 Manufacturing in the Bangladesh Economy, 1970 to 2019 (selected years)

Year	*Manufacturing, value added (constant 2010 prices: Mil. US$)*	*Manufacturing, value added (Annual % growth)*
1970	2,342.50	3.55
1975	2,237.62	-10.92
1980	2,856.31	2.32
1985	3,573.45	5.49
1990	4,621.18	7.86
1995	6,871.29	10.78
2000	9,011.70	4.70
2005	12,423.82	7.86
2010	18,584.40	6.65
2015	29,752.67	10.31
2016	33,231.00	11.69
2017	36,874.85	10.96
2018	41,816.87	13.40
2019	47,755.13	14.20

Source: World Bank (2020).

An indication of production growth of some of the key industry sectors can be obtained from Table 2.6. While only two manufacturing sectors (beverages and tobacco products) had low or negative growth rates in several years since 2013/14, the others are generally showing positive growth rates and for several items (pharmaceuticals, food, and rubber products) rapid growth occurred, the respective average annual growth rates over the period from 2006–07 to 2019/20 are 5.34 per cent, 8.39 per cent, and 4.18 per cent.

Table 2.7 shows the output produced by the top 15 manufacturing sub-sectors at the four-digit BSIC Code level in 2011/12 (based on the latest *Survey of Manufacturing Industries*, as available).

As in output, there has also been a gradual increase in the employment share in manufacturing which was 9.5 per cent in 1999/2000 (Table 2.3). The corresponding figure gradually increased to 14.4 per cent in 2015/16 and has remained unchanged in 2016/17.

However, the ready-made garments sectors (wearing apparel, knitwear, etc.) are also strong in employment (Table 2.8). These sectors alone (BSIC codes 1410 and 1430) provided over half of the total manufacturing employment in the country in 2018. Significantly weaker are the manufacture of bricks (8.57 per cent), textile fibres (5.48 per cent), jute textiles (3.45 per cent), iron and steel (2.05 per cent), and handloom textiles (2.03 per cent), etc.

2.5 Manufacturing: Export Growth

Table 2.9 shows the share in exports of the major manufacturing sub-sectors from 1972–73 to 2018–19. In the early years, jute goods occupied the dominant position, with about 90 per cent of total exports in 1972–73. This was followed

Table 2.6 Index of Industrial Production, 2006–07 to 2018–19 (2005–06 = 100)

Major Industry Group	*2006–07*	*2008–09*	*2010–11*	*2012–13*	*2013–14*	*2014–15*	*2015–16*	*2016–17*	*2017–18*	*2018–19*
General Index of Manufacturing	108.76	127.47	157.89	195.19	213.22	236.11	267.88	297.89	342.47	392.82
Food products	106.64	113.63	138.66	219.10	241.52	333.07	385.10	410.42	501.16	562.70
Beverages	109.23	122.56	152.37	189.81	243.19	230.06	269.75	257.61	240.41	272.74
Tobacco products	101.51	105.07	112.30	144.66	149.65	147.37	135.48	139.57	138.51	138.59
Wearing apparel (RMG)	112.12	144.75	200.80	265.83	293.70	304.76	338.70	343.74	388.62	443.05
Textiles	111.56	127.99	139.51	142.41	139.68	122.81	138.90	168.39	195.19	200.27
Leather and related products	105.76	115.48	129.02	139.76	147.83	140.48	125.44	194.13	292.22	348.58
Paper and paper products	111.81	145.30	169.70	160.43	151.95	174.68	181.08	183.67	185.38	187.58
Chemicals and chemical products	99.11	70.29	70.80	84.62	80.41	77.49	92.60	104.04	100.50	133.22
Pharmaceuticals and medicinal chemicals	105.19	128.33	164.97	178.79	230.60	290.98	319.26	424.30	507.53	670.41
Rubber and plastic products	108.20	135.26	191.97	244.87	263.84	292.69	338.14	359.79	411.94	442.63
Basic metals	111.48	136.44	111.50	136.41	150.20	187.13	202.85	174.04	185.27	188.14
Fabricated metal products except machinery	110.31	119.41	137.71	149.03	164.33	182.30	200.53	246.01	274.34	298.00
Furniture	100.86	102.20	103.19	109.14	101.12	116.35	132.02	551.44	184.81	193.84

Sources: GoB (2014: 274); GoB (2021: 292).

Note: The Table shows the index of industrial production of the top 15 manufacturing sub-sectors based on the latest *Survey of Manufacturing Industries*, as available.

Table 2.7 Top 15 Manufacturing Sub-sectors (value by gross output), 2012 (Values in Mil. Taka)

BSIC code	*Sub-Sectors*	*Value by Gross Output, Mil Tk.*	*Rank*	*% of Gross output*
1410	Manufacture of wearing apparel, except fur apparel	1,252,278.73	1	23.21
2410	Manufacture of basic iron and steel	766,035.35	2	14.20
1430	Manufacture of knitted and crocheted apparel	561,918.45	3	10.42
1311	Preparation and spinning of textile fibres	288,632.63	4	5.35
2394	Manufacture of cement, lime, and plaster	225,579.60	5	4.18
1063	Manufacture of rice/rice milling	180,097.71	6	3.34
1040	Manufacture of vegetable and animal oils and fats	162,870.02	7	3.02
2431	Casting of iron and steel	137,990.02	8	2.56
2732	Manufacture of other electronic and electric wires and cables	107,980.24	9	2.00
1313	Finishing of textiles (dying, bleaching etc.)	107,896.71	10	1.99
2100	Manufacture of pharmaceuticals, medicinal chemicals, and botanical products (Allopathic)	107,633.11	11	1.99
2397	Manufacture of bricks/blocks and tiles	106,465.57	12	1.97
1314	Manufacture of jute and jute textiles	100,829.32	13	1.87
1312	Weaving of textiles(excluding handloom products)	78,502.16	14	1.46
2012	Manufacture of fertilizers and nitrogen compounds	58,872.45	15	1.09
	Total	**4,243,582.07**		**78.65**

Source: BBS (2013: 188–96).

Note: Appendix Table A.1 shows gross output along with some other important values of the various major manufacturing sub-sectors.

by leather and leather goods, though with a significantly lower share (8.46 per cent). However, over the years, the picture has completely changed, these two sub-sectors occupying only 1.80 per cent and 0.42 per cent, respectively, in 2018–19. It is now the garments sector which has the dominant share; it has increased from only 0.24 per cent in total exports in 1972–73, to as high as 40.20 per cent in 2018–19 (and together with knitwear, the total share in exports is over 86 per cent in 2018–19). Thus, Bangladesh has come out of its

Table 2.8 Top 15 Manufacturing Sub-sectors: ranking based on employment, 2012

BSIC code	*Sub-Sectors*	*Number*	*Rank*	*% of Share*
1410	Manufacture of wearing apparel, except fur apparel	1,840,159	1	36.69
1430	Manufacture of knitted and crocheted apparel	909,500	2	18.13
2397	Manufacture of bricks/blocks, tiles	429,772	3	8.57
1311	Preparation and spinning of textile fibres	274,616	4	5.48
1314	Manufacture of jute textiles	173,283	4	3.45
2410	Manufacture of basic iron and steel	102,903	6	2.05
1315	Manufacture of handloom textiles	101,584	7	2.03
1313	Finishing of textiles (dying, bleaching etc.)	99,425	8	1.98
1063	Manufacture of rice/rice milling	83,978	9	1.67
2100	Manufacture of pharmaceuticals, medicinal chemicals, and botanical products (allopathic)	62,643	10	1.25
1520	Manufacture of footwear	56,819	11	1.13
1071	Manufacture of bakery products	42,376	12	0.84
1077	Manufacture/processing of tea and coffee	41,139	13	0.82
1312	Weaving of textiles (excluding handloom products)	33,143	14	0.66
1392	Manufacture of made-up textile articles, except apparel	26,667	15	0.53
	Total	**4,278,007**		**85.28**

Source: BBS (2013: 188–96).

heavy dependence on primary production manufactured exports, though the export concentration is as high as before.

The matter of concentration is also exposed when viewed in terms of the direction of exports (Table 2.10). In 2018–19, over 40 per cent of the total exports took place in three of the developed countries (USA, Germany, and United Kingdom).

2.6 Manufacturing: Ownership Distribution

Table 2.11 illustrates that the Bangladesh manufacturing sector is dominated by local private ownership. In 2012, the share of local private enterprises in net fixed assets in manufacturing was 83.07 per cent, while in gross output and gross value added, the respective share was 87.95 per cent and 88.73 per cent. In all these counts, the share of government-owned enterprises is significantly lower, respectively 6.69 per cent, 2.55 per cent, and 2.32 per cent, while the respective figures for foreign-owned enterprises are 4.97 per cent, 6.26 per cent, and 5.90 per cent. In terms of salaries and

Table 2.9 Major Manufactured Exports during 1972–73 to 2018–19 (selected years) Value in "000" US$

Commodity	*1972–73*	*1980–81*	*1989–90*	*1999–00*	*2009–10*	*2014–15*	*2018–19*
Ready-made garments	480.52 (0.24)	3,100 (0.6)	609,000 (50.71)	3,082,557 (58.35)	6,013,000 (39.25)	13,065,000 (43.63)	17,245,000 (40.20)
Knitwear	NA	NA	15,000 (1.25)	1,269,835 (24.04)	6,483,000 (42.32)	12,427,000 (41.50)	16,889,000 (43.29)
Jute goods	181,116.88 (89.89)	368,400 (72.1)	331,000 (27.56)	265,849 (5.03)	540,000 (3.53)	757,000 (2.53)	704,000 (1.80)
Leather and leather goods	17,051.59 (8.46)	57,200 (11.2)	179,000 (14.90)	249,924 (4.73)	430,000 (2.81)	587,000 (1.96)	165,000 (0.42)
Chemical products	NA	11,100 (2.2)	23,000 (1.92)	93,529 (1.77)	103,000 (0.67)	112,000 (0.37)	205,000 (0.53)
Naphtha, furnace oil, and bitumen	NA	48,600 (9.5)	17,000 (1.42)	11,396 (0.22)	301,000 (1.97)	78,000 (0.26)	204,000 (0.52)
Engineering products	NA	NA	12,000 1.00	7,626 (0.14)	311,000 (2.03)	447,000 (1.49)	341,000 (0.87)
Handicrafts	NA	3,700 (0.7)	5,000 (0.42)	5,161 (0.10)	4,000 (0.03)	9,000 (0.03)	20,000 (0.05)
Other manufactured commodities	2,844.16 (1.41)	19,100 (3.7)	100,000 (0.83)	297,186 (5.63)	1,135,000 (7.41)	2,461,000 (8.22)	2,969,000 (7.61)
Total Manufactured Exports	1,615.5 (100)	511,100 (100)	1,201,000 (100)	5,283,063 (100)	15,320,000 (100)	29,943,000 (100)	39,014,000 (100)
Manufactured Exports as % of Total Exports	59.60	71.57	78.8	91.84	94.54	95.94	96.24

Sources: GoB (1978:78); GoB (n.d.: 59); GoB (2005b: 290); GoB (2019: 355–56); and GoB (2021: 348).

Note: The % distribution is shown within brackets.

Table 2.10 Bangladesh Exports to Major Countries 2018–2019

Major Countries	*2018–19*	
	Export Earnings (Bil. $)	*Percentage*
United States	6.87	16.98
Germany	6.17	15.23
United Kingdom	4.16	10.29
Spain	2.55	6.36
France	2.22	5.47
Italy	1.64	4.05
Japan	1.37	3.37
Canada	1.34	3.31
Netherlands	1.28	3.15
Poland	1.27	3.14
Others	11.64	28.73
Total	**40.51**	**100.00**

Source: GoB (2020a: 34).

Note: Over 71% of Bangladesh's exports limited to only ten countries.

wages paid, the share of local private ownership was about 90 per cent, while that in government ownership was less than 2 per cent. However, in the case of foreign-owned enterprises, the share in terms of manufacturing employment was 5.71 per cent, and in terms of wages and salaries paid, 6.04 per cent. It is true that at an early stage, in some sectors including pharmaceuticals and footwear there was a heavy dominance of foreign ownership (not shown in the Table 2.11), however over the years even in these sectors, local ownership has grown rapidly.

In the growth of manufacturing that has taken place in Bangladesh, a major outcome is the emergence of a group of local entrepreneurs willing to take up the challenge. Indeed, they have been instrumental in the manufacturing growth of the country, producing over 87 per cent of the total manufacturing output of the country in (Table 2.11). However, in the early years, the manufacturing activities which were confined mostly to jute processing were mainly in the hands of the Europeans and Anglo-Indians and, later, some Marwaries (from Rajasthan), who were already engaged in the jute trade, became more closely involved (Iftikhar-ul-Awwal, 1982: 143–44). Following the creation of Pakistan, there was an in-flow of entrepreneurs from West Pakistan, investing mainly in jute manufacturing and also in leather manufacturing (producing mostly wet blue, an initial form of leather processing). The failure of local industrialists to emerge created the myth that there was little prospect of a native entrepreneurial class to create the growth of the country's industry and commerce. However, through the dynamism which the local entrepreneurs are now demonstrating, the old myth has been totally shattered, and this can be seen vividly, for example, in the growth of the pharmaceuticals industry. Hitherto, this industry was dominated by the MNCs as late as 1985, but by 2011 the narrative had changed; all the top ten manufacturing

Table 2.11 Distribution by Ownership: Fixed Assets, Gross Output and Value Added, 2012

Ownership	*No. of estab.*	*Net Fixed Assets*		*Gross Output*		*Gross Value Added*		*Total Persons Engaged*		*Salary/Wages and Benefits*	
	Number	(In Mil. Tk.)	%	(In Mil. Tk.)	%	(In Mil. Tk.)	%	Number	%	(In Mil. Tk.)	%
Government	103	79,582.65	6.69	138,025.29	2.55	36,319.88	2.32	84,205	1.68	11,225.13	1.97
Local Private	42,231	986,922.45	83.07	4,744,56.55	87.95	1,386,765.89	88.73	4,533,684	90.39	510,399.55	89.69
Government and private jointly	35	11,359.93	0.96	16,499.04	0.31	5,173.93	0.33	20,806	0.41	2,302.29	0.40
Joint venture (local and foreign)	160	51,239.36	4.31	158,154.65	2.93	42,465.39	2.72	90,876	1.81	10,788.75	1.90
Foreign	263	59,003.35	4.97	337,664.74	6.26	92,221.98	5.90	286,365	5.71	34,351.16	6.04
Total	42,792	1,188,107.74	100	5,394,906.28	100	1,562,947.08	100	5,015,936	100	569,066.89	100

Source: BBS (2013: 180).

Note: % distribution: Computed.

firms in the Bangladesh pharmaceutical industry were of local ownership (Amin and Sonobe, 2013: 35). Indeed, the emergence of the local entrepreneurial class, able to lead the industrial development of the country, can truly be considered as a major success story of Bangladesh. As in the NGO sector where Bangladesh has emerged a world leader, besides winning Nobel Prizes, the Bangladeshi industrialists are truly demonstrating their ability to advance the country's manufacturing growth.

In the state sector, the units are operated under state corporations, as shown in Table 2.12. In terms of sales revenue, BCIC (Bangladesh Chemical Industries Corporation) is the largest unit, while BTMC (Bangladesh Textile Mills Corporation) has the lowest relevant figure. However, only BSEC (Bangladesh Steel and Engineering Corporation) appears to be making profit. Also, BJMC (Bangladesh Jute Mills Corporation) has been experiencing serious problems recently and therefore the government has decided to close down the production of all the jute mills under this state corporation (Ahsan and Mahmud, 2020).

As may be seen from Table 2.13, the government-owned enterprises have very low rate of return (VA-W/K), only 3.15 per cent, while these have the highest capital intensity and also the highest wage rate. However, in local private enterprises, the rate of return was 8.88 per cent, and in foreign enterprises, the figure was as high as 9.81 per cent.

2.7 Challenges and Concerns

For a long time, the Bangladesh economy used to be dominated by agriculture and, in exports, by some agriculture-based items such as jute goods. The area now forming Bangladesh was a hinterland of Calcutta, the provincial capital of the then Bengal, with almost all large-scale manufacturing centred around there. There was, however, a thriving cottage and small-scale manufacturing industry mainly based on textile weaving, with artisans famous for their weaving skill. However, the then East Bengal used to supply large quantities of raw jute for the jute mills which were located mainly in and around Calcutta. Following the creation of Pakistan in 1947, in the former East Pakistan (now Bangladesh), the limited industralization which took place was chiefly for the processing of jute. So, in the export composition, the domination by the primary products continued. Now, the Bangladesh situation is completely different, the economy having moved from primary export dependence to manufactured goods.

However, one also needs to be aware of the various concerns and challenges that the sector is experiencing. A major issue is the concentration of exports in terms of product and market. A recent study by Faiz and Maitra (2020: 28) reveals sharply the case of product concentration: "The dependence on a single sector (ready-made garments) has increased over the last 30 years. This indicates that only one sector has grown, and (the) other sectors are stagnant which is very risky for an economy". Over the last 30 years, the contribution of the garments sector has increased from 40.96 per cent of the total exports to 84.21 per cent, while in the case of jute and jute goods (formerly the country's dominant export item), the

Table 2.12 State Ownership of Manufacturing Enterprises, 2018–19

Particulars	*Production*	*Sales Revenue (Million Tk.)*	*Cost of Sales (Million Tk.)*	*Operating profit/ loss (Million Tk.)* *	*Net profit/ loss (Million Tk.)* *
BCIC (Mil. mt.)	1.142	23,148.50	25,741.90	(2,593.40)	(4,854.80)
BTMC (Mil. mt.)	3.41	95.70	191.60	(95.90)	(6,302.20)
BSFIC (Mil. mt.)	4.792	6,473.30	8,915.60	(2,442.30)	(6,302.20)
BJMC (Mil. mt.)	1.304	11,748.70	15,789.90	(4,041.20)	(4,815.10)
BSEC (In Nos.)	2,180.0	7,238.10	6,462.40	775.70	775.70

Source: GoB. (2021: 295).

Note
* Figures shown in brackets indicate losses.

Table 2.13 Performance Indicators for Manufacturing Enterprises by Ownership, 2012

Ownership	*VA/L*	*K/L*	*VA/K*	*W/L*	*(VA-W)/K*
All	311.6	236.9	1.315	113.45	0.840
Government	431.3	945.1	0.456	133.31	0.315
Local Private	305.9	217.7	1.405	112.58	0.888
Government and Private Jointly	248.7	546.0	0.455	110.66	0.253
Joint Venture (local and foreign)	467.3	563.8	0.829	118.72	0.618
Foreign	322.0	206.0	1.563	119.96	0.981

Source: BBS (2013: 180).

Notes: These are the author's estimates based on the data in SMI (2012, p. 180). L = Total persons engaged, W = Salary wages and benefit, K = Net fixed asset, and VA = Gross value added. VA/L = gross value added per employed worker. W/L = employment cost per worker including wages, salaries, benefits and social security. K/L = the value of fixed assets (land, buildings, machines, transport equipment) per workers. VA/K = the ratio of value added to fixed assets, the inverse of the fixed-capital/income ratio.

export share has decreased from 29.71 per cent in 1989 to 2.01 per cent in 2018, and in the case of other main export items, the export share has declined or has remained low or negligible (Faiz and Maitra, 2020: 30; GoB, 2021: 16).

The cheap labour costs that prevail in Bangladesh is considered the main factor helping the growth of exports in garment manufacturing in Bangladesh. Indeed, compared to many other competitors, Bangladeshi entrepreneurs enjoy significantly cheaper labour costs, and this has greatly encouraged them to continue to specialize in garments, a sector which heavily depends on labour inputs (Faiz and Maitra, 2020). The favourable trade conditions, especially the *Most Favoured Nation* (MFN) facility given to Bangladesh as a least-developed country, have also greatly enhanced the growth exports in this sub-sector. However, unfavourable tariff regimes do exist for the non-traditional sectors, so there is an anti-export bias for these sub-sectors. Furthermore, the failure of Bangladesh to attract large FDI inflows has been a constraint to export diversification (Ibid: 31).

Bangladesh's export destination is also concentrated, with only a few countries featuring strongly (Table 2.11). Indeed, according to data from the Export Promotion Bureau, in the fiscal year 2018–19, over 70 per cent of Bangladeshi exports went to the USA, Germany, the UK, Spain, France, Italy, Canada, Japan, the Netherlands, and Poland. Such a high concentration can prove to be detrimental; hence, the urgency to diversify.

While recognizing the emergence of a local entrepreneurial class, playing a major role in the growth of the manufacturing sector of the country, one also needs to raise the concern arising from the loan-default culture which has been a disturbing development in Bangladesh. The seriousness of the crisis can perhaps be gleaned from a statement made by the Bangladesh Finance Minister in January 2020, naming three of the top loan defaulters, all of which are involved in manufacturing (The Daily Star, 2020). The number of loan defaulters in

Bangladesh stood at 8,238 in November 2020. At current prices, the total amount of the defaulted loans in Bangladesh was Taka 224,814.1 Mil. in end-December 2008, while the respective figure was Taka 1,162,883.1 Mil. in end-September 2019, i.e. the total amount of the default loans as a percentage of the total loans given by the banks increased from 10.79 per cent to 11.99 per cent over the corresponding period. It is true that the loan defaulters are not confined to the manufacturing sector alone, but at the top of the list of loan defaulters, there are a number of firms that belong to sub-sectors such as footwear and leather.

Another major issue is that Bangladeshi exports consist mostly of low-technology manufactured goods, and this is particularly striking in the context of the relevant development taking place in various Asian growing economies. For example, in 2016, 61 per cent of South Korea's exports consisted of high-technology products, and the corresponding figure in the Philippines, China, Thailand, Vietnam, and India were 61 per cent, 52 per cent, 50 per cent, 39 per cent, and 17 per cent, respectively, while in Bangladesh it was less than 1 per cent, i.e. machinery and electronics. What is particularly concerning is that, in Bangladesh this figure has remained unchanged since 1965. In the case of India, the corresponding figure gradually increased from 2 per cent in 1965 to 7 per cent in 1985, to 10 per cent in 2000, and further to 17 per cent in 2016; and in the case of South Korea the jump was simply astounding from 3 per cent in 1965 to 61 per cent in 2016. (Chang and Zach, 2018: 11).

The extremely low share of high-technology exports of Bangladesh is however not surprising, given that a serious national commitment to technology promotion has been missing and it has, obviously, not helped the cause of technological capability building. Fortunately, in the agricultural sector of Bangladesh, there is now evidence of significant success, thanks to some dedicated technology development and absorption initiatives undertaken over many years. In particular, Bangladesh Agricultural Research Institute (BARI), established in 1978, has been playing a major role in technology absorption and development in the country. Thus, various technological developments that have taken place in Bangladesh's agriculture have greatly helped to achieve some spectacular successes in productivity growth, especially in a number of crops (Ahmed, 1998; Hossain et al., 2006). Unfortunately though, the state of technological capability building in the Bangladesh manufacturing sector was found to be deficient, with the amount spent on R&D remaining negligible (Sahota, 1991; Huq and Islam, 1993; and Huq 2021b). Obviously, this conflicts with the national objective of vigorously promoting the manufacturing sector, and converting Bangladesh into a high-income country, with the industrial sector playing a leading role in helping fulfill the objective set out by the government of Bangladesh (GoB, 2020c).

Another issue of particular concern, as expressed in various quarters, is the slow pace of trade liberalization which, presumably, has been affecting export growth.[2] This concern was earlier voiced by the World Bank and has recently been strongly focused on by Ahmed and Sattar (2019), arguing for speeding up the process of liberalization and, in the process, removing the anti-export bias of the non-RMG sectors. This view has also been stated in the 7th Five-Year Plan (GoB, 2015: 39). However, many others are found to take a different approach.[2] While there is an appreciation that the growth performance of Bangladesh has been significantly influenced by the liberalization measures, there is also a belief that the liberalization of the tariff regime alone is unlikely to be sufficient for promoting export and economic growth. Indeed, various studies using historical data have failed to find a conclusive relationship between trade liberalization and growth in the context of the Bangladesh economy. Some simulation exercises based on applied general equilibrium models such as those of Khondker and Raihan (2004) and Annabi et al. (2006) have not shown any significant growth dividend from further trade liberalization of tariffs in Bangladesh. Also, the relationship between trade liberalization and employment has been a contentious issue, and one in which it is difficult to establish a direct linkage, as there are many channels through which trade liberalization can influence the labour market, directly or indirectly (see, e.g., Begum and Shamsuddin (1998); and Razzaque et al., 2003). The studies of Razzaque et al. (2003) and Raihan (2007), though overcoming some of the methodological problems of earlier studies, have also found no significant effect of trade liberalization on the export-growth relationship. Furthermore, Raihan's study (2007) of the manufacturing sector of Bangladesh for the 1977–98 period, found no evidence of any statistically significant positive 'trade liberalisation-growth nexus'. Not surprisingly, as observed by Raihan (2008: 2), there is a "continuing debate over the future direction of trade liberalisation in Bangladesh. Questions have been raised over whether Bangladesh ought to undertake further drastic wholesale liberalisation of trade or adopt a more gradual approach." A number of others including Mahmud (1998), Rashid (2000), and Huq (2020) appear to support the viewpoint that a much slower pace of liberalization is warranted. It is, therefore, not difficult to appreciate the strong emphasis on a conscious strategy of industrialization as put forward by Sobhan (1991), while advancing the case for industrial development in Bangladesh. Indeed, in the context of Bangladesh, to improve competitiveness, there are many other factors including improvement in rent-seeking behaviour, easing customs clearance, improving the serious transport bottlenecks. Furthermore, as observed by Huq (2021a: 142): "The available evidence seems to suggest that the growth performance of Bangladesh has not been achieved by liberalisation measures alone. The state's role in providing various incentives has been highly instrumental, but the emphasis on state support should in no way undermine the great benefits which have followed from trade liberalisation".

Another important challenge for the economy is to expedite the growth in employment and, given the high importance attached to manufacturing, this sector is expected to play an important role in this regard. As found by Moazzem and Reza (2020), the overall employment elasticity in the manufacturing sector is not very encouraging, only 0.28. However, the extensive estimates, as made by these authors, show that "the country's employment growth and its relative concentration is strongly associated with the growth and gravity of different export-oriented industries. … … (Furthermore) both the labour-intensive and capital-intensive industries under different export categories of industries, experienced growth in employment" (Ibid: 169). Hence, for increasing the growth in employment, the urgency is to encourage the growth of this type of export-oriented industries.

2.8 Concluding Remarks

The manufacturing sector of Bangladesh has witnessed some remarkable changes especially over the last three decades. While the jute sector – the erstwhile mainstay of the economy for foreign exchange earnings and also the main large-scale manufacturing activity – declined over the years, garments manufacturing emerged rapidly, and in the process has replaced jute, not only as a major foreign exchange earner but also as the main employer in the manufacturing sector. The vibrant nature of local enterprise has been clearly demonstrated and the entrepreneurs appear to be responding enthusiastically to encouragements offered by the state.

Indeed, the rapid change in manufacturing demonstrates the commendable ability of the economy to achieve some significant movements of labour and capital. This also means that by the 1990s Bangladesh had already emerged as a manufacturing export-earning country, with over 80 per cent of exports consisting of manufactured items, albeit the majority of the products produced with relatively simple technology. There are a number of highly positive features and the momentum needs to be maintained.

In the case of the Bangladesh economics (which, in the past, depended heavily on static comparative advantage focusing on specialization in primary goods), a positive move has definitely taken place with an approach towards dynamic comparative advantage. In this context, those specifically who initiated the move towards garment manufacturing deserve special praise. Similarly, the 1982 National Drug Policy was a major move for the country, helping to lay the foundations of the local pharmaceutical industry. However, there is an urgency to build on the realized gains. In particular, the competitive position needs to be maintained, and these demand serious considerations based on close and deep research investigations. Furthermore, the various concerns and challenges need to be attended urgently.

Notes

1 The article is taken mainly from Ch 8 (Manufacturing) of a forthcoming volume on *The Economy of Bangladesh: 50 Years of Economic Development* (by M M Huq, M K Mujeri and Q Shahabuddin), hopefully to be published soon. The author would like to acknowledge the extensive research support kindly provided by Bisaw Nath Roy and Jewel Sarker. Roy Grieve, Eric Rahim and Michael Tribe read an earlier draft and made some valuable comments. Also special thanks to Rose Mary Harley for kindly editing an earlier draft!
2 The arguments below are mostly taken from Huq (2020: 139–40).

References

Ahmed, R. (1998). Assessment of Past Agriculture Policies. Chapter 3 in R. Faruquee (ed), *Bangladesh Agriculture in the 21st Century*. Dhaka: University Press Limited.

Ahmed, S. and Z. Sattar. (2019). *Bangladesh Trade Policy for Growth and Employment: Collected Essays*. Dhaka: Policy Research Institute of Bangladesh.

Ahsan, N. and A. Mahmud (2020). Stopping Production at BJMC Jute Mills-1: Decision Farsighted, Closure to Save Taxpayers' Money. *The Dhaka Tribune* (9 July, 2020).

Amin, N. and T. Sonobe (2013). The Success of The Industrial Development Policy in The Pharmaceutical Industry in Bangladesh, GRIPS Discussion Paper13-07. *National Graduate Institute for Policy Studies*. Tokyo: National Graduate Institute for Policy Studies.

Annabi, et al (2006). WTO Agreements and Domestic Policy Reforms – Implications for Poverty in Bangladesh: A Study in a Dynamic Sequential CGE Framework, in Hertel, T. and Winters, A. (eds.), *Poverty and the WTO: Impacts of the Doha Development Agenda*. Washington DC: World Bank and Palgrave Macmillan.

Bakht, Z. (ed) (1991). *The Bangladesh Development Studies*, special issue: "Industrial Policies and State of Industrialization in Bangladesh". 19(1/2), March–June 1991. Dhaka: BIDS.

BBS (Bangladesh Bureau of Statistics) (2011). *Report on Labour Force Survey 2010*. August, 2011. Ministry of Planning, Government of the People's Republic of Bangladesh. Dhaka: Bangladesh Bureau of Statistics.

BBS (2013). *Survey of Manufacturing Industries (SMI) 2012*. Statistics, Planning and Statistics and Information Division (SID). Dhaka: Bangladesh Bureau of Statistics.

BBS (2015). *Report on Labour Force Survey (LFS) Bangladesh 2013*. October, 2015. Ministry of Planning, Government of the People's Republic of Bangladesh. Dhaka: Bangladesh Bureau of Statistics.

BBS (2018). *Report on Labour Force Survey (LFS) 2016–17*. January, 2018. Ministry of Planning, Government of the People's Republic of Bangladesh. Dhaka: Bangladesh Bureau of Statistics.

BBS (2019). *Statistical Year Book Bangladesh 2018*. Statistics and Information Division, Ministry of Planning. Dhaka: Bangladesh Bureau of Statistics.

BBS (2020). *Survey of Manufacturing Industries 2019*. Planning and Statistics and Information Division. Dhaka: Bangladesh Bureau of Statistics.

Begum, S. and A. F. M. Shamsuddin (1998). Exports and Economic Growth in Bangladesh. *Journal of Development Studies*. 35(1), pp. 89–114.

Chang, H.-J. and K. Zach (2018). *Industrial Development In Asia: Trends In Industrialization And Industrial Policy Experiences Of Developing Asia*, (WIDER Working Paper 2018). Retrieved from: https://www.wider.unu.edu/sites/default/files/wp2018-120.pdf (Accessed: 21 February, 2020).

Daily Star (2020). The Big Scammers Top Defaulters' List. (*The Daily Star*, Dhaka, 23 January) 2020. https://epaper.thedailystar.net/Home/ArticleView?eid=1&edate=23/01/2020&pgid=9057 (Accessed: 20 December 2021).

Faaland, J. and J. R. Parkinson (1976). *Bangladesh: The Test Case of Development*. London: Hurst and Company.

Faiz, M. and P. Maitra. (2020). *Concentration and Diversification of Export Economy of Bangladesh: Comparison and Policy Implication with Other Asian Countries*. South Asian Journal of Social Studies and Economics. September 2020.

GoB (Government of Bangladesh) (1975). *Bangladesh Economic Survey 1973-74.* Government of The People's Republic of Bangladesh. Dhaka: Ministry of Finance.

GoB (1978). *The Two-Year Plan of Bangladesh, 1978-1980.* Government of People's Republic of Bangladesh. Dhaka: Planning Commission. September, 1978.

GoB (1982). *New Industrial Policy 1982.* 1 June 1982. Government of the People's Republic of Bangladesh. Dhaka: Ministry of Industries.

GoB (1986). *Revised Industrial Policy 1986.* Government of the People's Republic of Bangladesh. Dhaka: Ministry of Industries.

GoB (1997). *The Fifth Five Year Plan of Bangladesh, 1997–2002.* Government of People's Republic of Bangladesh. Dhaka: Planning Commission.

GoB (1999). *Industrial Policy 1999.* Government of the People's Republic of Bangladesh. Dhaka: Ministry of Industries.

GoB (2005a). *Industrial Policy 2005.* March 2005. Government of the People's Republic of Bangladesh. Dhaka: Ministry of Industries.

GoB (2005b). *Bangladesh Economic Review 2005.* December, 2005. Government of Peoples' Republic of Bangladesh. Dhaka: Bangladesh Government Press.

GoB (2011). *Sixth Five Year Plan FY2011-FY2015: Accelerating Growth and Reducing Poverty.* December, 2011. Government of People's Republic of Bangladesh. Dhaka: Planning Commission.

GoB (2012). *Making Vision 2021: A Reality Perspective Plan of Bangladesh 2010–2021*, April 2012. Dhaka: General Economics Division.

GoB (2014). *Bangladesh Economic Review 2014.* December, 2014. Government of Peoples' Republic of Bangladesh. Dhaka: Bangladesh Government Press.

GoB (2015). *Seventh Five Year Plan FY2016-FY2020: Accelerating Growth, Empowering Citizens.* December, 2015. Government of People's Republic of Bangladesh. Dhaka: Planning Commission.

GoB (2017). *Bangladesh Economic Review 2017.* December, 2017. Government of Peoples' Republic of Bangladesh. Dhaka: Bangladesh Government Press.

GoB (2019). *Bangladesh Economic Review 2019.* June, 2019. Government of Peoples' Republic of Bangladesh. Dhaka: Bangladesh Government Press.

GoB (2020a). *Export Data.* July-January 2019–20. Government of Bangladesh, Dhaka 2020. Dhaka: Export Promotion Bureau Retrieved.

GoB (2020b). *Eighth Five Year Plan FY2020-FY2025: Promoting Prosperity and Fostering Inclusiveness.* December, 2020. Government of People's Republic of Bangladesh. Dhaka: Planning Commission.

GoB (2020c). *Making Vision 2041 a Reality: Perspective Plan of Bangladesh 2021-41.* Dhaka: Bangladesh Government Press, March 2020.

GoB (2021). *Bangladesh Economic Review 2021.* August, 2021. Government of Peoples' Republic of Bangladesh. Dhaka: Bangladesh Government Press.

GoB (n.d.). *Bangladesh Economy: Recent Macroeconomic Trend.* Dhaka: Ministry of Finance. Online Portal https://mof.portal.gov.bd/sites/default/files/files/mof.portal.gov.bd/page/fbec0015_547a_4cd0_ad6d_4e1f8fd07ba4/appendices.pdf

Hossain, M., M. L. Bose, and B. A. A. Mustafi. (2006). Adoption and Productivity Impact of Modern Rice Varieties in Bangladesh. *The Developing Economies*, 44(2).

Huq, M. (2021a). Liberalised Trade Policy with State Commitment to Growth: The Case of Bangladesh, in M. Tribe (ed), *Economic Neoliberalism and International Development.* London and New York: Routledge.

Huq, M. (2021b). Technological Capability Building: A Note *Foro. Science and Technology, Special Issue*, July–August, 2021. 5(4), pp. 50–62.

Huq, M. and J. Love (2000). Bangladesh Industrialisation since Independence, in M. Huq and J. Love (eds.), *Strategies for Industrialisation: The Case of Bangladesh.* Dhaka: University Press Ltd.

Huq, M. and K. M. N. Islam (1991). Transfer of Technology to Less Developed Countries: A Case Study of the Fertilizer Industry in Bangladesh. *Science, Technology and Development*, 9(1/2).

Huq, M. and K. M. N. Islam (1992). *Fertilizer Manufacture in Bangladesh: An Industry Study with Particular Reference to Choice of Technology.* Dhaka: University Press Ltd.

Huq, M. and M. Tribe (2018). *The Economy of Ghana: 50 Years of Economic Development.* London: Palgrave Macmillan.

Huq, M., K. M. N. Islam and N. Islam (1993). *Machinery Manufacturing in Bangladesh: An industry study with particular reference to technological capability.* Dhaka: University Press Ltd.

Iftikhar-ul-Awwal, A. Z. M. (1982). *The Industrial Development of Bengal, 1900–1939.* New Delhi: Vikas Publishing House Pvt Ltd.

Islam, N. (1999). Tropical Doctor, 29(2), April 1999. Access from online: https://journals.sagepub.com/doi/pdf/10.1177/004947559902900206

Khan, A. R. (2015). *The Economy of Bangladesh: A Quarter Century of Development.* London: Palgrave Macmillan.

Khondker, B. H. and S. Raihan (2004). Welfare and Poverty Impacts of Policy Reforms in Bangladesh: A General Equilibrium Approach, Paper Presented at the Seventh Annual Global Economic Conference (GTAP), The World Bank, Washington DC, USA, 17–19 June 2004.

Mahmud, W. (1998). Bangladesh: Structural Adjustment and Beyond. Paper presented at the International Conference on Adjustment and Beyond: the Reform Experience in South Asia, jointly organized by the Bangladesh Economic Association and the International Economic Association, Dhaka, 30 March-1 April 1998.

Moazzem, K. G. and M. M. M. Reza (2020). "Growth of Manufacturing Employment in the Changing Context of Trade and Trade-Related Policies", in M. Muqtada (ed), *Quest for Inclusive Growth in Bangladesh: An Employment-focused Strategy.* Singapore: Springer, pp. 137–173

Nath, N. C. (2012). Manufacturing Sector of Bangladesh-Growth, Structure and Strategies for Future Development. Paper for Presentation at the Biennial Conference "Global Economy and Vision 2021", held at the Institution of Engineers (12–14 July, 2012). Dhaka: Centre for Policy Dialogue (CPD).

Raihan, S. (2007). *Dynamics of Trade Liberalization in Bangladesh: Analysis of Policies and Practices.* Dhaka: Pathak Shamabesh.

Raihan, S. (2008). *Trade Liberalization and Poverty in Bangladesh.* Macao Regional Knowledge Hub Working Papers, No. 15, December 2008.

Rashid, M. A. (2000). Impact of Trade Reforms on Industrial Productivity and Employment, in Centre for Policy Dialogue, Structural Adjustment Participatory Review Initiative, Bangladesh (a report prepared for presentation in the Second National Forum of Bangladesh SAPRI held in Dhaka, March 13–15, 2001).

Razzaque, A., B. H. Khondker, N. Ahmed and M. K. Mujeri (2003). *Trade Liberalization and Economic Growth: Empirical Evidence on Bangladesh.* MAP Technical Paper. Dhaka: Bangladesh Institute of Development Studies.

Robinson, E. A. G. (1973). *Economic Prospects of Bangladesh*. London: Overseas Development Institute.

Sahota (1991). An Assessment of the Impact of Industrial Policies in Bangladesh. *Bangladesh Development Studies*, XIX (1 and 2), Mar–June 1991, pp. 157–199. Dhaka: Bangladesh Institute of Development Studies.

Sobhan, R. (1991). An Industrial Strategy for Industrial Policy: Redirecting the Industrial Development of Bangladesh in the 1990s. *Bangladesh Development Studies*, 19(1/2): March-June 1991.

World Bank (2019). *World Development Indicators*. July 2018. Washington, DC: The World Bank.

World Bank (2020). *World Development Indicators*. April 2020, Washington DC: Washington, The World Bank.

World Bank (2021). *World Development Indicators*. April 2020, Washington DC: Washington, The World Bank.

Table 2 A1 Performance Indicators for Some Selected Major Manufacturing Sub-sectors, 2012 (BSIC 4 digit) (Values at '000 Taka: Current Prices)

BSIC code	*Industry*	*L*		*W*		*K*		*I*		*GVO*		*VA*		*VA/L*	*W/L*	*K/L*	*VA/GVO*	*W/VA*	*VA/K*	*(VA-W)/K*
		Number	*%*	*Values*	*%*	*Values*	*%*	*Values*	*%*	*Values*	*%*	*Values*	*%*							
1	*2*	*3*	*4*	*5*	*6*	*7*	*8*	*9*	*10*	*11*	*12*	*13*	*14*	*15*	*16*	*17*	*18*	*19*	*20*	*21*
1410	Manufacture of wearing apparel, except fur apparel	1,840,159	36.7	209,993,839	36.9	217,092,300	18.3	859,416,843	22.8	1,252,278,730	23.2	376,929,990	24.1	204.8	114.1	118.0	0.3	0.6	1.7	0.8
2410	Manufacture of basic iron and steel	102,903	2.1	15,259,872	2.7	81,533,034	6.9	577,453,142	15.3	766,035,352	14.2	183,567,288	11.7	1783.9	148.3	792.3	0.2	0.1	2.3	2.1
1430	Manufacture of knitted and crocheted apparel	909,500	18.1	103,126,470	18.1	107,968,907	9.1	379,111,187	10.1	561,918,447	10.4	176,816,245	11.3	194.4	113.4	118.7	0.3	0.6	1.6	0.7
1311	Preparation and spinning of textile fibres	274,616	5.5	28,392,467	5.0	75,092,849	6.3	205,370,655	5.5	288,632,625	5.4	81,208,200	5.2	295.7	103.4	273.4	0.3	0.3	1.1	0.7
2394	Manufacture of cement, lime and plaster	21,757	0.4	3,069,674	0.5	52,368,791	4.4	168,546,215	4.5	225,579,602	4.2	55,319,316	3.5	2542.6	141.1	2407.0	0.2	0.1	1.1	1.0
1063	Manufacture of rice/rice milling	83,978	1.7	9,178,447	1.6	32,789,861	2.8	126,776,847	3.4	180,097,710	3.3	51,744,820	3.3	616.2	109.3	390.5	0.3	0.2	1.6	1.3
2397	Manufacture of bricks / blocks, tiles	429,772	8.6	42,112,922	7.4	21,375,362	1.8	55,466,030	1.5	106,465,571	2.0	48,180,669	3.1	112.1	98.0	49.7	0.5	0.9	2.3	0.3
1040	Manufacture of vegetable and animal oils and fats	15,046	0.3	2,269,034	0.4	10,218,228	0.9	117,207,782	3.1	162,870,021	3.0	42,836,689	2.7	2847.0	150.8	679.1	0.3	0.1	4.2	4.0
1313	Finishing of textiles (dying, bleaching etc.)	99,425	2.0	11,575,498	2.0	30,506,861	2.6	70,090,495	1.9	107,896,710	2.0	35,773,189	2.3	359.8	116.4	306.8	0.3	0.3	1.2	0.8
1314	Manufacture of jute textiles	173,283	3.5	19,975,606	3.5	67,414,574	5.7	66,144,604	1.8	100,829,322	1.9	32,949,014	2.1	190.1	115.3	389.0	0.3	0.6	0.5	0.2

2431	Casting of iron and steel	17,205	0.3	2,547,027	0.4	16,285,238	1.4	104,979,845	2.8	137,990,015	2.6	32,800,124	2.1	1906.4	148.0	946.5	0.2	0.1	2.0	1.9
2100	Manufacture of pharmaceuticals, medicinal chemicals and botanical products (Allopathic)	62,643	1.2	10,038,432	1.8	67,620,074	5.7	74,084,821	2.0	107,633,107	2.0	31,852,328	2.0	508.5	160.2	1079.5	0.3	0.3	0.5	0.3
2732	Manufacture of other electronic and electric wires and cables	11,623	0.2	1,692,078	0.3	7,226,588	0.6	78,618,068	2.1	107,980,235	2.0	28,794,867	1.8	2477.4	145.6	621.7	0.3	0.1	4.0	3.8
1312	Weaving of textiles (excluding handloom products)	47,555	0.9	5,386,533	0.9	27,310,613	2.3	54,904,118	1.5	78,502,159	1.5	22,432,012	1.4	471.7	113.3	574.3	0.3	0.2	0.8	0.6
1061	Manufacture of grain mill products except rice milling	14,565	0.3	1,894,251	0.3	4,699,155	0.4	37,718,262	1.0	53,681,801	1.0	15,395,683	1.0	1057.0	130.1	322.6	0.3	0.1	3.3	2.9
1315	Manufacture of handloom textiles	101,584	2.0	9,386,307	1.6	9,095,801	0.8	18,924,203	0.5	34,236,018	0.6	14,983,978	1.0	147.5	92.4	89.5	0.4	0.6	1.6	0.6

Source: BBS (2013: 188–196).

Note: These are the author's estimates based on the data in SMI 2012 (BBS, 2013: 181–182). L= Total persons engaged, W= Salary wages and benefits, K=Net fixed assets, I– Industrial cost, VA=Gross value added, GVO=Gross Output. Columns 4,6,8,10,12,14 = values in %. Columns 5, 7,9,11,13,15,16, 17 = values in thousand Taka (current prices). Columns 18,19,20, 21 = ratios. VA/L = gross value added per employed worker. W/L = employment cost per worker including wages, salaries, benefits and social security. K/L = value of fixed assets (land, buildings, machines, transport, equipment) per workers. VA/ GVO = ratio of gross value added to gross value of output. W/VA = ratio of employment cost to value added. VA/K = ratio of value added to fixed assets, the inverse of the fixed -capital/ income ratio. The last column is a crude measure of gross pre-tax rate of return on capital (or rather fixed capital).

3 Remittances, Foreign Aid, and Economic Growth in Bangladesh: An Empirical Analysis[1]

S A Abbas, E A Selvanathan, and S Selvanathan

3.1 Introduction

Foreign aid and remittances are the two most important external sources of development finance for many developing countries. Over the last few decades, foreign aid flows worldwide have increased gradually while remittance flows have risen phenomenally. For example, during the period 1980–2018, the aid flows have increased by almost five times globally. In the same period, remittance flows worldwide have increased by more than 17 times (Source: World Development Indicators (WDI), 2020). A large volume of remittance receipts was witnessed globally; however, a greater surge was observed in Europe and Central Asia, East Asia and the Pacific, and the South Asian regions. Due to rapid growth in remittances worldwide, policymakers have taken a great deal of interest in its effectiveness.

There is a large amount of literature on the determinants as well as on the role of foreign aid and remittances on the economic growth and well-being of developing countries. Remittance flows – private financial flows, have been found to play an important role in income and consumption smoothing, fiscal stabilization, investment, economic growth, and unemployment reduction. In addition, it also improves the income distribution in developing countries. Foreign aid has also been found to enhance government welfare expenditures, economic growth, and inequality reduction; however, the literature provides mixed opinions. The impact is found to be much stronger in countries with better established institutions, political stability, and governance quality. Hence, the two financial flows are crucial for fiscal sustainability and economic development of low-income countries. Apart from the important contribution of these flows to economic growth and development, little is known about the relationship between foreign aid and remittances.

Like many developing countries, Bangladesh has also received a large amount of aid and remittance flows over the last few decades. There are some studies that have examined the impact of remittances and aid flows on the economic growth and development of Bangladesh. This chapter applies the dynamic econometric techniques to recent data and examines the impact of foreign aid as well as

DOI: 10.4324/9781003231912-6

remittance flows on economic growth in Bangladesh. In particular, the present study employs the Autoregressive Distributed Lag (ARDL) method to investigate the aid-growth and remittance-growth relationships for Bangladesh.

This chapter is organized as follows. Section 3.2 presents the literature review on the impacts of both financial flows (foreign aid and remittances) on economic growth as well as on the relationship between them. Section 3.3 presents a preliminary data analysis of foreign aid, remittances, and economic growth in Bangladesh while also presenting a comparison of the results in the context of overall South Asia and major countries within the region, since Bangladesh is located in South Asia. Section 3.4 discusses the methodological framework and presents the estimation results. The last section concludes the chapter and offers important policy implications.

3.2 Literature Review

In this section, we review the recent literature on the link between economic growth, foreign aid, and remittances with reference to Bangladesh.

3.2.1 Foreign Aid and Economic Growth

Financial flows, in particular, foreign aid and remittances, have long been the subject of discourse among policymakers due to their important role in influencing economic growth and development in developing countries and regions. Earlier studies by development economists documented the positive and significant role of foreign aid in promoting growth in developing countries. For example, Papanek (1973) studying the cross-country analysis of 34 developing countries for the 1950s and 51 countries for the 1960s, found a significant and positive relationship between foreign aid and economic growth. Later, Mosley (1980) re-examined Papanek's work considering the panel data of 56 developing countries for the period 1969–1977. His study did not find the growth-enhancing effect of aid significant in overall developing countries, however, the aid-growth relationship is found to be positive and significant only for the poorest countries. Following this, employing the empirical approaches of the aforementioned studies, Dowling and Hiemenz (1983) using the three-year averaged panel data of 52 developing countries for the period 1968–1979, found foreign aid to be effective in promoting growth only in Asian countries.

The second stream of aid-growth literature linked aid effectiveness with favourable macroeconomic policy and a set institutional quality framework. For example, Durbarry et al. (1998) analyzing the large panel data of 68 developing countries for the period 1970–1993, documented that aid promotes growth conditional upon stable macroeconomic policies although the results differ according to income, geography, and the aid volumes. Burnside and Dollar (2000) studying the four-year average data of 56 developing countries for the period 1970–1993, found that aid improves economic growth with good fiscal, monetary, and trade policies. They contributed to the literature by interacting aid with policy variables. However, Lensink and White (2000) analyzing the World Bank's "*Assessing Aid*" report, contended that the "good policies" condition is arguable since aid is fungible and policies differ across aid-recipient countries. Hansen and Tarp (2001) reinvestigated the aid-growth nexus using various econometric techniques on five-year averaged data of 56 developing countries for the period 1974–1993 and reported the positive impact of growth in "all conditions" and particularly through the investment channel. Further, they also determined the negative returns of aid in quadratic form and found aid to have a positive impact initially on economic growth; however, at a later stage (of high aid-dependency), it reduces growth. Reproducing the estimates of earlier studies, they concluded that the aid-growth relationship is sensitive to modelling techniques and the choice of a set of controls. In another study, Lensink and White (2001) using panel data of 111 developing countries for the period 1975–1992, confirm the non-linear effects of aid on growth. Collier and Dollar (2002), considering four-year averaged data of 59 developing countries for the period 1974–1999, reported the effectiveness of aid combined with a good set of policies but found it ineffective in a poor policy framework as aid allocation is impacted by inefficient disbursement. Clemens et al. (2004) reassessing the earlier studies' models, found a significant positive impact of aid on growth in the short-run irrespective of income levels and institutional quality. Likewise, Dalgaard et al. (2004), studying panel data of 65 aid-receiving developing countries for the period 1974–1997, found foreign aid, in general, effective in the long run; however, the size of aid-effectiveness depends on macroeconomic policies, structural features and aid volumes. Tezanos et al. (2013), analyzing the growth effects of aid in 32 developing countries of Latin America and the Caribbean region for the period 1992–2007, found aid to be effective in increasing (inequality-adjusted) per capita income. Maruta et al. (2020), examining the large panel data set of 74 developing countries (from the South America, Asia, and Africa regions) for the period 1980–2016, found (sectoral) aid significant in promoting growth when linked with institutional quality. They also found educational aid to be effective in South America, health aid in Asia, and agriculture aid to be growth-enhancing in Africa.

In contrast to the earlier two streams, one group of literature views that foreign aid negatively impacts economic growth by increasing the debt burden on poor countries, reducing domestic resource mobilization, and governance problems with an expansion of public sector spending. For example, Rajan and Subramanian (2008), studying cross-country analysis of 68 developing countries for the period 1960–2000, indicated aid ineffectiveness under specific policies and geographical regions. Likewise, Chong et al. (2009), using panel data of 60 developing countries over the 1971–2002 period, found that aid does not increase income (or reduce poverty). Moreover, Young and Sheehan (2014), analyzing a large panel data set of 116 developing countries for the period 1970–2010, concluded that aid does not significantly affect growth even when controlled for institutions. Their findings suggest that aid flows are detrimental to economic and political institutions. Further, Bird and Choi (2020), studying panel data of 51 developing countries over the 1976–2015 period, found the insignificant (rather ambiguous) effect of aid on economic growth in developing countries.

Studies examining the impact of aid on economic growth in Bangladesh show mixed results. For instance, Rahman (1984), examining a two-sector model for the period 1972–1984, found a positive impact of foreign aid on economic growth. Hossain (2014), applying the ordinary least square estimation method on 33 years of data (1980–2012) under different government regimes, also documented the positive but limited impact of aid on growth. Likewise, Ahamad et al. (2019), using the Autoregressive Distributed Lag (ARDL) model on time series data for the period 1981–2016, recorded a significantly positive effect of aid on income growth both in the short and long run. On other hand, Hossain et al. (2019), using the vector error correction method to analyze the data over the period 1972–2015, failed to report any significant effect of foreign aid on income growth both in the short and long run while Hassan et al. (2016), applying the dynamic and fully modified ordinary least squares approaches on annual Bangladesh data for the period 1976–2012, asserted a negative impact of aid on growth. Some studies also analyzed the loans and grant elements of foreign aid disbursed to Bangladesh. For example, Islam (1992), applying the ordinary least squares method on time series data for the period 1972–1988, concluded that foreign aid is ineffective overall; however, the disaggregated analysis of aid suggests that loans positively influence growth while grants bring negative impact. Quazi (2005), employing the dynamic least square approach on annual Bangladesh data over the period 1973–1999, found a marginal impact of aid on growth. His disaggregated analysis of aid reveals the positive impact of the loans on growth while grants do not show any significant impact.

3.3 Remittances and Economic Growth

Remittances – private financial flows – have been found to be important for their crucial role in macroeconomic stabilization, income and consumption investment, unemployment reduction, and physical and human capital development. Most studies analyzing the remittance flows have found significant in promoting economic growth. For example, Adams and Page (2005), analyzed a panel data set of 71 developing countries for the period 1980–1998, and found remittance flows significant in improving income and reducing poverty. Acosta et al. (2008), studying panel data of 59 developing countries over the 1970–2000 period, also found significant and positive impact of remittances on economic growth. Giuliano and Ruiz-Arranz (2009), considering a large panel data set of 100 developing countries over the period 1975–2002, asserted that remittances promote growth through investment channels by offering liquidity (when the financial system has limited coverage) in developing countries. Cooray (2012) studied panel data from five major South Asian countries (namely Bangladesh, India, Nepal, Pakistan, and Sri Lanka) for the period 1970–2008, and found remittances to be effective in promoting growth in that region. Further,

Nyamongo et al. (2012), using a panel data set from 36 African countries for the period 1980–2009, also contended that remittances significantly improve growth in African countries. Imai et al. (2014), using a panel data set from 24 Asia-Pacific countries over the years 1989–2009 period, found a positive significant impact of remittances on growth and well-being in Asia Pacific countries. Likewise, Chowdhury (2016), studying the panel data of top-33 remittance-receiving countries for the period 1979–2011, revealed remittance flows to be effective in influencing growth. Meyer and Shera (2017), analyzing panel data consisting of seven high-remittances countries over the 1993–2013 period, found a robust positive impact of remittances on growth in high remittance-receiving countries. Williams (2018), considering a large panel data set of 109 developing countries for the 1975–2014 period, also documented the significant and positive impact of remittances on economic growth specifically in countries with strong democratic institutions.

The literature also reports the ineffectiveness of remittance flows in contribution to economic growth. For example, Catrinescu et al. (2009), analyzing the large panel data set comprising 135 developing countries for the period 1984–2003, failed to report the robust long-run growth effects of remittances. Their findings suggest that remittances contribute to growth only in countries with strong political and economic policies and good institutions. Likewise, Rao and Hassan (2011), studying the panel data of 40 remittance-receiving countries for the period 1960–2007, did not find any direct significant growth effects of remittances; however, marginal indirect growth effect is found through investment and financial development channels of remittance flows. In contrast to traditional literature, Bird and Choi (2020) recorded growth-reducing effect of remittances in a panel analysis of 51 developing countries for the period 1976–2015.

Due to impressive flows of remittances, researchers have shown a great deal of interest in examining its impact on economic growth in Bangladesh. For example, Salim (1992) documented that remittance flows finance import payments and government investment, thus helping to promote growth. Ahmed and Uddin (2009), applying the Granger causality tests on annual data from 1976–2005, found remittances to be significant and positively influencing growth in the short run. Studies have also examined the causal relationship between remittances and output in Bangladesh. For example, Kumar and Stauvermann (2014) determined the bi-directional (two-way) causality between remittances and economic output while Siddique et al. (2012) found the uni-directional causality running from remittances to growth when applying Granger causality tests on Bangladesh data for the periods 1979–2012 and 1975–2006. The literature also reveals a non-linear relationship between remittances and productivity or economic growth. For instance, Hassan et al. (2016), employing the dynamic and fully modified ordinary least squares estimation methods on the 1976–2012 annual data, revealed a non-linear (U-shaped) effect of remittances on Total Factor Productivity (TFP). They found a negative impact on TFP until remittances reach closer to 8% (of GDP) and then a positive impact when the remittance to GDP ratio exceeds 14%. Likewise, Hassan and Shakur (2017), applying the ordinary least squares, instrumental two-stage least squares, and generalized method of moment techniques on time series data for the period 1976–2012, also examined the non-linear (U-shaped) relationship between remittances and GDP growth, i.e., remittances initially reduce growth and later at a higher level, remittances positively influence GDP growth. In contrast to earlier studies, Sutradhar (2020), employing the fixed and random effects methods on panel data of four South Asian countries (namely Bangladesh, India, Pakistan, and Sri Lanka), found a growth-reducing effect of remittances in Bangladesh.

3.4 Foreign Aid and Remittances

There is a large amount of literature on the determinants of foreign aid and remittances and their corresponding impact on the growth and overall well-being of developing countries. However, little is known about the relationship between foreign aid and remittances since a limited number of studies attempted to examine the link between these financial flows. A few research studies suggest a positive relationship between foreign aid and remittances. For example, Arvin and Lew (2012), using the cross-sectional data of 56 remittance-receiving countries for the year 2005, and Driffield and Jones (2013), studying the large panel data set of developing countries for the period 1984–2007, found a positive (complementary) relationship between the two financial flows. Contrary to earlier, some studies also indicate a negative association between foreign aid and remittances. For instance, Amuedo-Dorantes et al. (2007), analyzing the panel data of 92 developing countries for the period 1990–2003, and Bettin et al. (2015), studying the large panel data set of 79 developing countries (receiving remittances from 103 Italian provinces) over the 2005–2011 period, determined a negative relationship – indicating a degree of substitution between these two financial flows. Adding to the literature, some studies also connect the two flows through different transmission channels. For example, Kpodar and Le Goff (2012), examining the panel data of 90 aid-recipient countries for the period 1970–2005, suggested that remittances reduce the demand for aid if they are invested largely into physical and human capital. The migrants' network (lobby channel) produces a positive impact of remittances on aid. In contrast, Abbas et al. (2021), analyzing a panel data set of 50 (aid-recipient) developing countries over the (1980–2016) period, reported that foreign aid, in general, negatively influences remittance flows in developing countries. Further, their findings suggest that foreign aid promoting human capital investment positively impacts remittances as well to its impact on growth, which attracts remittance flows. The migration channel of aid promotes remittances only in the poor (least developed) countries.

3.5 Preliminary Data Analysis[2]

South Asia is a small region comprising only eight developing countries namely Afghanistan, Bangladesh, Bhutan, India, Maldives, Nepal, Pakistan, and Sri Lanka, but constitutes about a quarter of the world population. With a lack of

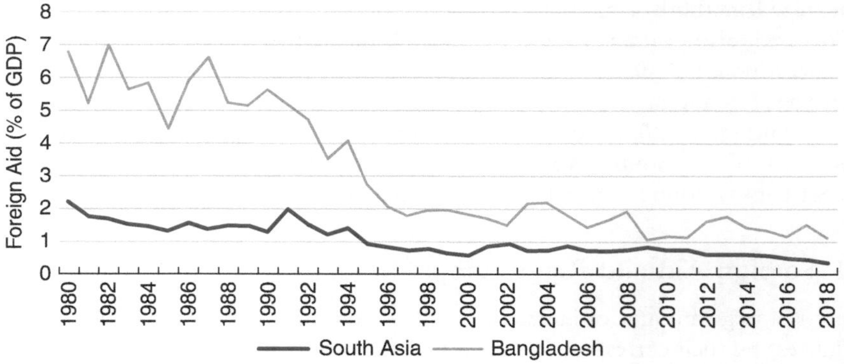

Figure 3.1 Foreign aid, South Asia vs Bangladesh, 1980–2018.

Source: *World Development Indicators*, World Bank database, various years.

resources and a large population, the South Asian region faces food security issues, poverty, and many other development challenges. During the period 2011–2018, on average, the region received about 10% of total foreign aid disbursed worldwide. Due to high labour exports, on average, South Asia receives a large volume of remittances and held almost a 21% share of world remittances during the 2011–2018 period (source: WDI, 2020).

Figure 3.1 presents the foreign aid flows (as a percentage of GDP) in overall South Asia and Bangladesh during the period 1980–2018. As can be seen, foreign aid is declining over time both in Bangladesh and South Asia. However, a greater reduction in aid is seen in Bangladesh from 1980 to the mid-1990s from almost 7% (of GDP) to just 2%. In recent times it has fallen close to 1% in Bangladesh. The foreign aid (as a percentage of GDP) in the South Asia region has fallen from a lower base of 2% in the early 1980s to close to 0.5% in recent times. Despite the decline, the level of foreign aid (as a percentage of GDP) in Bangladesh remains well above the South Asia level.

Figure 3.2 shows the remittance flows (as a percentage of GDP) in overall South Asia and Bangladesh over the 1980–2018 period. As can be seen, after the early 1980s, remittances received by Bangladesh have remained higher compared to the South Asia region. The remittance flows have increased gradually in South Asia since 1990. However, a greater surge can be seen in Bangladesh from early 2000 until 2012 where the remittances exceeded 10.5% of GDP. Afterwards, remittance flows declined to around 6% in 2018.

Figure 3.3 below presents the comparison of GDP growth (annual %) between the overall South Asia region and Bangladesh during the 1980–2018 period. As can be seen, despite the fluctuations, there is a marginal improvement in GDP growth in South Asia over time. However, Bangladesh has performed much better than the region in terms of achieving and sustaining a high GDP growth

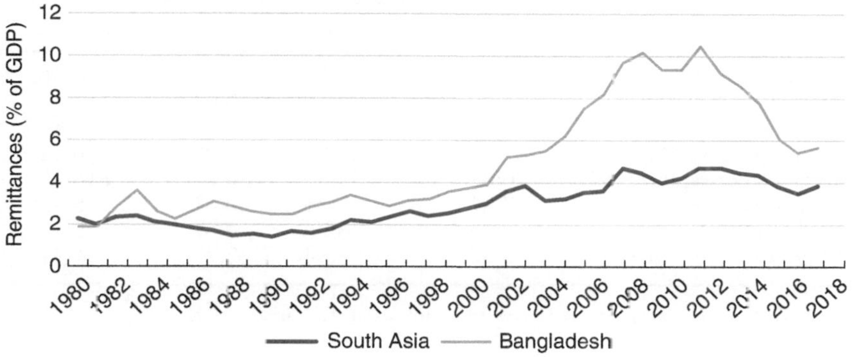

Figure 3.2 Remittances, South Asia vs Bangladesh, 1980–2018.

Source: *World Development Indicators*, World Bank database, various years.

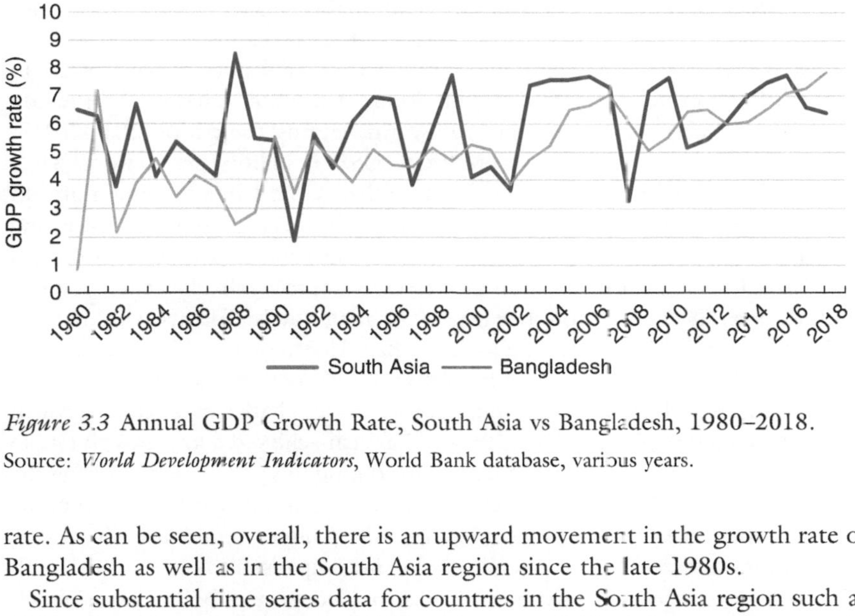

Figure 3.3 Annual GDP Growth Rate, South Asia vs Bangladesh, 1980–2018.

Source: *World Development Indicators*, World Bank database, various years.

rate. As can be seen, overall, there is an upward movement in the growth rate of Bangladesh as well as in the South Asia region since the late 1980s.

Since substantial time series data for countries in the South Asia region such as Afghanistan, Bhutan, Maldives, and Nepal is not available, below we focus on the four major countries in the region, namely, Bangladesh, India, Pakistan, and Sri Lanka that account for most of the region's population, economy (GDP), and receipts of financial flows. Below in Table 3.1, we compare India, Pakistan, and Sri Lanka in relation to aid, remittance flows, and economic growth indicators with Bangladesh using the data (averaged) for the period 2011–2018. As can be seen, in absolute aid flows (billion US$), Pakistan and India received almost similar amounts

Table 3.1 Selected indicators, four South Asian countries, average (2011–2018)

Indicators	*Bangladesh*	*India*	*Pakistan*	*Sri Lanka*
Aid (US$ billion)	2.57	2.74	2.75	0.36
Aid per capita (US$)	16.50	2.10	14.04	17.43
Aid (% of GDP)	1.37	0.13	1.09	0.49
Remittances (US$ billion)	14.12	68.89	17.29	6.64
Remittance per capita (US$)	90.87	52.88	86.99	316.70
Remittances (% of GDP)	7.87	3.24	6.61	8.49
GDP growth (%)	6.73	6.76	4.62	5.28
GDP per capita growth (%)	5.55	5.54	2.45	4.41

Source: *World Development Indicators*, World Bank database, various years.

on average during the period 2011–2018, while Bangladesh falls a little behind them. Sri Lanka received very low volumes of aid during this period. However, in the per capita form of aid, Sri Lanka received higher aid followed by Bangladesh and Pakistan. Analyzing the aid as a percentage of GDP, Bangladesh received more flows than any other country in the regional comparison. Both Bangladesh and Pakistan received aid of more than 1% of their GDP during this period. However, Sri Lanka and India had very low aid flows with respect to their economy.

India is the largest recipient of remittances (in absolute dollar terms) in the world. Presently, these four major South Asian countries fall in the top 15 remittance-receiving countries of the world. During the period 2011–2018, on average, Pakistan received more than US$17 billion per annum while Bangladesh received remittances worth more than US$14 billion per annum. In per capita terms, Sri Lanka stands out among South Asian countries, receiving remittances of more than US$300. Bangladesh and Pakistan are quite close with US$91 and US$87 per capita remittance receipts, respectively. As a percentage of GDP, during 2011–2018, on average, remittance flows remained very high in Sri Lanka with 8.5% per annum and in Bangladesh with 7.9% per annum, followed by Pakistan and India with 6.6% and 3.2% per annum, respectively.

Further, Table 3.1 indicates that India and Bangladesh have almost similar growth rates and are high performers in the region. Pakistan achieved a low growth rate in comparison with other its regional counterparts during this period. Summarizing the above discussion of Table 3.1, it is clear that, overall, as a proportion of economy size, Bangladesh has received more aid and relatively higher remittance flows (after Sri Lanka) and achieved high economic growth in comparison to other major South Asian countries. In per capita terms, Sri Lanka received more of both financial flows.

We now further analyze the foreign aid and remittance flows to Bangladesh. Table 3.2 presents the decade-wise flows of foreign aid to Bangladesh from different sources. Broadly, foreign aid is disbursed by bilateral donors and multilateral agencies. Further, bilateral aid is disbursed by the Development Assistance Committee (DAC) members of the Organisation for Economic Cooperation and Development (OECD) and non-DAC donors comprising some emerging and high-income developing countries. United Nations and

Table 3.2 Composition of aid to Bangladesh by sources, average (decade-wise)

Period	*Bilateral Aid (%)*		*Multilateral Aid (%)*
	DAC	*Non-DAC*	
1980–1989	62.36	4.95	32.69
1990–1999	58.63	0.88	40.50
2000–2009	51.07	0.89	48.04
2010–2018	58.25	-2.68	44.43

Source: OECD statistics, various years.

international financial institutions (such as the Asian Development Bank, International Monetary Fund, the World Bank, etc.) provide multilateral aid to developing countries. As can be seen from Table 3.2, the bilateral aid from DAC donors constitutes a major share in aid disbursed to Bangladesh. The share of bilateral aid has reduced marginally over time while it has reduced largely from the non-DAC donors. The negative sign indicates the return of loans with no fresh flows. The share of multilateral aid flows as a proportion of total aid to Bangladesh has increased by almost 12% in the last four decades.

Further, we analyze the sectoral composition of aid disbursed to Bangladesh in recent times. Table 3.2 presents the aid disbursed to different sectors during the years 2011, 2015, and 2018. As can be seen, more than two-thirds of the aid disbursed to Bangladesh comprises social and economic infrastructure and services programmes. Social infrastructure mainly focuses on the education and health sectors while economic infrastructure primarily aims to improve the energy and transport and communication sectors. In the last few years, the share of social infrastructure and services has reduced to half while the share of economic infrastructure and services has improved substantially during this period. The share of food aid has also seen a sizable reduction in recent years (Table 3.3).

Table 3.3 Composition (%) of aid to Bangladesh by sectors, various years

	Percentage of Aid		
Sectors	*2011*	*2015*	*2018*
Social Infrastructure and Services	49.04	26.58	23.80
Economic Infrastructure and Services	30.88	44.40	54.47
Production Sectors	6.99	9.77	5.20
Multisector	5.72	16.05	1.47
Programme Assistance	4.04	0.88	1.19
Action Relating to Debt	0.02	0.01	0.00
Humanitarian Aid	3.13	2.10	13.05
Unallocated/Unspecified	0.16	0.20	0.82
Total	100.00	100.00	100.00

Source: OECD statistics, various years.

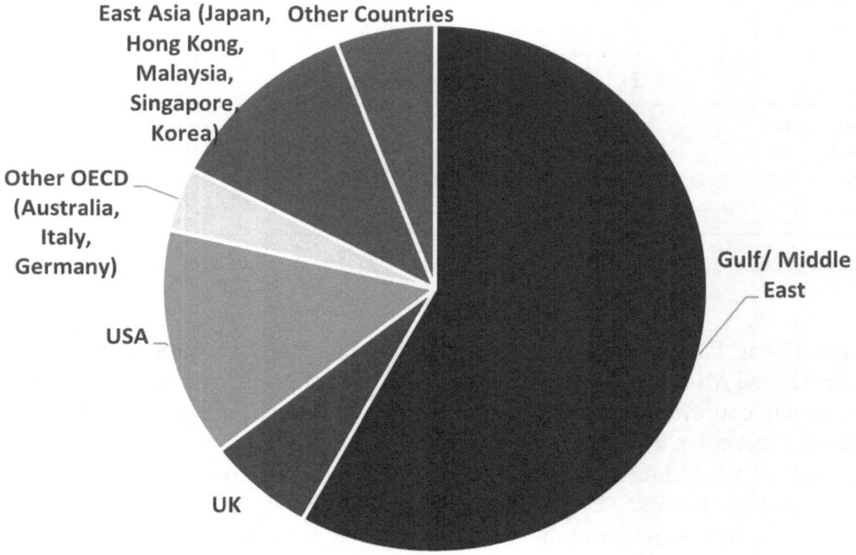

Figure 3.4 Remittance Share (%) from Major Migrant Destinations, Average (2011–2018).

Source: Bangladesh Bank (2020), Department of Statistics.

After analyzing the aid flows from different sources and for different sectors, we now analyze the remittances from the major Bangladesh migrants host countries. Figure 3.4 presents the share of remittance flows from notable migrant destinations averaged for the period 2011–2018. The pie chart indicates that migrants to Gulf and Middle East regions contribute 58% of the total remittances to Bangladesh. Importantly, remittances from the Kingdom of Saudi Arabia and the United Arab Emirates comprised more than 63% (on average) of the total remittances from the Gulf region. Other important migrant destinations in the Gulf/Middle East region are Kuwait, Oman, Qatar, and Bahrain. The combined remittances from the United Kingdom and the USA accounted for almost 20.5% per annum of the total remittances to Bangladesh. Other OECD destinations such as Australia, Italy and Germany contributed 3.9% per annum in total remittances destined to Bangladesh during the 2011–2018 period. Notably, Italy was the source of more than 82% of remittances from the other OECD countries category.

Overall, OECD countries (including the United Kingdom and the USA) constitute almost a quarter of the total remittances. East Asia is also an important source of remittance flows to Bangladesh with almost 11.6% share of total remittances, on average. Malaysia stands out as an important country in East Asia, contributing more than 70% of the total East Asian share of remittances.

We now compare the historical trends of aid and remittance flows to Bangladesh. Figure 3.5 below presents the volumes of foreign aid and remittance flows to

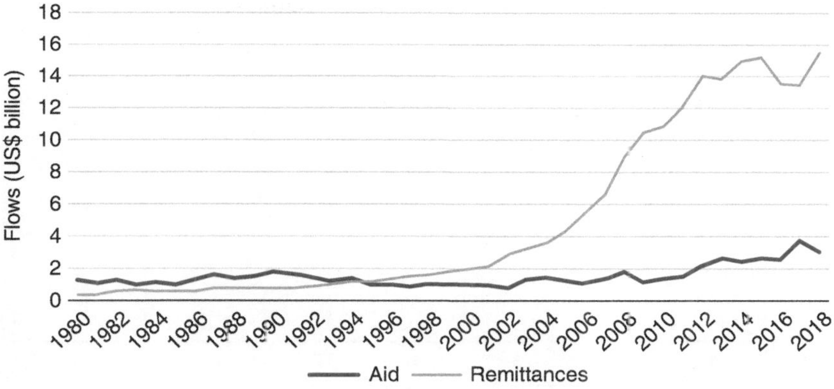

Figure 3.5 Foreign Aid and Remittance Flows, Bangladesh, 1980–2018

Source: *World Development Indicators*, World Bank database, various years.

Bangladesh over the 1980–2018 period. As can be seen, foreign aid remained higher than remittances until the early 1990s and then became comparable during the mid-1990s. Subsequently, remittances increased substantially while aid, after a period of stability, improved gradually over time. Since the early 2000s, we see a phenomenal rise in remittance flows to Bangladesh until 2012, and then with some fluctuations, the remittances stabilized around US$14 billion in recent times.

We also compare the two flows as a proportion of GDP for the period 1980–2018 in Figure 3.6. As can be seen, foreign aid was higher than remittances until the mid-1990s and then remittances surpassed the aid flows in Bangladesh.

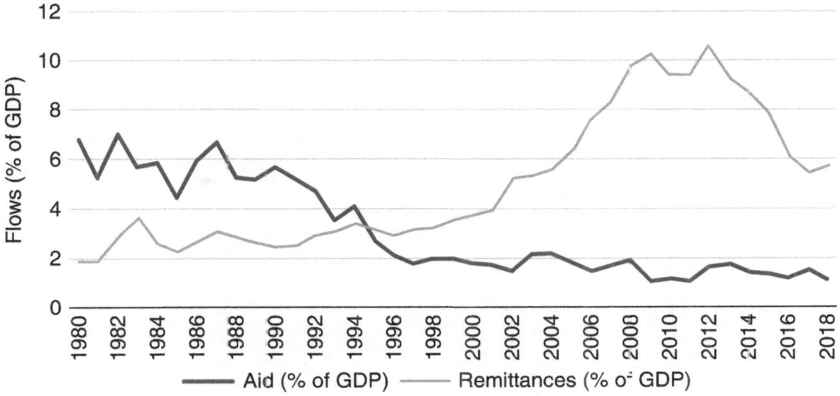

Figure 3.6 Foreign Aid and Remittance Flows as a percentage of GDP, Bangladesh, 1980–2018.

Source: *World Development Indicators*, World Bank database, various years.

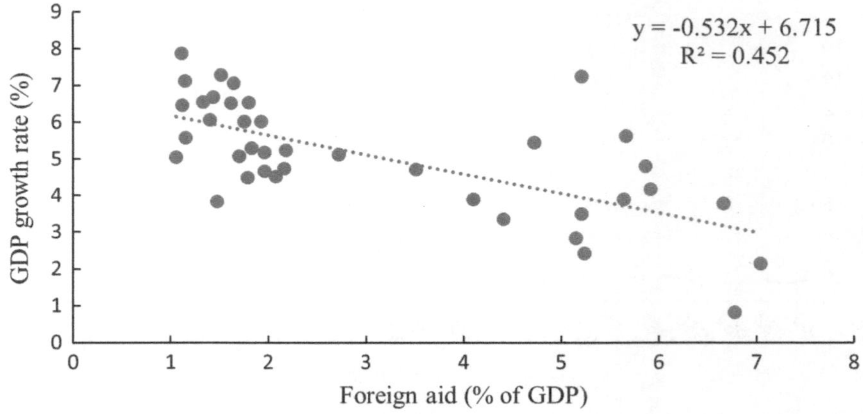

Figure 3.7 GDP Growth Rate vs Foreign Aid, Bangladesh, 1980–2018.

Foreign aid (as a percentage of GDP), in general, falls sharply from the 1980s until the late 1990s. Afterwards, aid flows fall marginally over time. Remittances (as a percentage of GDP) increased slightly over time until 2010. Subsequently, remittance flows, while showing some fluctuations, increased phenomenally until 2012 and then fell sharply while remaining much higher than aid receipts.

We now present the scatter plot in Figure 3.7 to examine the relationship between foreign aid and GDP growth. The graph indicates a negative relationship between the GDP growth rate and foreign aid in Bangladesh.

Further, we analyze the relationship between remittances and GDP growth using the scatter plot in Figure 3.8. The graph suggests a positive relationship between GDP growth rate and remittance flows in Bangladesh.

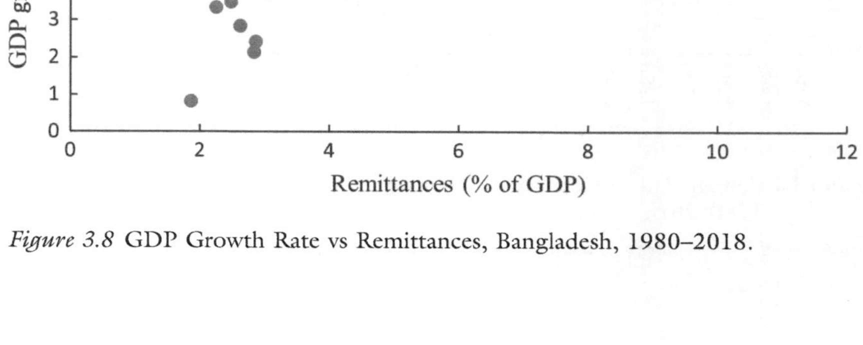

Figure 3.8 GDP Growth Rate vs Remittances, Bangladesh, 1980–2018.

3.6 Modelling the Relationship and Estimation Results

For model estimation, we first test whether all the variables in the model are stationary (that is, no unit root). To achieve this, we test the stationarity of each variable under consideration (foreign aid, remittances, and GDP growth rate) using the unit root test. For the three variables, we use the data collected for Bangladesh from the World Development Indicators (WDI) for the period 1983–2018. Table 3.4 presents the unit root test results using three different methods, namely, Augmented Dickey-Fuller (ADF) test, the Phillips-Perron (PP) test, and Kwiatkowski-Phillips-Schmidt-Shin test (KPSS). For the ADF and PP tests, the null hypothesis is H_0: There is a unit root (or, the series is non-stationary). The null hypothesis for the KPSS test is H_0: Series is stationary. As can be seen, all three test results indicate that GDP growth rate is stationary in its level form (that is, I(0)) and foreign aid is stationary in its first-difference form (that is, I(1)). The ADF and KPSS test results indicate that remittances is I(0) while PP test results indicate that it is I(1). As the three variables are either I(0) or I(1), and not of a higher order than 1, we model the relationship between the three variables using the ARDL framework.

Before setting up the model equation(s), we also determine the direction of causality between GDP growth rate (GDPG), remittances (REM), and foreign aid (AID). For this, we select the appropriate lag length based on Akaike Information Criteria (AIC) and apply the Granger Causality test. Table 3.5 presents the pair-wise Granger causality test results for testing the null hypothesis, Ho: no causal relationship between the variables. The results in Table 3.5 indicate that among the three variables, there is only a one directional causality from (a) remittances to GDP growth and (b) aID to GDP growth. Therefore, from here onwards, we model the GDP growth rate variable as a function of remittances and aid variables.

We model the relationship between the three variables using the ARDL framework as the three variables are either I(0) or I(1). One of the attractions of the use of the ARDL framework is that the ARDL bounds test approach can be used to test cointegration (Pesaran, Shin, and Smith 2001; Pesaran and Shin 1997) instead of the traditional cointegration testing methods (see, for example, Engle and Granger 1987; Johansen 1988; and Johansen and Juselius 1990). Another attraction of the bounds test approach is that the order of time-series variables included in the ARDL model can be either I(0) or I(1). The bounds test approach also allows the variables to have different optimum lag lengths and it employs a single reduced form equation. In addition, bounds test can also be used in small sample situations, and the long-run and short-run models can be estimated simultaneously. The critical values are computed based on the assumption that the variables under consideration are either I(0) and I(1). Critical values for large samples can be found in Pesaran et. al. (2001) and for small samples in Narayan (2005). The decision rule for the bounds test is that if the test statistic is above the I(1) critical value, we conclude that the variables are cointegrated and if the test statistic is below the I(0) critical value, there is no

Table 3.4 Unit root test results: ADF, PP and KPSS tests

Variable		*Unit root test*			*Conclusion*
		ADF	*PP*	*KPSS*	
GDP Growth (%)	Level	–5.368 (0.001)	–5.357 (0.001)	0.058 (0.146)	I(0)
Remittances (% of GDP)	Level	–4.355 (0.008)	–1.428 (0.835)	0.098 (0.146)	I(0)
	1st Difference		–4.303 (0.002)		I(1)
Foreign Aid (% of GDP)	Level	–2.491 (0.330)	–2.403 (0.372)	0.168 (0.146)	
	1st Difference	–4.277 (0.002)	–9.645 (0.000)	0.282 (0.463)	I(1)

Note: For the ADF and PP tests, p-values are given in parentheses. For the KPSS test, the critical values at the 5% level are given in parentheses.

Table 3.5 Granger causality test results, Bangladesh, 1983–2018

Null Hypothesis	*F-Statistic*	*p-value*	*Conclusion*
REM does not Granger cause GDPG	4.307	0.046	REM → GDPG
GDPG does not Granger cause REM	0.827	0.370	GDPG → REM
AID does not Granger cause GDPG	7.297	0.011	AID → GDPG
GDPG does not Granger cause AID	2.297	0.139	GDPG → AID
AID does not Granger cause REM	1.212	0.279	AID → REM
REM does not Granger cause AID	0.511	0.480	REM → AID

cointegration among the variables. If the value of the test statistic is between the I(0) and I(1) critical values, the result is inconclusive. Even though the bounds test allows the time-series variables to be either I(0) or I(1), it is required to validate that they are not of a higher order. The unit root test results presented in Table 3.4 provide this validation.

The ARDL (p,q,r) formulation of the relationship between GDP growth rate (dependent variable) and the independent variables, remittances and aid, can be written as

$$\Delta GDPG_t = \alpha_1 + \beta_1 GDPG_t + \beta_2 REM_t + \beta_3 AID_t + \sum_{j=1}^{p} \gamma_{1j}\, \Delta GDPG_{t-j} + \sum_{j=0}^{q} \gamma_{2j}\, \Delta REM_{t-j} + \sum_{j=0}^{r} \gamma_{3j}\, \Delta AID_{t-j} + u_t. \quad (3.1)$$

Using the ARDL bounds test, we test the long-run (or the cointegrating) relationship between GDPG, REM, and AID based on a non-standard F-test by testing the null and the alternative hypotheses, H_0: $\beta_1 = \beta_2 = \beta_3 = 0$ (no cointegration) vs H_A: At least one of β_1 or β_2 or $\beta_3 \neq 0$ (existence of cointegration) using the critical values for I(0) and I(1) provided in Pesaran et al. (2001) and Narayan (2005). If the calculated value of the F-statistic is greater than the I(1) critical value, then it should be concluded that there is support for cointegration. If cointegration between the three variables, GDPG, REM, and AID, exists, then an error-correction model can be used to estimate the speed of adjustment of the disequilibrium caused by previous period shocks that re-converges to the long-run equilibrium. The error correction model which corresponds to Equation (3.1) can be written as

$$\Delta GDPG_t = \alpha_1 + \sum_{j=1}^{p} \gamma_{1j} \Delta GDPG_{t-j} + \sum_{j=0}^{q} \gamma_{2j} \Delta REM_{t-j} + \sum_{j=0}^{r} \gamma_{3j} \Delta AID_{t-j} + \delta ECT_{t-1} + v_t. \quad (3.2)$$

Based on the Akaike Information Criteria (AIC), between the three variables, we identified an ARDL (1, 3, 0) model suitable for estimation. Table 3.6 presents the estimation results together with the bounds test F-statistic and diagnostics

Table 3.6 Error correction model estimation results, Bangladesh, 1983–2018

Dependent variable: GDP Growth Rate (%)
Method: ARDL (1,3,0)

Independent variables	Long-run coefficient	Short-run coefficient
Constant	4.860*	3.823*
	(0.853)	(1.112)
AID	−0.247*	
	(0.145)	
REM	0.228*	
	(0.097)	
D(REM)		−0.027
		(0.225)
D(REM(-1))		−0.114
		(0.230)
D(REM(-2))		0.514*
		(0.218)
Error Correction Term (ECT(-1))	−0.787*	
	(0.162)	
Bounds test F-statistic = 5.34,	0.791	
Critical values at 5%: I(0) = 2.84 and I(1) = 4.26		
Jarque-Bera test (*p*-value)		
Breusch-Godfrey LM test (*p*-value)	0.928	
Breusch-Pagan-Godfrey test (*p*-value)	0.621	
Ramsey's RESET test (*p*-value)	0.641	

Note
* Represents significance at the 5% level. Standard errors are given in parentheses.

test results for serial correlation and heteroskedasticity. As can be seen, there is no evidence of serial correlation or heteroskedasticity. The value of the bounds test F-statistic is 5.34 with critical values at the 5% level corresponding to I(0) = 2.84 and to I(1) = 4.86. As F-statistic = 5.34 > 4.86 = I(1) critical value, we conclude that the variables of interest are cointegrated at the 5% level of significance. This means that there is a long-run relationship between GDP growth, remittances, and aid. The CUSUM and CUSUMSQ plots in Figure 3.9 confirms the stability of the model and the estimation results.

The first half of Table 3.6 presents the estimation results corresponding to the long-run equilibrium and short-run relationship and the estimates for the error correction term. As can be seen, the error correction coefficient is in the range of −1 to 0 (as it should be) and is statistically significant. This result further confirms the findings of cointegration between GDP growth, remittances, and foreign aid. The estimates of the long-run and short-run coefficients for the remittance's variable are positive and are statistically significant at the 5% level. For example, the estimated coefficient 0.228 for the long-run remittance variable means that a 1% increase in remittances as a percentage of GDP in Bangladesh will result in an increase of 0.228% in GDP growth rate. The estimated coefficient of the foreign

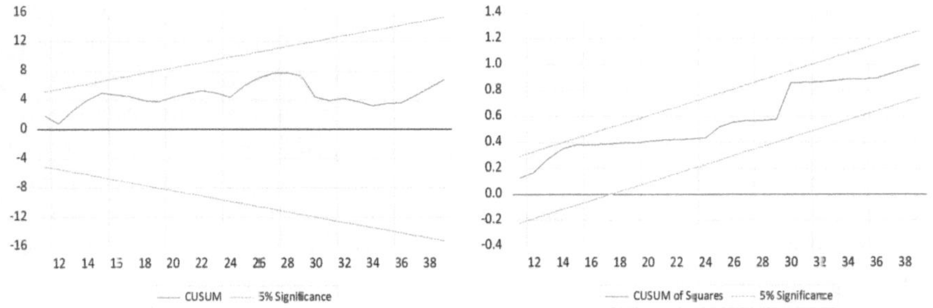

Figure 3.9 Cumulative Sum (CUSUM) and CUSUM of Square test results.

aid variable coefficient is negative and statistically significant in the long run. The estimated long-run coefficient is –0.247 which means that a 1% increase in foreign aid as a percentage of GDP in Bangladesh will result in a decrease of 0.247% in GDP growth rate. The error correction coefficient is –0.786 which means that approximately 78.6% of the disequilibrium caused by previous period shocks are corrected within one period.[2]

3.7 Concluding Comments

This chapter, applying dynamic modelling, examines the impact of the financial flows, foreign aid, and remittances, on economic growth in Bangladesh. The Autoregressive Distributed Lag (ARDL) modelling technique has been used to determine the short-run and long-run effects of aid and remittance flows on GDP growth rate. The estimation results indicate a negative significant impact of aid on GDP growth in the long run. The results also reveal a positive and significant influence of remittances on GDP growth both in the short run and long run.

The increased foreign aid may significantly raise the debt burden of poor developing countries. Further, in the long-run, it can also cause governance problems and reduction in foreign investment (due to increased vulnerability on account of high aid-dependency) leading to growth reduction. Since remittances support the household expenditure (particularly on education) to develop human capital, this may benefit the developing countries in the long run. Likewise, apart from consumption, remittances can also be a source of investment that reduces unemployment by creating economic opportunities and helps to improve income and economic growth of developing countries. Thus, a positive and significant effect of remittances on GDP growth is expected.

The findings of this chapter offer important insights to policymakers in developing countries, particularly in Bangladesh, and international financial institutions. The high aid-dependency reduces growth in low-income developing countries by increasing their debt burden, leading to ineffective governance and corruption. Therefore, the developing countries should be given foreign aid to the level which sustains effectiveness and does not excessively raise their debt burden. On the other hand, remittance flows support the household income and consumption and stabilize the fiscal balances, which increases the GDP growth rate by contributing both at micro and macro levels. Importantly, the positive effect of remittance flows from the migrant-network channels on growth is significant due to its potential to positively contribute to human capital development and investment. Therefore, policymakers should facilitate channels of remittance transfers and improve measures to reduce the associated transaction costs, which can further increase the remittance flows to low-income developing countries leading to high economic growth.

Notes

1 The authors would like to acknowledge the financial support from the Griffith Asia Institute, Griffith University, Australia, to carry out this project. They also thank Ms Tanya Parker for her research assistance.
2 In this study, due to data unavailability, we have used data only for the period 1983–2018 (36 observations). When using the results from this study, this data size limitation should be kept in mind. However, the diagnostic tests we have performed on the estimation results gives assurance that the results are of reasonably good quality.

References

Abbas, S. A., Selvanathan, E. A., Selvanathan, S., and Bandaralage, J. S. (2021). Are remittances and foreign aid interlinked? Evidence from least developed and developing countries. *Economic Modelling*, *94*, 265–275.

Acosta, P., Calderón, C., Fajnzylber, P., and Lopez, H. (2008). What is the impact of international remittances on poverty and inequality in Latin America? *World Development*, *36*(1), 89–114.

Adams, R. H., and Page, J. (2005). Do international migration and remittances reduce poverty in developing countries? *World Development*, *33*(10), 1645–1669.

Ahamad, K. M. U., Chowdhury, N. F. H., and Muzib, M. (2019). Aid-growth nexus in Bangladesh: An evidence from the ARDL bound testing approach. *Journal of Economics and Sustainable Development*, *10*(6).

Ahmed, H. A., and Uddin, M. G. S. (2009). Export, imports, remittance and growth in Bangladesh: An empirical analysis. *Trade and Development Review*, *2*(2).

Amuedo-Dorantes, C. P., Susan, and Vargas-Silva, C. (2007). *Remittances and the macroeconomy: The case of small island developing states.* UNU-WIDER. United Nations University.

Arvin, B. M., and Lew, B. (2012). Do happiness and foreign aid affect bilateral migrant remittances? *Journal of Economic Studies*, *39*(2), 212–230.

Bangladesh Bank (2020). Department of Statistics, Bangladesh, Dhaka; https://www.bb.org.bd/en/index.php/econdata/index

Bettin, G., Presbitero, A. F., and Spatafora, N. L. (2015). Remittances and Vulnerability in Developing Countries. *The World Bank Economic Review*, lhv053. doi:10.1093/wber/lhv053

Bird, G., and Choi, Y. (2020). The effects of remittances, foreign direct investment, and foreign aid on economic growth: An empirical analysis. *Review of Development Economics*, *24*(1), 1–30.

Burnside, C., and Dollar, D. (2000). Aid, policies, and growth. *American Economic Review*, *90*(4), 847–868.

Catrinescu, N., Leon-Ledesma, M., Piracha, M., and Quillin, B. (2009). Remittances, institutions, and economic growth. *World Development*, *37*(1), 81–92.

Chong, A., Gradstein, M., and Calderon, C. (2009). Can foreign aid reduce income inequality and poverty?. *Public Choice*, *140*(1-2), 59–84.

Chowdhury, M. (2016). Financial development, remittances and economic growth: Evidence using a dynamic panel estimation. *Margin: The Journal of Applied Economic Research*, *10*(1), 35–54. doi:10.1177/0973801015612666

Clemens, M. A., Radelet, S., and Bhavnani, R. R. (2004). Counting chickens when they hatch: The short term effect of aid on growth. *Center for Global Development working paper*, *44*.

Collier, P., and Dollar, D. (2002). Aid allocation and poverty reduction. *European Economic Review*, *46*(8), 1475–1500.

Cooray, A. (2012). The impact of migrant remittances on economic growth: Evidence from South Asia. *Review of International Economics*, *20*(5), 985–998.

Dalgaard, C. J., Hansen, H., and Tarp, F. (2004). On the empirics of foreign aid and growth. *The Economic Journal*, *114*(496).

Dowling, J. M., and Hiemenz, U. (1983). Aid, savings, and growth in the Asian region. *The Developing Economies*, *21*(1), 3–13.

Driffield, N., and Jones, C. (2013). Impact of FDI, ODA and migrant remittances on economic growth in developing countries: A systems approach. *The European Journal of Development Research*, *25*(2), 173–196.

Durbarry, R., Gemmell, N., and Greenaway, D. (1998). *New evidence on the impact of foreign aid on economic growth* (No. 98/8). CREDIT Research paper.

Engle, R. F., and Granger, C. W. (1987). Co-integration and error correction: representation, estimation, and testing. *Econometrica: journal of the Econometric Society*, *55*(2), 251–276.

Giuliano, P., and Ruiz-Arranz, M. (2009). Remittances, financial development, and growth. *Journal of Development Economics*, *90*(1), 144–152.

Hansen, H., and Tarp, F. (2001). Aid and growth regressions. *Journal of Development Economics*, *64*(2), 547–570.

Hassan, G. M., Chowdhury, M., and Bhuyan, M. (2016). Growth effects of remittances in Bangladesh: Is there a U-shaped relationship?. *International Migration*, *54*(5), 105–121.

Hassan, G. M., and Shakur, S. (2017). Nonlinear effects of remittances on per capita GDP growth in Bangladesh. *Economies*, *5*(3), 25.

Hossain, B. (2014). The effect of foreign aid on the economic growth of Bangladesh. *Journal of Economics and Development Studies*, *2*(2), 93–105.

Hossain, S., Mitra, R., and Abedin, T. (2019). Aid and Growth in Bangladesh: A Reassessment. *Journal of European Economy*, *17*(4), 422–440.

Imai, K. S., Gaiha, R., Ali, A., and Kaicker, N. (2014). Remittances, growth and poverty: New evidence from Asian countries. *Journal of Policy Modeling*, *36*(3), 524–538.

Islam, A. (1992). Foreign aid and economic growth: An econometric study of Bangladesh. *Applied Economics*, *24*(5), 541–544.

Johansen, S. (1988). Statistical analysis of cointegration vectors. *Journal of Economic Dynamics and Control*, *12*(2–3), 231–254.

Johansen, S., and Juselius, K. (1990). Maximum likelihood estimation and inference on cointegration—with appucations to the demand for money. *Oxford Bulletin of Economics and Statistics*, *52*(2), 169–210.

Kpodar, K., and Le Goff, M. (2012). Do remittances reduce aid dependency? *Development*, *34*, 1–23.

Kumar, R. R., and Stauvermann, P. J. (2014). Exploring the nexus between remittances and economic growth: a study of Bangladesh. *International Review of Economics*, *61*(4), 399–415.

Lensink, R., and White, H. (2000). Aid allocation, poverty reduction and the Assessing Aid report. *Journal of International Development*, *12*(3), 399–412.

Lensink, R., and White, H. (2001). Are there negative returns to aid?. *Journal of Development Studies*, *37*(6), 42–65.

Maruta, A. A., Banerjee, R., and Cavoli, T. (2020). Foreign aid, institutional quality and economic growth: Evidence from the developing world. *Economic Modelling*, *89*, 444–463.

Meyer, D., and Shera, A. (2017). The impact of remittances on economic growth: An econometric model. *EconomiA*, *18*(2), 147–155. doi:10.1016/j.econ.2016.06.001

Mosley, P. (1980). Aid, savings and growth revisited. *Oxford Bulletin of Economics and Statistics*, *42*(2), 79–95.

Narayan, P. K. (2005). The saving and investment nexus for China: Evidence from cointegration tests. *Applied Economics*, *37*(17), 1979–1990.

Nyamongo, E. M., Misati, R. N., Kipyegon, L., and Ndirangu, L. (2012). Remittances, financial development and economic growth in Africa. *Journal of Economics and Business*, *64*(3), 240–260. doi:10.1016/j.jeconbus.2012.01.001

OECD Statistics. https://stats.oecd.org/

Papanek, G. F. (1973). Aid, foreign private investment, savings, and growth in less developed countries. *Journal of Political Economy*, *81*(1), 120–130.

Pesaran, M. H., and Shin, Y. (1997). An autoregressive distributed lag modelling approach to cointegration analysis. Revised version of a paper presented at the Symposium at the Centennial of Ragnar Frisch, The Norwegian Academy of Science and Letters, Oslo, March 3–5, 1995.

Pesaran, M. H., Shin, Y., and Smith, R. J. (2001). Bounds testing approaches to the analysis of level relationships. *Journal of Applied Econometrics*, *16*(3), 289–326.

Quazi, R. M. (2005). Effects of foreign aid on GDP growth and fiscal behavior: An econometric case study of Bangladesh. *The Journal of Developing Areas*, *38*(2), 95–117.

Rahman, M. A. (1984). *Foreign Aid and Self-reliant Growth: The Case of Bangladesh.* Centre for Social Studies, Dhaka University.

Rajan, R. G., and Subramanian, A. (2008). Aid and growth: What does the cross-country evidence really show? *The Review of economics and Statistics*, *90*(4), 643–665.

Rao, B. B., and Hassan, G. M. (2011). A panel data analysis of the growth effects of remittances. *Economic Modelling*, *28*(1–2), 701–709.

Salim, R. A. (1992). Overseas remittances in Bangladesh: Importance, potentialities and policy options. *Jahangirnagar review, Part II, social science XIII and XIV. Jahangirnagar University, Dhaka.*

Siddique, A., Selvanathan, E. A., and Selvanathan, S. (2012). Remittances and economic growth: Empirical evidence from Bangladesh, India and Sri Lanka. *Journal of Development Studies, 48*(8), 1045–1062.

Sutradhar, S. R. (2020). The impact of remittances on economic growth in Bangladesh, India, Pakistan and Sri Lanka. *International Journal of Economic Policy Studies, 14*(1), 275–295.

Tezanos, S., Quiñones, A., and Guijarro, M. (2013). Inequality, aid and growth: Macroeconomic impact of aid grants and loans in Latin America and the Caribbean. *Journal of Applied Economics, 16*(1), 153–177.

Williams, K. (2018). Are remittances good for economic growth? The role of political institutions. *Applied Economics Letters, 25*(1), 56–60.

World Development Indicators (2020). The World Bank database. https://databank.worldbank.org/source/world-development-indicators.

Young, A. T., and Sheehan, K. M. (2014). Foreign aid, institutional quality, and growth. *European Journal of Political Economy, 36*, 195–208.

4 Impact of COVID-19 on the Ready-Made Garments Industry of Bangladesh

Rubaiyat Shaimom Chowdhury, S M Sohrab Uddin, Shafiqul Islam, and Md Samsul Alam

4.1 Introduction

Today, "Made in Bangladesh" tag is very much familiar to Ready-Made Garments (RMG) throughout the globe. Bangladesh is the second-highest exporter of RMG, just behind China (Alam et al. 2017). Currently, 144 Leadership in Energy and Environmental Design (LEED) green garment factories, certified by the US Green Building Council (USGBC), are available in Bangladesh, which include nine out of the world's top ten green garment factories (BGMEA 2020). In addition, Bangladesh is holding 39 out of the top 100 green industrial projects globally, and 500 more factories are obtaining LEED certification. But the picture is not always the same. When Bangladesh achieved independence through a brutal war against Pakistan in 1971, it was one of the poorest countries in the world. The country was heavily dependent on primary industries, including agriculture and firming, and there was almost no major industry during the initial phase after independence. Most of the world thought Bangladesh would be locked in a 'below poverty level equilibrium trap'. However, at present, Bangladesh is close to becoming a middle-income country, and its journey from a least developed country (LDC) to a middle-income country is a story of the success of the RMG sector.

The export-oriented RMG sector plays a significant role in the transformation of the Bangladesh country. It earns foreign currency for the nation and opens an entirely new job sector for its citizens, especially women. The RMG entrepreneurs using their entrepreneurship capabilities and the continuous support from the government, make it possible for the country. Specifically, the export-oriented RMG sector started its journey as a non-traditional export sector in the late 1970s; 1978 to be exact. Reaz Garments was the first garment factory that exported RMG worth US$69,000 to the USA. By 2019, the RMG export reached US$30 billion in aggregate, followed by which the sector started to experience the devastating impact of the ongoing pandemic created by COVID-19.

Like every other country, Bangladesh faces a pandemic and needs to take preventive measures to save lives. The initiatives undertaken by the government of Bangladesh and other countries seemingly have an impact on the RMG

DOI: 10.4324/9781003231912-7

export. This chapter examines the effect of COVID-19 on the RMG sector; the actions needed to combat the pandemic, and the sector's historical background.

The remaining part of the chapter is divided into six sections. The RMG sector in Bangladesh is briefly described in Section 4.2. Section 4.3 examines the economic impact of the RMG sector. Section 4.4 discusses the sector's response to COVID-19. Section 4.5 indicates the initiatives undertaken by the government of Bangladesh for the RMG sector, particularly for combating the ongoing pandemic. Section 4.6 portrays the results derived from the industry as a result of the introduction of various stimulus packages, and the last section concludes the chapter with a few policy implications.

4.2 Starting the Journey of the RMG Sector in Bangladesh and the Challenges It Faced

The RMG sector of Bangladesh initiated its journey in the late 1970s, to be specific, after the independence in 1971. The first footstep in the export-oriented garments business was noticed in 1977 when Reaz and Jewel Garments made their first shipment (Alam et al. 2016; 2017). During that time, Bangladesh did not have any reputation or prior history of exporting garment products to the world market. It was very tough for Bangladesh to convince the market participants of its capability to deliver the desired products on time. In 1978, the Daewoo Corporation, one of the largest garment companies in South Korea at that time, signed a joint venture contract with Desh Garments of Bangladesh. Afterward, official production started in Bangladesh to export RMG in the international market. It was an important incident in the development of the sector as the Daewoo-Desh joint venture helped Bangladesh to overcome the problem of entry barriers by using the Daewoo's brand name and business network (Rock 2001). Bangladesh also used its resources, predominantly the availability of labour at the cheapest cost, very effectively to build the reputation of delivering quality products according to the stipulated time, which contributes positively to become a reliable supplier of RMG products for the world.

When the garment sector was trying to strengthen its position in the world market, the Bangladesh government also extended its assistance by formulating different timely and effective policies. During 1980–1990, the government of Bangladesh came up with various friendly policies, including import tariff exemptions, free warehouse facilities, and the initiation of back-to-back letters of credit (L/C). Besides, international support has come through the implementation of quota under the Multi-Fibre Agreement (MFA), which provided immense help to the industry in achieving and maintaining its growth and development in the early stages. Accordingly, the sector experienced an exponential rate of growth during 1991–1994.

However, the world's RMG sector entered in a transition period in 1995. It was a ten-year transition phase where the quota under the MFA would be abolished within 2004, which has made the competition even more challenging for countries like Bangladesh (Alam et al. 2019a). The level of competition enhanced even further when China joined the World Trade Organization (WTO) in 2001. Many researchers, such as Dowlah (1999) and NordÃ (2004), thought that Bangladesh would face a significant problem after the withdrawal of the quota. The sector had faced a decrease in orders, and correspondingly the size of the industry shrunk. As per their analysis, Bangladesh would not be as attractive as it was before 2004. But these competitive forces could not shrink the industry's growth at last; rather, the RMG sector successfully maintained a rapid growth by exporting high-quality products over the period 1995–2004. As a result, renowned brands like Walmart, JCPenney, and Gap relocated some of their factories in Bangladesh and placed some orders as third parties while other competitors, including China and India, faced difficulties due to the imposition of quotas under the MFA (Rock 2003). The government of Bangladesh extended various financial and non-financial supports to the sector to face the post-MFA challenges. As a result, Bangladesh became the second-largest RMG exporter after China in 2011.

The challenges faced by the sector did not end here. Later, Rana Plaza accident and the consequent tragedy had created a big challenge for the industry's reputation in 2013. There was a question raised on the working condition of the factories, followed by which the USA suspended the Generalized System of Preferences (GSP) for Bangladesh in July 2013 (Sokou & Schneider 2013). Furthermore, the RMG sector faced both national and international pressures during the period 2014–2016, and as a response, different actions have been taken by the RMG sector for improving the working environment for the workers. The supports provided by the government of Bangladesh and other international organizations were also noticeable.

Before the pandemic period, Bangladesh's RMG sector faced tremendous competition from Vietnam and Myanmar for its business. Vietnam was aggressively approaching Bangladesh's second position of exporting RMG products globally, just behind China. Bangladesh was fighting to hold its ground, and then the COVID-19 pandemic began. Further discussion will be made on this issue in the sections below.

4.3 Overview of RMG Sector and Influence on Bangladesh

4.3.1 Influence of RMG Sector on Bangladesh Economy

The RMG sector influences the Bangladesh economy in several ways. It has an impact on gross domestic product (GDP), export revenue, employability, and women empowerment. The economy of Bangladesh is heavily dependent on the RMG export as it earns a significant portion of the foreign earnings for the country (Robbani 2000). Overall, according to Majumder (2021), the industry pays US$5 billion in wages to workers, along with other contributions. Table 4.1 shows that the RMG industry has exported more than twice of the entire nation's export over the period 1983–1984 to 2019–2020. According to the table, the percentage of the RMG export was 3.89% in 1983–1984, which reached 83.00%

Table 4.1 Percentage of RMG Out of Total Exports of Bangladesh (in million $)

Year	*Export of RMG*	*Total Export*	*% of RMG Export*
1983–1984	31.57	811.00	3.89
1984–1985	116.2	934.43	12.44
1985–1986	131.48	819.21	16.05
1986–1987	298.67	1076.61	27.74
1987–1988	433.92	1231.20	35.24
1988–1989	471.09	1291.56	36.47
1989–1990	624.16	1923.70	32.45
1990–1991	866.82	1717.55	50.47
1991–1992	1182.57	1993.90	59.31
1992–1993	1445.02	2382.89	60.64
1993–1994	1555.79	2533.90	61.40
1994–1995	2228.35	3472.56	64.17
1995–1996	2547.13	3882.42	65.61
1996–1997	3001.25	4418.28	67.93
1997–1998	3781.94	5161.20	73.28
1998–1999	4019.98	5312.86	75.67
1999–2000	4349.41	5752.20	75.61
2000–2001	4859.83	6467.30	75.14
2001–2002	4583.75	5986.09	76.57
2002–2003	4912.09	6548.44	75.01
2003–2004	5686.09	7602.99	74.79
2004–2005	6417.67	8654.52	74.15
2005–2006	7900.80	10526.16	75.06
2006–2007	9211.23	12177.86	75.64
2007–2008	10699.80	14110.80	75.83
2008–2009	12347.77	15565.19	79.33
2009–2010	12496.72	16204.65	77.12
2010–2011	17914.46	22924.38	78.15
2011–2012	19089.73	24301.90	78.55
2012–2013	21515.73	27027.36	79.61
2013–2014	24491.88	30186.62	81.13
2014–2015	25491.40	31208.94	81.68
2015–2016	28094.16	34257.18	82.01
2016–2017	28149.84	34655.90	81.23
2017–2018	30614.76	36668.17	83.49
2018–2019	34133.27	40535.04	84.21
2019–2020	27949.19	33674.09	83.00

Source: Export Promotion Bureau, Bangladesh.

in 2019–2020. Most importantly, the sector earns the highest export revenue and makes the highest contribution toward the employment generation of the country. The number of garments factories from 1985 to 2018 reported in Figure 4.1 demonstrates the importance of the RMG sector for the country.

The RMG sector of Bangladesh started slowly with a low rate of growth during the 1980s. However, it proliferated between 1991 and 2013, with factories rising from 834 to 5876. After 2013, a sharp decline was noticed in 2014, though an

Figure 4.1 Bangladesh's Apparel Export to the World from 1993–2020 (values in million $).

Source: BGMEA (2020).

immediate recovery was observed from 2015. This is evidence of the substantial depth of the sector. In terms of employment, the industry employed 0.12 million people in 1985, and that number climbed to 4.00 million nearly without interruption until 2018. Among these 4 million workers, the majority are female. Thus, the RMG industry plays a vital role in women's empowerment in Bangladesh.

4.3.2 Dependence on Woven and Knit to Export RMG Products

Bangladesh's RMG export can be classified into two broad sectors, woven and knit. At the beginning, during 1993–1994, Bangladesh was focused on the woven exports. The difference in export was significant. In 1994, Bangladesh exported $1544.89 million of woven goods, whereas knit exports were only $341.53 million. The picture changed during 2007 as the nation has shipped $4608.4 million of woven and $4741.93 million of knit products. Even in 2019, the year of the COVID-19 pandemic, Bangladesh has exported its highest apparel export. During that time, it has exported $33072.4 million, out of which $13242.4 million was woven and $14228.4 million was knit products. For the coronavirus pandemic, Bangladesh lost its exports, and in 2020 it only exported $27470.7 million in total.

To get a clearer picture of the apparel export items, one can classify those as shirts, trousers, jackets, T-shirts, and sweaters. Bangladesh had started its apparel export with shirts, trousers, jackets, and T-shirts and added sweaters in later years to its export line. In 1995, Bangladesh exported $0 of sweaters, and in 2019 it increased its export to $4255.92 million. Still, the sweater is not the highest exporting item; the T-shirt was the highest exported product in 2019, worth

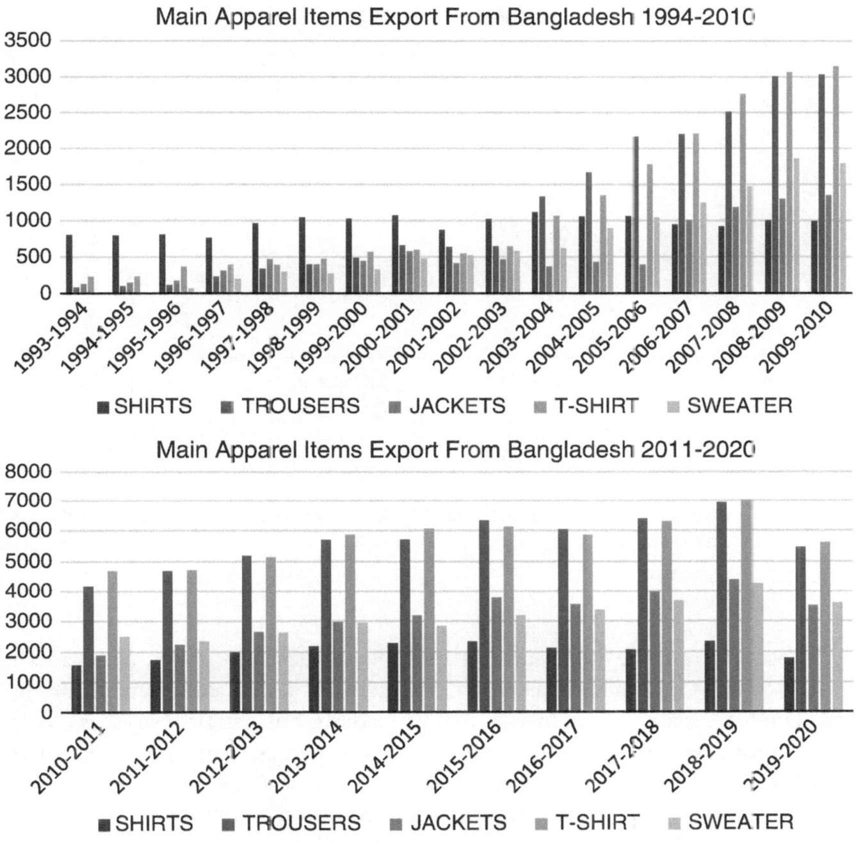

Figure 4.2 Main Apparel Items Export from Bangladesh (1993–2020, values in million $).

Source: BGMEA (2020).

$7011.26 million, just a step ahead of trousers with an export worth of $6939.61 million in the same year (Figure 4.2).

4.4 Traditional and Non-Traditional Export Market Influence on Bangladesh RMG Products

Bangladesh exports its RMG products in different world markets. These markets are mainly divided into two types: traditional market and non-traditional market. The traditional market includes all European Union (EU) countries, the USA market, and the Canadian market. Any other market that excludes traditional market is under non-traditional market. Australia, China, India, Japan, and Russia are some of the non-traditional markets (Figure 4.3).

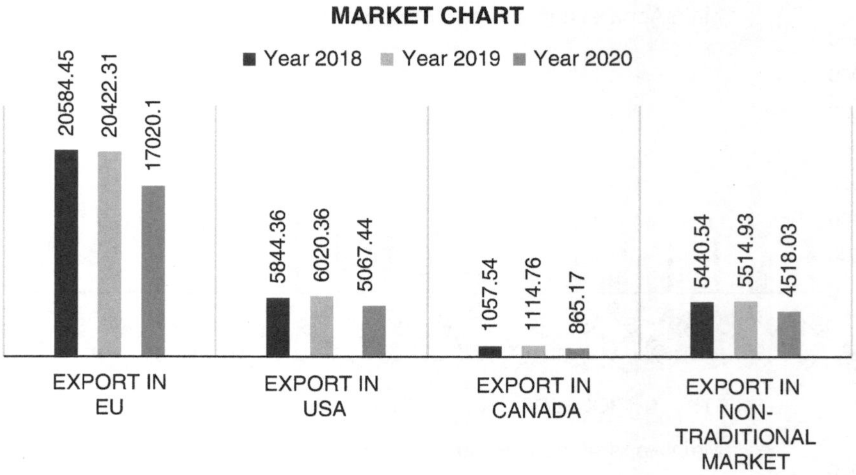

Figure 4.3 Tradition and Non-Traditional Market Comparison (2018–2020, values in million $).

Source: BGMEA (2020).

EU countries are the biggest market for Bangladesh. In 2018, Bangladesh exported $20584.45 million in the EU market, but it reduced dramatically in 2020. The USA is a potential market for Bangladesh, but Bangladesh faces a very tough competition because of the GSP and other issues. Bangladesh exported $1114.76 million worth of products in 2019 in Canada. The amount is not very impressive compared to other traditional and even non-traditional markets, but the Canadian market has an excellent prospect for Bangladesh.

4.4.1 RMG Sector's Employability and Women Empowerment

After the agricultural sector, the RMG sector created the highest number of jobs in Bangladesh. It had started to grow slowly in the 1980s, but after the end of the 1990s and the beginning of the 2000s, it experienced rapid growth. Figure 4.4 explains the journey from 0.05 million of the workforce to 4 million year by year. The number of factories also increased throughout the time period. In 1984, it was only 384 apparel factories, whereas in 2006 it was 4220. Bangladesh experienced the highest number of functional factories in 2012. After that, there was a sharp decline to 4222, but we have seen the recovery in 2019.

The RMG workers work in different production sections like sewing, knitting, cutting, finishing, drying, packaging and printing, washing, and embroidery. But the participation rate as per gender is not the same throughout the departments. We have compared the participation of workers as per gender in two different time frames (Figure 4.5). We can observe the men and women participation in various

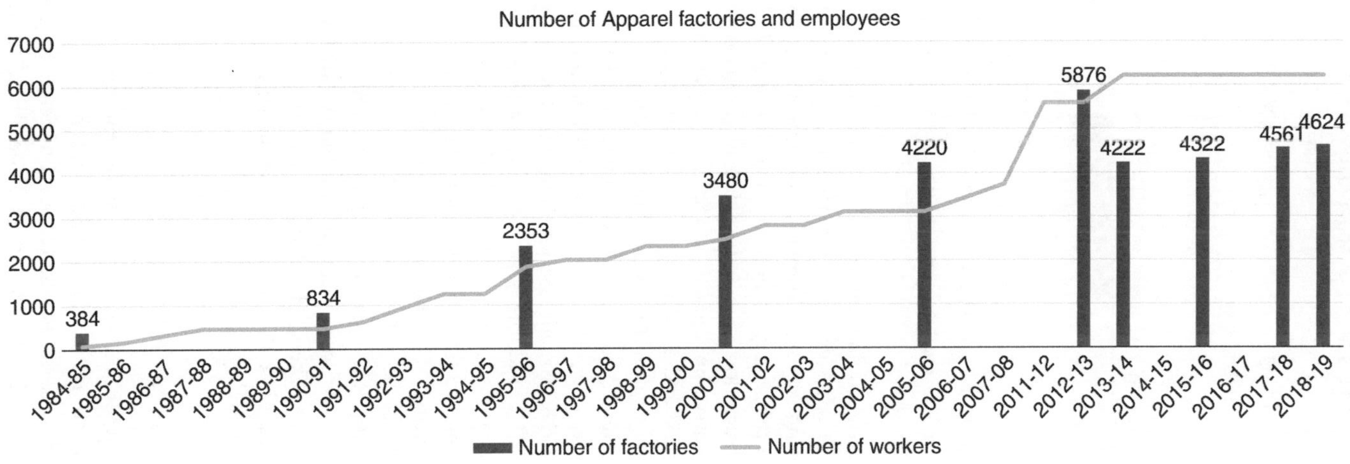

Figure 4.4 Number of Workers (1985–85 to 2018–19, values in millions) and Number of Factories.

Source: Prepared by authors using BGMEA employment figures for 2019, available online.

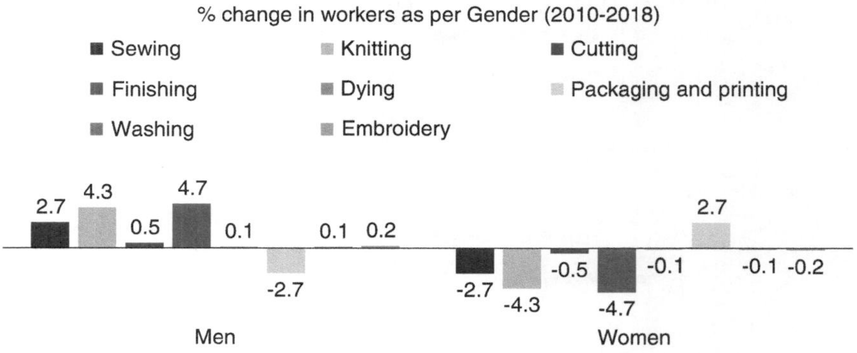

Figure 4.5 Percentage Change in RMG Workers as per Gender from 2010–2018.

Source: Prepared by authors using ILO and UN women (enterprise level survey) study on the RMG sector in Bangladesh, 2018.

departments in 2010 and then again find the workers' participation in 2018. From a survey on a total of 1892 and 2784 workers in 2010 and 2018, it was found that women are good in the sewing section. Women work almost two times more in number compared to men in the sewing section. It is true for both 2010 and 2018 statistics. On the other hand, men dominate in the dying and embroidery section. In 2010, 177 and 305 men worked in these two sections, respectively, where the women participation was only 3 and 4. The same trend continued in 2018.

International Labor Organization (ILO)'s baseline study found that the rate of participation of women in the RMG sector is declining. In 2018, women represented 61.17% of the sector's workforce, whereas in 2010, the representation was 2.9% higher than in 2018. Except for printing and packaging, women's participation decreased in 2018 in all other production sections.

Though women's participation decreases in the RMG sector, this is still the major sector that allows women to start their first job. The RMG is the very first job of women who have tried to start earning (Figure 4.6). Around 42.1% of women were engaged in household activities, and 29.7% were unemployed before starting their careers in the RMG sector. Adding students who were 23.2% of the RMG sector's women workforce, it can be said that the RMG sector is the first job for 95% of the women workers. The RMG sector also plays a vital role in empowering women and changing the socio-cultural structure of Bangladesh and the country's economic stability.

4.4.2 Working Conditions in the RMG Sector

From the beginning of the RMG industry, the 1970s, the working conditions were poor in Bangladesh. In 30 fire incidents, 530 workers were killed between 1990 to 2013. Besides, 1383 workers also died in several incidents, including the Rana Plaza collapse (Sammilita Garments Sramik Federation, Annual Report,

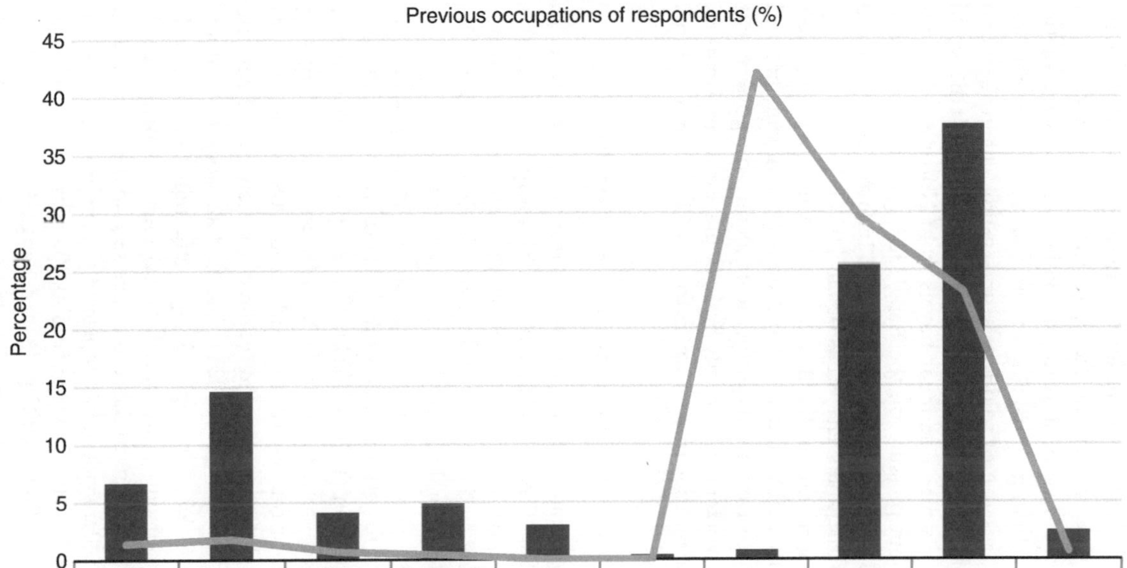

	Self-employed in agriculture	Day labourer	Self-employed in business	Employee in non-RMG work	Rickshaw/van /auto driver	Transport workers	Household activities	Unemployed	Student	Other
Men	6.7	14.6	4.1	4.9	3	0.4	0.8	25.4	37.6	2.5
Women	1.4	1.8	0.7	0.4	0	0	42.1	29.7	23.2	0.7

Figure 4.6 RMG Workers' Previous Work Experience.

Source: Prepared by authors using ILO and UN women (workers' survey) study on the RMG sector in Bangladesh, 2018.

2014). Not only the accidents and incidents but also the poor pay to the workers also shocked the world. Before 2018, the minimum wage for workers was BDT5300 ($67) per month, which only covers 35% of the estimated living wage of BDT15100 ($188) per month. After 2018, the new wage scale was introduced where the minimum wage is BDT8000 ($90). However, it is not a very big jump, but still a good move toward improvement.

According to Ahmed et al. (2014), 5% of the workers of the RMG sector belong to any union. They decided to keep their distance from the union to secure their jobs. That is why they do not have their voice for higher wages. Most of the factories are involved in long working hours, delay in promotion, irregular salaries, very low overtime payments, absence of paid leaves, and insufficient medical and maternity benefits (Kamal et al. 2010). The accidents and incidents push the world to rethink the issue. Twenty-six major garment buyers from North America, including GAP and JCPenny, put pressure on the Bangladesh garments to ensure health and safety issues in 2013. These alliances visited 1326 factories till 2015 to provide electricity, fire, and structural safety issues (Galib 2019). Until then, with the involvement of the purchasing group, the Bangladesh Garment Manufacturers and Exporters Association (BGMEA) and the Bangladesh government, fire and safety issues have been nearly resolved. Even during the pandemic, the government provides vaccines to garment workers on a priority basis, even without registration. Also, the government offers loans to garment owners for providing wages on time.

4.5 Backward Linkages of the Bangladesh RMG Sector

Specific industries require significant intermediate inputs from other industries to produce their final output. This is referred to as backward linkage. Bangladesh's apparel sector relies on four backward links: cotton production; yarn manufacturing; weaving and knitting; and dyeing, printing, and finishing. Cotton is the first backward linkage that the apparel industry requires, and Bangladesh is heavily dependent on cotton import. Due to the shortage of land in Bangladesh and cotton's low growing season for six months, only 1–2% of Bangladesh's total cropland is used to produce cotton (USDA 2021). The Bangladesh RMG sector mainly produces products from cotton (nearly 80%), whereas viscose, polyester, and other materials are used for the rest of the production; 90% of the yarn demanded by the knit RMG and 40% of the yarn required for the woven RMG are fulfilled by the imported cotton (USDA 2021). Bangladesh does not import cotton from one source (Figure 4.7). Through 433 spinning mills and 796 textile weaving mills (Cotton Development Board, CDB, Government of Bangladesh), Bangladesh is trying to be self-sufficient in the sector. The second part of backward linkage is the yarn production. Bangladesh has improved in yarn production in the last two decades. In 2004, the demand for yarn was 630,000 tons, and Bangladesh could produce 430,000 tons (USDA 2021). As per Bangladesh Textile Mills Association (2018), the demand for yarn was 2100 thousand tons out of which 1350 thousand tons could be supplied domestically. Still, Bangladesh depends around 30% on imports, mainly from India, China, Vietnam, and Pakistan. The

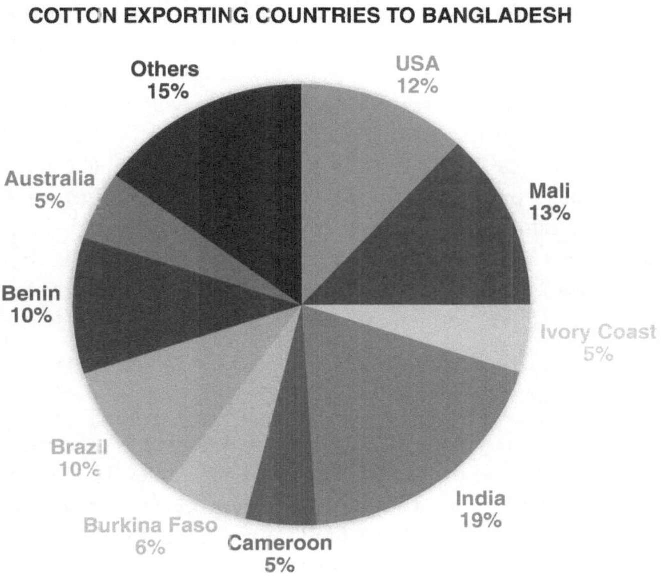

Figure 4.7 Cotton Exporting Countries to Bangladesh.

Source: Bangladesh Bank (2020).

third part is weaving and knitting, where yarn is converted to fabric. Fabric cost is 75% of the apparel raw material cost. Bangladesh consistently increases its fabric production capacity. In 2004, it could produce 2500 million metres, whereas by the end of 2018, the capacity increased to 6587 million metres. But the domestic consumption of fabric rises even faster as the fabric consumption increased from 4200 million metres in 2004 to 7400 million metres in 2018.

The gap is filled up through imported fabric from China, India, Pakistan, and Thailand. Bangladesh government takes different steps such as cash incentives, and withdrawal of import duties on capital machinery and spare parts for fabric and other textile manufacturing. It allows to capitalize on the capacity to increase fabric production. The fourth and final stage of the backward linkages of the apparel are dyeing, printing, and finishing. Bangladesh is self-sufficient and can fulfill its demand entirely in this stage. The industry is meeting up the order not only in quantity but also with a world-class quality.

4.6 Status of Global Agreement Available for Bangladesh

4.6.1 GSP Facility

The EU is the largest export market for the Bangladesh apparel products. Till now, Bangladesh enjoys GSP facilities to export in EU countries and will continue to enjoy till 2024 when Bangladesh will no longer be an LDC officially. But the good news is that the EU agrees to give Bangladesh GSP Facilities till 2027. After withdrawing GSP facilities, Bangladesh will lose 12.5% duty privileges in the EU market and, at the same time, needs to pay an extra 6.5% tariff for export. However, it is expected that, after 2027, Bangladesh will acquire the eligibility to get GSP-plus facility. Bangladesh had a GSP facility in the USA market, but that was suspended in 2013 after the Ranna Plaza incident due to poor labour rights and unsafe working conditions in factories. The US government gave 16 conditions to fulfill in order to retain the GSP status. Bangladesh fulfilled all those 16 conditions but still could not get back the GSP facility in the US market. However, the government of Bangladesh has taken the initiative to sign a Free Trade Agreement (FTA) with the USA.

4.6.2 FTA

Bangladesh has been trying to sign as many FTA as possible to have a better trade option in international trade. Currently, six FTAs are on the table. The Asia-Pacific Trade Agreement, Preferential Tariff Arrangement-Group of Eight Developing Countries, and South Asian Free Trade Area have already been signed and in effect. Trade Preferential System of the Organization of the Islamic Conference has been signed but not in effect. Bangladesh is also continuing negotiations on Multi-Sectoral Technical & Economic Cooperation (BIMSTEC) Free Trade Area and Pakistan-Bangladesh Free Trade Agreement. Bangladesh is also trying to have FTAs with China, Bhutan, Thailand, Turkey, Malaysia, Sri Lanka, Nepal, and India.

4.6.3 Trans-Pacific Partnership (TPP) Deal

The TPP consists of 12 major players in world trade including Australia, Brunei, Canada, Chile, Japan, Malaysia, Mexico, New Zealand, Peru, Singapore, the USA, and Vietnam. It contributes 40% to the world economy. Though recently the USA pulled itself out from the TPP, but TPP still has excellent control over the world economy. Vietnam, a member of the TPP, is a major disadvantage for Bangladesh as Vietnam is a close competitor for the RMG products in the US market. When the USA left TPP, it was supposed to put Bangladesh in an advantageous position, but the scenario was just opposite. Currently, the US government is considering more protective measures, which may impose additional duty, and if it happens, Bangladesh will lose its competitive edge in the US market.

4.7 Impact of COVID-19 on the RMG Sector

Before the pandemic, the declining trend of apparel prices and the consistently increasing production cost has remained vital concerns for the global trade of RMG. Some of the challenges faced by the RMG sector of Bangladesh, in

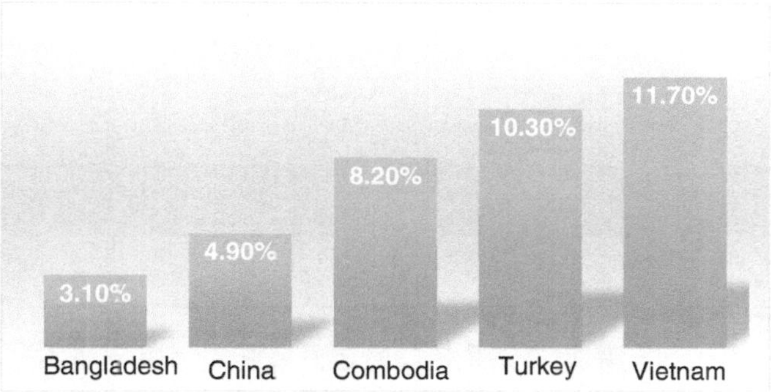

Figure 4.8 Export Growth to the USA in January and February of 2020.
Source: Centre for Policy Dialogue (CPD).

particular, include overvalued exchange rates and a lack of diversified products. The overvalued exchange rates made the RMG products more expensive for buyers. A few economists and market observers opine that the overvalued exchange rate is one of the biggest reasons for Bangladesh not taking advantage of the USA-China trade war. The small basket of apparel products of Bangladesh at times outperformed by the automation adopted by the competitors. In this regard, Figure 4.8 reports a 3.1% growth rate in the apparel export to the USA by Bangladesh, which is low as compared to other major players in the world market.

Undoubtedly, the COVID-19 hits almost all of the sectors of an economy, and the RMG sector of Bangladesh is no exception. A study made by McKinsey & Company's State of Fashion in 2020 showed that 65% of the consumers planned to decrease their expenditure on apparel goods in Europe and the USA. They also forecast 30% decline in the global garments sector due to the pandemic. This reflects the decrease in the demand side, which in turn directly affects the producers.

The year 2020 was a very challenging year for the world's business as well as for the Bangladesh RMG Sector. COVID-19 situation changes every prediction about growth and business style. Figure 4.9 reflects that 2020 growth was negative for all EU countries except Hungary and Latvia. Latvia is the minor consumer of Bangladesh RMG products among the EU countries with $0.81 million import in 2020. Hungary is also not a big market. On average, it lost 23% of its export earnings in 2020 due to the COVID -19 pandemic in the EU market (excluding Hungary and Latvia).

Immediately after the coronavirus outbreak in March 2020, roughly 1150 factories in Bangladesh experienced export suspension or cancellation from the buyers and retailers in the international arena, which was equivalent to US$3.18 billion (Majumder 2021). These mainly were pending work orders. The production costs were also higher than before because of the COVID-19's strict

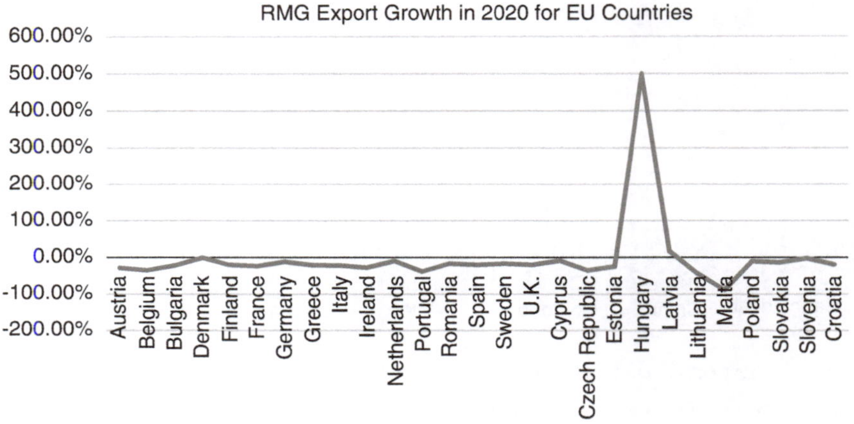

Figure 4.9 RMG Export Growth in 2020 for EU Countries.
Source: BGMEA (2020).

adherence to health rules, including practices for safety and hygiene, as well as social isolation. Most importantly, these protocols for the workers need to be assured not only at their workplaces but also at the places where they reside and commute. In contrast to the increasing production cost, the aggregate unit price of apparel exported by Bangladesh was reduced by 2.17% on a year-to-year basis during January–September, 2020. Specifically, the price was declined by 3.18% in the US market, whereas in the EU market, the price was dropped by 1.13% for the same time period (Majumder 2021). As a result, several factories faced financial distress created by bank liability, accrued wages, and unmet overhead and other operating expenses, which led to bankruptcy and the permanent closure of many of these garment factories. According to BGMEA, the factories that were temporarily closed for the pandemic, which was approximately 268 in number, could only run at their 55% capacity after they had returned to business.

To have an idea about the impact on the RMG sector, Table 4.2 highlights the changes in earnings from the sector for the period July 2018 to May 2020. According to the table, the woven sector observed a decline of 19.22% in its earnings, whereas the knitwear category faced a decrease of 18.74% in the earnings growth rate. In aggregate, the growth rate in earnings was decreased by 18.99%. Most importantly, the pandemic causes the highest negative growth for the RMG sector in the last five years. Undoubtedly, the decline in the growth rate is associated with the unemployment of the workers of this sector.

4.8 Stimulus Packages Introduced for Fighting Back

The Bangladesh government has announced 23 economic stimulus initiatives to combat the effects of the current pandemic, nine of which are linked directly to

Table 4.2 Changes in Earnings from the RMG Sector (in billion $)

Time Period/ Category	*Earnings from July, 2018–May, 2019*	*Earnings from July, 2019–May, 2020*	*Growth (%)*	*Shortfall from Govt Target (%)*
Earnings from Woven	16.04	12.96	–19.22	—
Earnings from Knitwear	15.68	12.74	–18.74	—
Total	31.72	25.70	–18.99	26.31

Source: Export Promotion Bureau, Bangladesh.

the Bangladesh Bank, the country's central bank (Bangladesh Bank 2021). The size of the stimulus packages in aggregate is equivalent to nearly BDT (the currency of Bangladesh) 1.24 trillion, which is 4.44% of the country's GDP. Various initiatives have been undertaken by targeting the RMG sector. Notable initiatives include wage and salary support of BDT50 billion for the export-oriented industries, stimulus package of BDT400 billion for working capital financing of badly affected companies from the industrial and service sector, subsidizing the rate of interest for working capital loan by 4.50%, refinancing fund of BDT50 billion for providing pre-shipment credit facility to export-oriented industries, usage period of input imports has been extended to 360 days from 180 days under supplier's/buyer's credit, permission to open back-to-back/usance L/C with a realization clause, the prescribed realization period for export proceeds has been extended from 120 days to 210 days, lengthening the time period for submitting the bill of entry from 120 days to 180 days, and discounting of the export bill at 10% of Free on Board (FOB) value. In addition, the Export Development Fund (EDF) limit for disbursements has been increased to $30 million from $25 million with an extended time period for repayment and with a reduced rate of interest, easing the process of obtaining cash incentive against foreign remittances, and ensuring Mobile Financial Services (MFS) wallets for unbanked workers are also included in the policy initiatives adopted by the government. The following table provides a detailed description of each of the initiatives (Table 4.3).

4.9 The Impact of Stimulus Packages on the RMG Sector

Table 4.4 indicates the implementation status of various stimulus packages till January 31, 2021. It shows that the wage and salary support of BDT50 billion was fully disbursed by the government as committed in the year 2020. BDT302.07 billion of the working capital loans segregated for the adversely affected large industries and service sectors were also paid, which is 91.54% of the total committed amount for this category. Similarly, BDT91.32 billion of EDF

Table 4.3 Policy Initiatives Undertaken by the Government of Bangladesh

Initiatives	*Details*
Paying Workers'/Stuffs' Wages and Salaries	An amount of BDT50 billion was formed for the export-oriented industries with an export of at least 80% of their production. The fund can be used for paying the wages and salaries for up to three months with effect from April 2, 2020. The loan amount needs to be paid within two years with a grace period of six months.
Financing Working Capital	A stimulus package of BDT300 billion was declared for the badly affected companies from industrial and service sector on April 5, 2020. Later on, an additional amount of BDT30 billion was added for paying the wages of the workers for July 2020, which led to an aggregate of BDT330 billion. It was enhanced further to BDT400 billion on October 29, 2020.
Subsidizing the Interest Rate	The prevailing interest rate of 9.00% for working capital financing was subsidized by 4.50% by the government for lessening the interest rate burden.
Refinance Schemes	With an objective of providing pre-shipment credit facility to export-oriented industries and with a validity of three years, Bangladesh Bank created a refinancing fund of BDT50 billion with effect from April 13, 2020. In addition, with a similar validity period, Bangladesh Bank established a refinancing scheme of BDT150 billion for ensuring working capital financing for large industrial and service sectors on April 23, 2020.
Usance Period of Input Imports	The period for industrial importers was lengthened from 180 days to 360 days under the supplier's/buyer's credit. It will remain valid until June 30, 2021. In addition, the quarterly repayments on usance terms for periods exceeding 180 days against imports were waived.
Back-to-Back/Usance L/C	It was permitted to open such L/C with a realization clause. The payment in foreign currency for inland L/C can be made through the Nostro Accounts of the commercial banks rather than through Bangladesh Bank clearing accounts, which will remain valid until June 30, 2021.
Realization of Export Proceeds	The prescribed period was extended from 120 days to 210 days from the date of shipments for RMG and textile goods with a validity up to June 30, 2021.

(*Continued*)

Table 4.3 (Continued)

Initiatives	*Details*
Submission of Bill of Entry	The time period for submitting the bill of entry was extended to 180 days from 120 days from the date of payments. It will remain effective till June 30, 2021.
Repatriation of Export Bills	Based on bona fide grounds, it was allowed to repatriate the bills at a discounted price of 10% of FOB value for a period up to June 30, 2021.
EDF	The corresponding EDF limit for disbursements has been increased to $30 million from $25 million until the end of June 2021 for all the member factories of BGMEA and Bangladesh Textile Mills Association (BTMA). The deadline for repaying the EDF loan was extended from 90 days to 180 days, which will be applicable till June 30, 2021. Furthermore, with effect from April 1, 2020; the interest rate for the EDF loan disbursed within March 31, 2021 was reduced to 2.00%, which was further declined to 1.75%.
Cash Incentive against Foreign Remittances	No submission of document is required for obtaining the cash incentives against the foreign remittances for an amount equivalent to $5000 or BDT500 thousand. Previously, the permissible amount was $1500, or BDT150 thousand.
MFS Wallets	With effect from April 20, 2020; the MFS provides were instructed to launch new wallets for the workers who do have any formal bank accounts. Furthermore, the charge applied for the cash-out of salaries was reduced to 0.8% from 1.85%.

Source: Constructed by the authors based on Bangladesh Bank (2021) and different circulars issued by the Bangladesh Bank.

loans has already been disbursed for the designated sectors; 71.62% of the total allocation. However, the implementation of the pre-shipment credit refinancing scheme and working capital loans for different types of industries at the Export Processing Zones (EPZs) remain insignificant since only 2.72% and 1.47% of the respective disbursements were made.

Because of the government's support and the wholehearted negotiations made by the BGMEA, most of the orders that were either cancelled or postponed have been reinstated by the internationally reputed brands. For example, 85–90% of the $3.18 billion in cancelled orders are returned; however, 20–50% discounts have been imposed (Majumder 2021). Due to the wage and salary support, owners of garment factories were able to pay their workers even though factories were halted for 40 consecutive days during March–April, 2020.

Table 4.4 Implementation Status of the Stimulus Packages by the End of January 2021

Packages	*Amount (in BDT billion)*	*Disbursement (in BDT billion)*	*Implementation in %*
Working Capital Loans for Adversely Affected Large Industry and Service Sector	330	302.07	91.54
Working Capital Loans for 'A', 'B' and 'C' Type Industries	70	1.03	1.47
Payment of Allowances and Salaries to the Workers/Stuffs of Export-Oriented Industries	50	50	100
Pre-shipment Credit Refinancing Scheme	50	1.36	2.72
EDF	127.50	91.32	71.62

Source: Bangladesh Bank (2021).

Many new wallets were opened, leading to a total number of accounts of almost 3.8 million. In this regard, BGMEA conducted a survey in April 2020 for identifying the extent to which the MFS covers the RMG workers. According to the responses from 752 factories, 67% provided wages in cash, 5% by bank transfer, 5% through MFS, and the remaining 23% adopted multiple modes of payment (Rafique 2021). Furthermore, only 43% of the workers have maintained MFS accounts and, in most cases, with minimal use. However, due to the government's initiative in April 2020, 2.5 million workers opened MFS wallets for receiving their wages in just 25 days.

Table 4.5 highlights the individual and collective RMG export during 2020 from woven and knitwear categories. Seemingly, the situation has been improving since July onward, particularly for the knitwear category as the growth rates in all of the months, except October and December, compared to the similar month of the year 2019, are favourable. The aggregate export has been consistently higher than $2240 million from June–December 2020. The growth rates in the aggregate export also marked positive growth in August and September 2020.

4.10 Conclusions

The above analyses suggest that the RMG sector has been well equipped, although challenges from COVID-19 exist in Bangladesh. Due to the pandemic, the RMG sector is greatly affected, orders are cancelled, workers are economically affected,

Table 4.5 RMG Export during 2020 (in million $)

Month	*Woven*	*Knit*	*Total*
January	1625.00 (–1.19)	1414.22 (–4.96)	3039.22 (–2.98)
February	1505.58 (–3.27)	1278.70 (–5.45)	2784.28 (–4.28)
March	1200.37 (–20.88)	1055.83 (–19.27)	2256.20 (–20.14)
April	194.55 (–84.50)	180.12 (–85.97)	374.67 (–85.25)
May	622.16 (–62.19)	608.38 (–61.92)	1230.54 (–62.06)
June	1075.31 (–9.89)	1164.95 (–3.41)	2240.26 (–6.63)
July	1494.66 (–8.43)	1750.28 (4.30)	3244.94 (–1.98)
August	1103.52 (–5.14)	1364.50 (9.80)	2468.02 (2.58)
September	1064.54 (–2.49)	1348.88 (7.96)	2413.42 (3.09)
October	985.50 (–14.43)	1338.22 (–2.19)	2323.72 (–7.78)
November	1110.12 (–10.48)	1334.47 (4.97)	2444.59 (–2.66)
December	1261.05 (–18.07)	1389.82 (–0.45)	2650.87 (–9.69)
Total	13242.36 (–240.96)	14228.37 (–166.53)	27470.73 (–197.78)

Source: Export Promotion Bureau, Bangladesh.

Note: The figures in parentheses represent the growth rate compared to similar month of the year 2019.

many of them lose their jobs, and a significant number of small and medium enterprises (SMEs) are closed or stopped production. However, because of the stimulus packages, the effects are reduced to a manageable level. Nevertheless, problems arise in operationalization. The operationalization process identifies and selects affected firms and workers and disburses the funds through the proper banking channel. Institutional challenges in ensuring transparency and accountability have little deviated from achieving exactly accurate targets.

The banking sector needs to be taken care of with a stimulus package, as they are affected badly by COVID-19. In addition, the stimulus packages should cover the worker's health and safety and present financial assistance. It is also necessary to ensure proper distribution of the stimulus packages so that the target group can receive the benefits. Furthermore, the Bangladesh RMG sector should accommodate cooperation and collaborative efforts among global brands/retailers, the government of Bangladesh, ILO, and BGMEA. This cooperation requires long-term support from the global supply chain.

This chapter's contribution is that it has analyzed the history of the RMG sector, portrayed the COVID-19 impacts, and described the stimulus packages in detail. It has concluded the present scenario of the RMG sector and suggested some measures. However, direct interviews or direct face-to-face data collection from the stakeholders has not been made by the present study. Instead, it is a desk study based on secondary data. Further research can explore the impact of COVID-19 on the Bangladesh RMG sector and outcomes of stimulus packages through the analysis of qualitative and quantitative data using sophisticated techniques.

References

Ahmed, N. (2009). "Sustaining ready-made garment exports from Bangladesh." *Journal of Contemporary Asia*, *39*(4): 597–618.

Ahmed, F., Greenleaf, A., & Sacks, A. (2014). "The paradox of export growth in areas of weak governance: The case of the ready made garment sector in Bangladesh." *World Development*, *56*: 258–271.

Alam, M. S., & Natsuda, K. (2016). The competitive factors of the Bangladeshi garment industry in the post-MFA era. *Canadian Journal of Development Studies/ Revue canadienne d'études du développement*, *37*(3): 316–336.

Alam, M. S., Selvanathan, E. A., & Selvanathan, S. (2017). "Determinants of the Bangladesh garment exports in the post-MFA environment." *Journal of the Asia pacific Economy*, *22*(2): 330–352.

Alam, M. S., Selvanathan, E. A., Selvanathan, S., & Hossain, M. (2019a). "The apparel industry in the post-multifiber arrangement environment: A Review." *Review of Development Economics*, *23*(1): 454–474.

Alam, M. S., Selvanathan, E. S., Selvanathan, S., & Hossain, M. (2019b). "Causal relationship between apparel exports and macroeconomic factors." *Applied Economics*, *51*(25): 2687–2702.

Bangladesh Bank. (2021). "Policy measures of Bangladesh bank in response to the COVID-19 pandemic." Bangladesh Bank. Dhaka: Bangladesh.

BGMEA employment figures for (2018). available online, http://bgmea.com.bd/home/pages/TradeInformation

BGMEA (2020). BGMEA Sustainability Report. (2020). "Bangladesh Garment Manufacturers and Exporters Association (BGMEA)" Dhaka, Bangladesh.

Bangladesh Garment Manufacturers and Exporters Association (BGMEA) (2020). "BGMEA Refutes Accusations." *The Guardian*, 11 July.

Dowlah, C. A. F. (1999). "The future of the readymade clothing industry of Bangladesh in the post-Uruguay round world." *World Economy*, *22*(7): 933–953.

Frederick, S., & Staritz, C. (n.d). "Developments in the global apparel industry after the MFA phaseout".

Galib, Sabbir Ahmed, Kabir, Md Humayun, Abdullah, Shah, & Khan, Mohd. (2019). "A Study on the Occupational Safety and Health in Perspective of Disaster Management Approach: Research on Ready-Made Garments Sector of Bangladesh." 196–218. 10.5281/zenodo.3545009.

ILO and UN Women. (2018). "Enterprise level survey." *Study on the Ready-made Garment Sector in Bangladesh*, A survey Report in 2018.

Kamal, M., Billah, M. M., & Hossain, S. (2010). "Labor Unrest and Bangladesh Labor Act 2006: A study on ready made garment factories in Gazipur." *Journal of Business and Technology*, *5*(2): 1–18.

Majumder, F. H. (2021). "Covid-19 and the RMG industry: The pandemic effect." *The Apparel Story*. Bangladesh Garment Manufacturers and Exporters Association (BGMEA): Dhaka, Bangladesh.

NordÃ, G. (2004). *The Correspondence Principle and Structural Stability in Non-Maximum* (No. *12224700000000422*). UCLA Department of Economics.

Rafique, M. (2021). "Digital payment to Usher in new era in Bangladesh garment industry." *The Apparel Story*. Bangladesh Garment Manufacturers and Exporters Association (BGMEA): Dhaka, Bangladesh.

Rahman, S. (2020). "Revisiting empowerment: Rising female unemployment in the Bangladesh garment sector", Accessed 27 April 2020. Manuscript at: DOI: 10.1177/194277861801100203

Robbani, M. G. (2000). "World trade organization and the ready-made garment industry of Bangladesh: A critical analysis." *Journal of Business Studies*, *2*(2): 16–27

Robbins, A. J., & Campbell, T. (2010). *Organizational Behaviour*. Pearson Education Ltd.

Rock, M. (2001). "Globalisation and Bangladesh: The case of export-oriented garment Manufacture." *South Asia: Journal of South Asian Studies*, *24*(1): 201–225.

Rock, M. (2003). "Labour conditions in the export-oriented garment industry in Bangladesh." *South Asia: Journal of South Asian Studies*, *26*(3): 391–407.

Sammilita Garments Sramik Federation, Annual Report. (2014). https://www.fairlabor.org/sites/default/files/documents/reports/2014_fla_apr_0.pdf

Sokou, K., & Schneider, H. (2013). "US Suspends Bangladesh's Trade Privileges Due to Labor Concerns." *Washington Post (Washington, DC)*, *27*.

Trading Economics (https://tradingeconomics.com/bangladesh/living-wage-family#:~:text=Living%20Wage%20Family%20in%20Bangladesh%20is%20expected%20to%20reach%2013300.00,according%20to%20our%20econometric%20models)

UN (2020). World Economic Situation and Prospects. (2020). Briefing, No. 136. Accessed 15 May 2020 at: https://www.un.org/development/desa/dpad/publication/world-economic-situation-and-prospects-april-2020-briefing-no-136/

U.S. Department of Agriculture, USDA. (2021). https://www.usda.gov/oce/ag-outlook-forum

WTO. (2019). *World Trade Statistical Review*. Geneva: World Trade Organization.

5 Energy Consumption and GDP Nexus in Bangladesh

Maneka Jayasinghe, S Selvanathan, and E A Selvanathan

5.1 Introduction

In the past two decades, Bangladesh has achieved significant economic growth. Rapid economic growth, together with an increasing population, has resulted in a notable increase in energy consumption in the country (Islam and Khan 2017). The relationship between economic growth and energy consumption has received significant attention in the economic growth literature (see, for example, Mozumder and Marathe 2007, Jayasinghe and Selvanathan 2021, Selvanathan et al. 2020). This is because while energy is an impetus for economic growth, excessive energy consumption is also detrimental to environmental sustainability (Jafari et al. 2012). Due to various country-specific socio-economic characteristics and differences in various policy frameworks countries are adhering to, there is no consensus on the relationship between energy consumption and economic growth in the literature (Mozumder and Marathe 2007; Ozturk and Acaravci 2011). In this context, a revisit on the interrelationship between energy consumption and other economic activities in Bangladesh is timely.

Natural gas is the main energy source of Bangladesh and the power generation sector is heavily dependent on that (Government of Bangladesh 2016). In recent years, there have been significant efforts by the government to reduce the dependence on fossil-fuel-based energy. As a result, arrangements have been made to build three nuclear power plants with a life span of 60 years by 2024. Additionally, by 2021, another coal power plant will be set up to meet the increasing demand for energy in the country (Islam and Khan 2017). Intending to promote renewable energy in the country, the government of Bangladesh established the Sustainable and Renewable Energy Development Authority (SREDA) in 2014. Among other initiatives, the solar home system programme implemented by a state-owned institution, Infrastructure Development Company Limited (IDCOL) currently provides solar energy for about 11% of the total population of Bangladesh (IDCOL 2015). Currently, energy from renewable energy sources, such as solar, wind, and hydro energy, and biomass contribute to only less than 2% of the total energy generation in the country (Islam and Khan 2017).

In addition to renewable energy, energy conservation is another area of great concern of the government of Bangladesh, as it is key to ensure sustainable

DOI: 10.4324/9781003231912-8

development in the country. According to the energy efficiency and conservation master plan, the government of Bangladesh expects a 20% improvement in energy efficiency, which will reduce the electricity demand by 8 GW, compared to base value by 2030. This, in turn, will contribute to 2.3 trillion BDT worth reduction in fuel imports in the country (JICA 2015). Given that the country is focusing on energy conservation and rapid economic growth, while tackling other socio-economic challenges, it is important to revisit the relationship between energy consumption and other key economic indicators in the country, such as GDP, capital formation, and labour force.

To this end, using data for the period 1990–2014, this chapter aims at testing several hypotheses on the causal relationship between energy consumption and economic growth (measured by GDP), capital formation and labour. These include whether (a) GDP causes energy consumption, (b) capital formation increase the demand for energy consumption, (c) labour force level impacts on the energy consumption, (d) energy consumption causes economic growth, (e) energy consumption increases capital formation, and (f) energy consumption affects the level of the Bangladesh labour force.

This chapter is organized as follows. Section 5.2 presents a brief review of existing literature on the causality between energy consumption and GDP. The methodology adopted for the empirical analysis is given in Section 5.3. Section 5.4 presents preliminary data analysis, while Section 5.5 presents estimation results and discussion. Section 5.6 provides concluding remarks.

5.2 Review of Literature

There is a significant body of empirical literature on the relationship between energy consumption and economic growth based on data from various countries. These findings could be broadly divided into four groups: (a) growth hypothesis, (b) conservation hypothesis, (c) feedback hypothesis, and (d) neutrality hypothesis (Ozturk and Acaravci 2011). Ozturk and Acaravci (2011) and Soytas and Sari (2003) noted that the empirical findings of the relationship between energy and economic growth depends on the model specification, econometric techniques used, and the country characteristics. Below we discuss the empirical literature with respect to the above four hypotheses.

The growth hypothesis implies the presence of unidirectional causality running from energy consumption to economic growth. For example, evidence for growth hypothesis was found in a number of studies; in India (Masih and Masih 1996; Asafu-Adjaye 2000); Indonesia (Asafu-Adjaye 2000); Turkey, France, Germany, and Japan (Soytas and Sari 2003); China (Wolde-Rufael 2004); Taiwan (Yang 2000); and Korea and Philippines (Yu and Choi 1985). In this case, as energy consumption plays a vital role in economic growth, any disruption to energy supply can have an adverse impact on the economy.

The conservation hypothesis suggests that there is a unidirectional causality running from economic growth to energy consumption. Many studies found support for the conservation hypothesis. For example, Abosedra and Baghestani

(1989) found support in the United States, Aqeel and Butt (2001) in Pakistan, Cheng and Lai (1997) in Taiwan, Cheng (1999) in India, Jumbe (2004) in Malawi, Masih and Masih (1996) in Indonesia, and Soytas and Sari (2003) in Italy and Korea. Mozumder and Marathe (2007) found similar results in Bangladesh between 1971 and 1999. The presence of the conservation hypothesis implies that energy conservation policies could be implemented with limited or no adverse impact on the economy.

The feedback hypothesis implies that there is bidirectional causality between energy consumption and economic growth. Evidence for feedback hypothesis was found in Japan (Erol and Yu 1988), Canada (Ghali and El-Sakka 2004), Taiwan (Hwang and Gum 1991), South Korea (Glasure 2002; Oh and Lee 2004), and Argentina (Soytas and Sari 2003). Some studies have found that there is no causal relationship between energy and economic growth, supporting the neutrality hypothesis. See, for example, Fatai et al. (2002) in New Zealand; Masih and Masih (1996) in Malaysia, Singapore, and Philippines; Stern (1993), Yu and Hwang (1984), and Yu and Jin (1992) in the United States.

The next section presents the methodology and research hypotheses established based on the literature review.

5.3 Methodology

Since this chapter aims to analyze the nexus between energy consumption and GDP, we consider the Vector Error Correction Model (VECM) under the Autoregressive Distributed Lag (ARDL) framework. One of the advantages in using the ARDL model approach is that we can estimate the long-run and short-run relationships simultaneously.

Following Lee (2005) and Odhiambo (2010), we include the variables: energy consumption (in kg of oil equivalent per-capita, E), per-capita GDP (PCGDP, constant LCU), per-capita gross capital formation (PCGCF, constant LCU), and total labour force – people ages 15 and above, which include those who are currently employed and those who are unemployed but seeking work (L) to investigate the long-run relationship between energy consumption and GDP. We consider the following four linear functional relationships between the above four variables (all in log-form).

5.3.1 Energy

$$\ln E_t = \delta_0 + \delta_1 \ln PCGDP_t + \delta_2 \ln PCGCF_t + \delta_3 \ln L_t + e_t \tag{5.1}$$

In Equation (5.1), we would expect δ_1 and δ_2 to be positive as more energy is required to enhance GDP and GCF through increased domestic production and δ_3 to be negative, as if labour and energy are substitutes (Murry and Nan 1990), increased labour force may reduce the need for energy.

5.3.2 GDP

$$\ln PCGDP_t = \delta_0 + \delta_1 \ln E_t + \delta_2 \ln PCGCF_t + \delta_3 \ln L_t + e_t \quad (5.2)$$

In Equation (5.2), we would expect δ_1 and δ_2 to be positive, as additional energy and GCF are expected to increase the level of GDP and, δ_3 can be expected to be either positive or negative as up to a certain point an increase in labour would increase GDP at an increasing rate and then starts to decline.

5.3.3 Gross Capital Formation

$$\ln PCGCF_t = \delta_0 + \delta_1 \ln E_t + \delta_2 \ln PCGDP_t + \delta_3 \ln L_t + e_t \quad (5.3)$$

In equation (5.3), we would expect δ_1, δ_2, and δ_3 all to be positive as anincrease in energy consumption, GDP, and labour would tend to increase the requirement for GCF.

5.3.4 Labour

$$\ln L_t = \delta_0 + \delta_1 \ln E_t + \delta_2 \ln PCGDP_t + \delta_3 \ln PCGCF_t + e_t \quad (5.4)$$

In equation (5.4), we would expect δ_1 to be negative, as an increase in energy consumption would decrease the demand for labour, and δ_2 and δ_3 to have positive signs, as increased GDP and capital both would increase the demand for labour.

By estimating long-run equations (5.1–5.4) above, we test the following six hypotheses. Using Equation (5.1):

H_1: Conservation hypothesis (unidirectional causality running from GDP to energy)
H_2: Capital increases energy consumption
H_3: Labour reduces energy consumption

Using Equation (5.2):

H_4: Growth hypothesis (unidirectional causality running from energy to GDP)

Using Equation (5.3):

H_5: Energy consumption increases capital formation

Using Equation (5.4):

H_6: Energy consumption reduces the demand for labour

The ARDL (p, q, r, s) formulas corresponding to long-run relationships (1)–(4) can be written as

$$\Delta(\ln E_t) = b_0 + b_1 \ln E_{t-1} + b_2 \ln PCGDP_{t-1} + b_3 \ln PCGCF_{t-1} + b_4 \ln L_{t-1} + \sum_{j=1}^{p} \gamma_{1j}\Delta(\ln E_{t-j}) + \sum_{j=0}^{q} \gamma_{2j}\Delta(\ln PCGDP_{t-j}) + \sum_{j=0}^{r} \gamma_{3j}\Delta(\ln PCGCF_{t-j}) + \sum_{j=0}^{s} \gamma_{4j}\Delta(\ln L_{t-j}) + u_t \quad (5.5)$$

$$\Delta(\ln PCGDP_t) = b_0 + b_1 \ln E_{t-1} + b_2 \ln PCGDP_{t-1} + b_3 \ln PCGCF_{t-1} + b_4 \ln L_{t-1} + \sum_{j=1}^{p} \gamma_{1j}\Delta(\ln PCGDP_{t-j}) + \sum_{j=0}^{q} \gamma_{2j}\Delta(\ln E_{t-j}) + \sum_{j=0}^{r} \gamma_{3j}\Delta(\ln PCGCF_{t-j}) + \sum_{j=0}^{s} \gamma_{4j}\Delta(\ln L_{t-j}) + u_t \quad (5.6)$$

$$\Delta(\ln PCGCF_t) = b_0 + b_1 \ln E_{t-1} + b_2 \ln PCGDP_{t-1} + b_3 \ln PCGCF_{t-1} + b_4 \ln L_{t-1} + \sum_{j=1}^{p} \gamma_{1j}\Delta(\ln PCGCF_{t-j}) + \sum_{j=0}^{q} \gamma_{2j}\Delta(\ln E_{t-j}) + \sum_{j=0}^{r} \gamma_{3j}\Delta(\ln PCGCF_{t-j}) + \sum_{j=0}^{s} \gamma_{4j}\Delta(\ln L_{t-j}) + u_t \quad (5.7)$$

$$\Delta(\ln L_t) = b_0 + b_1 \ln E_{t-1} + b_2 \ln PCGDP_{t-1} + b_3 \ln PCGCF_{t-1} + b_4 \ln L_{t-1} + \sum_{j=1}^{p} \gamma_{1j}\,\Delta(\ln L_{t-j}) + \sum_{j=0}^{q} \gamma_{2j}\Delta(\ln PCGDP_{t-j}) + \sum_{j=0}^{r} \gamma_{3j}\Delta(\ln PCGCF_{t-j}) + \sum_{j=0}^{s} \gamma_{4j}\Delta(\ln E_{t-j}) + u_t \quad (5.8)$$

We determine the number of lags p, q, r, s in each equation based on the AIC and SIC criteria.

The ARDL bounds test can be used to test the long-run (or the co-integrating) relationship between energy consumption, GDP, capital and labour based on a non-standard F-test by testing the null and the alternative hypotheses.

H_0: $\beta_1 = \beta_2 = \beta_3 = \beta_4 = 0$ (no co-integration)
H_A: At least one of β_1 or β_2 or β_3 or $\beta_4 \neq 0$ (existence of co-integration).

We use the critical values provided in Pesaran et al. (2001). There are two sets of critical values: one based on the assumptions that all variables are I(0) and the other based on the assumptions that all variables are I(1). If the calculated F-statistic is above the I(1) critical value, the null hypothesis should be rejected and concluded that there is support for co-integration. If the calculated F-statistic is below the I(0) critical value, the null hypothesis should not be rejected and concluded that there is no support for co-integration. If the calculated F-statistic is between the I(0) critical value and the I(1) critical value, the test result is inconclusive.

There are two points worth noting in relation to the bounds test: (a) even though the bounds test approach does not generally require the order of the integration of all the variables to be I(0) or I(1), it does require that none of the variables in the model equation are of order I(2) or higher. To ensure that none of the variables are I(2) or higher, we perform the unit root tests: (b) if some or all of the variables in a regression model are non-stationary in their level form, then a least squares regression model with these variables may produce spurious results. As the bounds test results also reveal whether the variables of energy consumption, economic growth, capital, and labour are co-integrated, we can use the bounds test results to confirm whether the model estimation results are spurious or not. It is because even if the variables in the regression model are integrated of order 1, that is I(1), if they are co-integrated, then the least squares estimation results would still be valid.

If co-integration exists between energy consumption, GDP, capital, and labour, then we can use an error correction (EC) model to estimate the speed of adjustment of the disequilibrium caused by previous period shocks that re-converges to the long-run equilibrium. The EC models that correspond to equations (5.5–5.8) can be written as

$$\begin{aligned}\Delta(\ln E_t) = \gamma_0 + + \sum_{j=1}^{p} \gamma_{1j}\Delta(\ln E_{t-j}) + \sum_{j=0}^{q} \gamma_{2j}\Delta(\ln PCGDP_{t-j}) \\ + \sum_{j=0}^{r} \gamma_{3j}\Delta(\ln PCGCF_{t-j}) + \sum_{j=0}^{s} \gamma_{4j}\Delta(\ln L_{t-j}) \\ + \mu EC_{t-1} + u_t\end{aligned} \tag{5.9}$$

$$\begin{aligned}\Delta(\ln PCGDP_t) = \gamma_0 + \sum_{j=1}^{p} \gamma_{1j}\Delta(\ln PCGDP_{t-j}) + \sum_{j=0}^{q} \gamma_{2j}\Delta(\ln E_{t-j}) \\ + \sum_{j=0}^{r} \gamma_{3j}\Delta(\ln PCGCF_{t-j}) + \sum_{j=0}^{s} \gamma_{4j}\Delta(\ln L_{t-j}) \\ + \mu EC_{t-1} + u_t\end{aligned} \tag{5.10}$$

$$\begin{aligned}\Delta(\ln PCGCF_t) = \gamma_0 + \sum_{j=1}^{p} \gamma_{1j}\Delta(\ln PCGCF_{t-j}) + \sum_{j=0}^{q} \gamma_{2j}\Delta(\ln E_{t-j}) \\ + \sum_{j=0}^{r} \gamma_{3j}\Delta(\ln PCGDP_{t-j}) + \sum_{j=0}^{s} \gamma_{4j}\Delta(\ln L_{t-j}) \\ + \mu EC_{t-1} + u_t\end{aligned} \tag{5.11}$$

$$\Delta(\ln L_t) = \gamma_0 + \sum_{j=1}^{p} \gamma_{1j}\Delta(\ln L_{t-j}) + \sum_{j=0}^{q} \gamma_{2j}\Delta(\ln E_{t-j}) + \sum_{j=0}^{r} \gamma_{3j}\Delta(\ln PCGDP_{t-j}) + \sum_{j=0}^{s} \gamma_{4j}\Delta(\ln PCGCF_{t-j}) + \mu EC_{t-1} + u_t \quad (5.12)$$

where EC_{t-1} is the error correction term derived from the long-run relationship (1)–(4) and for equations (5.9–5.12), respectively. The coefficient γ_{ij} measures the short-run dynamics associated with the long-run relationships and coefficient μ is the speed of adjustment that measures the long-run effect. Using the EC models (9)–(12), we can test two forms of Granger causality, namely (a) short-run causality by performing Wald test on the short-run γ_{ij} coefficients to identify whether individual independent variables have any causal relationship with the dependent variable; and (b) a long-run causality using a t-test on the EC coefficient, μ, to identify whether independent variables collectively have any causal relationship with the dependent variable. Following Page (1954), we also test the stability of the EC model using cumulative sum (CUSUM) and cumulative sum of squares (CUSUMQ).

5.4 Preliminary Data Analysis

The data for the four variables, energy consumption (E), per-capita GDP (PCGDP), per capita gross fixed capital formation (PCGCF), and total labour force (L) for Bangladesh for the period of 1990–2014, were collected from the World Bank open data (World Bank 2019). Figures 5.1–5.4 present the time-series

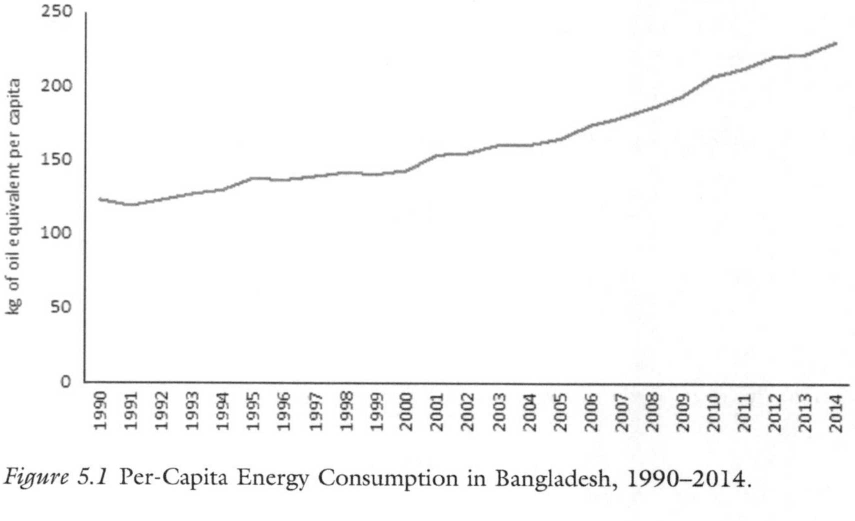

Figure 5.1 Per-Capita Energy Consumption in Bangladesh, 1990–2014.

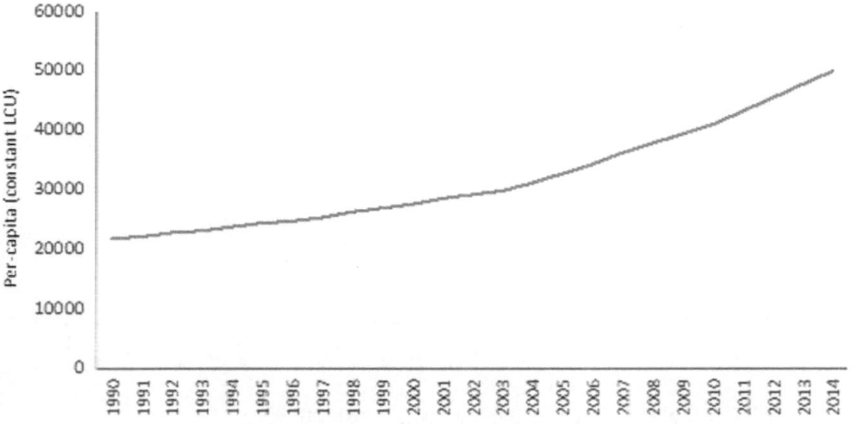

Figure 5.2 Real Per-Capita GDP in Bangladesh, 1990–2014.

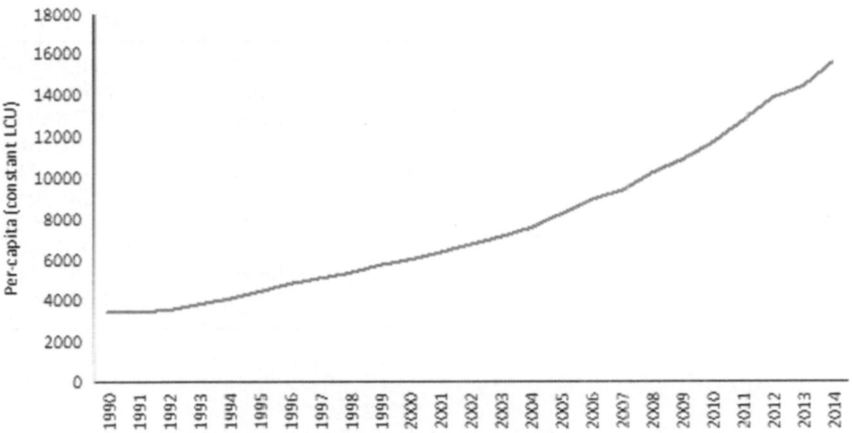

Figure 5.3 Per-capita gross capita formation in Bangladesh, 1990–2014.

plots of the data. Table 5.1 presents the values of the four variables for a number of selected years and the summary statistics. As can be seen, all four variables have gradually increased over time. Per-capita energy consumption, per-capita GDP, and the total labour force in Bangladesh have almost doubled over the last 25 years, while the per-capita gross capital formation has quadrupled. In the rest of the analysis of this chapter, we use all variables in natural logarithm form.

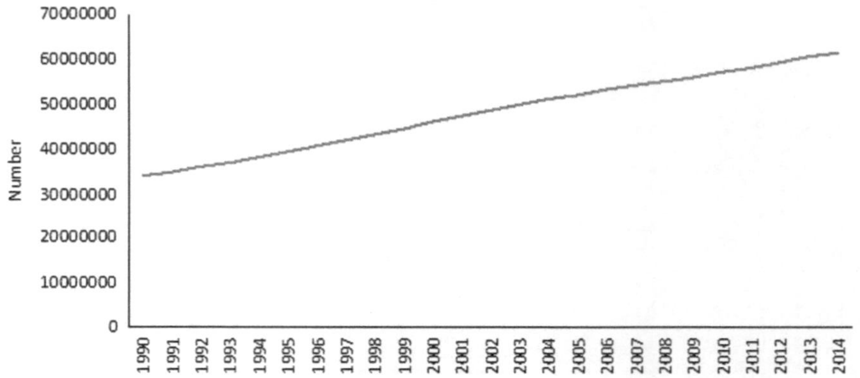

Figure 5.4 Total Labour force in Bangladesh, 1990–2014.

Table 5.1 Summary Statistics

(1)	*Energy (kg of oil equivalent per capita)* *(2)*	*PCGDP (constant LCU)* *(3)*	*PCGCF (constant LCU)* *(4)*	*Labour (number)* *(5)*
1990	123	21653	3497	33853862
1995	138	24205	4443	39492646
2000	143	27645	6063	45978639
2005	164	32522	8254	52170458
2010	207	41138	11722	56913121
2014	229	50099	15697	61288304
Minimum	119	21653	3497	33853862
Mean	163	31771	7781	47928542
Maximum	229	50099	15697	61288304
Standard Deviation	34	8654	3710	8575662

5.5 Estimation Results

As discussed in Section 5.3, to apply the ARDL bounds test on models (9)–(12), we need to ensure that none of the variables in our models is integrated of order 2, (I(2)) or higher. In order to investigate that we performed the unit root tests, we present the unit root test results based on three commonly used unit root tests, namely, the Augmented Dickey and Fuller (1979) (ADF) test, Phillips and Perron (1988) (PP) test, and KPSS (Kwiatkowski et al. 1992) test. The first two tests, ADF and PP tests, test the null hypothesis H_0: series has a unit root (or equivalently the series is non-stationary), whereas the null hypothesis for the KPSS test is H_0: series has no unit roots (that is the series is stationary).

Table 5.2 presents the unit root test results based on the above three tests. As can be seen, all the variables are either stationary in the level form (I(0)) or the

Table 5.2 Stationarity Test Results for Bangladesh

		ADF test			*PP test*			*KPSS*		*Conclusion*
		Test stat	*Critical Value (5%)*	*p-value*	*Test stat*	*Critical Value (5%)*	*p-value*	*Test stat*	*Critical Value (5%)*	
(1)	*(2)*	*(3)*	*(4)*	*(5)*	*(6)*	*(7)*	*(8)*	*(9)*	*(10)*	*(11)*
Energy	Level	−1.993	−3.603	0.577	−1.993	−3.603	0.577	0.179	0.146	Non-stationary
	First Diff	-5.711	−2.986	0.000*	−5.711	−2.986	0.000*	0.317	0.463*	Stationary, I(1)
PCGDP	Level	0.134	−3.603	0.999	0.041	−3.603	0.999	0.195	0.146	Non-stationary
	First Diff	−2.708	−2.986	0.087**	−2.667	−2.986	0.094**	0.618	0.739**	Stationary, I(1)[a]
PCGCF	Level	−3.353	−3.603	0.081	−3.353	−3.603	0.081	0.185	0.146	Non-stationary
	First Diff	−3.476	−2.986	0.018*	−3.380	−2.986	0.022*	0.399	0.463*	Stationary, I(1)
Labour	Level	−2.484	−2.998	0.132	−6.147	−2.992	0.000*	0.195	0.146	Non-stationary
	First Diff	−1.722	−1.956	0.080**	−1.512	−1.956	0.120	0.622	0.739**	Stationary, I(1)[a]

Notes:
ADF and PP tests: H_0: series is non-stationary, KPSS: H_0: series is stationary.
* Significant at 5% level.
** Significant at 10% level.
[a] Stationary at 10% level.

Table 5.3 ARDL Bounds Test Results

ARDL Model	*Null hypothesis*	*F-Test statistic*	*Critical values at 5% level of significance*	
			I(0)	*I(1)*
(1)	*(2)*	*(3)*	*(4)*	*(5)*
ARDL (1, 2, 2, 1)	F (Energy/PCGDP, PCGCF, Labour)	6.39	2.45	3.63
ARDL (1, 0, 1, 2)	F (PCGDP/Energy, PCGCF, Labour)	19.73	3.27	4.31
ARDL (1, 3, 2, 0)	F (PCGCF/Energy, PCGDP, Labour)	4.26	3.38	4.23
ARDL (2, 0, 2, 0)	F (Labour/Energy, PCGDP, PCGCF)	5.00	3.27	4.31

first differenced form (I(1)), and therefore, the ARDL bounds test approach can be applied for further analysis.

Table 5.3 presents the bounds test results for co-integration. As can be seen, all the calculated values of the F-test statistic are higher than the bounds test upper limit – I(1) critical value – at the 5% level of significance. This means that all the variables combinations under consideration are co-integrated.

Table 5.4 presents the long-run estimation results (for models (1)–(4) and (9)–(12)) and diagnostic test results for serial correlation, heteroscedasticity, and normality. As can be seen, the results indicate that serial correlation is not an issue in any of the estimated models at 5% level of significance. Based on the Breusch-Pagan-Godfrey (B-P-G) test, we do not reject the null hypothesis of no heteroscedasticity at the 5% level of significance, indicating that there is no issue of heteroscedasticity. Jarque-Bera (J-B) test results indicate that, generally, the normality assumption is satisfied at the 5% except PCGCF, which is significant at 1% level of significance. In addition, the Ramsay rest test results indicate that the null hypothesis that model specification is correct is not rejected at 5% and 1% (for PCGCF) level of significance.

The long-run estimation results presented in Column 2 of Table 5.4 for the energy equation (5.1) reveals that PCGDP and PCGCF have a positive and significant impact on energy consumption. For example, a 1% increase in per-capita GDP and per-capita gross capital formation increases energy consumption by 0.697%, and 0.103%, respectively. Therefore, we find support for the hypotheses H_1: conservation hypothesis (unidirectional causality running from GDP to energy) and H_2: capital increases energy consumption in Bangladesh in the long run. Column 2 results also indicate that labour force has a negative and significant impact on energy consumption, supporting H_3: labour reduces energy consumption. The estimate of labour coefficient reveals that a 1% increase in total labour reduces energy consumption by 0.164%. Such a negative relationship between energy and labour is expected when labour

Table 5.4 Long-Run Estimation Results

Independent Variables	*Dependent variable*			
(1)	*Energy* *(2)*	*PCGDP* *(3)*	*PCGCF* *(4)*	*Labour* *(5)*
Constant		22.877** (0.087)		16.803* (0.000)
Trend			−0.080 (0.119)	
Energy		−0.290 (0.771)	0.878* (0.011)	−0.343 (0.207)
PCGDP	0.697* (0.000)		1.398* (0.013)	−0.262 (0.393)
PCGCF	0.103** (0.073)	1.127 (0.142)		0.633* (0.000)
Labour	−0.164* (0.001)	−1.169 (0.163)	2.851* (0.023)	
EC	−0.939* (0.000)	−0.161* (0.000)	−0.812* (0.000)	−0.052* (0.000)
Serial Correlation (B-G LM)	1.941 (0.183)	0.376 (0.693)	0.878 (0.448)	2.779 (0.100)
Heteroscedasticity (B-P-G)	0.837 (0.596)	1.342 (0.294)	0.759 (0.664)	0.776 (0.617)
Normality (J-B)	0.926 (0.629)	0.768 (0.681)	7.583[a] (0.023)	3.243 (0.198)
Ramsey Reset Test	0.699 (0.417)	0.554 (0.468)	8.518[a] (0.015)	3.302 (0.091)

Notes:
p-values are given in parenthesis.
* Significant at the 5% level.
** Significant at the 10% level. Breusch-Godfrey serial correlation LM (B-G LM) test H_0: No Serial correlation; Breusch-Pagan-Godfrey (B-P-G) Test H_0: No heteroscedasticity; Jarque-Bera (J-B) test H_0: Data is normally distributed; Ramsey Reset test H_0: The model is correctly specified.
[a] Null hypothesis not rejected at the 1% level of significance.

and energy consumption are substitutes. Column 3 results for the PCGDP equation (5.2) reveal that none of the variables has a statistically significant impact on PCGDP. Since the energy coefficient is statistically insignificant, we have no support for the H_4: growth hypothesis (unidirectional causality running from energy to GDP) in the long-run.

Column 4 of Table 5.4 results for the PCGCF equation (5.3) indicate that all variables, energy consumption, per-capita GDP, and labour force, positively contribute to the per-capita gross capital formation and this result is statistically significant. The estimates indicate that a 1% increase in energy consumption increases capital formation by 0.878%, a 1% increase in per-capita GDP increases capital formation by 1.398%, and a 1% increase in labour force increases capital formation by 2.851%. To this end, we find evidence to support H_5: energy consumption increases capital formation in Bangladesh. Column 5 results on labour equation (5.4) reveal that per-capita gross capital formation positively and significantly influences the labour force. The point estimate reveals that a 1% increase in the capital formation increases the total labour force by 0.633%. Column 5 results also indicate that energy consumption has a negative impact on the labour force, but it is not statistically significant. Although based on earlier results, we found that labour could act as a substitute to energy, it is also evident that energy does not necessarily have a significant adverse impact on labour force and hence the employment level in Bangladesh. This indicates that we do not find evidence to support H_6: energy consumption reduces demand for labour in Bangladesh. In summary, the long-run results indicate that there is a bidirectional causality between (energy, GCF) and (GCF, labour) and a unidirectional causality from GDP to energy, labour to energy, and GDP to GCF.

All the EC coefficient estimates reported in Table 5.4 are in the range –1 to 0 as they should be and are all statistically significant. These EC estimates reveal that in Bangladesh, short-run deviations in the long-run relationships models for energy, PCGDP, PCGCF, and labour are corrected within a year at a rate of 93.9%, 16.1%, 81.2%, and 5.2%, respectively. All EC terms are statistically significant, and this indicates that there is a collective long-run causality from all the variables on the right-hand side towards the respective left-hand side variable in each model (1)–(4). As can be seen in Figures 5.5, 5.6, 5.7, and 5.8, in the majority of instances, the stability of the EC models can be confirmed using CUSUM and CUSUMQ.

Table 5.5 presents the short-run Granger causality results. As can be seen, in the short run, there is bidirectional causality among (energy and GCF), (GDP and GCF), and (labour and GDP). The short-run causality test results also indicate that there is a unidirectional causality from GDP to energy. Similar results were observed earlier in the long-run relationship as well. This result provides evidence for the presence of conservation hypothesis (H_1: unidirectional causality running from GDP to energy) in Bangladesh. Our results with respect to H_1 is in line with Mozumder and Marathe (2007) on Bangladesh. On the other hand, we do not find any causal relationship running from energy to GDP in Bangladesh either in the short run or long run (see Table 5.4), and therefore, we find no evidence for the presence of growth hypothesis (H_4: growth hypothesis, unidirectional causality running from energy to GDP). In addition, short-run causality test results also indicate a unidirectional causality running from labour to energy, which we also found in the long run as well (see Table 5.4) in Bangladesh.

Findings imply that Bangladesh can adapt energy conservation policies either in the short-run or long-run with limited or no adverse impact on GDP and labour force.[1]

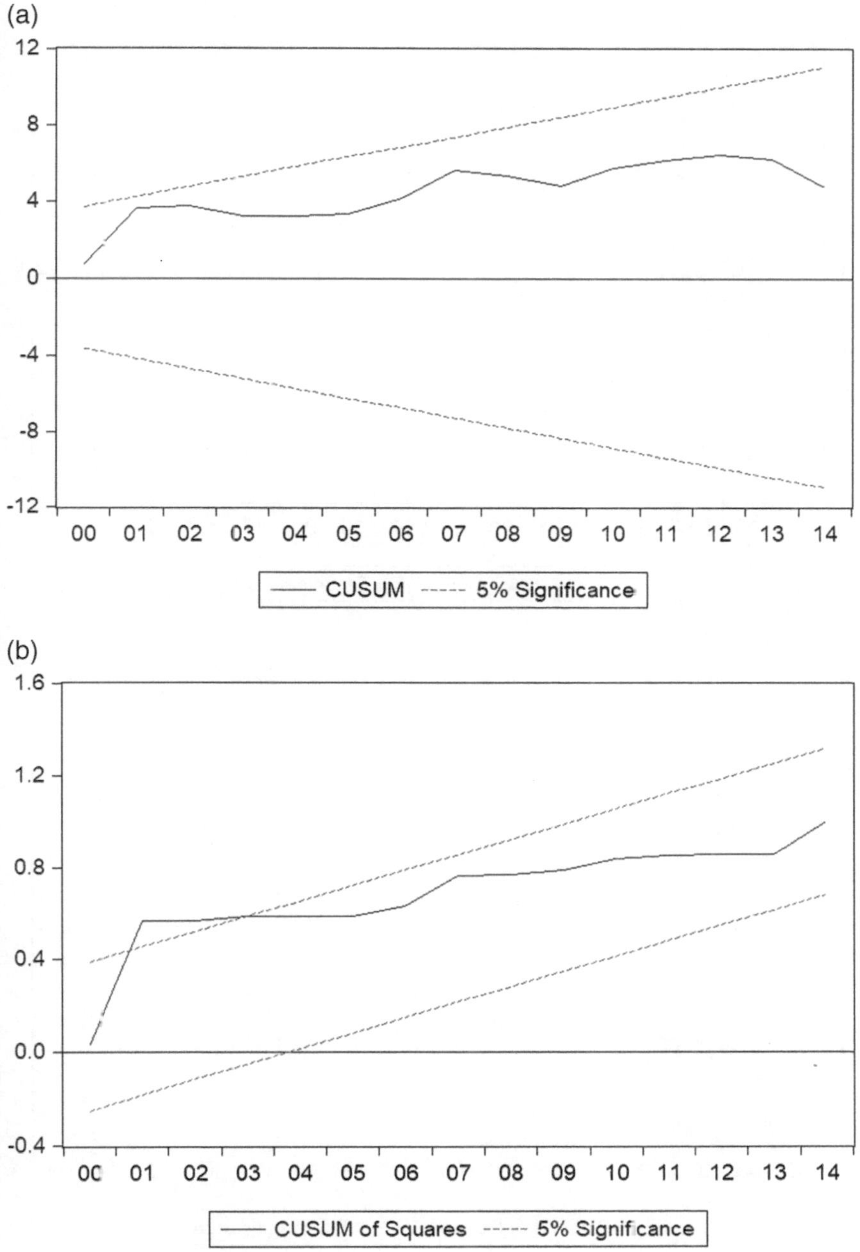

Figure 5.5 CUSUM and CUSUM of Squares for Energy.

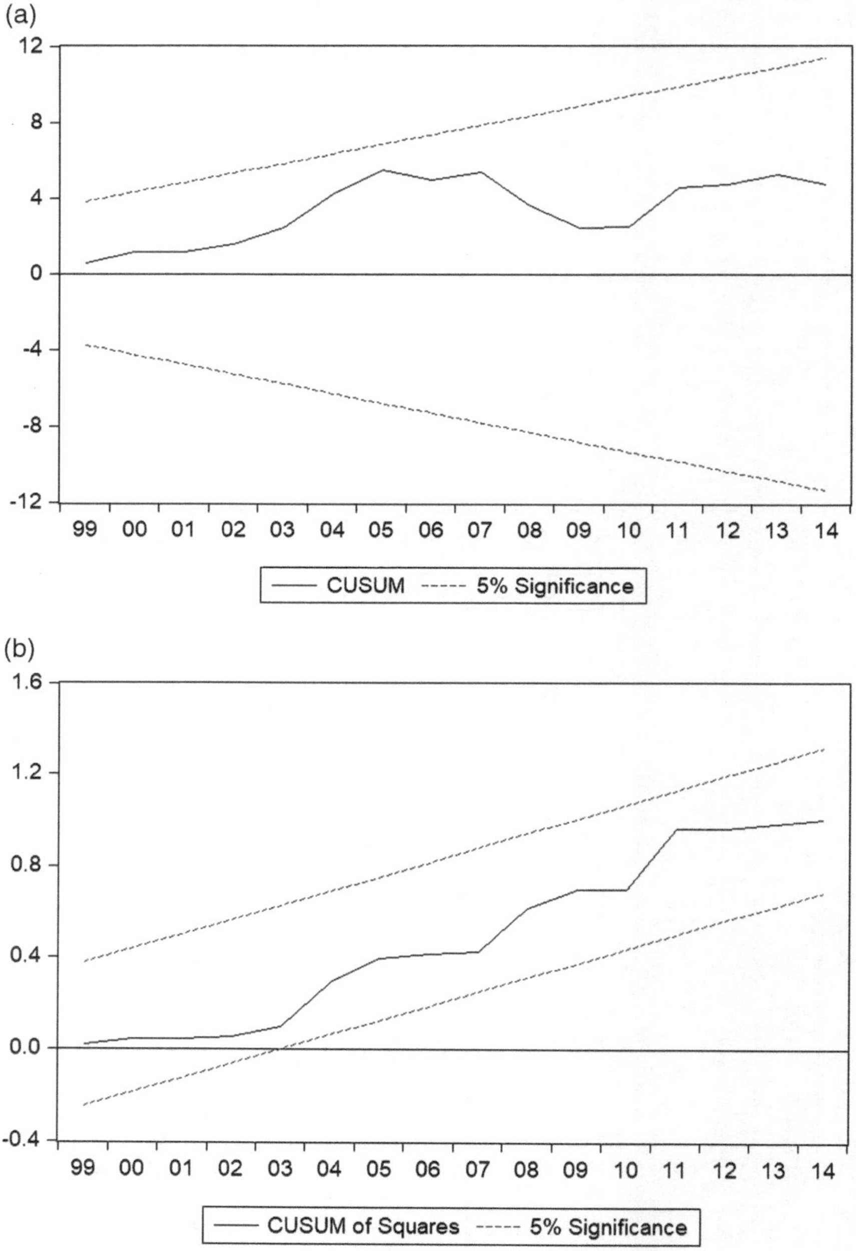

Figure 5.6 CUSUM and CUSUM of Squares for Per-Capita GDP.

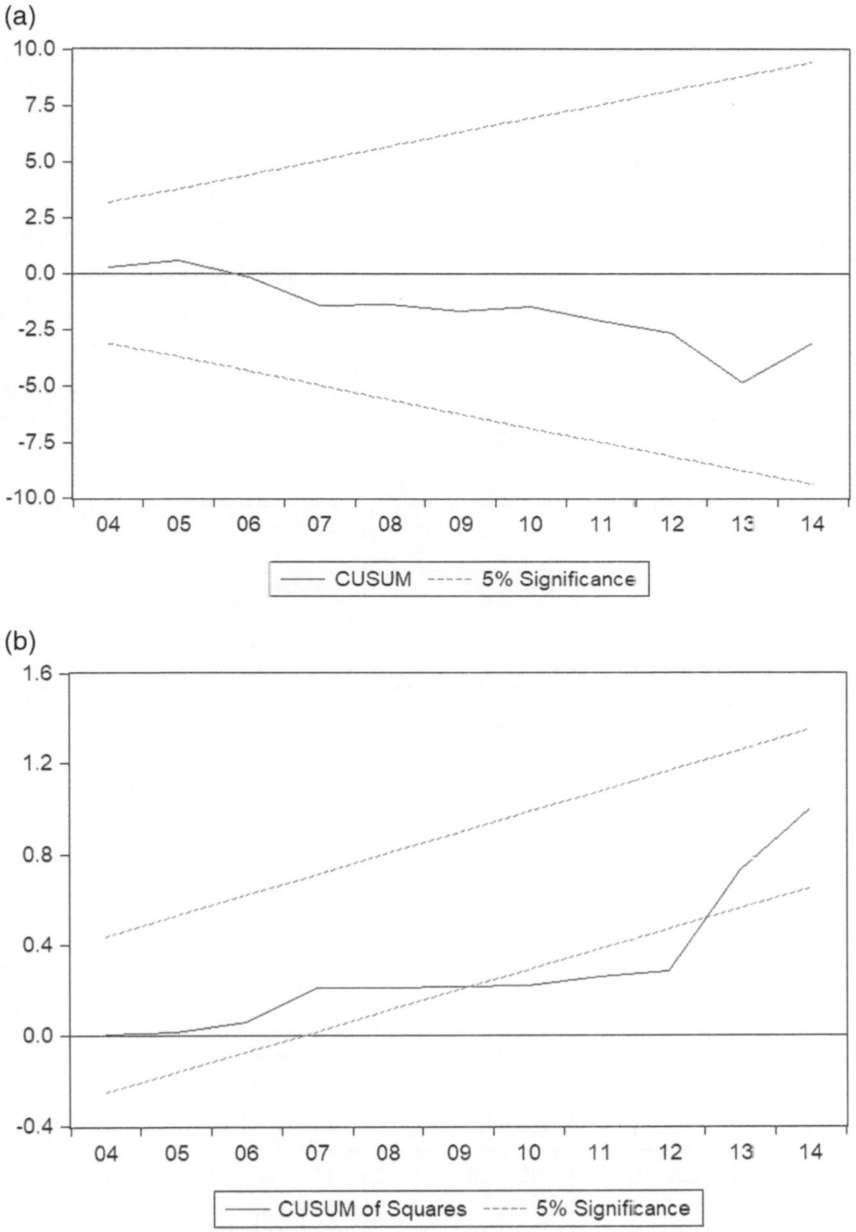

Figure 5.7 CUSUM and CUSUM of Squares for Per-Capita GCF.

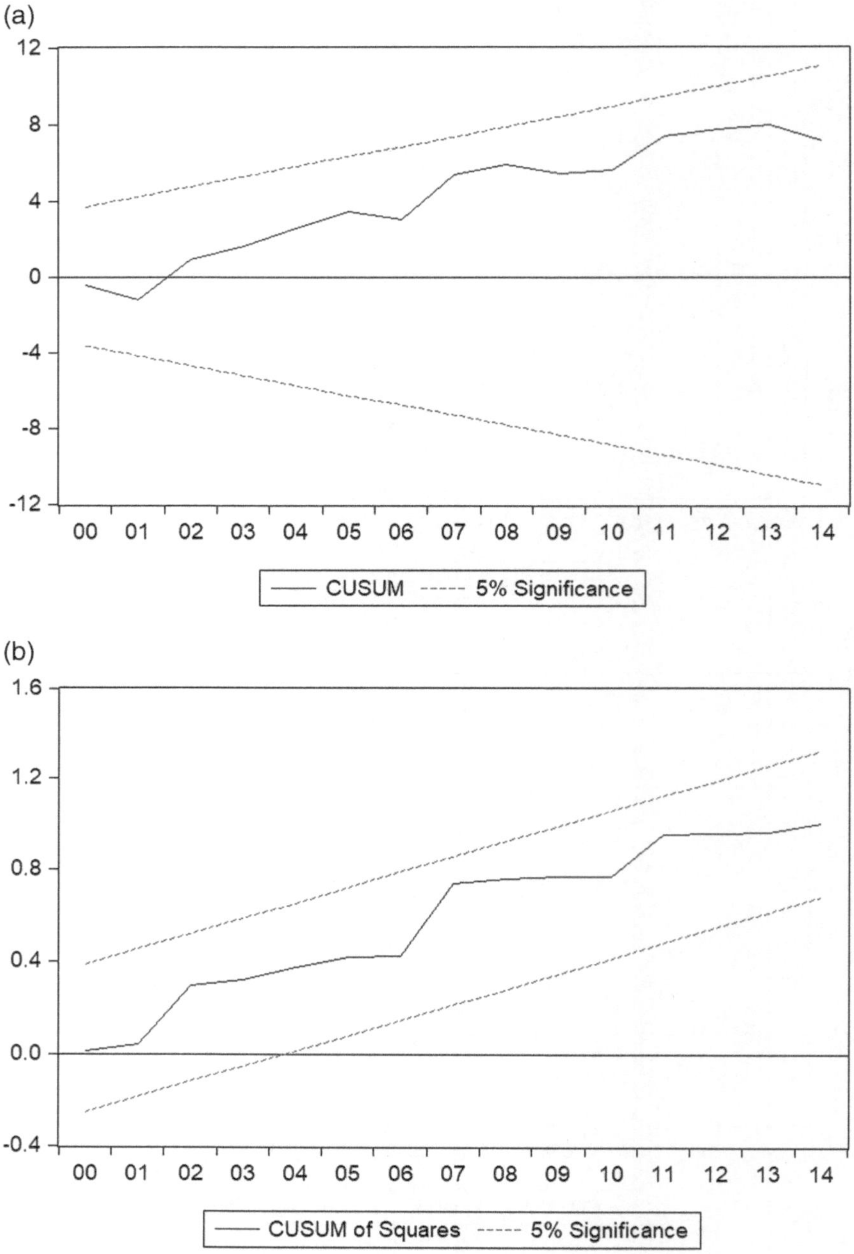

Figure 5.8 CUSUM and CUSUM of Squares for Labour.

Table 5.5 Results for the Granger Causality Test

Dependent Variable	*Short-run results χ^2 Statistics*				*Short-run Granger causality test conclusion*
(1)	*D(Energy)* *(2)*	*D(PCGDP)* *(3)*	*D(PCGCF)* *(4)*	*D(Labour)* *(5)*	*EC* *(6)*
D(Energy)		23.082* (0.000)	19.144* (0.000)	10.056* (0.007)	PCGDP→ E GCF → E L → E
D(PCGDP)	0.953 (0.621)		10.314* (0.006)	17.245* (0.000)	GCF → PCGDP L→ PCGDP
D(PCGCF)	7.897* (0.019)	12.404* (0.002)		6.619* (0.037)	E → GCF PCGDP → GCF L → GCF
D(Labour)	0.234 (0.889)	6.353* (0.042)	3.190 (0.203)		PCGDP→L

Dependent Variable	*Short-run results χ^2 Statistics*				*Short-run Granger causality test conclusion*
(1)	*D(Energy)* *(2)*	*D(PCGDP)* *(3)*	*D(PCGCF)* *(4)*	*D(Labour)* *(5)*	*EC* *(6)*
D(Energy)		23.082* (0.000)	19.144* (0.000)	10.056* (0.007)	PCGDP→ E GCF → E L → E
D(PCGDP)	0.953 (0.621)		10.314* (0.006)	17.245* (0.000)	GCF → PCGDP L→ PCGDP
D(PCGCF)	7.897* (0.019)	12.404* (0.002)		6.619* (0.037)	E → GCF PCGDP → GCF L → GCF
D(Labour)	0.234 (0.889)	6.353* (0.042)	3.190 (0.203)		PCGDP→L

Notes:
p-values are given in parenthesis.
* Significant at the 5% level.

5.6 Conclusions and Policy Implications

There is a growing interest in promoting renewable energy consumption and adopting energy conservation policies in Bangladesh. However, as it is widely accepted that energy consumption plays a significant role in economic growth, an in-depth analysis of energy and GDP nexus in Bangladesh, using the most recent data, is timely.

This chapter, using data for the period 1990–2014, tested six hypotheses on the short-run and long-run causal relationship between energy consumption and economic growth (measured by GDP), capital formation, and labour: (1) the conservation hypothesis (unidirectional causality running from GDP to energy), (2) capital increases energy consumption, (3) labour reduces energy consumption, (4) growth hypothesis (unidirectional causality running from energy to GDP), (5) energy consumption increases capital formation, and (6) energy consumption reduces the demand for labour.

Our results revealed a unidirectional causality running from GDP to energy in the short run as well as long run, supporting the conservation hypothesis in Bangladesh. Results also revealed that capital increases energy consumption, labour reduces energy consumption, and energy consumption increases capital formation in the long run. Nevertheless, no unidirectional causal relationship was found running from energy to GDP in the short run or long run, suggesting that the growth hypothesis is not valid in Bangladesh. Furthermore, we found no evidence that energy consumption reduces the demand for labour.

Note

1 In this study, due to data unavailability, we have used data only for the period 1990–2014 (25 observations). When using the results from this study, this data size limitation should be kept in mind. However, the diagnostic tests we have performed on the estimation results give assurance that the results are of reasonably good quality.

References

Abosedra, S., and Baghestani, H. 1989. New Evidence on the Causal Relationship Between United States Energy Consumption and Gross National Product. *Journal of Energy Development*, *14*, 285–292.

Aqeel, A., and Butt, M. S. 2001. The Relationship Between Energy Consumption and Economic Growth in Pakistan. *Asia Pacific Development Journal* 101–110.

Asafu-Adjaye, J. 2000. The Relationship between Energy Consumption, Energy Prices and Economic Growth: Time-series Evidence from Asian Developing Countries. *Energy Economics*, *22*, 615–625.

Cheng, B. S. 1999. Causality Between Energy Consumption and Economic Growth in India: An Application of Cointegration and Error-correction Modeling. *Indian Economic Review*, *34*(1), 39–49.

Cheng, B. S., and Lai, T. W. 1997. An Investigation of Co-integration and Causality Between Energy Consumption and Economic Activity in Taiwan. *Energy Economics*, *19*, 435–444.

Dickey, D., and Fuller, W. 1979. Distribution of the Estimators for Autoregressive Time Series with a Unit Root. *Journal of the American Statistical Association*, *74*, 427–431.

Erol, U., and Yu, E. S. H. 1988. On the Causal Relationship Between Energy and Income for Industrialized Countries. *Journal of Energy Development*, *13*, 113–122.

Fatai, K., Oxley, L., and Scrimgeour, F. 2002. *Energy Consumption and Employment in New Zealand: Searching for Causality*. Paper presented at the NZAE Wellington.

Ghali, K. H., and El-Sakka, M. I. T. 2004. Energy Use and Output Growth in Canada: A Multivariate Cointegration Analysis. *Energy Economics*, *26*(2), 225–238.

Glasure, Y. U. 2002. Energy and National Income in Korea: Further Evidence on the Role of Omitted Variables. *Energy Economics*, *24*, 355–365.

Government of Bangladesh. 2016. Power System Master Plan Dhaka: Ministry of Power, Energy and Mineral Resources Dhaka. https://policy.asiapacificenergy.org/node/3219.

Hwang, D., and Gum, B. 1991. The Causal Relationship Between Energy and GNP: The Case of Taiwan. *Journal of Energy Development*, *16*, 219–226.

IDCOL. 2015. *Annual Report*. Dhaka: IDCOL.

Islam, S., and Khan, M. Z. R. 2017. A Review of Energy Sector of Bangladesh *Energy Procedia*, *110*, 611–618.

Jafari, Y., Othman, J., and Nor, A. H. S. M. 2012. Energy Consumption, Economic Growth and Environmental Pollutants in Indonesia. *Journal of Policy Modeling*, *34*(6), 879–889.

Jayasinghe, M. and Selvanathan, E. A. (2021). Energy Consumption, Tourism, Economic Growth and CO_2 Emissions Nexus in India. *Journal of the Asia Pacific Economy*, *26*(2), 361–380.

JICA. 2015. *Energy Efficiency and Conservation Master Plan up to 2030*. Dhaka: Japan International Cooperation Agency (JICA).

Jumbe, C. B. L. 2004. Cointegration and Causality Between Electricity Consumption and GDP: Empirical Evidence from Malawi. *Energy Economics*, *26*, 61–68.

Kwiatkowski, D., Phillips, P. C. B., Schmidt, P., and Shin, Y. 1992. Testing the Null Hypothesis of Stationarity Against the Alternative of a Unit Root. *Journal of Econometrics*, *54*(1–3), 159–178.

Lee, C.-C. 2005. Energy Consumption and GDP in Developing Countries: A Cointegrated Panel Analysis. *Energy Economics*, *27*, 415– 427.

Masih, A. M. M., and Masih, R. 1996. Energy Consumption, Real Income and Temporal Causality: Results from a Multi-country Study Based on Cointegration and Error Correction Modeling Techniques. *Energy Economics*, *18*, 165–183.

Mozumder, P., and Marathe, A. 2007. Causality Relationship Between Electricity Consumption and GDP in Bangladesh. *Energy Policy*, *35*, 395–402.

Murry, D. A., and Nan, G. D. 1990. The Energy Consumption and Employment Relationship: A Clarification. *The Journal of Energy and Development*, *16*(1), 121–131.

Odhiambo, N. M. 2010. Electricity Consumption, Labour Force Participation rate and Economic Growth in Kenya: An Empirical Investigation. *Problems and Perspectives in Management*, *8*(1), 31–38.

Oh, W., and Lee, K. 2004. Causal Relationship Between Energy Consumption and GDP Revisited: The Case of Korea 1970–1999. *Energy Economics*, *26*, 51–59.

Ozturk, I., and Acaravci, A. 2011. Electricity Consumption and Real GDP Causality Nexus: Evidence from ARDL Bounds Testing Approach for 11 MENA Countries. *Applied Energy*, *88*, 2885–2892.

Page, E. S. 1954. Continuous Inspection Schemes. *Biometrika*, *41*, 100–115.

Pesaran, M. H., Smith, R. J., and Shin, Y. 2001. Bounds Testing Approaches to the Analysis of Level Relationships. *Journal of Applied Econometrics*, *16*, 289–326.

Phillips, P., and Perron, P. 1988. Testing for a Unit Root in Time Series Regression. *Bimetrika*, *75*, 335–346.

Selvanathan, E. A., Jayasinghe, M., and Selvanathan, S. (2020). 'Dynamic Modelling of Inter-relationship between Tourism, Energy Consumption, CO_2 Emissions and Economic Growth in South Asia. *International Journal of Tourism Research*, *23*(4), 597–610.

Soytas, U., and Sari, R. 2003. Energy Consumption and GDP: Causality Relationship in G-7 Countries and Emerging Markets. *Energy Economics*, *25*, 33–37.

Stern, D. I. 1993. Energy and Economic Growth in the USA. *Energy Economics 15*, 137–150.

Wolde-Rufael, Y. 2004. Disaggregated Industrial Energy Consumption and GDP: The Case of Shanghai, 1952–1999. *Energy Economics*, *26*, 69–75.

World Bank. 2019. World Bank Open Data. https://data.worldbank.org/

Yang, H. Y. 2000. A Note on the Causal Relationship Between Energy and GDP in Taiwan. *Energy Economics*, *22*, 309–317.

Yu, E. S. H., and Choi, J. Y. 1985. The Causal Relationship Between Energy and GNP: An International Comparison. *Journal of Energy Development*, *10*, 249–272.

Yu, E. S. H., and Hwang, B. K. 1984. The Relationship Between Energy and GNP: Further Results. *Energy Economics*, *6*, 186–190.

Yu, E. S. H., and Jin, J. C. 1992. Cointegration Tests of Energy Consumption, Income and Employment. *Resources and Energy*, *14*, 259–266.

6 Determinants of Sustainable Foreign Direct Investments in Bangladesh

Maneka Jayasinghe, S Selvanathan, and E A Selvanathan

6.1 Introduction

During the last two decades, Bangladesh has seen significant changes in the volume and the composition of Foreign Direct Investments (FDIs). In particular, since the year 2000, Bangladesh FDI inflows experienced a tenfold increase from US$m 280 in 2000 to US$m 2,831 in 2015. Currently, FDI is about 2% of Gross Domestic Production (GDP) of the country. In this chapter, we use the Autoregressive Distributed Lag (ARDL) framework to identify the determinants of FDI in Bangladesh during the period of 1986–2017. The estimation results reveal that per capita GDP, infrastructure, and trade openness positively and significantly determine the level of FDI inflows into Bangladesh. Granger causality test results revealed that in the long run, infrastructure has a bidirectional relationship with FDI, while trade openness and per capita GDP have unidirectional causality with FDI. The error correction coefficient estimate reveals that approximately 81% of the disequilibrium caused by previous period shocks are corrected within one period.

Foreign Direct Investment (FDI) is widely considered to be catalyst of economic development. A significant body of literature discusses how FDI contributes to productivity gains, particularly in developing countries, by means of new investments, improved technology, management expertise, and expansion of export markets (Asiedu 2002; Dunning 2009; Meyer 2003; Sahoo 2006). Chen (2000) describes FDI as investment in which a firm acquires a substantial controlling interest in a foreign firm or sets up a subsidiary in a foreign country. Alternatively, UNCTAD (2006) defines FDI as an

> investment that involves a long-term relationship and reflects a lasting interest and control by a resident entity in one economy (foreign direct investor or parent enterprise) in an enterprise resident in an economy other than that of the foreign direct investor (FDI enterprise or affiliate enterprise or foreign affiliate).

FDI has a considerable number of economic benefits on the host country through enhanced technological transfer, optimal utilization of human

DOI: 10.4324/9781003231912-9

capabilities and natural resources, enhanced competitiveness in the global markets, diversified production and export capacities, provision of backward and forward linkages, and augmenting employment opportunities. These potential benefits of FDI have encouraged developing countries to focus on attracting FDI by creating a conducive environment for foreign investors.

Studies have shown that FDI played an important role, particularly in the context of technology transfers in the remarkable economic development and success in a number of South East Asian countries – Hong Kong, Singapore, South Korea, and Taiwan, followed by Indonesia, Malaysia, and Thailand (Bende-Nabende, Ford, & Slater 2001; Sung & Uk 2008). The experience of Asian tigers has encouraged many developing countries to embark on an economic policy regime that promotes FDI. To this end, host countries provide various incentives, such as fiscal incentives, financial incentives, and other non-financial incentives. More specifically, these include provision of tax concessions, government grants, subsidized credit, duty-free import of materials, infrastructure facilities, preferential treatment on foreign exchange, and setting up free trade zones or export processing zones (Quader 2009). While these liberalized economic policies have enhanced FDI inflows into many developing countries around the globe, particularly in Asian countries since early 2000, not all countries in the region have been equally successful in attracting FDI and the competition among countries to attract FDI continues to grow. It is in this context that many researchers and policymakers have started investigating what factors determine successful FDI inflows into various countries.

6.1.1 Determinants of FDI: Global and Asian Experience

Empirical studies on the determinants of FDI reveal that FDI inflow is influenced by an extensive set of factors depending on the country. For example, using pooled cross-section and time-series data for 49 less-developed countries over 1970–95, Gastanaga, Jeffrey, and Pashamova (1998) found that factors such as taxes and tariffs the degree of openness to international capital flows, exchange rate distortions, contract enforcement, nationalization risk, bureaucratic delay, and corruption and location in the host country significantly influence FDI inflow into the countries they examined. Frenkel, Funke, and Stadtmann (2004) also found that distance and characteristics of both home and host country are vital in determining the level of FDI inflows in 22 emerging economies they examined. Bellak, Leibrecht, and Riedl (2008) found that labour costs are an important determinant of FDI in a number of Central and Eastern European countries they examined. Asiedu (2002) found that while a higher return on investment and better infrastructure promotes FDI inflows into non–Sub-Saharan African countries, these factors do not have a significant effect on FDI inflow into Sub-Saharan African countries. Furthermore, Asiedu (2002) also found that trade openness is an important determinant of FDI in both Sub-Saharan African countries and non–Sub-Saharan African countries. Using annual time-series data for the period of 1960–2005, Ang (2008) identified that GDP growth rate, level of financial development, infrastructure development, and trade openness positively and significantly influence FDI inflows into Malaysia.

When considering FDI inflows in the Asian region, in recent years, China and India have become major destinations for most of the FDI inflows in the region. Wei (2005) found that larger domestic market and higher international trade ties with OECD countries are the main factors that attract FDI inflows to China, while cheaper labour, lower country risk, and geographic closeness to OECD countries promote FDI inflows to India. Xing (2006) revealed that devaluation of the Chinese Renminbi (RMB) and the pegging of the RMB to the dollar both enhanced the competitiveness of China in attracting FDI. Bhavan, Xu, and Zhong (2011) found that factors such as trade openness index, human development index, population, and infrastructure have significant positive effects on FDI inflow in South Asian countries, such as Pakistan, India, Bangladesh, and Sri Lanka.

6.1.2 Determinants of FDI: Bangladesh Experience

Since 1990s, following the trend in a number of neighbouring countries, Bangladesh also implemented various economic policies directed towards attracting FDI into the country. These policy initiatives have undoubtedly promoted a healthy level of FDI inflows in Bangladesh over the last few decades. A number of studies have investigated what factors determine FDI inflows to the country and which factors act as obstacles in promoting FDI inflows. Nevertheless, these studies have found mixed results with respect to the determinants of FDI inflows in Bangladesh. For example, while Quader (2009) found that GDP growth positively influences FDI inflows in Bangladesh, Shaheena (2014) found that per capita gross domestic product (GDP) does not affect the level of FDI in the country. However, both Quader (2009) and Shaheena (2014) show that trade openness is one of the most influencing factors of FDI inflows in the country, while low wage rate is also another contributing factor for enhanced FDI inflows. Additionally, Quader (2009) also identified that net export and tax rate also promoted FDI inflows during 1990–2006. Quader (2009) findings are based on the UNCTAD's inward FDI performance index and inward FDI potential index framework. Qamruzzaman (2015), using regression approach, found that during the period of 1980–2010, trade and foreign exchange liberalization, infrastructure availability, and sound economic and political conditions increase FDI inflows and their effects are much higher and prominent with respect to FDI inflows in the manufacturing sector. Aziz, Sarkar, and Mahmud (2014) found that while market size and trade balance positively and significantly influence FDI inflows, labour productivity has a positive but insignificant influence on FDI inflows into Bangladesh. Shah (2013), using a descriptive analysis, focused on ten determinants of FDI in Bangladesh; 1- market size, 2- economic environment, 3- growth, 4- trade performance, 5- competitiveness, 6- labour costs and productivity, 7- infrastructure, 8- political risk, 9- tax, and 10- regulatory policies and also found that factors such as poor infrastructure, low skilled labour, unreliable energy supply, corruption, political instability and disturbances, unfriendly legal system, and inefficient institutions act as major impediments for FDI inflows in the country.

The objective of this chapter is to identify the determinants of FDI inflows into Bangladesh. Nevertheless, the analysis in this chapter differs from the existing studies on the determinants of FDI inflows in Bangladesh in two ways; firstly, this chapter uses both the Autoregressive Distributed Lag (ARDL) framework and regression approach, and investigates the unidirectional and bi-directional causality between the variables used in the analysis; secondly, the analysis in this chapter uses more recent data, covering the period of 1986–2017. The remainder of this chapter is organized as follows. Section 6.2 presents a detailed description of the time-series trend in a number of socio-economic and demographic indicators in Bangladesh and a detailed comparison of some of these indicators with five neighbouring countries in the region, namely China, India, Pakistan, and Sri Lanka. Section 6.3 presents the methodology used in this study, while Section 6.4 presents the estimated results. Section 6.5 provides concluding remarks.

6.2 Trends in Socio-economic and Demographic Indicators

In this section, first we analyze the trend in a number of socio-economic and demographic indicators in Bangladesh and then make a comparison of the Bangladesh trend with that of a number of other countries in the region, namely China, India, Pakistan, and Sri Lanka.

6.2.1 Trends in Socio-economic and Demographic Indicators Bangladesh

Table 6.1A presents statistics on real GDP in US$m (column 2), GDP growth rate (column 3), final consumption expenditure as percentage of GDP) (column 4), real GDP per capita in US$ (column 5), exports in US$m (column 6), imports in US$m (column 7), exports as a percentage of GDP (column 8), imports as a percentage of GDP (column 9), trade openness defined as the sum of exports and imports as a percentage of GDP (column 10), FDI in US$m (column 11), FDI as a percentage of GDP (column 12), official exchange rate (1US$ equivalent in Bangladesh Taka, period average) (column 13), and inflation rate (column 14) for selected years during the period 1970 to 2017 in Bangladesh. Figures 6.1A–D graphically present the corresponding complete time-series data for the same period.

As can be seen in column 2 in Table 6.1A and Figure 6.1A, GDP has increased 2.5 times between 1970 to 2000 (from US$m26411 in 1970 to US$m 67013 in 2000), doubled again between 2000 and 2013, and continued to increase steadily from US$m 138597 in 2013 to US$m 179992 in 2017. As shown in column 2, the GDP has fallen slightly during the early 1970s when Bangladesh

Table 6.1A Socio-economic and demographic indicators, Bangladesh, 1970–2017

Year	*GDP (U$m)*	*GDP Growth rate (%)*	*Final consumption expenditure (% of GDP)*	*GDP per capita (constant 2010 USD)*	*Exports (US$m)*	*Imports (US$m)*	*Exports (% of GDP)*	*Imports (% of GDP)*	*Trade Openness*	*FDI (US $m)*	*FDI (% of GDP)*	*Official exchange rate (LCU per US$, period average)*	*Rate of inflation*
(1)	*(2)*	*(3)*	*(4)*	*(5)*	*(6)*	*(7)*	*(8)*	*(9)*	*(10)*	*(12)*	*(13)*	*(14)*	*(15)*
1970	26411	5.6	92.8	398.71	878	11726	3.3	44.4	47.7	–	–	7.87	
1975	23324	-4.1	99.1	375.83	720	2545	3.1	10.9	14.0	1.5	0.01	12.19	
1980	28627	0.8	97.9	337.60	1224	4553	4.3	15.9	20.2	8.5	0.03	15.45	
1985	35275	3.3	85.5	366.67	932	2274	2.6	6.4	9.1	-6.7	-0.02	27.99	
1990	42421	5.6	84.1	383.81	1332	3115	3.1	7.3	10.5	3.2	0.01	34.57	6.13
1995	52934	5.1	86.9	403.75	2482	4622	4.7	8.7	13.4	1.9	0.00	40.28	10.30
2000	67013	5.3	80.0	456.24	4027	6403	6.0	9.6	15.6	280.4	0.42	52.14	2.21
2005	85860	6.5	78.9	525.07	12052	19037	14.0	22.2	36.2	760.5	0.89	64.33	7.05
2010	115279	5.6	79.2	630.05	18472	25106	16.0	21.8	37.8	1232.3	1.07	69.65	8.13
2011	122731	6.5	79.4	666.40	23892	32426	19.5	26.4	45.9	1264.7	1.03	74.15	11.40
2012	130735	6.5	78.8	698.56	26886	35836	20.6	27.4	48.0	1584.4	1.21	81.86	6.22
2013	138597	6.0	78.0	725.77	27546	36273	19.9	26.2	46.0	2603.0	1.88	78.10	7.53
2014	146997	6.1	77.9	757.67	28427	36697	19.3	25.0	44.3	2539.2	1.73	77.64	6.99
2015	156630	6.6	77.8	797.41	27623	37872	17.6	24.2	41.8	2831.2	1.81	77.95	6.19
2016	167771	7.1	75.0	839.51	28230	35186	16.8	21.0	37.8	2332.7	1.39	78.47	5.51
2017	179992	7.3	74.7	879.58	27568	36198	15.3	20.1	35.4	2151.4	1.20	80.44	5.70
Mean	65249	4.3	85.8	469.05	7437	11552	7.7	15.3	23.0	486.2	0.39	42.92	6.32

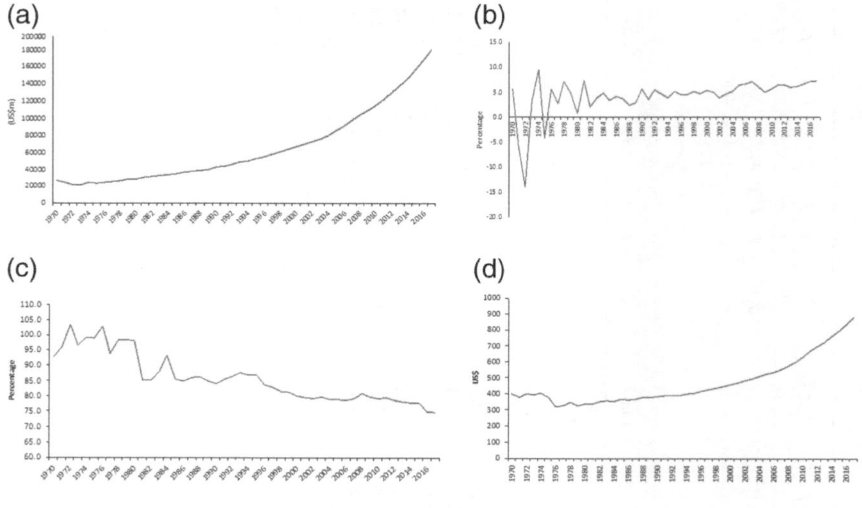

Figure 6.1 (A) GDP (Constant 2010 US$ million), Bangladesh, 1970–2017. (B) GDP Growth Rate (%), Bangladesh 1970–2017. (C) Final Consumption Expenditure (% GDP), Bangladesh, 1970–2017. (D) GDP per Capita (Constant 2010 US$), Bangladesh, 1970–2017.

gained independence, but from 1980 onwards GDP has grown at a steady rate from 0.8% in 1980, to around 5% during the 1990s, to around 6% during the 2000s and to 7.3% in 2017. Throughout the sample period, the GDP has grown at an annual rate of 4.3%. Figure 6.1B graphically depicts these fluctuations in GDP growth in the early 1970s and the steady growth thereafter. Final consumption as a proportion of GDP (in column 4 and Figure 6.1C) has steadily declined from 92.8% in 1970 to 74.7% in 2017 with an average of 85.8% over the sample period. The per capita GDP of Bangladesh experienced some fluctuations during period of 1970–1985 and then increased at an increasing rate to $880 (constant 2010 US$, column 5 and Figure 6.1D) by 2017.

As can be seen in Figure 6.2A and Figure 6.2B and in columns 6–9 of Table 6.1A, Bangladesh imports exceed exports by a significant amount in the 1970s and then the difference between the two became smaller until 2004 and the gap started widening from then onwards. Trade openness (in column 10 and Figure 6.2C), (imports + exports) as a percentage of GDP, has fallen from a high of 48% in 1970 to a low of 9% during mid-1980 and continued to increase to around 48% by 2012 and started to decline to a low level of 35% in 2017.

As shown in Figures 6.3A and B and column 12 of Table 6.1A, the amount of FDI Bangladesh had received is negligibly small until 2000. However, from 2000 onwards, the net FDI inflow in Bangladesh experienced a tenfold increase from US$m 280 in 2000 to US$2,831 in 2015. During 2015–2017, a slight decline of FDI inflows was observed. In terms of FDI as a proportion of GDP, it has increased

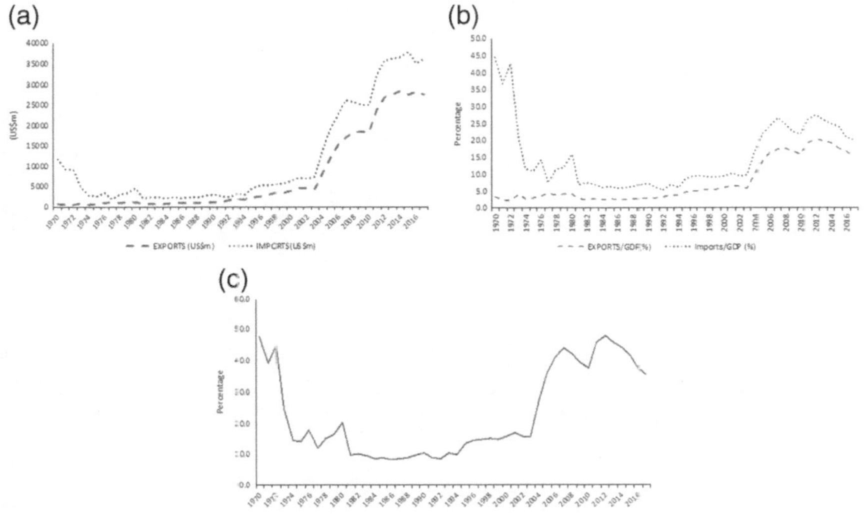

Figure 6.2 (A) Exports and Imports (Constant 2010 US$ m), Bangladesh, 1970–2017. (B) Exports and Imports (% of GDP), Bangladesh, 1970–2017. (C) Trade Openness, Bangladesh, 1970–2017.

from 0.4% in 2000 to 1.9% in 2013 and has fallen since then to 1.2% in 2017. As in column 14 of Table 6.1A and Figure 6.4A, the official exchange rate (Bangladesh Taka per US$) has seen a tenfold increase from 1US$ = 7.9 Taka in 1970 to 1US$ = 80 Taka in 2017. As can be seen in Figure 6.4B (and column 15 of Table 6.1A), the rate of inflation has fluctuated between 2% (in 2000) and 11.4% (in 2017) with a decreasing trend in later part of the sample period.

In summary, over the sample period 1970 to 2017, on average, Bangladesh GDP has grown at a rate of 4.3% per annum, while exports and imports as a proportion of GDP, respectively, have grown at 7.7% and 15.3% per annum. Trade openness has grown with an annual average of 23%. FDI as percentage of GDP has increased at a rate of 0.4% per annum. The inflation has fluctuated throughout the sample period with an annual average rate of 6.3% (between 1987 to 2017) per annum.

Table 6.1B presents data on population growth rate (column 2), life expectancy at birth of males in years (column 3), life expectancy at birth of females in years (column 4), fixed telephone subscriptions per 100 people (column 5), mobile cellular subscriptions per 100 people (column 6), electric power consumption kwh per capita (column 7), fossil fuel energy consumption as a percentage of total energy consumption (column 8), and net energy imports as a percentage of energy used (column 9) for selected years during the period 1970 to 2017. Complete time-series data for the same period for the respective indicators are graphically presented in Figures 6.5–6.7.

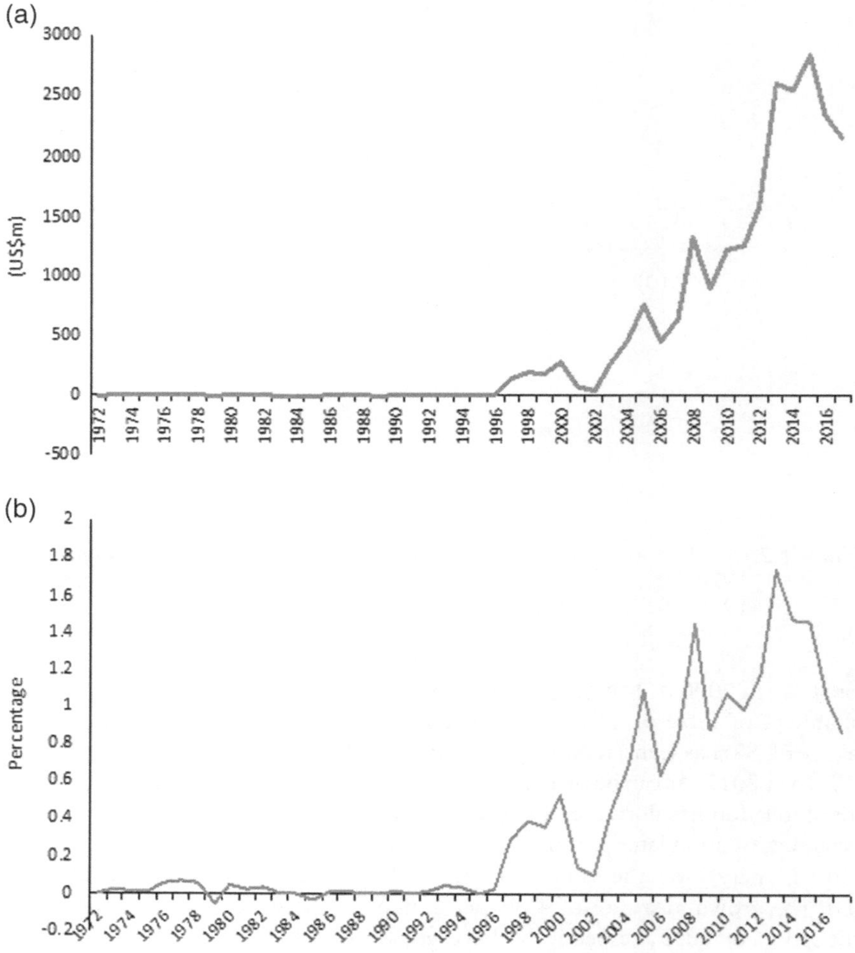

Figure 6.3 (A) Foreign Direct Investment, Net Inflows (BoP, current US$ m) Bangladesh, 1970–2017. (B) FDI, Net Inflows (% of GDP), Bangladesh, 1972–2017.

As can be seen in Figure 6.5A and Table 6.1B, population growth had a sharp fall during the early 1970s and then gradually increased until the mid-1980s and then continued with a declining trend. The population growth in Bangladesh more than halved over the last three decades and has fallen from 2.7% in 1985 to 1.1% in 2017. The life expectancy at birth of males and females (columns 3 and 4 of Table 6.1B and Figure 6.5B) started at the same level at around 47 years in 1970s. However, it could be observed that a gap between the life expectancy of

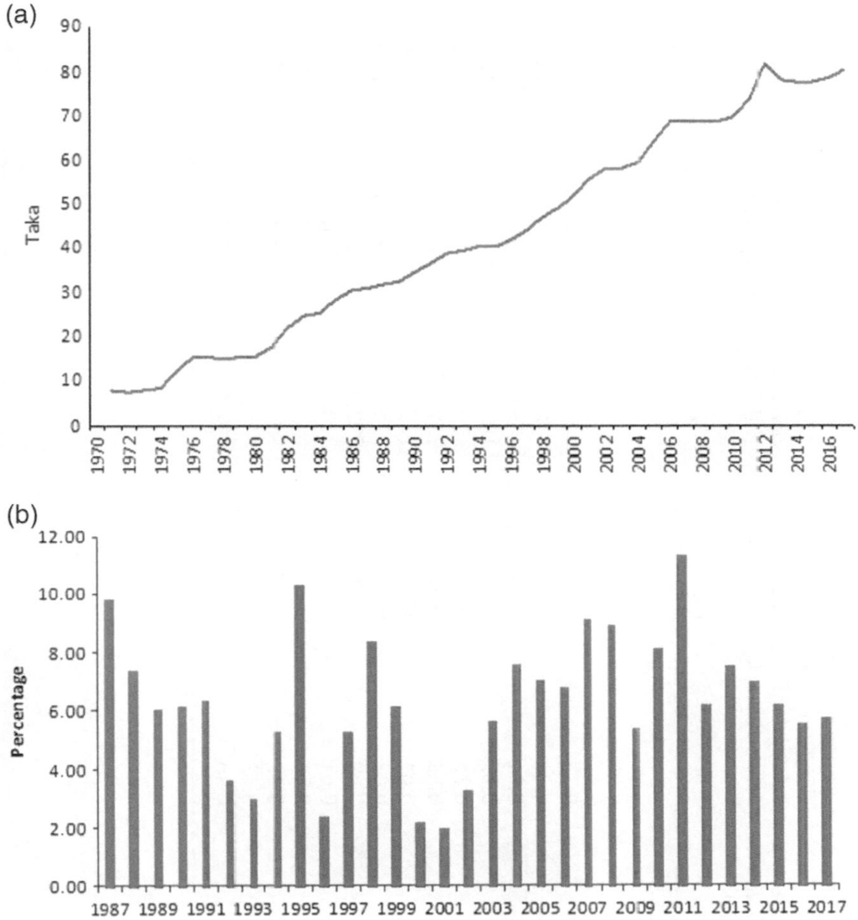

Figure 6.4 (A) Official Exchange Rate (BT per US$ period average), Bangladesh 1970–2017. (B) Rate of Inflation (%), Bangladesh, 1987–2017.

males and females started emerging in favour of females since early 2000 and in 2017 the gap was widened and is around 4 years (71.2 years for males versus 74.6 years for females). As depicted in Figures 6.6A and B and columns 5 and 6 of Table 6.1B, while fixed telephone subscriptions (per 100 people) have increased from 0.08 in 1970 to 0.84 in 2010 and then went on a declining path to 0.43 in 2017, mobile cellular subscriptions (per 100 people) have increased at an impressively faster rate from 0.00 in 1995 to 91.7 in 2017. Electric power consumption (kWh per capita) has increased at an alarming rate from 10.7 kWh per capita in 1970 to 310.4 kWh per capita in 2014. As depicted in Figure 6.7B,

Table 6.1B Socio-economic and demographic indicators, Bangladesh, 1970–2017

Year (1)	*Population Growth rate (%)* (2)	*Life expectancy at birth, male (years)* (3)	*Life expectancy at birth, female (years)* (4)	*Fixed telephone subscriptions (per 100 people)* (5)	*Mobile cellular subscriptions (per 100 people)* (6)	*Electric power consumption (kWh per capita)* (7)	*Fossil fuel energy consumption (% of total)* (8)	*Energy imports, net (% of energy use)* (9)
1970	2.54	47.4	47.6	–	–	10.7	–	–
1975	2.01	48.8	48.9	0.08	–	17.0	20.7	14.3
1980	2.78	53.3	53.7	0.12	–	18.7	27.3	17.8
1985	2.68	55.3	55.8	0.16	–	32.6	35.0	19.1
1990	2.47	58.1	58.8	0.21	–	48.4	43.9	16.3
1995	2.15	61.6	62.2	0.24	0.00	75.9	46.7	14.2
2000	1.96	65.0	65.7	0.37	0.21	101.5	56.6	21.6
2005	1.49	67.3	68.7	0.75	6.27	170.7	61.0	18.1
2010	1.12	69.0	71.5	0.84	44.64	239.8	66.4	13.6
2011	1.15	69.3	72.1	0.64	54.82	257.6	67.6	12.8
2012	1.17	69.7	72.6	0.62	62.40	274.9	69.0	12.4
2013	1.18	70.0	73.1	0.69	73.97	292.8	71.0	14.5
2014	1.16	70.3	73.5	0.61	79.59	310.4	71.6	16.9
2015	1.12	70.6	73.9	0.54	81.50		72.7	17.8
2016	1.08	70.9	74.3	0.47	83.45		72.9	15.0
2017	1.05	71.2	74.6	0.43	91.67		73.8	16.8
Mean	1.19	60.1	61.2	0.36	26.29	94.5	48.3	16.6

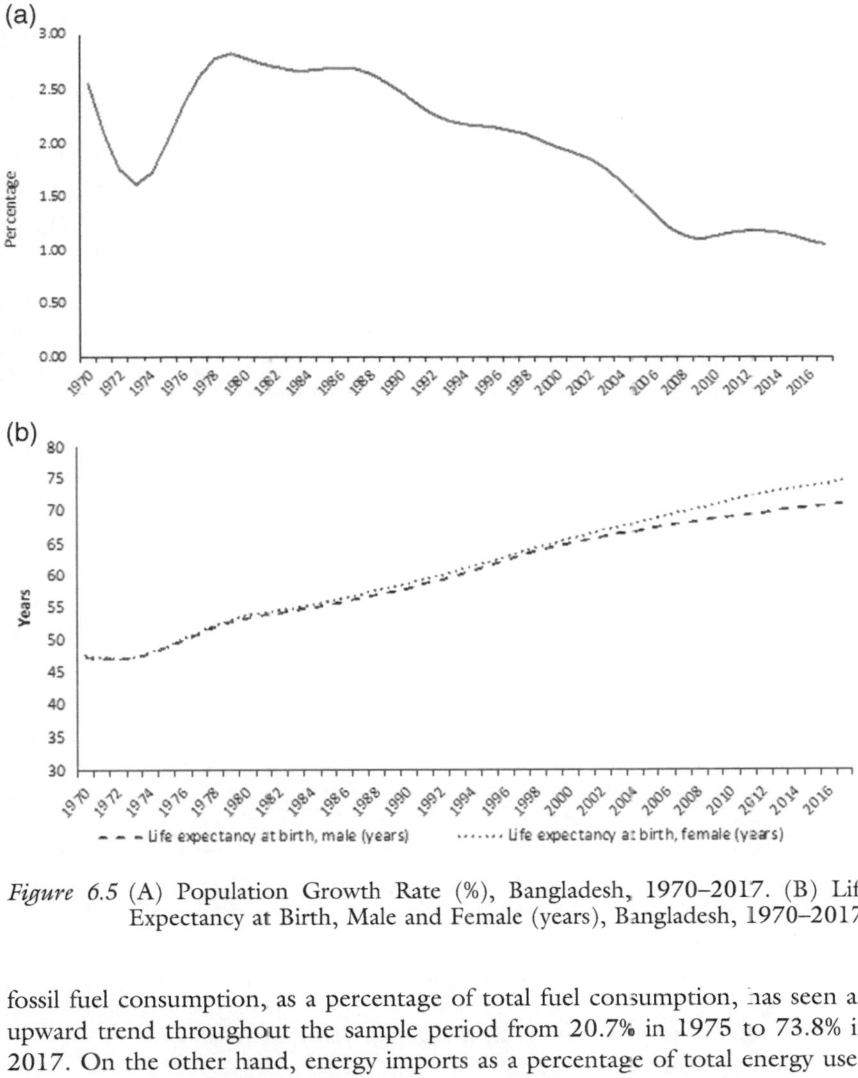

Figure 6.5 (A) Population Growth Rate (%), Bangladesh, 1970–2017. (B) Life Expectancy at Birth, Male and Female (years), Bangladesh, 1970–2017.

fossil fuel consumption, as a percentage of total fuel consumption, has seen an upward trend throughout the sample period from 20.7% in 1975 to 73.8% in 2017. On the other hand, energy imports as a percentage of total energy used have fluctuated throughout the sample period with an annual average of about 17%.

In summary, the population has increased at a rate of 2% per annum, while the life expectancy at birth of both males and females has improved with a more favourable outcome for women. Mobile cellular subscriptions (per 100 people) have increased tremendously, replacing fixed telephone subscriptions (per 100 people). Electric power consumption (kwh per capita) has increased about 20 times over the last five decades.

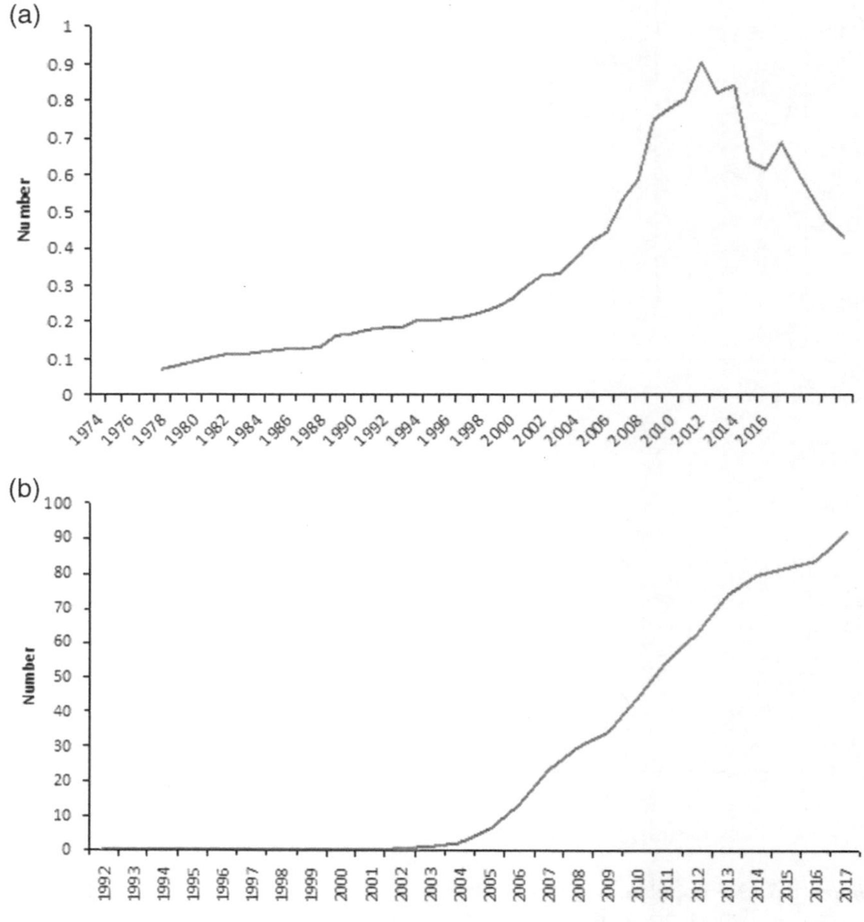

Figure 6.6 (A) Fixed Telephone Subscriptions (per 100 people), Bangladesh, 1974–2017. (B) Mobile Cellular Subscriptions (per 100 people).

6.2.2 Trends in Socio-economic and Demographic Indicators: A Comparative Analysis

Now we compare the trend in socio-economic and demographic indicators in Bangladesh against those of a number of countries in the region, namely China, India, Pakistan, and Sri Lanka. Table 6.2 presents the GDP growth rate in the five countries. Among the five economies, China has the highest average economic growth (9.6% per annum), followed by India (6.5% per annum), Bangladesh (5.8% per annum), and Sri Lanka (5.6% per annum). Pakistan has the lowest economic growth of 4.2% per annum. It is also noticeable from the coefficient of variation (CV) values presented in the last row of Table 6.2 that the Bangladesh economy

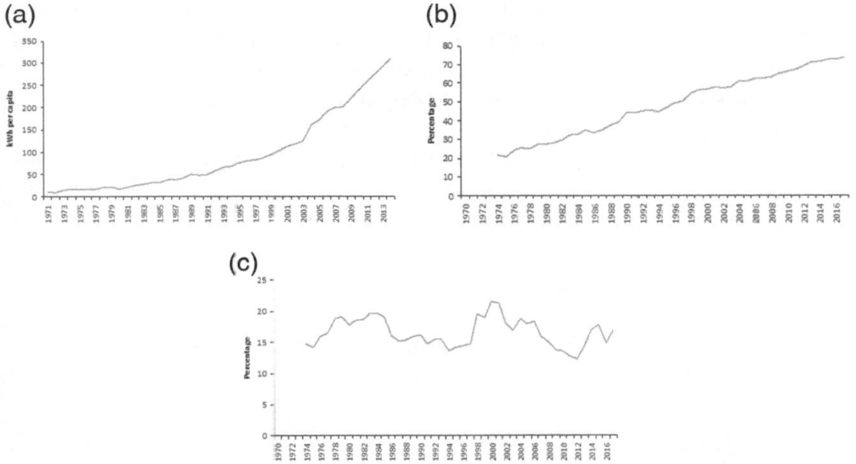

Figure 6.7 (A) Electric Power Consumption (kWh per capita), Bangladesh, 1972–2014. (B) Fossil Fuel Energy Consumption (% of total), Bangladesh, 1970–2017. (C) Energy Imports, Net (% of energy uses), Bangladesh, 1970–2017.

Table 6.2 GDP growth rate, 2000–2015

Year (1)	*GDP growth (annual %)*				
	Bangladesh	*China*	*India*	*Pakistan*	*Sri Lanka*
2000	5.3	8.5	3.8	4.3	6.0
2001	5.1	8.3	4.8	2.0	-1.5
2002	3.8	9.1	3.8	3.2	4.0
2003	4.7	10.0	7.9	4.8	5.9
2004	5.2	10.1	7.9	7.4	5.4
2005	6.5	11.4	7.9	7.7	6.2
2006	6.7	12.7	8.1	6.2	7.7
2007	7.1	14.2	7.7	4.8	6.8
2008	6.0	9.7	3.1	1.7	6.0
2009	5.0	9.4	7.9	2.8	3.5
2010	5.6	10.6	8.5	1.6	8.0
2011	6.5	9.5	5.2	2.7	8.4
2012	6.5	7.9	5.5	3.5	9.1
2013	6.0	7.8	6.4	4.4	3.4
2014	6.1	7.3	7.4	4.7	5.0
2015	6.6	6.9	8.0	4.7	5.0
Mean	5.8	9.6	6.5	4.2	5.6
SD	0.9	2.0	1.8	1.8	2.5
CV	15.0	20.5	28.2	44.2	45.6

grows at a stable rate, as with China and India economies; however, the GDP growth rate is somewhat unstable in Pakistan and in Sri Lanka compared to the other three countries. The CV value for Sri Lanka and Pakistan are about three times that of Bangladesh. Figure 6.8 shows a comparison of economic growth rate across the five countries on four selected years: 2000, 2005, 2010, and 2015.

Table 6.3 presents the exports as a proportion of GDP for the five countries. As can be seen, the average values are 27.6% for Sri Lanka, 27% for China, 20% for

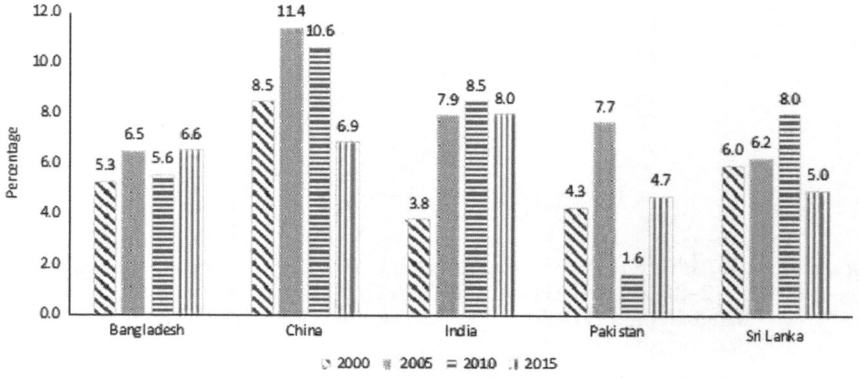

Figure 6.8 GDP Growth (annual %), 2000–2015.

Table 6.3 Exports of goods and services, 2000–2015

Year (1)	*Exports of goods and services (% of GDP)*				
	Bangladesh	*China*	*India*	*Pakistan*	*Sri Lanka*
2000	12.3	20.9	13.0	13.4	39.0
2001	13.4	20.3	12.6	14.7	37.3
2002	12.4	22.6	14.3	15.2	34.9
2003	11.4	27.0	14.9	16.7	34.7
2004	11.1	31.1	17.9	15.7	35.3
2005	14.4	33.8	19.6	15.7	32.3
2006	16.4	36.0	21.3	14.1	30.1
2007	17.0	35.4	20.8	13.2	29.1
2008	17.7	32.5	24.1	12.4	24.8
2009	16.9	24.5	20.4	12.4	21.3
2010	16.0	26.3	22.4	13.5	19.6
2011	19.9	26.5	24.5	14.0	20.9
2012	20.2	25.4	24.5	12.4	19.8
2013	19.5	24.5	25.4	13.3	20.3
2014	19.0	23.5	23.0	12.2	21.1
2015	17.3	21.3	19.8	10.6	21.0
Mean	15.9	27.0	19.9	13.7	27.6
SD	3.1	5.2	4.3	1.6	7.2
CV	19.2	19.3	21.4	11.6	26.0

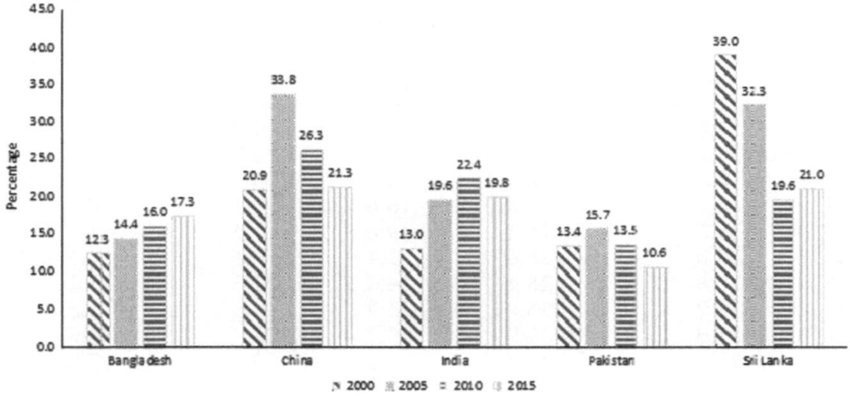

Figure 6.9 Exports of Goods and Services (% GDP), 2000–2015.

India, 16% for Bangladesh, and 13.7% for Pakistan. While Pakistan's exports as a percentage GDP is the lowest among the five countries, based on the CV values, Pakistan also has the lowest variability over the years. The CV values of other four countries are almost double that of Pakistan. Although Bangladesh exports (as a % of GDP) ranks fourth among the five countries under consideration in this chapter, Figure 6.9 clearly shows that unlike the other four countries, Bangladesh has experienced a steady growth in exports (as a % of GDP).

Table 6.4 presents imports as a proportion of GDP for the five countries. As can be seen, the imports as a percentage of GDP is highest for Sri Lanka (36.7%), whereas in the other four countries, this value varies between 18.4% (Pakistan) to 23.2% (India). Based on the CV values, Pakistan has the lowest variability (13.9%) over the years and the CV value for India is twice that of Pakistan. As can be seen in Figure 6.10, Bangladesh has experienced a steady growth in imports (as a % of GDP) over the sample period.

Statistics on merchandise trade (% of GDP) for the five countries are given in Table 6.5. As can be seen, the average values over the sample period for Bangladesh is 36.9%, China is 48.6%, and India is 31.6%. While Pakistan has the lowest percentage of 31%, Sri Lanka has the highest merchandise trade of 53.3%. Based on CV values, Pakistan has the lowest fluctuations in merchandise trade (% of GDP) (CV = 11.5%), while India has the highest fluctuations (CV = 27%). Figure 6.11 presents a graphical comparison of merchandise trade (% of GDP) for the five countries in the four 5-year intervals starting from 2000.

The inflation rates (GDP deflator) for the five countries given in Table 6.6 show that China has the lowest average inflation rate of 3.6% over sample period. Bangladesh and India have an average inflation rate at about 6%, while that of Sri Lanka and Pakistan is around 10%. The variability is the lowest in Bangladesh (CV = 26.8%) and the highest is for China (CV = 81.2%). A graphical

Table 6.4 Imports of goods and services, 2000–2015

Year (1)	*Imports of goods and services (% of GDP)*				
	Bangladesh	*China*	*India*	*Pakistan*	*Sri Lanka*
2000	17.0	18.5	13.9	14.7	49.6
2001	18.7	18.2	13.4	15.7	43.6
2002	16.6	20.1	15.2	15.3	41.4
2003	16.2	24.8	15.6	16.1	40.7
2004	15.7	28.4	19.6	14.6	44.2
2005	20.0	28.4	22.4	19.6	41.3
2006	21.8	28.4	24.5	21.5	41.1
2007	22.9	26.7	24.9	19.8	39.5
2008	25.0	24.9	29.3	23.2	38.5
2009	23.2	20.1	25.9	19.7	27.8
2010	21.8	22.6	26.9	19.4	26.8
2011	27.5	24.1	31.1	19.0	34.1
2012	27.9	22.7	31.3	20.4	31.7
2013	26.8	22.1	28.4	20.1	28.9
2014	25.5	21.4	26.0	18.7	29.2
2015	24.7	18.1	22.1	17.1	28.5
Mean	22.0	23.1	23.2	18.4	36.7
SD	4.2	3.6	6.0	2.6	7.1
CV	19.0	15.7	25.9	13.9	19.3

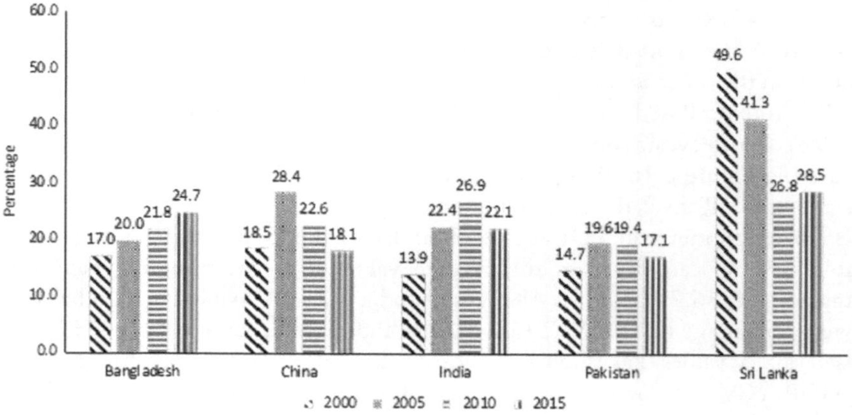

Figure 6.10 Imports of Goods and Services (% GDP), 2000–2015.

comparison of inflation across the five countries for the four selected periods during 2000–2015 is given in Figure 6.12.

Table 6.7 presents the military expenditure (% of GDP) across the five countries. The military expenditure (% of GDP) in Bangladesh varied between

Table 6.5 Merchandise trade, 2000–2015

Year (1)	*Merchandise trade (% of GDP)*				
	Bangladesh	*China*	*India*	*Pakistan*	*Sri Lanka*
2000	28.6	39.2	20.0	26.9	71.7
2001	28.0	38.1	19.3	26.9	68.5
2002	26.9	42.2	20.5	29.2	65.3
2003	29.0	51.3	21.6	30.0	62.5
2004	31.2	59.0	24.9	32.0	66.4
2005	33.4	62.2	29.6	37.8	62.2
2006	38.8	64.0	31.9	34.1	60.6
2007	39.0	61.3	31.2	33.1	58.9
2008	42.8	55.7	43.0	36.8	55.0
2009	36.0	43.2	31.5	29.3	41.3
2010	40.8	48.7	34.4	33.4	39.0
2011	47.2	48.1	42.1	32.5	46.7
2012	44.5	45.2	43.0	30.6	41.7
2013	44.1	43.3	42.0	30.2	38.0
2014	41.4	41.0	38.5	29.6	38.7
2015	38.2	35.7	31.4	24.4	36.5
Mean	36.9	48.6	31.6	31.0	53.3
SD	6.6	9.2	8.5	3.6	12.6
CV	17.9	19.0	27.0	11.5	23.7

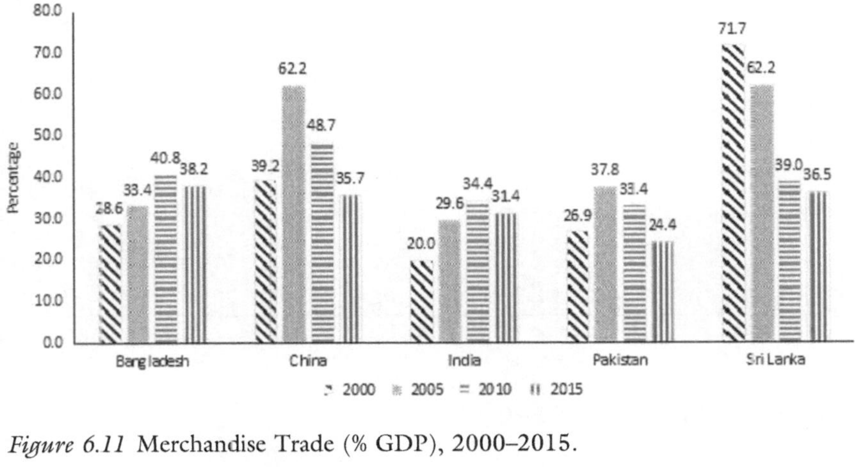

Figure 6.11 Merchandise Trade (% GDP), 2000–2015.

1.1% and 1.4%, with an average of 1.2% and CV = 8.8%, China varied between 1.8% to 2.2% with an average of 2% and the lowest CV = 5.5%, India varied between 2.3% to 3.1% with an average of 2.7% and CV = 7.7%, Pakistan varied between 3.1% to 4.2% with an average of 3.6% and CV = 16.4%, and Sri Lanka

Table 6.6 GDP deflator, 2000–2015

Year (1)	*Inflation, GDP deflator (annual %)*				
	Bangladesh	*China*	*India*	*Pakistan*	*Sri Lanka*
2000	3.4	2.1	3.6	24.9	7.3
2001	3.3	2.0	3.2	7.9	13.7
2002	3.9	0.6	3.7	2.5	8.1
2003	5.8	2.6	3.9	4.4	8.7
2004	4.6	7.0	5.7	7.7	8.8
2005	4.6	3.9	5.6	7.0	10.4
2006	5.9	3.9	8.4	19.1	11.3
2007	6.5	7.8	6.9	7.3	14.0
2008	7.9	7.8	9.2	13.2	16.3
2009	6.8	-0.1	7.0	20.7	5.9
2010	7.1	6.9	10.5	10.9	22.8
2011	7.9	8.2	8.7	19.6	3.8
2012	8.2	2.4	7.9	6.0	10.8
2013	7.2	2.2	6.2	7.0	6.2
2014	5.7	0.8	3.3	7.4	2.9
2015	5.9	0.1	2.3	4.1	0.6
Mean	5.9	3.6	6.0	10.6	9.5
SD	1.6	3.0	2.5	6.8	5.5
CV	26.8	81.2	41.5	64.3	57.9

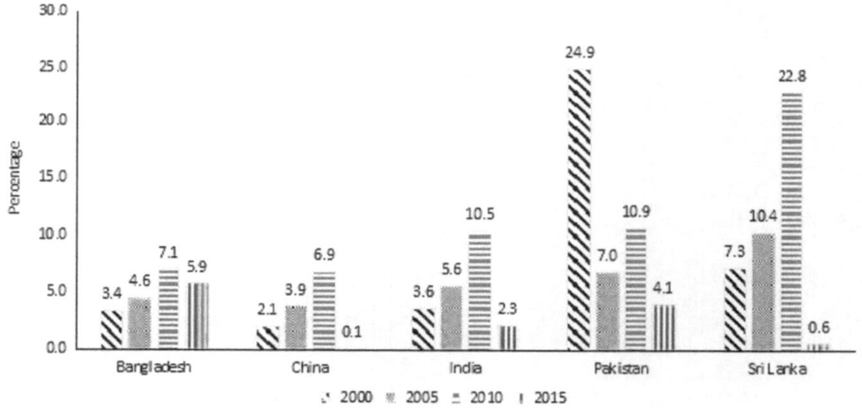

Figure 6.12 GDP Deflator, 2000–2015.

varied within a larger band between 2.2% to 5% with an average of 3% and the highest variation has been reflected by the corresponding CV = 25.4% during the period of 2000–2017. The average military expenditure in China and India is about twice as that of Bangladesh, and in Pakistan and Sri Lanka it is about three

Table 6.7 Military expenditure, 2000–2015

Year (1)	*Military expenditure (% of GDP)*				
	Bangladesh	*China*	*India*	*Pakistan*	*Sri Lanka*
2000	1.4	1.9	3.1	4.0	5.0
2001	1.3	2.1	2.9	4.1	4.3
2002	1.2	2.2	2.8	4.2	3.3
2003	1.1	2.1	2.7	4.1	2.9
2004	1.1	2.1	2.8	4.0	3.0
2005	1.1	2.0	2.8	3.9	2.6
2006	1.1	2.0	2.5	3.7	2.8
2007	1.1	1.9	2.3	3.4	3.3
2008	1.1	1.9	2.6	3.1	3.7
2009	1.2	2.1	2.9	3.1	3.6
2010	1.3	1.9	2.7	3.1	2.7
2011	1.4	1.8	2.7	3.1	2.7
2012	1.3	1.8	2.5	3.3	2.2
2013	1.3	1.9	2.5	3.3	2.2
2014	1.3	1.9	2.5	3.3	2.4
2015	1.4	1.9	2.4	3.4	2.6
Mean	1.2	2.0	2.7	3.6	3.1
SD	0.1	0.1	0.2	0.4	0.8
CV	8.8	5.5	7.7	11.4	25.4

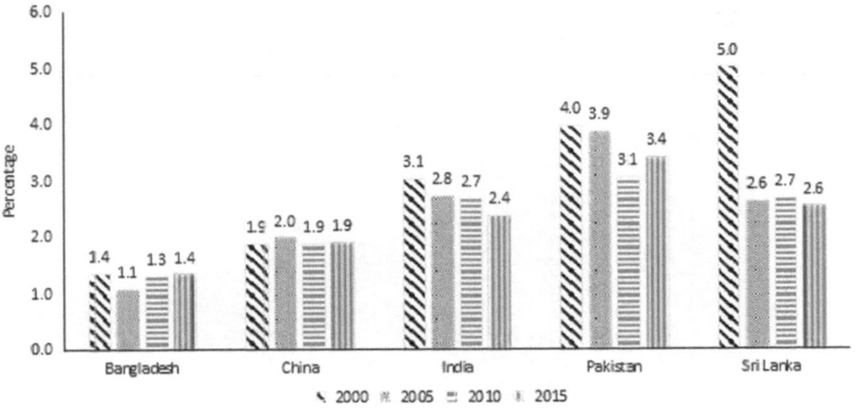

Figure 6.13 Military Expenditure (% of GDP), 2000–2015.

times Bangladesh. The variation in military expenditure in Sri Lanka is about three times as that of Bangladesh. Figure 6.13 shows a comparison of military expenditure (% of GDP) for the five countries every five-year period starting from 2000. Bangladesh displays the lowest military expenditure (% of GDP) among the five countries.

Table 6.8 shows the FDI and net inflows (as % of GDP) received by each country over 2000–2017. As can be seen, on average, China attracted the highest FDI of 3.5% per annum and Bangladesh has the lowest rate of FDI of 0.9% per annum. The variability over the years is high for Pakistan (CV = 81%) and the

Table 6.8 Foreign direct investment, net inflows, 2000–2015

Year (1)	*Foreign direct investment, net inflows (% of GDP)*				
	Bangladesh	*China*	*India*	*Pakistan*	*Sri Lanka*
2000	0.53	3.48	0.77	0.42	1.06
2001	0.15	3.51	1.06	0.52	1.09
2002	0.10	3.61	1.01	1.14	1.19
2003	0.45	3.49	0.61	0.64	1.21
2004	0.69	3.48	0.77	1.14	1.13
2005	1.10	4.55	0.89	2.01	1.12
2006	0.64	4.51	2.13	3.11	1.70
2007	0.82	4.40	2.07	3.67	1.86
2008	1.45	3.73	3.62	3.20	1.85
2009	0.88	2.56	2.65	1.39	0.96
2010	1.07	3.99	1.64	1.14	0.84
2011	0.98	3.70	2.00	0.62	1.46
2012	1.19	2.82	1.31	0.38	1.38
2013	1.74	3.03	1.52	0.58	1.25
2014	1.47	2.56	1.70	0.76	1.13
2015	1.45	2.19	2.09	0.60	0.84
Mean	0.9	3.5	1.6	1.3	1.3
SD	0.5	0.7	0.8	1.1	0.3
CV	52.4	20.3	49.9	81.0	25.4

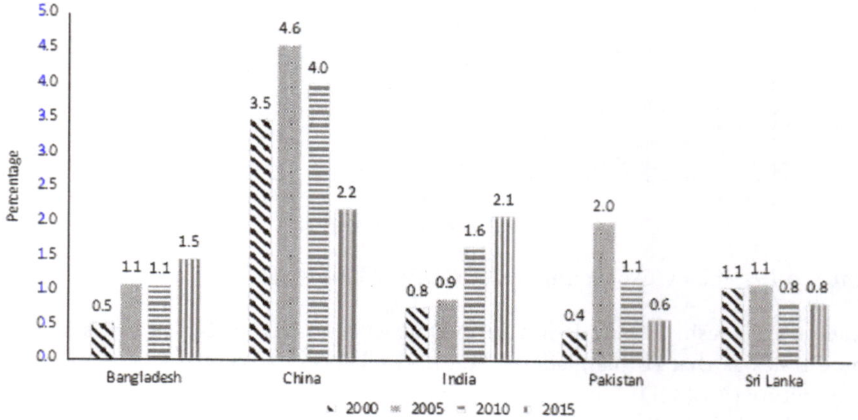

Figure 6.14 Foreign Direct Investment, Net Inflows (as % of GDP), 2000–2015.

Table 6.9 Population growth, 2000–2015

Year (1)	*Population growth (annual %)*				
	Bangladesh	*China*	*India*	*Pakistan*	*Sri Lanka*
2000	2.0	0.8	1.8	2.3	0.6
2001	1.9	0.7	1.7	2.2	0.7
2002	1.8	0.7	1.7	2.1	0.8
2003	1.8	0.6	1.7	2.1	0.8
2004	1.6	0.6	1.6	2.1	0.8
2005	1.5	0.6	1.6	2.1	0.8
2006	1.3	0.6	1.5	2.0	0.7
2007	1.2	0.5	1.5	2.0	0.7
2008	1.1	0.5	1.5	2.0	0.7
2009	1.1	0.5	1.4	2.1	0.6
2010	1.1	0.5	1.4	2.1	0.6
2011	1.2	0.5	1.3	2.1	0.6
2012	1.2	0.5	1.3	2.1	0.5
2013	1.2	0.5	1.2	2.1	0.8
2014	1.2	0.5	1.2	2.1	0.9
2015	1.1	0.5	1.2	2.0	0.9
Mean	1.4	0.6	1.5	2.1	0.7
SD	0.3	0.1	0.2	0.1	0.1
CV	22.9	16.6	13.7	3.0	15.6

lowest variability is for China (CV = 20.3%). Figure 6.14 plots the FDI and net inflows (as % of GDP) for the five countries for the selected five-year intervals: 2000, 2005, 2010, and 2015.

Annual population growth rates of the five countries are displayed in Table 6.9. As can be seen, on average, China and Sri Lanka have the lowest population growth rate of 0.6% and 0.7%, respectively, followed by Bangladesh (1.4%) and India (1.5%). The population growth rate in Bangladesh and India is almost double that of China and Sri Lanka. The highest population growth rate of 2.1% is seen in Pakistan. The stable population growth rate in Pakistan is reflected by the corresponding lowest CV value of 3% with minimum fluctuations, while the highest fluctuation in population growth rate is seen in Bangladesh with CV = 22.9%. A graphical comparison of the population growth rates across the five countries for the years 2000, 2005, 2010, and 2015 is shown in Figure 6.15.

Table 6.10 presents the per capita electric power consumption (in kWh) for the five countries over the 2000–2015 period. Numbers in the table show that, on average, Bangladesh consumes 198 kWh per capita, China 2324 kWh per capita, India 561 kWh per capita, Pakistan 442 kWh per capita, and Sri Lanka 413 kWh per capita. The electricity consumption figures over the period 2000–2015 varied highly for China (CV = 42.8%) and varied only slightly for Pakistan (CV = 8.7%). Figure 6.16 plots the per capita electric power consumption (in kWh) for the five countries for the period 2000–2015. As can be clearly seen in the diagram, among the selected countries, Bangladesh consumes

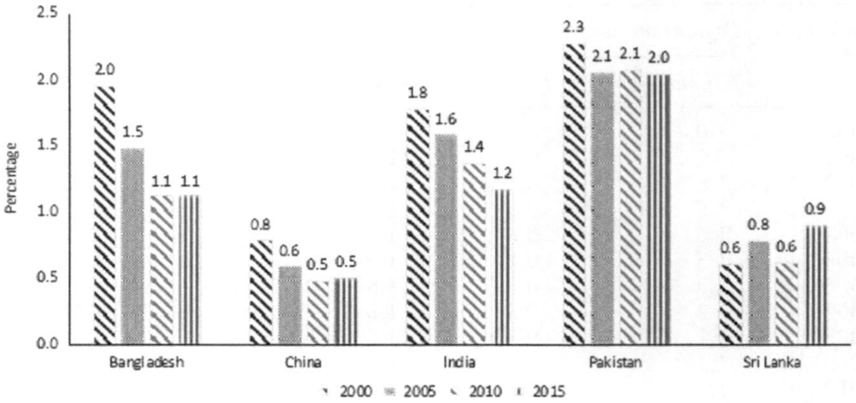

Figure 6.15 Population Growth (annual), 2000–2015.

Table 6.10 Electric power consumption, 2000–2015

Year (1)	*Electric power consumption (kWh per capita)*				
	Bangladesh	*China*	*India*	*Pakistan*	*Sri Lanka*
2000	101	993	395	372	295
2001	112	1077	395	378	291
2002	119	1195	412	385	303
2003	125	1379	432	410	326
2004	160	1586	453	429	355
2005	171	1782	469	463	401
2006	191	2039	511	487	404
2007	200	2326	543	481	421
2008	201	2446	563	443	427
2009	219	2612	600	459	426
2010	240	2944	642	465	461
2011	258	3298	699	455	504
2012	275	3475	725	450	524
2013	293	3773	766	482	526
2014	310	3927	806	471	531
2015	101	993	395	372	295
Mean	198.4	2323.5	560.7	442.0	413.0
SD	67.5	994.3	139.5	38.6	85.5
CV	34.0	42.8	24.9	8.7	20.7

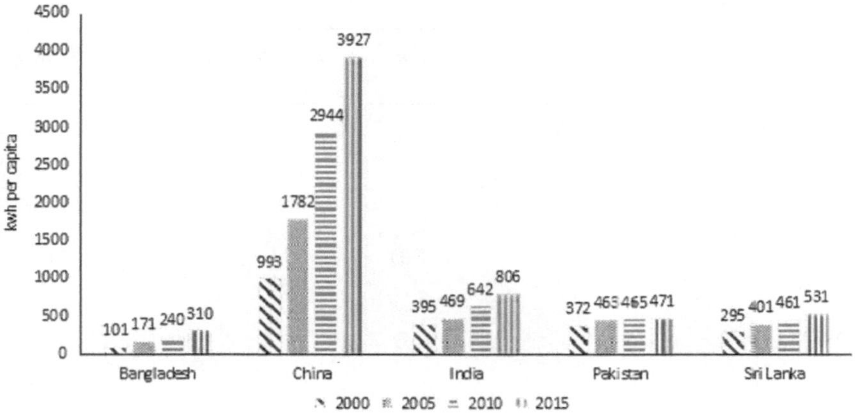

Figure 6.16 Electric Power Consumption (kWh per capita), 2000–2015.

the lowest per capita electric power during the sample period, which is only 10% of China's electricity consumption.

6.2.3 FDI Inflows into Bangladesh

Table 6.11 presents the gross FDI inflows (in millions of US$) into Bangladesh by major countries and into major sectors for the period October–December 2018. As can be seen, Netherlands contribute almost all FDI (98%) of the food sector. In the power sector, major FDI contributors are China (80%) and Singapore (13%). The largest contributor in the banking sector is the United Kingdom (50%). The telecom sector has a number of contributors, where Norway (68%) is the largest contributor, followed by Sweden (15%) and Malaysia (13%). Taiwan contributes most of the FDI (88%) to the leather sector, while the textile sector is dominated by Korea (24%), Hong Kong (20%), China (10%), Norway (7%), and the United Kingdom (7%).

Figure 6.17A to C shows the sector-wise FDI inflows to Bangladesh for selected years: 2010, 2013, and 2016. As can be seen, the FDI inflows have seen a clear and gradual increased in power, food, and other sectors, while those in the telecom, textile, and banking sectors have seen some fluctuations. While in 2010, the telecom sector received the highest FDI inflows; by 2016, it changed to the "other" sector. Figure 6.18 shows the sector-wise FDI inflows to Bangladesh in 2017. Compared to the years 2010, 2013, and 2016 presented in Figure 6.17A to C, we could observe some notable changes in the sector-wise FDI inflows in Bangladesh by 2017. For example, the agricultural sector that attracted FDI inflows in previous years does not belong to the top FDI attracting sector any more in 2017. In contrast, trading and computing sectors that were not in the top FDI attracting sector in previous years have

Table 6.11 FDI gross inflows classified by major countries and major sectors, Oct–Dec 2018

Sector *Country*	*Food*	*Power*	*Banking*	*Telecom*	*Leather Products*	*Textile*
Netherlands	607.15 (98)					12.19 (7)
China		199.29 (80)				16 (10)
United Kingdom			43.13 (50)			11 (7)
Norway				60.34 (68)		
Taiwan					42.26 (88)	
Korea						38.85 (24)
Singapore		32.12 (13)				
Hong Kong						32.61 (20)
Malaysia				11.26 (13)		
Sweden				12.84 (15)		
Total Gross FDI Inflows (in US$m)	621.21	250.47	87.03	88.54	48.01	164.96

Source: Foreign investment and External Debt (FIED), Statistics Department, Bangladesh Bank.

Notes: The percentage of each country in the total gross FDI inflows of FDI to each sector is in parentheses.

attracted a total of 8% FDI inflows in the country in 2017. The food sector, however, has continued to attract an increasing level of FDI inflows into Bangladesh in 2017 as well.

Figure 6.19 shows the FDI inflows to Bangladesh by country in 2017. The United Kingdom is the main FDI source country in Bangladesh with 15% FDI of total FDI inflows to Bangladesh, followed by Singapore and Norway (9%). Additionally, South Korea, USA, Hong Kong, India, and the Netherlands are also important FDI partners of the country.

6.3 Determinants of FDI in Bangladesh: Data and Methodology

We used data on the following variables: FDI net flows as proportion of GDP, real GDP, real per capita GDP, trade openness defined as (imports + exports)/GDP, and fixed and mobile telephone combined subscriptions as a proxy for infrastructure for the sample period 1986–2017 in our modelling. The data for all these

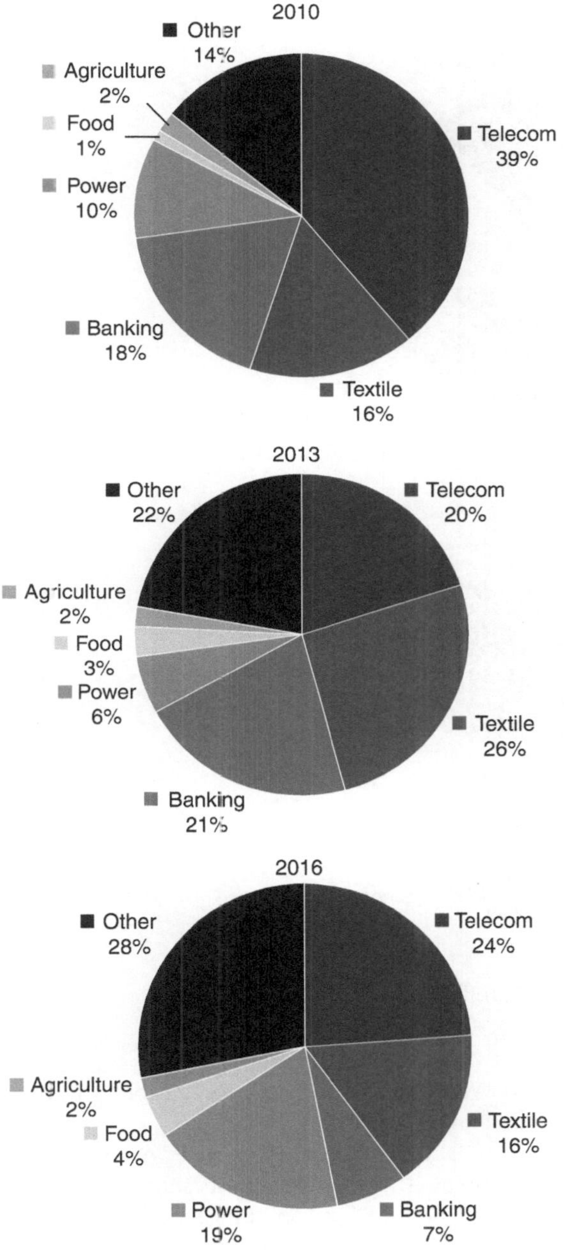

Figure 6.17 (A) Sector-Wise FDI Inflows in Bangladesh, 2010. (B) Sector-Wise FDI Inflows in Bangladesh, 2013. (C) Sector-Wise FDI Inflows in Bangladesh, 2016.

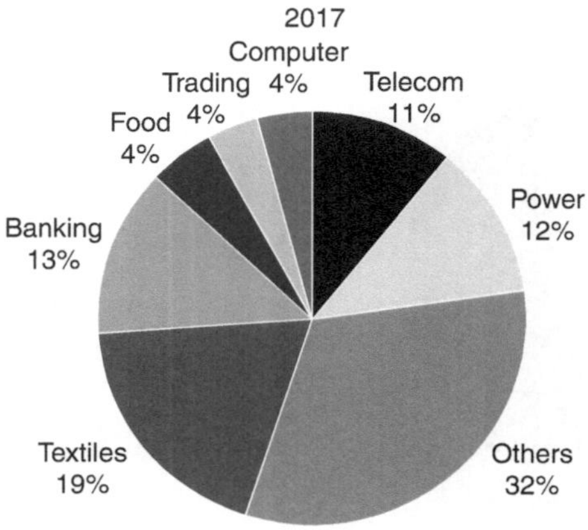

Figure 6.18 Sector-Wise FDI Inflows in Bangladesh, 2017.

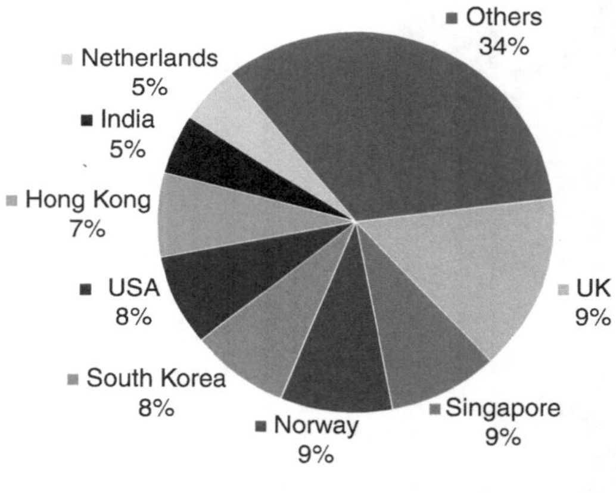

Figure 6.19 Country-Wise FDI Inflows in Bangladesh, 2017.

variables are collected from the World Bank's open database. Table 6.12 presents summary statistics of these variables.

Figure 6.20A to C present the scatter plots: FDI vs trade openness, FDI vs infrastructure, and FDI vs per capita GDP. All three plots show a clear positive association and considerably high fitted R^2 values. Since trade openness, per capita GDP and infrastructure appear to explain most of the variation in the FDI inflows to Bangladesh by means of R^2, we propose the following econometric model consisting of these three variables as the main determinants of FDI inflows into Bangladesh. The selection of variables is also in line with the literature as

Table 6.12 Summary statistics

	Mean	*SD*	*Min*	*Max*
FDIGDP = FDIGDP	0.58	0.61	0.00	1.88
PCGDP (constant 2010 US$)	609	209	387	1093
INFRA (telephone subscriptions per 100 people)	22.51	31.98	0.18	92.09
TRADEOP = (imports + exports)/GDP	0.25	0.15	0.09	0.48

Notes: FDIGDP is FDI as proportion of GDP, PCGDP is the per capita GDP, INFRA is the infrastructure proxied by telephone (fixed line plus mobile) subscriptions per 100 people, and TRADEOP is trade openness calculated as (imports + exports)/GDP.

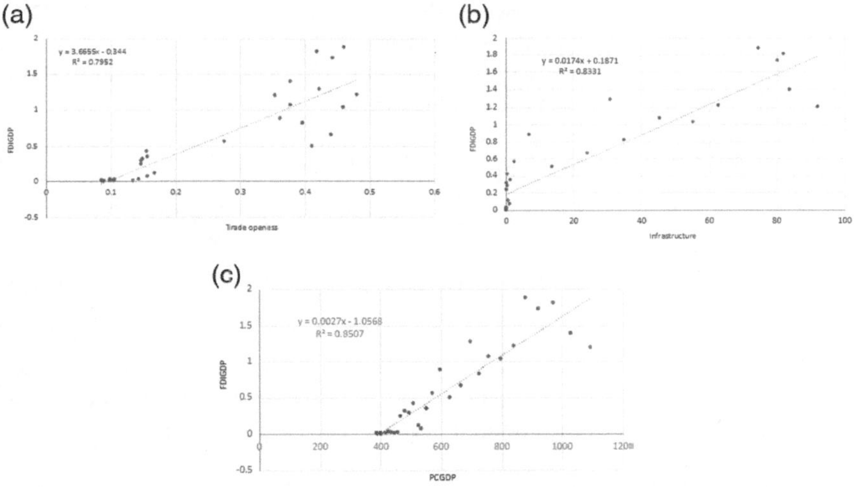

Figure 6.20 (A) FDI vs. Trade Openness. (B) FDI vs. Infrastructure. (C) FDI vs. Per Capita GDP.

these are the most commonly identified explanatory variables in the literature (for example see, Asiedu 2002).

The long-run relationship between FDI and GDP, TRADEOP (Trade openness), and INFRA (infrastructure) can be written as

$$FDIGDP_t = \alpha_1 + \beta_1 PCGDP_t + \beta_2 TRADEOP_t + \beta_3 INFRA_t + e_t \qquad (6.1)$$

where FDIGDP is FDI as proportion of GDP, PCGDP is per capita GDP, TRADEOP is the trade openness calculated as (imports + exports)/GDP, and INFRA is proxied by fixed and mobile telephone combined subscriptions.

Equation (6.1) can be estimated by the least squares method, provided that either all of the variables are stationary I(0) in their level form or even if the variable are non-stationary and I(1) but are cointegrated. Otherwise, the results may be spurious.

As such, we first investigate the cointegration of the variables of Equation (6.1) in two ways.

Under the first method, we estimate the model by LS and test the stationarity of the estimated residuals using the Granger cointegration test. If the residual series is stationary, I(0), then we conclude that the variables involve in model (1) are cointegrated.

Another way of investigating the cointegration is using the Autoregressive Distributed Lag (ARDL) bound test framework proposed by Pesaran, Smith, and Shin (2001). The attraction of the ARDL bounds test approach is that it does not require all the variables of the model to be integrated of the same order, that is, all I(0) or all I(1).

The long-run relationship between the four variables, FDIGDP, PCGDP, TRADEOP, and INFRA, is given by Equation (6.1).

The ARDL (p, q, r) formulations involving the four variables FDIGDP, PCGDP, TRADEOP, and INFRA can be written as

$$\begin{aligned}\Delta(FDIGDP_t) = {} & \alpha_1 + \beta_1 FDIGDP_{t-1} + \beta_2 PCGDP_{t-1} + \beta_3 TRADEOP_{t-1} \\ & + \beta_4 INFRA_{t-1} + \sum_{j=1}^{p} \gamma_{1j}\Delta(FDIGDP_{t-j}) + \sum_{j=0}^{q} \gamma_{2j}\Delta(PCGDP_{t-j}) \\ & + \sum_{j=0}^{r} \gamma_{3j}\Delta(TRADEOP_{t-j}) + \sum_{j=0}^{s} \gamma_{4j}\Delta(INFRA_{t-j}) + u_t \qquad (6.2)\end{aligned}$$

The ARDL bounds test can be used to test the long-run (or the cointegrating) relationship between FDIGDP, PCGDP, TRADEOP, and INFRA based on a non-standard F-test by testing the null and the alternative hypotheses:

H_0: $\beta_1 = \beta_2 = \beta_3 = \beta_4 = 0$ (no cointegration)
H_A: At least one of β_1 or β_2 or β_3 or $\beta_4 \neq 0$ (existence of cointegration).

using the critical values provided in Pesaran et al. (2001). There are two sets of critical values based on the assumptions that all variables are I(0) and that all variables are I(1). If the calculated F-statistic is above the I(1) critical value, then the null hypothesis should be rejected and conclude that there is support for cointegration. If the calculated F statistic is below the I(0) critical value, then the null hypothesis should not be rejected and conclude that there is no support for cointegration. If the calculated F-statistic is between the I(0) critical value and the I(1) critical value, then the test result is inconclusive.

If we find cointegration between FDIGDP, PCGDP, TRADEOP, and INFRA, then we can use an error-correction model to estimate the speed of adjustment of the disequilibrium caused by previous period shocks that re-converges to the long-run equilibrium. The error correction models which correspond to Equation (6.2) can be written as

$$\Delta(\text{FDIGDP}_t) = a_1 + \sum_{j=1}^{p} \gamma_{1j}\Delta(\text{FDIGDP}_{t-j}) + \sum_{j=0}^{q} \gamma_{2j}\Delta(\text{PCGDP}_{t-j}) + \sum_{j=0}^{r} \gamma_{3j}\Delta(\text{TRADEOP}_{t-j}) + \sum_{j=0}^{r} \gamma_{4j}\Delta(INFRA_{t-j}) + \mathrm{d}EC_{t-1} + u_t \quad (6.3)$$

where EC_{t-1} is the error correction term derived from the long-run relationship specified in equation (6.1). The coefficient γ_{ij} measures the short-run dynamics associated with the long-run relationships and coefficient δ is the speed of adjustment that measures the long-run effect.

Using the error correction model (3), we can also test various forms of Granger causality between each pair of variables. The following two points are worth noting in relation to the bound test. If some or all of the variables in a regression model are non-stationary in their level form, then the least squares estimation results using a regression model involving these variables may be spurious. As the bound test results will also reveal whether the variables FDIGDP, PCGDP, TRADEOP, and INFRA are cointegrated, we can use the bound test results to verify whether the model estimation results are spurious or not. However, even if the variables in the regression model are integrated of order 1, that is I(1), if they are co-integrated, then the least squares estimation results would still be valid.

6.4 Estimation Results

Table 6.13 presents the results of the Augmented Dickey and Fuller (1979) (ADF) test, Phillips and Perron (1988) PP unit root test, and KPSS (Kwiatkowski et al. 1992) test. For the ADF and PP tests, the null hypothesis is

Table 6.13 Unit-root test for the error term

Null hypothesis H0: Errors has a unit root (or errors are non-stationary)			
	Test statistic	*p-value*	*Decision*
ADF Test	–4.13	0.0121	e is I(0)
Phillips-Perron Test	–5.62	0.0002	e is I(0)
Null hypothesis H0: Errors are stationary			
	Test statistic	*Critical Value*	*Decision*
KPSS Test	0.299	0.463	e is I(0)

Table 6.14 ARDL bound test results for cointegration between FDIGDP, PCGDP, TRADEOP, and INFRA

		Critical Values		*H_0: No Serial correlation*	
Dependent Variable	*F-test Statistics*	*I (0)*	*I (1)*	*F-test Statistic*	*p-value*
(1)	*(2)*	*(3)*	*(4)*	*(5)*	*(6)*
FDIGDP	9.18	4.01	5.07	1.67	0.20
EC(−1) −0.807 (*p*-value = 0.000)					

that the time series has a unit root (or the series is non-stationary), while the null hypothesis for the KPSS test is that the time series has no unit root (or the series is stationary). Based on all three test results, we can conclude that the errors are stationary and hence there is a cointegrating relationship between the four variables, FDIGDP, PCGDP, TRADEOP, and INFRA exists.

Table 6.14 presents the bound test results for testing cointegration. As can be seen, the value of the F-test statistics is larger than the bound test upper limit – I(1) critical value – at the 5% level of significance. This means that the variables FDIGDP, PCGDP, TRADEOP, and INFRA are cointegrated. Furthermore, the results presented in Table 6.14 also reveal that serial correlation is not a major issue with our estimation results. The error correction coefficient estimate is −0.807 and is negative as it should be and is statistically significant. This result further confirms the earlier findings of cointegration between the four variables FDIGDP, PCGDP, TRADEOP, and INFRA. The error correction coefficient −0.807 means that approximately 81% of the disequilibrium caused by previous period shocks are corrected within one period.

Table 6.15 presents the Granger causality test results. As can be seen, among all the variables, only infrastructure (INFRA) appeared to have a bidirectional causal relationship with FDI. On the other hand, per capita GDP (PCGDP) has a unidirectional causal relationship with FDI and infrastructure (INFRA), while trade openness (TRADEOP) has a unidirectional relationship with FDI, per capita GDP (PCGDP), and infrastructure (INFRA).

Table 6.16 presents the least squares regression estimation results for the long-run relationship given by Equation (6.1). As can been, all the three determinants, per capita GDP (PCGDP), infrastructure (INFRA), and trade openness (TRADEOP), impact positively on attracting FDI into Bangladesh. All coefficient estimates are statistically significant at the 5% or 10% level of significance. The three model variables, per capita GDP, infrastructure, and trade openness, alone explains 91% of the variation in GDP coming into Bangladesh.

Table 6.15 Long-run Granger causality test results: Null hypothesis Ho: X does not Granger cause Y

	FDIGDP		*PCGDP*		*TRADEOP*		*INFRA*	
	F-test	*Conclusion*	*F-test*	*Conclusion*	*F-test*	*Conclusion*	*F-test*	*Conclusion*
FDIGDP			4.510* (0.017)	PCGDP --> FDIGDP	6.859* (0.003)	TRADEOP --> FDIGDP	7.080* (0.002)	INFRA --> FDIGDP
PCGDP	0.386 (0.683)	FDIGDP -/-> PCGDP			4.080* (0.025)	TRADEOP --> PCGDP	0.228 (0.800)	INFRA -/-> PCGDP
TRADEOP	0.668 (0.519)	FDIGDP -/-> TRADEOP	0.838 (0.440)	PCGDP-/-> TRADEOP			1.640 (0.207)	INFRA -/-> TRADEOP
INFRA	8.684* (0.001)	FDIGDP --> INFRA	4.629* (0.016)	PCGDP--> INFRA	6.294* (0.004)	TRADEOP--> INFRA		

Notes: *p*-values are in parentheses.
* Reject the null hypothesis.

Table 6.16 Least squares estimation results

Variable	*Coefficient*	*Std. Error*	*Prob.*
Constant	−0.583	0.162	0.001
PCGDP	0.001	0.000	0.003
TRADEOP	1.0254	0.297	0.001
INFRA	0.006	0.003	0.051
Adjusted R-squared		0.91	
Breusch-Godfrey Serial Correlation LM Test:			
F-statistic	2.5	*p*-value = 0.0948	

Note: dependent variable: FDIGDP.

6.5 Conclusions

The objective of this chapter was to identify the major determinants of foreign direct investment (FDI) in Bangladesh. In doing so, firstly, we examined the time-series trend in a number of socio-economic and demographic indicators in Bangladesh during the period of 1970–2017. We also presented a detailed discussion of the performance of these indicators in Bangladesh in comparison to five other neighbouring countries in the region, namely China, India, Pakistan, and Sri Lanka. We then presented the theoretical model adapted for the empirical analysis of this paper. The empirical analysis of this paper is based on the ARDL bound test framework.

The Augmented Dickey and Fuller (1979) test, Phillips and Perron (1988) unit root test, and KPSS (Kwiatkowski et al. 1992) test results indicated that the errors are stationary at the first difference. The ARDL bound test results also revealed that the variables, FDIGDP, PCGDP, TRADEOP, and INFRA, are cointegrated and that serial correlation is not a major issue with our estimation results. The error correction coefficient estimate reveals that approximately 81% of the disequilibrium caused by previous period shocks are corrected within one period. We then performed the Granger causality test, which revealed that only infrastructure has a bidirectional relationship with FDI, while all the other variables appeared to have unidirectional causality in the long run. The least squares regression results revealed that per capita GDP, infrastructure, and trade openness positively and significantly impact FDI inflows into Bangladesh.[1]

The empirical findings of this study provide some important policy insights with respect to attracting more FDI inflows to Bangladesh. For example, as the infrastructure variable coefficient indicates a positive relationship with FDI, further government investments in improving infrastructure facilities may facilitate an increased inflow of FDI into the country. In particular, infrastructure investments in energy, green technologies, information technology, and human capital development need to receive increased attention from policymakers to enhance a conducive environment for FDI inflows. Improving trade openness is another important area of attention by policymakers to facilitate increased FDI into Bangladesh. Simplified and improved transparency in bureaucratic procedures, simplified tariff structures, reduced financial fragility, and well-established accounting and regulatory frameworks need to be at the forefront of the policy agenda to further improve trade openness in the country.

Note

1 Due to unavailability of data, we have used data only for the period 1986–2017 (32 observations). When using the results from this study, this sample size limitation should be kept in mind. However, The diagnostic tests we have performed on the estimation results gives assurance that the results are of reasonably good quality. The authors wish to thank the Griffith Asia Institute at Griffith University, Australia for providing funds to undertake this research project.

References

Ang, J. B. (2008), Determinants of Foreign Direct Investments in Malaysia. *Journal of Policy Modeling*, 30, 185–189.

Asiedu, E. (2002), On the Determinants of Foreign Direct Investment to Developing Countries: Is Africa Different? *World Development*, 30(1).

Aziz, M. S., Sarkar, P., & Mahmud, M. A. L. (2014), Determinants of Foreign Direct Investment In Bangladesh and Empirical Analysis. *European Journal of Business and Management*, 6(27), 101–117.

Bellak, C., Leibrecht, M., & Riedl, A. (2008), Labor Costs and FDI Flows into Central and Eastern European Countries: A Survey of the Literature and Empirical Evidence. *Structural Change and Economic Dynamics*, 19, 17–37.

Bende-Nabende, A., Ford, J., & Slater, J. (2001), FDI, Regional Economic Integration and Endogenous Growth: Some Evidence from Southeast Asia. 6(3).

Bhavan, T., Xu, C., & Zhong, C. (2011), Determinants and Growth Effect of FDI in South Asian Economies: Evidence from a Panel Data Analysis. *Electronic Business Journal*, 10(1), 23–30.

Chen, John-ren. (2000), *Foreign direct investment/edited by John-ren Chen.* Macmillan Press; St. Martin's Press Houndmills, Basingstoke, Hampshire: New York

Dickey, D., & Fuller, W. (1979), Distribution of the Estimators for Autoregressive Time Series with a Unit Root. *Journal of the American Statistical Association*, 74, 427–431.

Dunning, J. H. (2009), Location and the Multinational Enterprise: A Neglected Factor? *Journal of International Business Studies*, 40(1), 5–19.

Frenkel, M., Funke, F., & Stadtmann, G. (2004), A Panel Analysis of Bilateral FDI Flows to Emerging Economies. *Economic System*, 28, 281–300.

Gastanaga, V. M., Jeffrey, B. N., & Pashamova, B. (1998), Host Country Reforms and FDI Inflows: How Much Difference do They Make? *World Development*, 26(7), 1299–1314.

Kwiatkowski, D., Phillips, P. C. B., Schmidt, P., & Shin, Y. (1992), Testing the Null Hypothesis of Stationarity Against the Alternative of a Unit Root. *Journal of Econometrics*, 54(1–3), 159–178.

Meyer, K. E. (2003), FDI Spill overs in Emerging Markets: A Literature Review and New Perspective, Foreign Direct Investment in Emerging Markets. Retrieved from

Pesaran, M. H., Smith, R. J., & Shin, Y. (2001), Bounds Testing Approaches to the Analysis of Level Relationships. *Journal of Applied Econometrics*, 16, 289–326.

Phillips, P., & Perron, P. (1988), Testing for a Unit Root in Time Series Regression. *Bimetrika*, 75, 335–346.

Qamruzzaman, M. (2015), Determinants of Foreign Direct Investment (FDI): Evidence from Bangladesh. *Pacific Business Review International*, 7(10), 97–105.

Quader, S. M. (2009), Foreign Direct Investment in Bangladesh: An Empirical Analysis on its Determinants and Impacts. Retrieved from

Sahoo, P. (2006), Foreign Direct Investment in South Asia: Policy, Trend, Impact and Determinants. Retrieved from

Shah, N. (2013), Determinants of Foreign Direct Investment: A Study on Bangladesh. *Journal of Economics and Sustainable Development*, 4(18), 11–18.

Shaheena, D. (2014), FDI Inflows in Bangladesh: Identifying its Major Determinants. *Journal of Economics and Finance*, 5(6), 1–13.

Sung, D. H., & Uk, H. (2008), U.S. and Japanese Foreign Direct Investment in East Asia: A Comparative Analysis. 36(3), 385–401.

UNCTAD. (2006), FDI from Developing and Transition Economies: Implications for Development. Retrieved from Geneva:

Wei, W. (2005), China and India: Any Difference in their FDI Performances? *Journal of Asian Economics*, 16, 719–736.

Xing, Y. (2006), Why is China so Attractive for FDI? The Role of Exchange Rates. *China Economic Review*, 17, 198–209.

Part III

Innovation and Opportunities

Part III focuses on Bangladesh's innovation and opportunities that were created before the pandemic hit the world in early 2020.

DOI: 10.4324/9781003231912-10

7 Nonfarm Employment and Household Calorie Consumption in Rural Bangladesh

Ripon Kumar Mondal, E A Selvanathan, S Selvanathan, and Moazzem Hossain

7.1 Introduction

Attaining food security[1] remains a significant unfulfilled aim of governments in many developing countries, despite numerous efforts by local, national, and international bodies (both governmental and non-governmental). According to the Food and Agricultural Organization (FAO 2019), 27% of the world population experienced some level of food insecurity in 2018, and the number of severely food insecure[2] people has been on the rise since 2015. Moreover, the prevalence of food insecurity is higher in countries where a larger proportion of the population lives in rural areas and mainly depend on agricultural production (FAO 2019). However, due to various challenges in the agricultural sector (such as seasonality of production, natural disasters, and decrease in arable land per capita), this sector has not been a sufficient vehicle for ensuring rural household food security. In rural areas where farming is the main labour market activity, farm households, in addition to their farm income/employment, usually maintain a portfolio of income sources, with nonfarm[3] employment being a major component of their drive to ensure food security (Barrett et al. 2001).

The contemporary contribution of past studies on the farm economy in developing countries may be limited, as such studies have largely assumed no other sources of income, but that farm income was available to farm households in order to meet their food security needs. This is increasingly not the case, and there is now increasing evidence that rural households incapable of producing sufficient food to meet their own requirements do have the choice of undertaking either nonfarm employment or to send family members to urban areas to seek employment and send back remittances (Davis et al. 2009). Nevertheless, there is a lack of universal agreement among researchers pertaining to the impact of nonfarm employment on rural household food security. For instance, participation of rural households in nonfarm employment could negatively affect the availability of food through lowering food production due to the possible competition of labour between farm and nonfarm employment (Chang and Mishra 2008; Pfeiffer et al. 2009). In contrast, rural households can enjoy improved food security through better access to food and/or intensifying

DOI: 10.4324/9781003231912-11

production due to a rise in their nonfarm income (Babatunde and Qaim 2010). Further, the increase in nonfarm income significantly contributes to the increase in agricultural production through intensifying major purchased agricultural inputs and reducing the technical inefficiency of production (Mondal et al. 2021). This increase in agricultural production could lead to an increase in food availability, which is an important dimension of food security. However, food security is a complex and multidimensional concept that encapsulates other dimensions alongside it, such as food availability and its access, utilization, or stability (FAO et al. 2014). Therefore, a better understanding of the linkage between nonfarm income and food security is an important topic to be investigated, especially in the case for Bangladesh which is highly dependent on agriculture for its food needs. Therefore, in this chapter, an attempt has been made to study the impact of nonfarm income on the utilization dimension of food security which could be measured through households' calorie consumption per day per adult equivalent in rural Bangladesh.

Rural livelihood literature is evident that rural nonfarm employment could be an influential factor to improve household welfare in many developing countries (see, for example, Al-Amin and Hossain 2019; Chang and Mishra 2008; Do et al. 2019; Hossain and Al-Amin 2018; Owusu et al. 2011; Rahut et al. 2015; Scharf and Rahut 2014; Seng 2015; Tran 2015; Tsiboe et al. 2016). Several studies indicated that nonfarm employment increases household's income as well as their food consumption (see, for example, Chang and Mishra 2008; Mishra et al. 2015; Seng 2015; Tran 2015). Some other studies examine the relationship between nonfarm employment and household food security in relation to various other aspects such as crop mortgage, decline in food stock, coping strategy, and micronutrient availability (see, for example, Babatunde and Qaim 2010; Do et al. 2019; Mabuza et al. 2016; Mishra and Khanal 2017; Owusu et al. 2011; Rahman and Mishra 2019).

Among different dimensions of food security, the utilization dimension could be measured using household calorie consumption per day per adult. However, much less is known regarding the impact of nonfarm employment on rural households' calorie consumption. A few studies have carried out empirical investigations into the relationship between nonfarm employment and household calorie consumption in different countries (Babatunde and Qaim 2010; Ruben and Berg 2001; Tsiboe et al. 2016), and to the best of our knowledge, there is only one study (Alam et al. 2018) that identified the determinants of food security of rural vulnerable households, among which nonfarm employment was a determinant. Since most of the total Bangladeshi population live in rural areas and ensuring food security is still a challenge to many rural households, it is pertinent to investigate the impact of rural nonfarm income on household calorie consumption in rural Bangladesh.

Despite Bangladesh achieving several milestones in reducing poverty and increasing its agricultural productivity, a quarter of the population is still considered to be food insecure (Magnani et al. 2015). Figure 7.1 presents the average calorie consumption (Kcal/day/AE) in rural areas in different survey

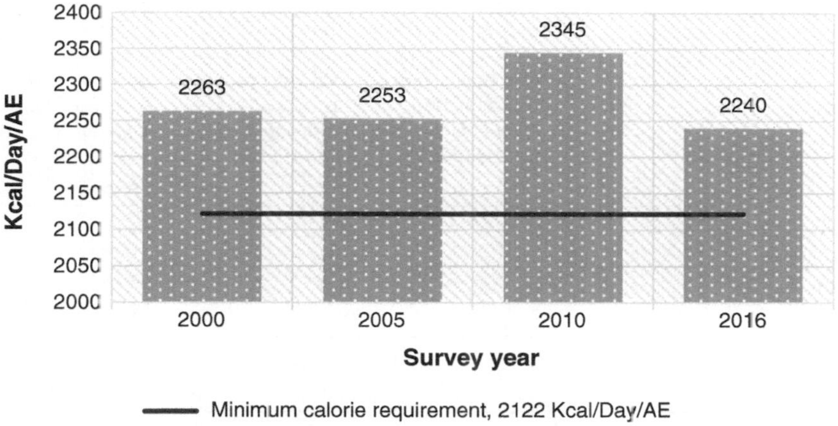

Figure 7.1 Average per capita per day calorie consumption, rural Bangladesh, 2000–2016.

Source: HIES 2016.

years conducted by the Bangladesh Bureau of Statistics. As can be seen, the average calorie consumption per capita in rural areas was about 2345 Kcal/day/AE in 2010, which declined to 2240 Kcal/Day/AE in 2016. Although the average calorie consumption (Kcal/Day/AE) in rural areas in 2016 is still beyond 2122 Kcal/day/day, the threshold level of food security measurement, maintaining food security remains a significant issue to address among rural poor households. Rural people are more vulnerable to sickness and different infectious diseases who consume less than the daily calorie requirement of 2122 Kcal/day/AE (Alam et al. 2018; Lim 2017, also see Table 7.1 below).

In addition, people spend most of their income meeting the demand for nonfood items rather than food items. However, the rise in nonfarm employment and the subsequent rise in nonfarm income could be used to increase agricultural production, though it could also primarily be used to increase households' nonfood expenditure. Therefore, there is debate about whether nonfarm income has any influence on household calorie consumption in rural Bangladesh. We are unaware, at this juncture, of any other study addressing this issue in relation to Bangladesh. Therefore, considering the increasing importance of nonfarm employment, this chapter addresses the need to study the linkage between rural nonfarm employment and household calorie consumption in Bangladesh. To investigate the possible link between nonfarm employment and household calorie consumption, the present study focuses on research question: *"Does nonfarm income has any influence on household calorie consumption in rural Bangladesh?"*

This chapter has been structured as follows: the next section presents the overview of rural nonfarm sector of Bangladesh. The subsequent sections present the details of the data sources; showcase the summary statistics of different

Table 7.1 Summary Statistics of Main Variables

Binary variables (1)	*Households without nonfarm income (49 observations) As a % of total households without nonfarm income* (3)	*Households with nonfarm income (95 observations) As a % of total households with nonfarm income* (2)	*Complete sample (144 observations) As a % of total households* (4)
Household has livestock	68	39	49
Access to credit	33	63	53
Access to electricity	59	81	74

Continuous variables (1)	*Mean* (2)	*Mean* (3)	*Mean* (4)
Calorie consumption (Kcal/day/AE)	2011	2322	2216
Nonfarm income (BDT/AE)	–	3756	2478
Farm income (BDT/AE)	2197	714	1218
Household head's (HH) age	44.4	41.7	42.6
HH years of schooling	3.2	4.0	3.8
Household size (AE)	3.2	3.7	3.5
Number of children	0.9	1.1	1.1
Dependency ratio	73.2	64.3	70.2
Farm size (hectare)	0.6	0.4	0.4
Household's distance from nearest market (km)	1.7	1.8	1.8

Source: Based on field survey data, 2019.

variables; the households expenditure patterns in rural Bangladesh; discusses the model (and its specifications) and the findings on the relationship between nonfarm income and household calorie consumption. The final section concludes the chapter.

7.2 The Rural Nonfarm Sector in Bangladesh

Although most Bangladeshis are still dependent on farm employment, the situation has been changing in the last two decades. The rural nonfarm sector has started playing a more significant role in terms of supplementing income as well as employment. According to the *Bangladesh Bureau of Statistics* (BBS 2018), the number of economically active workers aged above 15 years engaged in nonfarm employment has increased over time.[4] While 48.3% of the total labour force was employed in the nonfarm sector in 2000, this rate increased to 59.4% in 2017[5] and about 49.3% of the rural labour force was engaged in nonfarm employment in 2017. In addition, the average amount of arable land area per person has been in decline over the years. For instance, arable land area per person reduced by approximately 28.5% between 2000 and 2016 (World Development

Indicator 2019). There is limited room for arable land expansion in Bangladesh, and access to arable land for rural households is constrained further by population increase. Thus, the capacity of the agriculture sector to generate productive employment to ensure food security, as well as welfare for its expanding rural labour force, is becoming increasingly limited. Given these limitations, nonfarm employment activities have become increasingly important for the poor, who are being pushed out of agriculture due to limited land resources.

Although earnings from nonfarm employment are the main pathway to supplement household income to attain food security for poor rural households, unemployment remains an issue in Bangladesh. Based on an International Labour Organization (ILO) estimate, the unemployment level was about 4.4% of the Bangladesh labour force in 2017 (World Development Indicator 2019). The number of people unemployed in Bangladesh in 2017 was estimated at 2.7 million, of which 1.8 million were living in rural areas (BBS 2018). Therefore, creating employment opportunities, especially employment in the rural nonfarm sector, would be a good way to absorb the unemployed labour force in Bangladesh.

7.3 Data Description of Rural Households

Data used in this chapter are from a primary sample survey[6] of Bangladeshi rural households conducted during August 2018 to January 2019. The sample rural households for this study have been selected applying a multistage random sampling technique. The study areas are indicated in Figure 7.2. At the beginning stage, five (out of eight) divisions[7] namely Dhaka, Rangpur, Rajshahi, Sylhet, and Khulna have been randomly selected. In the second stage, one district from each division was selected randomly, for instance, the Tangail, Kurigram, Naogaon, Sylhet, and Khulna districts from Dhaka, Rangpur, Rajshahi, Sylhet, and Khulna divisions, respectively. In the third stage, one upazila (sub-district) was randomly selected from each district, namely the Kalihati, Rajarhat, Mahadebpur, Golapganj, and Dumuria upazila, respectively, from the Tangail, Kurigram, Naogaon, Sylhet, and Khulna district. In the fourth stage, one union was randomly selected from each upazila. In the next stage, two rural villages were randomly selected from each selected union.

In the final stage, we prepared a complete list of rural households in each village with the help of local government administrators and local political figures (the union chairman and ward member). From the list of households in each village, 14 households were selected randomly from each village, giving a total of 140 rural households from 10 villages. In addition, four sample households from the Rajarhat upazila of the Kurigram district were also collected for the convenience of data gathering. Therefore, a total of 144 sample households are included in this study. A pre-structured and pre-tested questionnaire was used to collect the required data from the sample household in a face-to-face interview. A wide range of information was collected through the survey questionnaire, including household demographic characteristics, socioeconomic characteristics, household farm and nonfarm income, consumption, and access to social amenities.

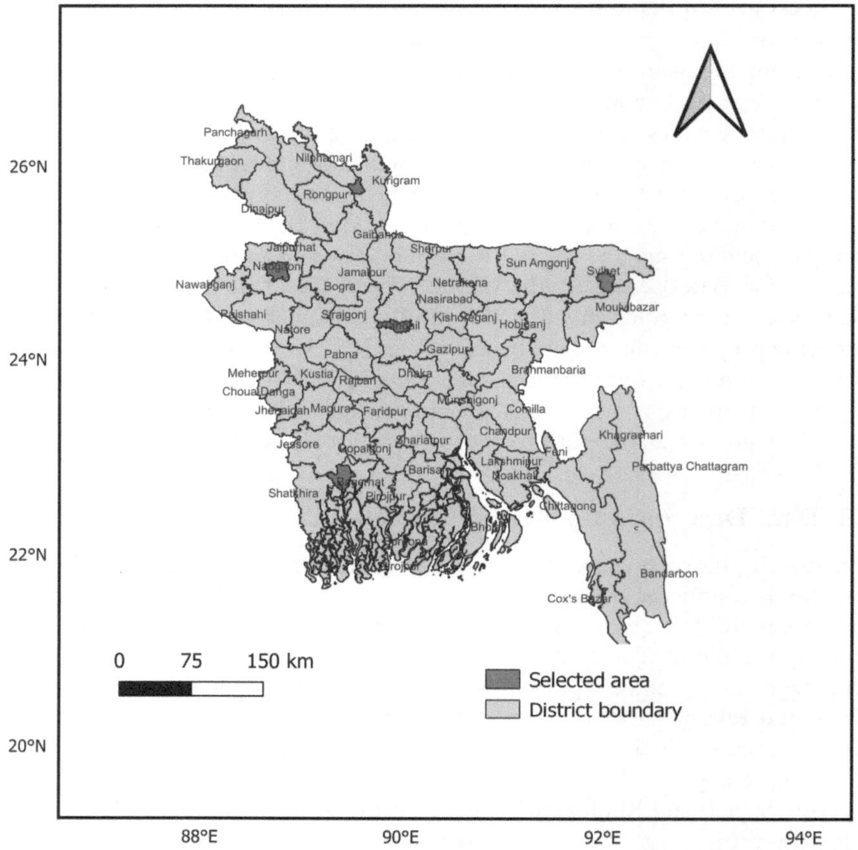

Figure 7.2 The Study Area (indicated by blue colour on the map of Bangladesh).
Source: The map is adapted from the Bangladesh Bureau of Statistics (BBS), 2018.

Households both self-sourced and purchased food items were considered to calculate the total quantity of food consumption at the household level. Total quantity of food consumed at the household level were converted into kilocalories using a locally available food composition table (Shaheen et al. 2013). The kilocalorie values were divided by the number of adult equivalents (AE)[8] in a household in order to make them comparable across households of different sizes (Alam et al. 2018; Bellù 2005; Miah et al. 2014). Household family members and guests were included or excluded in the calculation of the AE, depending on their presence or absence during the three-day recall period of data collection. In this chapter, the term ***kilocalorie*** is taken as calorie and daily kilocalorie consumption per adult equivalent is denoted as Kcal/day/AE.

7.4 Summary Statistics

Summary statistics of the variables used in this study for the households with nonfarm income and without, are presented in Table 7.1. From the top section of the table, it can be seen that approximately 68% of households without nonfarm income and about 39% of households with nonfarm income have livestock. In terms of access to credit, about 33% of households without nonfarm income and about 63% of households with nonfarm income have access to that facility. Besides, about 59% of households without nonfarm income has electricity in their household while about 81% of households have electricity who have nonfarm income.

It can be seen from the bottom half of Table 7.1, that the average calorie consumption in the households without nonfarm income (2011 Kcal/Day/AE) is lower than the calorie consumption in the households with nonfarm income (2322 Kcal/Day/AE). Column 3 also presents that the average monthly nonfarm income of nonfarm employed households is about BDT[9] 3,756 per adult equivalent. However, the average monthly farm income is higher (BDT 2,197/AE) in the households that do not have nonfarm income than in the households that have nonfarm income (BDT 714 /AE). The average age of the household head without nonfarm income (44.4 years) is higher than the average age of the heads of households with nonfarm income (41.7 years).

On average, years of schooling[10] for farm-employed household heads (3.2 years) are lower than those of nonfarm-employed household heads (4.0 years). The average size of the household (adult equivalent) is lower in households without nonfarm income (3.2) than in households with nonfarm income (3.7). In addition, the number of children up to 5 years of age are almost the same in both types of households. The average dependency ratio in households without nonfarm income is about 73.2, while dependency ration in households with nonfarm income is about 64.3%. In terms of the farm size per household, on average, farm employed households have access to 0.6 hectares of land, while nonfarm-employed households have access to 0.4 hectares[11] of land. The table also reveals that the average distance to the nearest market is about the same for both types of households (with and without nonfarm income).

In summary, households without nonfarm income consume less calories (Kcal/day/AE, which is below the required level) in a day than households with nonfarm income. Further, the household heads' average years of schooling, household size, and number of children are lower in households that do not have nonfarm income than in households that have nonfarm income. The average monthly farm income, household head's age, dependency ratio, and farm size are higher in households that do not have nonfarm income than in households that have nonfarm income.

7.5 Household Expenditure of Rural Areas of Bangladesh

Household expenditure data consists of food consumption expenditure and expenditure on different non-food items. This chapter considers a household to

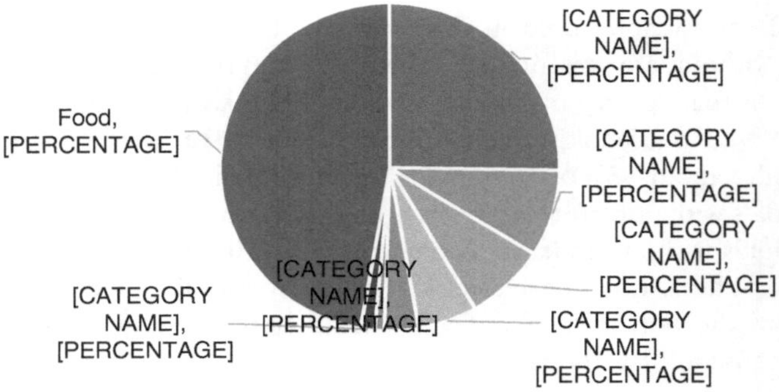

Figure 7.3 Graphical representation of the household monthly expenditure on different items as a percentage of the total monthly expenditure, rural Bangladesh, 2019.

Source: Based on field survey data, 2019.

be a unit that has a common arrangement for the cooking and partaking of food. Figure 7.3 presents the proportional distribution of household monthly expenditure on food and different nonfood items in rural settings. As can be seen in Figure 7.3, the expenditure share on food out of total monthly household expenditure is much higher among different expenditure categories in rural households. They spend on average about 47%[12] of their total expenditure on food while spending about 25% on housing. Figure 7.3 also reveals that the share of clothing expenditure (9%) and health expenditure (8%) out of total expenditures in rural households is almost the same. Besides, the share of transport expenditure is about 6%, whereas the share of education expenditure is about 3% out of total expenditures. The share of recreation expenditure and other nonfood expenditures out of total expenditures is about 1% in rural households.

Figure 7.4 presents the distribution of monthly expenditure on food and different nonfood items in BDT in rural households. It can be seen that the average monthly food expenditure is the highest, about BDT 5,500, followed by housing expenditure (BDT 2,900), expenditure in clothing, health, and transport. It can also be seen that rural households spend on average BDT 100 per month for recreation purposes, which is the lowest expenditure among different expenditure categories.

Figure 7.5 presents the share of different food groups of household monthly food expenditure. It covers a total of 305 food items that are classified under the following sub-groups.: 'cereal', 'pulses', 'vegetable', 'fish', 'meat', 'egg', 'milk', 'sugar', 'fat', 'fruit', 'outside-home food',[13] and 'tobacco'. Rural households spend about 25.8% of their total food expenditure on cereal consumption, while spending about 22.2% on vegetable consumption, 18.2% on fish consumption, and 9.4% on tobacco consumption.

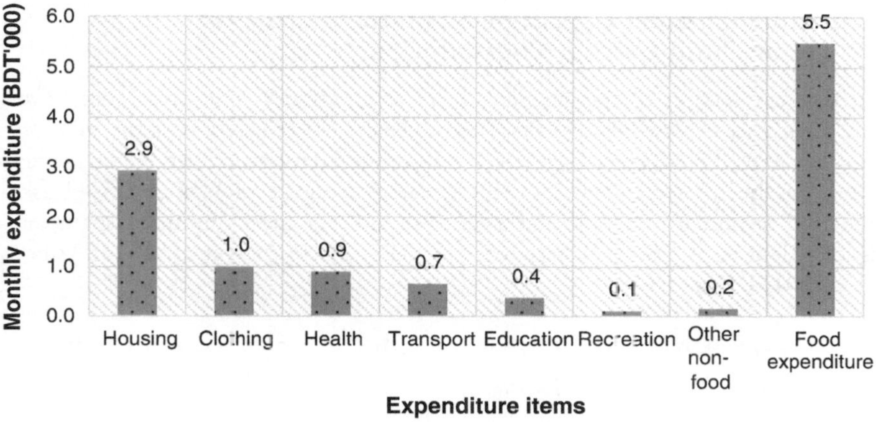

Figure 7.4 Household monthly expenditure on different items in (BDT '000), rural Bangladesh, 2019.

Note: BDT is the Bangladeshi currency. USD 1 = BDT 84 (This was the exchange rate during the period of data collection, 2019).

Source: Based on field survey data, 2019.

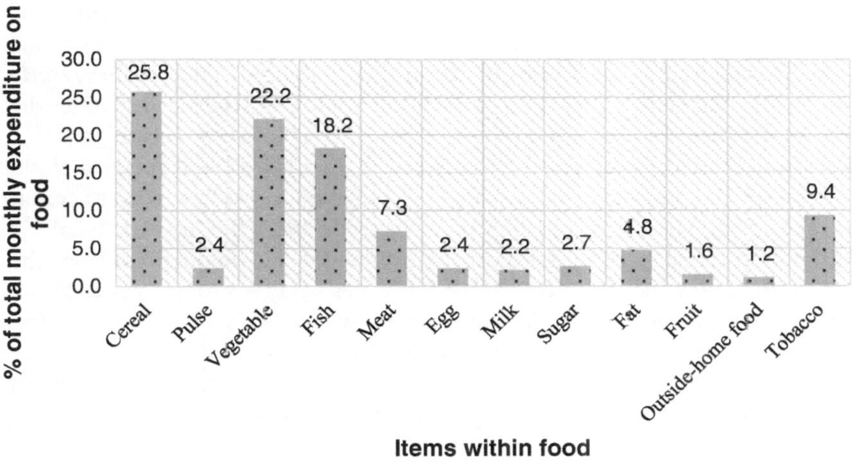

Figure 7.5 Graphical representation of rural households' monthly food expenditure on different food groups as a percentage of the total monthly food expenditure, 2019.

Source: Based on field survey data, 2019.

7.6 Modelling the Impact of Nonfarm Income on Household Calorie Consumption

In the first section of this chapter, a research question was presented: *"Does nonfarm income has any influence on household calorie consumption in rural Bangladesh?"* To answer this research question, the following regression framework has been used, where household calorie consumption is expressed as a function of nonfarm income and a set of household and community characteristics (Alam et al. 2018; Babatunde and Qaim 2010; Dev et al. 2016; Tsiboe et al. 2016). That is:

$$\begin{aligned} C_i = {} & \beta_0 + \beta_1 NFI_i + \beta_2 FI_i + \beta_3 Age_i + \beta_4 Age_i^2 + \beta_5 Edu_i + \beta_6 HS_i + \beta_7 HS_i^2 \\ & + \beta_8 Children_i + \beta_9 Dratio_i + \beta_{10} Elec_i + \beta_{11} FS_i + \beta_{12} Livestock_i \\ & + \beta_{13} Credit_i + \beta_{14} M\_dist_i + u_i \end{aligned} \tag{7.1}$$

where, C_i is the daily calorie consumption per adult equivalent (AE) for the household i. *NFI* is the average monthly nonfarm income (BDT '000) per adult equivalent and *FI* is the average monthly farm income (BDT '000) per adult equivalent for household i. The term u_i is the idiosyncratic error term. The variable *Age* is the age of the household head measured in completed years while the variable Age^2 is the squared age of the household head. *Edu* is the completed years of schooling of the household head. The variable household size (*HS*) is measured by the total number of household members in adult equivalent while HS^2 denotes the household size squared. The variable *Children* is the total number of children under 5 years of age in the household. The variable *Dratio* denotes the total dependency ratio in the household. This study also includes the variables electricity (*Elec*) access (1 = if the household has electricity, 0 = otherwise), *FS* (farm size measured in hectare), *Livestock* (1 = if the household has livestock, 0 = otherwise) and *Credit* (1 = if the household has access to credit, 0 = otherwise). The above variables may positively affect the household calorie consumption. Finally, the distance of the nearest market (kilometres) from the household, *M_dist*, has been controlled for in this study if a longer distance can be associated with lower calorie consumption in the household due to infrastructural constraints and lower physical access to food. This study also controlled for village level fixed effects in the estimation to capture the effects of regional heterogeneity on household calorie consumption.

7.7 Empirical Results

Estimation results for Equation (7.1) are reported in Table 7.2, column 2 shows that the average monthly nonfarm income is statistically significant and positively associated with household daily calorie consumption per adult equivalent. The coefficient of nonfarm income (74.61) indicates that an increase in monthly nonfarm income by BDT 1000 per AE results in an increase in the household's

Table 7.2 Estimated Coefficients for the Impact of Different Factors on the Households' Daily Calorie Consumption (Kcal/Day/AE)

	Calorie consumption per capita per day AE (C_i)		
Variables	*Coefficient*	*Robust Standard error*	*p-value*
(1)	*(2)*	*(3)*	*(4)*
Nonfarm income in BDT '000/AE (***NFI***, β_1)	74.61*	(14.02)	0.00
Farm income in BDT '000/AE (***FI***, β_2)	30.01*	(20.91)	0.01
Household head's (HH) age (***Age***, β_3)	13.47	(12.08)	0.27
HH Age squared (***Age***^{2}, β_4)	-0.12	(0.13)	0.37
HH years of schooling (***Edu***, β_5)	27.65*	(10.01)	0.01
Household size (AE) (***HS***, β_6)	166.90*	(45.61)	0.00
Household size squared (***HS***^{2}, β_7)	-6.32**	(3.36)	0.06
Number of children (***Children***, β_8)	-5.43	(61.62)	0.93
Dependency ratio ***(Dratio***, β_9***)***	-0.483	(0.72)	0.50
Access to electricity ***(Elec***, β_{10}***)***	117.65	(78.45)	0.14
Farm size in hectare (***FS***, β_{11})	9.51	(71.80)	0.89
Household has livestock (***Livestock***, β_{12})	158.92*	(62.35)	0.01
Access to credit (***Credit***, β_{13})	13.70	(55.55)	0.81
Household's distance from nearest market (km) (***M_dist***, β_{14})	-98.80**	(55.01)	0.09
Constant (β_0)	1,558.46*	(331.247)	0.00
Village level field effect	Yes		
Observations	144		
R-squared	0.63		
Omitted variable test (*p*-value)	0.17		
Mean VIF	1.91		

Source: Based on field survey data, 2019.

Note: OLS estimation has been used. Dependent variable: Calorie consumption per capita per day AE. '*' *denotes significant at the 5% level, and '**' denotes significant at the 10% level.* Hausman Endogeneity test for farm and nonfarm income: (F (2,114); *p*-value: 0.43).

average calorie consumption by 74.61 (Kcal/day/AE). It can also be seen that the average monthly farm income is also positively and significantly associated with household calorie consumption (Kcal/day/AE). However, its magnitude (30.01) is less than half that of nonfarm income. In addition, the two-sample mean test also suggests that average nonfarm income is significantly higher than average farm income. These findings suggest that the level of income from nonfarm employment sources is more important than the level of farm income for household calorie consumption (Kcal/day/AE). Although farm income also has a positive association with household calorie consumption, the scope to increase farm income is limited due to various challenges faced by the agricultural sector in rural areas of Bangladesh.

The coefficient of the variable of years of schooling is positively and significantly associated with household calorie consumption. The magnitude of this coefficient (27.65 in column 2) suggests that on average a one-year increase in the household head's years of schooling leads to 27.65 Kcal/day/AE increase in household calorie consumption. This finding indicates that education might be a common pathway to increase nonfarm income through participation in nonfarm employment. Further, this increased nonfarm income will increase the household's access to food by increasing purchasing power.

The variable of household size is statistically significant and positively associated with household calorie consumption while household size squared variable is negatively and significantly associated with calorie consumption. The above results indicate a nonlinear relationship of household size with household calorie consumption and up to a certain point the calorie consumption increases with increasing household size at a decreasing rate and then starts to decrease after that point. This finding is not surprising, because more family members in the household may create excess pressure on food consumption in the household. However, this will not be the case if the household is endowed with more earning members.

Among other control variables, this study finds that the variable livestock ownership is statistically significant and positively associated (158.92) with household calorie consumption. This finding indicates that, on average, calorie consumption is higher by 158.92 Kcal/day/AE in households that have livestock than in those households which do not. The most likely reason for this is that livestock is considered an important source of supplementary income for rural households in Bangladesh. In addition, homestead livestock may also be an important source of food, such as meat and milk, at the household level in rural areas in Bangladesh. The distance of the nearest market from the household is negatively and significantly (–98.80) associated with household calorie consumption. Therefore, a 1-kilometre increase in the distance of the nearest market from a household leads to a decrease in calorie consumption by 98.80 Kcal/day/AE. This may be because a shorter distance from the market means greater physical access to food, which could lead to a higher level of calorie consumption. Although the signs of other control variables (age, number of children, farm size, and access to credit) were in line with expectations, this study fails to find any significant relationship between these variables with household calorie consumption in rural Bangladesh.

To be sure that nonfarm income as well as farm income are not endogenous in relation to household calorie consumption, this study employed the Hausman endogeneity test to verify that the error terms are uncorrelated with these variables. Since the Hausman endogeneity test *p*-value, 0.43, is greater than 0.05 (F (2,114); *p*-value: 0.43), we are unable to reject the null hypothesis, H_o: no endogeneity issue associated with nonfarm income or farm income in relation to household calorie consumption.

As can be seen at the bottom of Table 7.2, the omitted variable test *p*-value is greater than the 5% level of significance that we are unable to reject the null hypothesis of Ho: no omitted variables in the model. Moreover, this study also tested the possible existence of multicollinearity among explanatory variables since severe multicollinearity could lead to imprecise parameter estimation (Kennedy 1998). The mean Variance Inflation Factor (VIF) for the explanatory variables is 1.91 (with a range from 1.61 to 2.59), which does not reach the conventional threshold of ten or higher used in regression diagnosis. The robustness of the findings presented in Table 7.2 has been checked and the results are presented in Table 7.3.

To check the robustness of the findings presented in Table 7.2, Equation (7.1) has been estimated, considering nonfarm employment as a dummy variable instead of NFI measured in local currency. It is assumed that nonfarm employment = 1 if the household has nonfarm income from any nonfarm employment sources; 0 = otherwise. The estimated results are presented in Table 7.3. As can be seen in column 2 of Table 7.3 the coefficient of nonfarm employment is statistically significant and positively associated with household calorie consumption. This finding indicates that, on average, calorie consumption in households that have nonfarm income is higher by 267.47 Kcal/day/AE compared with households that do not. Therefore, this finding confirms the positive impact of nonfarm income on household calorie consumption in rural areas.

7.8 Concluding Comments

In the last few decades, Bangladesh has experienced an increasing nonfarm employment participation in rural areas. Although Bangladesh has achieved self-sufficiency in cereal production, achieving food security remains a challenge. Especially the rural poor people become more vulnerable to food insecurity in Bangladesh. However, Bangladesh needs to achieve food security and end all forms of child malnutrition by 2030 to attain the second goal of the sustainable development goal (SDG-2). Considering the increase in rural nonfarm employment and high prevalence of food insecurity, this chapter analyzed the impact of nonfarm employment on household calorie consumption in rural Bangladesh. Field survey data of 144 rural households collected from five different districts of rural Bangladesh from August 2018 to January 2019 was used in this study. Findings of this study indicate a positive association between increase in nonfarm income and household calorie consumption in rural Bangladesh. Results also indicate that households that have nonfarm income consume more calories per day per adult equivalent compared to households that do not. Therefore, increase in nonfarm income could be associated with the increase in purchasing power, which leads to improved food security. This finding is in line with previous studies in other developing countries (the study

Table 7.3 Estimated Results of Robustness Check for the Impact of Nonfarm Employment on Households' Daily Calorie Consumption (Kcal/Day/AE)

Variable	*Calorie consumption per capita per day AE (C_i)*		
	Coefficient	*Robust Standard error*	*p-value*
(1)	*(2)*	*(3)*	*(4)*
Nonfarm employment (dummy variable)[a] (***NFI***, β_1)	267.47*	(78.38)	0.00
Farm income in BDT '000/AE (***FI***, β_2)	40.14**	(21.57)	0.07
Household head's (HH) age (***Age***, β_3)	11.60	(13.83)	0.40
HH Age squared (Age^2, β_4)	-0.12	(0.14)	0.37
HH years of schooling (***Edu***, β_5)	38.16*	(10.95)	0.00
Household size (AE) (***HS***, β_6)	168.38*	(49.16)	0.00
Household size squared (HS^2, β_7)	-7.13*	(3.47)	0.04
Number of children (***Children***, β_8)	-40.52	(67.04)	0.55
Dependency ratio (***Dratio***, β_9)	-0.42	(0.85)	0.62
Access to electricity (***Elec***, β_{10})	132.10**	(75.72)	0.08
Farm size in hectare (***FS***, β_{11})	51.62	(70.80)	0.47
Household has livestock (***Livestock***, β_{12})	157.27*	(69.52)	0.03
Access to credit (***Credit***, β_{13})	82.59	(65.43)	0.21
Household's distance from nearest market (km) (***M_dist***, β_{14})	-114.70**	(71.84)	0.10
Constant (β_0)	1,539.42*	(393.395)	0.00
Village level field effect	Yes		
Observations	144		
R-squared	0.55		
Omitted variable test (*p*-value)	0.14		
Mean VIF	1.99		

Source: Based on field survey data, 2019.

Note: [a]Nonfarm employment is a dummy variable (1 = if the household has any income from nonfarm employment sources, 0 = otherwise). OLS estimation has been used. *'*' denotes significant at the 5% level, and '**' denotes significant at the 10% level.*

on Nigeria by Babatunde and Qaim 2010; on Honduras by Ruben and Berg 2001; on Ghana by Tsiboe et al. 2016).

It is commonly believed that farm income has a more favourable effect on household calorie consumption than nonfarm income, especially in rural areas. Although both farm and nonfarm income seem to have a significant and positive impact on household calorie consumption in this study, the magnitude of nonfarm income is much higher than for farm income. Also, the two-sample mean test suggests that the average nonfarm income is significantly higher than the average farm income. Moreover, several challenges impose limitations on participation in farm employment in rural areas. For instance, the average size of farm holding is declining due to the increase in population over the past decades, which creates excess pressure on limited land resources. Therefore, the evidence presented in this chapter supports the idea that households can significantly improve their calorie consumption by increasing nonfarm income, which leads to improved food security for the household.

In terms of policy implications, the results from this study suggest that promising policy measures to boost nonfarm income should be emphasized to improve household calorie consumption in rural areas, and this will lead to improved food security in rural Bangladesh. For instance, infrastructural facilities could be improved to reduce the market distance from the household to increase the physical access to food. Moreover, education facilities could be improved, since improved education usually creates a pathway to participate in different types of nonfarm activities, which in turn increases household access to food as well as calorie consumption.

Notes

1 "Food security exists when all people, at all times, have physical and economic access to sufficient, safe and nutritious food that meets their dietary needs and food preferences for an active and healthy life" (World Food Summit 1996).
2 "Severe food insecurity is characterized by feeling hungry but not eating, or not eating for an entire day, due to lack of money or other resources" (FAO 2019). The pandemic, COVID-19, made it worse over 2020 and 2021.
3 Nonfarm employment refers to employment in all activities excluding agriculture/farm employment. It can take place at home, in factories or be performed by itinerant traders (Haggblade et al. 2007; Scharf and Rahut 2014; Shi et al. 2007).
4 By implication, this means that there has been a corresponding decrease in farm employment, as one is either engaged in farm or nonfarm activity.
5 This means the rate for farm employment decreased by as much as the increase in nonfarm employment, from 51.7% in 2000 to 40.6% in 2017.
6 The survey was carried out by a team of researchers headed by the author of this chapter while carrying out PhD research at Griffith University. Ethics approval was obtained from Griffith University Human Research Ethics Committee for this survey, GU ref no: 2018/527.
7 The administrative structure of Bangladesh consists of divisions, districts, upazilas, unions, and villages in descending order by size. There are 8 divisions, 64 districts, 492 upazilas, 4,554 unions, and 56,348 villages. (A new division was added as the eighth division in 2015, and 8 new upazilas and 56 unions were added from 2015 to 2018.)
8 Adult equivalent is measured by applying the equivalence scale (Bellù 2005).
9 BDT is the Bangladeshi currency. USD 1 = BDT 84 (This was the exchange rate during the period of data collection, 2019.)
10 Formal schooling is considered to measure the years of schooling for the household head (HH).
11 Since all households who have nonfarm income are not engaged in farming, the average farm size is higher for households without nonfarm income compared to households with nonfarm income.

12 The rural sample includes some households solely dependent on nonfarm employment. Most of the rural farm households produce limited crops (cereal and cash crops) and purchase other foods from the market. Furthermore, average income for rural households is much lower than for urban households. Therefore, the food share of rural households is higher than that of urban households. However, in terms of absolute value, urban households spend more on food than rural (please see Figure 7.4).

13 This category includes foods prepared and consumed outside of the home.

References

Alam, G. M. M., Alam, K., and Mushtaq, S. (2018). Drivers of Food Security of Vulnerable Rural Households in Bangladesh. *South Asia Economic Journal, 19*(1), 43–63.

Al-Amin, A. K. M. A., and Hossain, M. J. (2019). Impact of Non-farm Income on welfare in Rural Bangladesh: Multilevel Mixed-effects Regression Approach. *World Development Perspectives, 13*, 95–102.

Babatunde, R. O., and Qaim, M. (2010). Impact of off-farm income on food security and nutrition in Nigeria. *Food policy, 35*(4), 303–311.

Barrett, C. B., Reardon, T., and Webb, P. (2001). Nonfarm income diversification and household livelihood strategies in rural Africa: concepts, dynamics, and policy implications. *Food policy, 26*(4), 315–331.

BBS. (2018). *Statistical Yearbook of Bangladesh.* Retrieved from Bangladesh Bureau of Statistics, Ministry of Planning, Government of the People's Republic of Bangladesh.

Bellù, L. G. (2005). *Equivalence Scales Subjective Methods.* Agricultural Policy Support Service, Policy Assistance Division, FAO, Rome, Italy.

Bouis, H. E. (1994). The effect of income on demand for food in poor countries: Are our food consumption databases giving us reliable estimates?. *Journal of Development Economics, 44*(1), 199–226.

Chang, H.-H., and Mishra, A. (2008). Impact of off-farm labor supply on food expenditures of the farm household. *Food policy, 33*(6), 657–664.

Davis, B., Winters, P., Reardon, T., and Stamoulis, K. (2009). Rural nonfarm employment and farming: household-level linkages. *Agricultural Economics, 40*(2), 119–123.

Dev, T., Sultana, N., and Hossain, M. E. (2016). Analysis of the Impact of Income Diversification Strategies on Food Security Status of Rural Households in Bangladesh: A Case Study of Rajshahi District. *American Journal of Theoretical and Applied Business, 2*(4), 46–56.

Do, T. L., Nguyen, T. T., and Grote, U. (2019). Nonfarm employment and household food security: evidence from panel data for rural Cambodia. *Food Security, 11*, 703–718.

FAO. (2019). *The state of food security and nutrition in the world.* Retrieved from Food and Agricultural Organization, Rome, Italy.

FAO, IFAD, and WEP. (2014). *The state of food insecurity in the world.* Retrieved from Rome: Strengthening the Enabling Environment for food Security and Nutrition. Food and Agricultural Organization of the United State, FAO, Rome, Italy.

Haggblade, S., Hazell, P., and Reardon, T. (2007). *Transforming the rural nonfarm economy.* International Food Policy Research Institute and Johns Hopkins University Press, Washington DC.

Harrigan, J. (2008). Food insecurity, poverty and the Malawian starter pack: Fresh start or false start? *Food Policy*, *33*(*3*), 237–249.

Hossain, M. J., and Al-Amin, A. K. M. A. (2018). Non-farm Income and Consumption Expenditures in Rural Bangladesh: Empirical Evidence from Multilevel Regression Modelling. *Journal of Quantitative Economics*, *17*(2), 377–396.

HIES. (2016). *Household Income and Expenditure Survey*. Final report, Bangladesh Bureau of Statistics. Ministry of Planing, Government of the People's Republic of Bangladesh.

Kennedy, P. (1998). *A guide to econometrics* (4th ed.). The MIT Press, USA, Cambridge

Lim, S. S. (2017). Consumption vulnerability to prolonged illness. *Journal of International Development*, *29*, 351–369.

Mabuza, M. L., Ortmann, G. F., Wale, E., and Mutenje, M. J. (2016). The effect of major income sources on rural household food (in)security: Evidence from Swaziland and implications for policy. *Ecol Food Nutr*, *55*(2), 209–230.

Magnani, R., Oot, L., Sethuraman, K., Kabir, G., and Rahman, S. (2015). *USAID Office of Food For Peace Food Security Country Framework for Bangladesh (FY 2015–2019)*. Report. Washington, DC. FHI 360/FANTA.

Miah, M. A. M., Alam, Q. M., and Mohabbatullah, M. (2014). Household food security among indigenous hill people in Khagrachari hill district of Bangladesh. *BangladeshJ. Agric. Econs.*, *XXXVII*(1 & 2), 69–88.

Mishra, A. K., and Khanal, A. R. (2017). Assessing food security in rural Bangladesh: The role of a nonfar economy. *Frontiers of Economics and Globalization*, *17*, 241–257.

Mishra, A. K., Mottaleb, K. A., and Mohanty, S. (2015). Impact of off-farm income on food expenditures in rural Bangladesh: an unconditional quantile regression approach. *Agricultural Economics*, *46*(2), 139–148.

Mondal, R. K., Selvanathan E. A. and Selvanathan, S. (2020). Nexus between rural nonfarm income and household food security in Bangladesh, *Applied Economics*, *53*(10), 1184–1199.

Owusu, V., Abdulai, A., and Abdul-Rahman, S. (2011). Non-farm work and food security among farm households in Northern Ghana. *Food policy*, *36*(2), 108–118.

Pfeiffer, L., López-Feldman, A., and Taylor, J. E. (2009). Is off-farm income reforming the farm? Evidence from Mexico. *Agricultural Economics*, *40*(2), 125–138.

Rahman, A., and Mishra, S. (2019). Does Non-farm Income Affect Food Security? Evidence from India. *The Journal of Development Studies*, *56*(6), 1190–1209.

Rahut, D. B., Jena, P. R., Ali, A., Behera, B., and Chhetri, N. B. (2015). Rural nonfarm employment, income, and inequality: Evidence from Bhutan. *Asian Development Review*, *32*(2), 65–94.

Ruben, R., and Berg, M. V. D. (2001). Nonfarm employment and poverty alleviation of rural farm households in Honduras. *World Development*, *29*(3), 549–560.

Scharf, M. M., and Rahut, D. B. (2014). Nonfarm Employment and Rural Welfare: Evidence from the Himalayas. *American Journal of Agricultural Economics*, *96*(4), 1183–1197.

Schmidhuber, J. and Tubiello, F. N. (2007). Global food security under climate change, *Proceedings of National Academic Science*, USA, *104*(50), 19703–19708.

Seng, K. (2015). The Effects of nonfarm activities on farm households' food consumption in rural Cambodia. *Development Studies Research*, *2*(1), 77–89.

Shaheen, N., Rahim, A. T. M. A., Mohiduzzaman, M., Banu, C. P., Bari, M. L., and Tukun, A. B. (2013). *Food composition table for Bangladesh.* Retrieved from (NFPCSP Fianl Report). Dhaka:. National Food Policy Capacity Strengthening Programme, Dhaka, Bangladesh.

Shi, X., Heerink, N., and Qu, F. (2007). Choices between different off-farm employment sub-categories: An empirical analysis for Jiangxi Province, China. *China Economic Review*, *18*(4), 438–455.

Tran, T. Q. (2015). Nonfarm employment and household income among ethnic minorities in Vietnam. *Economic Research-Ekonomska Istraživanja*, *28*(1), 703–716.

Tsiboe, F., Zereyesus, Y. A., and Osei, E. (2016). Non-farm work, food poverty, and nutrient availability in northern Ghana. *Journal of Rural Studies*, *47*, 97–107.

World Development Indicator. (2019). *Warld Development Indicators.* The World bank, Washington D.C. Retrived from https://databank.worldbank.org/source/world-development-indicators.

World Food Summit. (1996). Rome Declaration on World Food Security and World Food Summit Plan of Action, 13–17 November 1996, Rome, Italy, Retrieved from http://www.fao.org/docrep/003/w3613e/w3613e00.h

8 Bangladesh's Agricultural Growth and Development Over Fifty Years

A M Muazzam Husain and Moazzem Hossain

8.1 Introduction

Bangladesh is blessed with quality soil and year-round relatively non-hostile weather for agriculture for which agriculture has always been the predominant sector of the economy. However, due to natural hazards like frequent floods, cyclones, and droughts, and due to its peculiar geophysical characteristics, the country has become highly vulnerable to natural disasters. As a result, the performance of its agriculture sector is often affected adversely and becomes unstable. A second problem is the excessive pressure of population, leading to small-scale farming and diminishing size of farm holdings. Third, area under cultivation has also been declining since the 1980s due to increase in demand for land for housing,, industry, and infrastructure development (BBS, 2019).

In recent years, however, according to a Report on Agriculture and Rural Statistics published by Bangladesh Bureau of Statistics (BBS) 2019, the land tenure ship has been found to be in four categories: own land (80%), land taken out (23%), land taken in (25%), and total land operated by farmer household is (82%) (BBS, 2019).

Besides limitations of land resources, the question of augmenting irrigation facilities also deserves special mention due to emerging problem of arsenic contamination found in tube-well irrigation water. Planned and economic exploitation of surface water sources will be required for future growth in agriculture. Again, with growth in the non-agricultural employment, the relative supply of labour is declining in agriculture too. This would have to be addressed through judicious expansion of mechanization in the agricultural sector. Of course, mechanization has been taking place and has contributed to increase in labour productivity in agriculture sector, and aggregate rate of growth of the sector has been fluctuating between 3.33% in 2015 and 3.90 in 2019 (PC, 2020). Among four major subsectors of agriculture (crops and horticulture, animal farming, forestry and fisheries), crops, and horticulture had been suffering from least growth rate over 2015 and 2019, between 1.83% and 1.90%, respectively. In terms of share of GDP, the agriculture sub-sector has been experiencing decline too. For example, the share of GDP declined was from 15.36% in 2015 to 13.61% in 2019. In contrast, the industrial sector grew from 29.19% in 2015 to 34.7% in 2019 (PC, 2020).

DOI: 10.4324/9781003231912-12

In spite of the disadvantages mentioned above, agriculture in this nation has been moving toward growth and modernization as seen in Korea and Taiwan in the 1960s and 1970s. There have been structural changes taken place in Bangladesh too. Increased adoption of modern technology and agriculture friendly public policy changes have contributed to significant growth over the last four decades. Some of these are discussed in the next section with trends of growth. Overall production has been increasing along with diversification. The country has recently shown signs of attaining self-sufficiency sustainably at least in food grain production. Some argue that the self-sufficiency has already been achieved. With the current pace of growth, it is now a reality that in agriculture, Vision 2021 agendas have been realized. Having said that, over the last three years (2019–2022), a global pandemic and untimely floods were major challenges to the agriculture sector. The impacts of the global pandemic have not been analyzed in this chapter due to uncertainties expected to continue in the years to come.

8.1.1 Bangladesh's Vision 2021 Agenda and Agriculture

The Vision 2021 agenda, worked out in 2000, in general, envisages that by 2021 all the basic needs of the country's total population will be met on a sustainable basis (Hossain et al., 2003). Specifically, in the agricultural sector, output growth will ensure self-sufficiency in food grains sustainably. There have been enough records showing diversification has been taking place in the sector as shown by increased production of higher value crops and non-crop agricultural produces, and exports of many high-value crops. Agriculture has been transforming from subsistence to commercial production since better marketing facilities have been established over the last two decades. For example, with a provision of more marketing facilities and rise in per capita income, the demand for vegetables, fruits, fish, and livestock products have been increased (PC, 2020). Overall, the agricultural growth rate has been increased by 3 to 4% per year. Along with higher productivity in agriculture, the growth rate in the industrial sector has risen too.

In realizing the development agendas for 2021, one of the goals to be achieved by Bangladesh agriculture was to provide food for its growing population, which has now reached to more than 170 million people. According to the United Nations (UN, 1998), by early 2020s, even with a reduced annual growth rate of 1.2%, the population will reach 173 million. Now, in accordance with population growth it has been claimed that by end of 2021, the population reached close to 180 million. Secondly, the agriculture sector must also provide surpluses to be able to supply raw materials for industry and provide goods for export to help earn valuable foreign currency. The country must also adopt strategies to minimize losses from natural calamities making agricultural sector sustainable. All of these have now become realities.

To explore the capacity of the agricultural sector to achieve the desired goals of 2021, the present chapter briefly analyzes the history of growth and performance of agriculture in Bangladesh to 2030 and the potentialities for accelerating growth further. In this context, some policy issues are also discussed, which are considered necessary for realizing the goals of agricultural development in this nation in years to come given uncertainties created by the COVID-19 pandemic since 2020. In this country, the first COVID-19 case was detected on 22 January 2020.

8.2 Growth Trends of Agriculture

8.2.1 Growth Over the Last Four Decades

Until the late 1960s, production and yield rates were very poor in agriculture due to the use of traditional methods and lack of access to modern inputs by farmers. Rice was the main cereal crop produced and jute was the principal cash crop. Among other minor crops were pulses, oilseeds, and spices. At about this time, with the introduction of the improved seed, fertilizer, and irrigation-based technology, the scenario slowly started to change. New High Yielding Varieties (HYVs) of rice started to replace *rabi* (winter) crops like pulses, oilseeds, and spices. Production of HYV rice started growing at a low pace. Wheat production also started to increase along with potato production. The crop sector was, nevertheless, dominated by rice which occupied 75% of the cropland (Hossain M, 1983).

The growth rate in food production has been boosted up since the mid-1980s, which coincided with major public policy changes in agricultural input procurement and distribution. Shallow tube-well use has been increased tremendously because of liberalization of import policy and privatization of irrigation equipment. Fertilizer distribution was also privatized and imports by the private sector had been allowed. Expansion of area under HYV rice replacing local low-yielding varieties and other *rabi crops* was mainly responsible for almost doubling the food grain production from 1969–70 to 1992–93 and there had been an increase in production through to 2014 (Kabir et al. 2015).

However, during the early 1990s, the growth rate in cereal crop production surprised everyone. Productivity indicators for both fertilizer and irrigation exhibited a declining trend of (–) 4.2% and (–) 6.9%, respectively (Abdullah and Shahabuddin, 1997). Privatization of input supply, reduction in subsidy, and other related factors raised the cost of production. At the same time, with increasing demand for food grains and greater stability in food grain prices, the relative profitability of cereal production declined for the producers. Undue public interference in the fertilizer distribution system created anomalies in its availability and prices. Public-sector development allocation to agriculture also declined. All of these, however, set a favourable stage for transformation of the agricultural sector toward diversification. In fact, one piece of evidence of the ongoing structural transformation of the agricultural sector is provided by the fact that while, in 1973–74 the share of the crop sub-sector was 80% of the total share of income from the agricultural sector, its share came down to 58% in 1998–99. It has now dropped to below 40%. During this period, the share of fisheries and the livestock sub-sectors continued to increase (Hossain and Bose, 2000; Sarkar and Rahman, 2020).

Table 8.1a Growth Rate of Agricultural Sector Between 1973–74 and 1998–99

Sector	*(Annual growth rate in percent)*			
	1997–98 to 1998–99	*1995–96 to 1998–99*	*1990–91 to 1998–99*	*1973–74 to 1989–90*
Agriculture	5.0	4.8	2.7	2.6
Crops	4.3	4.0	1.4	1.7
Forestry	4.1	4.2	3.8	3.8
Livestock	7.6	7.8	7.2	5.2
Fisheries	8.0	8.4	7.8	2.3

Source: BBS, *Statistical Yearbook of Bangladesh*, various issues; Monthly Statistical Bulletin, (December 1999), Biswas et al. (2020) and Sarkar and Rahman (2020).

In the crop sub-sector, the new seed policy of the government had opened up opportunities for the involvement of the private sector and the import of improved seed was liberalized. Higher productivity and growing demand helped in the expansion of area and production of maize, pulses, oilseeds, tubers, and especially vegetables. Another major change occurring in the agricultural sector during the 1990s is the high rate of growth in the non-crop sectors like livestock (including poultry), fisheries, and forestry.

After the mid-1990s, both crop and non-crop sub-sectors of agriculture again showed a trend of high growth. The rate of growth in food grain production was spectacular. While the average rate of long-term growth in the sub-sector was 2.6% per year from 1973–74 to 1989–90, the rate of growth was 4.0% per year from 1995–96 to 1998–99 and 5% from 1997–98 to 1998–99 (Table 8.1a). There was a spectacular rise in the production of food grains (rice and wheat) from 1995–96 to 1999–00 showing a growth rate of 7% per annum (Palmer-Jones, 1999). Total food grain production stood at 25 million MT in 1999–2000. The average yield of rice increased from 1.86 t/ha in 1996–97 to 2.16 t/ha in 1999–2000.

Table 8.1b presents agricultural growth rate since 2001. In 1999 the growth rate reached 5% (see Table 8.1a). In subsequent years, the rate dropped on average to 3.7%. The rate of growth bounced back to the 3.5% level since 2017 (PC, 2020).

Table 8.1c below presents crop production predictions by the Planning Commission for the next five years from 2020–21 to 2024–25. These targets are certainly attainable if one looks at the trend of overall growth of agriculture sub-sector presented in Tables 8.1a and 8.1b.

8 2.2 Analyzing Sources of Growth

There were several factors that contributed to the relatively fast rate of growth in the agricultural sector since 2000. One group of factors relates to improvement

Table 8.1b Growth Rate of Agricultural Sector Between 2001–02 and 2018

Sector	*(Annual growth rate in percent)*			
	2001–02 to 2005–06	*2007–08 to 2009–10*	*2013–14 to 2015–16*	*2017 to 2018*
Agriculture	3.3	4.7	3.2	3.5
Crops and Horticulture	3.6	4.9	1.8	2.5
Forestry	4.7	5.3	4.9	–
Fishing	2.6	4.1	6.1	6.4
Livestock	–	8.9	17.9	33.9

Source: Planning Commission FFYP and Sarkar and Rahman (2020).

Table 8.1c Projections of Productions of the Crop Sub-Sector for Eighth Five-Year Plan (in million MT, million bales for jute fibre)

Items	*2020–21*	*2021–22*	*2022–23*	*2023–24*	*2024–25*
Rice	39.29	39.89	40.49	41.11	41.73
Wheat	1.29	1.32	1.37	1.41	1.46
Potato	11.23	11.54	11.86	12.20	12.54
Oil Seed	1.18	1.21	1.23	1.26	1.29
Vegetables	9.44	20.48	21.58	22.74	23.96
Maize	5.67	5.95	6.25	6.56	6.89
Spices	4.03	4.11	4.19	4.28	4.36
Pulses	1.09	1.13	1.17	1.21	1.25
Jute	8.09	8.02	8.02	8.02	8.03

Source: Alam and PC (2021).

in the technology used for production. Farmers in Bangladesh, after prolonged period of exposure to improved technology, have become by this time, very much responsive to technology changes and market forces.

There has been large-scale substitution of traditional low-yielding seeds by improved seeds. This was facilitated by release of modern HYV seeds such as BR 28 and BR 29 by BRRI that contributed to a significant rise in rice yields. Imported hybrid rice seeds were introduced after the floods in 1998, though on a relatively small scale. Hybrid vegetable seeds were being used and hybrid maize seeds were also introduced. A favourable environment was also created for use of improved seeds by introducing more liberal seed policy by the government.

At the same time, the private sector and some NGOs also initiated promotional activities or improvement in the agricultural production technology. Several large NGOs involved in producing and/or marketing of improved seeds besides providing credit and extension services. The Government also played an important role by liberally providing agricultural credit facilities. Public sector support in fertilizer supply and distribution including provision of some subsidy helped improve the availability of fertilizers. Thus, public sector allocation in agriculture also increased. In fact, in the Fifth Five-Year Plan (1997–2002) of Bangladesh, agriculture, including rural development, is to receive the highest public-sector financial allocation (Planning Commission, 1998).

Interplay of several technological and market forces also contributed significantly to attaining high agricultural growth during this period. The high growth rate in the non-crop sub-sectors along with increased per capita income created additional demand for the crop sub-sector, which provided incentives for increased production. At the same time, increasing capital investment in agriculture facilitated this process. Mechanization in agriculture reached a critical stage to produce significant impact on production growth and increase in labour productivity. The number of rural households owning irrigation equipment increased from 274,000 in 1983–84 to 933,000 in 1996 and the number of equipment increased from 312,000 to 1,100,000 during the same period. Again, the number of rural households owning power tillers/tractors increased from 27,000 to 141,000 from 1983–84 to 1996 (Hossain and Bose, 2000). The use of power tillers also helped in reducing land preparation time and thus helped in increasing cropping intensity. These are increasing further in recent years too (see BBS, 2019).

Increasing replacement of draft animals by power tillers also helped create opportunities for dairy farming resulting in increased milk production. Changes in the food habit and increasing awareness of nutrition promoted by NGOs and the mass media along with initiation of exports of agricultural products also helped in the growth and diversification of agriculture (Husain A M, 2003).

8.2.2.1 Rice Crops

Table 8.2 below presents an account of production of clean rice from 1972 to 2014 in actual terms. Kabir et al. (2015) also provides projected requirements of clean rice from 2020 to 2050. This study found a significant momentum in rice production in two phases: phase one covers 1996–97 to 2000–01. Phase two spreads from 2009–10 to 2013–14 due to major policy intervention in agricultural sector. Table 8.2 also provides a prediction of clean rice production and requirements from 2020 to 2050.

The recent production of clean rice (2014) has been reached to almost 34.5 million tonnes. With the present rate of increase in production, it has been predicted that this amount will reach to 47.2 million tonnes in 2050, given no change in area of cultivated land. In contrast, the demand for clean rice would reach 44.6 million metric tonnes in 2050 with 2.6 million tonnes considered as surplus (Kabir et al., 2015).

It appears that the prediction of rice production in 2025 by the Planning Commission (PC), as shown in Table 8.1c above, is 41 million MT, which is well above the amount of 36 million MT projected by Kabir et al. (2015). The PC's

Table 8.2 Actual and Predicted Clean Rice Production from 1972 to 2050 in Million Tonnes

Year	*Rice Production (in MT)*	*Surplus/Deficit*
1972	10	Deficit
1978	13	Deficit
1984	15	Deficit
1990	17	Deficit
1996	18	Deficit
2002	24	Deficit
2008	25	Deficit
2014	34	Surplus
2020	35	Surplus
2026	36	Surplus
2032	40	Surplus
2038	42	Surplus
2044	45	Surplus
2050	47	Surplus

Source: Kabir et al. (2015).

prediction certainly sounds optimistic given the COVID-19 affected the production over 2020–2021 period. Moreover, it is hard to predict at this stage whether the COVID-19 pandemic could be restrained by 2025. However, one can safely say that the nation would continue enjoying surplus to 2050 with a reduced amount. Even in some bad years, the surplus could disappear altogether.

Although the country was suffering from deficit (production < consumption) in rice to 2008, in subsequent years the farmers have been benefiting from cultivation of rice due to adopting modern technology gradually since 1972. Of course, the deficit was met by importing food grains over these years. Most importantly, the adoption of HYV rice for three different types of rice in three seasons of a year had been the major reason of such an achievement. These are shown in Table 8.3 in terms of the benefit-cost ratio of modern variety rice cultivation over three seasons.

Benefit-cost ratios of three types of rice presented above certainly make it clear that, in recent years, farmers have been incurring loss in producing HYV rice. There were many studies addressed this issue over recent years. Three main reasons have been identified in these studies: loss of productivity, costs of inputs increased due to lack of adequate availability of seeds, chemical fertilizers, and so on, and lack of credit facilities in the right time at the right place due to corrupt practices. In recent years, most importantly, the price of uncleaned rice (paddy) in the peak season remains relatively low due to lack of marketing facilities, particularly manipulation in the market by middlemen in the harvest season has been seen uncontrolled and went against the interest of the farmers.

Table 8.3 Benefit-Cost Ratio of HYV Rice Cultivation in Different Season

Year	*1989–90*	*1998–99*	*2003–04*	*2005–06*	*2008–09*	*2010–11*	*2017–18*	*2018–19*
<u>Season</u>								
Aus	1.65	2.45	1.37	1.20	1.20	1.09	1.10	0.86
Aman	1.76	2.64	1.63	1.37	1.21	1.22	1.20	1.04
Boro	1.72	0.86	1.26	1.27	1.05	1.06	0.92	0.81

Source: AED and BRRI several issues.

8.2.3 Implications of Growth Trend

Some implications of the trend of growth in the Bangladesh agricultural sector may be summarized as follows:

- In spite of small farm size, natural calamities, and various inefficiencies encountered in the input supply situation, the farmers have been pushing forward the progress in both the crop and non-crop sub-sectors, though fluctuations in the rate of growth are observed. This indicates growing resilience and innovation of farmers, a positive sign of qualitative improvement in the farming sector have been witnessed.
- From small-scale subsistence farming, the agricultural sector is currently moving toward diversification which would pave the way for specialization. Diversification in the sector has been facilitated by increased demand caused by rising income and consequent profitability of new crop and non-crop products.
- Farmers have become increasingly responsive to changes in market forces and natural factors. They are showing evidence of shifting from low-return to high-return crops and non-crop enterprises. At the same time, they are adjusting to natural calamities by changing their cropping pattern and *shifting* from *aman* to *boro* season cropping.
- Favourable growth rate in agriculture has been supported by public sector policy adjustments, improved infrastructure and growing participation of the NGOs and the private sector in agriculture.
- The growth process has also been facilitated by increased capital investment in agriculture such as irrigation equipment, power tillers, provision of credit and improved seeds.
- With gradual shift of labour from crop to non-crop agriculture and other sectors, this growth process has also been facilitated by increasing labour productivity in agriculture through increased mechanization.

Thus, a favourable environment has been created through increased market orientation, gradual increase in mechanization and better adjustment capacity of the farmers, increasing involvement of the NGOs and the private sector in promoting agricultural production technology, improved inputs and exports, and supporting public policy changes in agriculture. This process needs to be strengthened for sustaining a high growth rate in the agricultural sector in the future. There is also a need for removing other existing weaknesses and bottlenecks in the sector for further strengthening of this growth process. Among the steps needed may be mentioned large-scale promotion of research and development activities, undertaking land improvement programs, further improvement in the agricultural extension system, accelerating the capital investment activities, and developing a strong marketing infrastructure including export promotion activities (Husain, A M M p. 82 2003).

8.3 Potentials vs Reality for Agricultural Production in the Past

8.3.1 Cereals

Considering the growth rate so far and the required growth rate until 2020, the prospects for meeting the target appear to be good as predicted in 2000 and subsequent years by the Planning Commission. Especially, with increasing production, supply and adoption of quality seeds and growing involvement of NGOs and the private sector in these areas, growth rates certainly will be accelerated further. According to new research findings, regular use of purchased seeds instead of seeds by farmers can increase yields by 12–17% (Pal et al., 2000). The seed project of the Department of Agricultural Extension is also contributing to an increase in the know-how and skill of the farmers on production and preservation of seeds at the village level. It has been found that by using cleaned seed from their own harvest, farmers can increase yields by 8–10% (Diaz et. al., 2000). With high-yielding varieties such *as* BR 28 and BR 29, prospects for raising yield rate of rice have become high. Hybrid seeds imported from India did not produce expected results for producers in terms of yield and profitability. Chinese hybrid seeds gave higher yield and profit but the grain quality is liable to impede its long-run adoption (Husain et al., 2001). Bangladesh has evolved over the years its own hybrid seeds to suit its peculiar agro-ecological conditions and consumer tastes and preferences. New varieties of both hybrid and inbred (HYV) rice seeds are being developed by the Bangladesh Rice Research Institute with a regular interval, which is giving higher yields. High-yielding varieties of wheat and the expansion in the *adoption* of hybrid maize have been helping in raising productivity and accelerating the growth rates of these cereals too.

Besides seeds, improvement in soil and crop management practices including use of balanced nutrients have been improving productivity. The involvement of NGOs and the private sector in providing better extension services to their client farmers along with the recent reform measures in the government agricultural extension system have been contributing to increased awareness and knowledge about better soil and crop management. Again, some NGOs have introduced an integrated extension system combining training, motivation, and provision of credit and other inputs as well as marketing services, which have shown better results than the traditional agricultural extension model (Husain M, p. 84 2003).

8.3.2 Roots and Vegetables

Recent developments in the production of potato include the production of tissue culture for improving quality of seeds and an increased demand for exports. Adequate infrastructure facilities including storage and export promotion will be needed. The public sector needs to support and facilitate these developments initiated by the NGO/private sector, which would contribute positively to accelerating production of potato. At present, a need for measures taken to promote surplus and quality potato export by the government is most urgent.

Vegetable production has also attained a high-growth rate due to use of improved seeds provided by the Bangladesh Agricultural Development Corporation (BADC), the NGOs, and the private sector. In the case of vegetable seeds, however, the private sector has so far shown more interest in dealing with imported seeds rather than going for production of quality seeds on profitability considerations. The government may provide more incentives for involving them in production of quality seeds by offering easy credit and other facilities. Many NGOs also motivate the rural people to increase consumption of vegetables for better nutrition. In this connection, the efforts of the mass media in changing food habits need to be further strengthened. Changes in food habit, increased income, and growing demand for exports are likely to promote production of roots and vegetable crops. Considering all these factors, the potentialities for accelerating production of these crops appear to be high (Husain A M M, 2003).

8.3.3 Pulses and Oilseeds

There has been very slow progress in raising the production level of pulses and oilseeds. However, with the introduction of high-yielding varieties of seeds and better crop management, their growth rate is also likely to be accelerated. Some new high-yielding varieties of seeds for pulses and mustard have already been released by public research institutions, but further strengthening of R&D activities are needed. Provision should be made to provide more incentives to scientists for evolving better varieties.

As a new oilseed crop, sunflower is being promoted. Improvement in the processing technology for extraction of oil would help increase production. Increased yield and profitability of improved mustard seed is expected to contribute expanding the adoption of improved seeds of mastered and thereby raise total production.

8.3.4 Fruits

The prospects for accelerating production of fruit crops are also high with a rise in income levels due to high-income elasticity of demand for fruits. However, R&D activities are needed to reduce their perishable character. Improvement in storage, transportation, packaging, and preservation are necessary to wastage and seasonal fluctuations in supply and prices. Export potentials may also be explored to help boost up production and raise growth rate.

8.3.5 Other Commodities

As income elasticities of some products like fish, meat, eggs, and milk indicate, with a rise in population and increase in income levels, demand for these commodities will expand. The present growth rate is already high. With favourable public support to the private sector, enforcement of quality control and necessary regulatory reforms in these subsectors, it may be possible to sustain their high growth rate to 2020 and onwards (Husain A M M, 2003).

8.4 Perspectives for Agricultural Development to 2030

8.4.1 Some Growth Projections for Cereal Production

In spite of stabilized consumer demand for food, population increase will require a continuous growth in food grain availability. To meet the increased demand for rice in 2020, the National Commission on agriculture estimates a growth rate of 1.7% per year. On the other hand, according to a research strategy document of the Bangladesh Agricultural Research Council (BARC), the annual growth rate of rice needed is 2.2% per year. This rate had to be achieved by a smaller number of producers and with a smaller area of land. Thus, the real growth rate per unit of land had to be even higher than those mentioned above. Hossain and Bose estimated the required growth rate in the production of different food items based on the income elasticities of demand derived from the Household Expenditure Survey data (see Hossain and Bose, 2000).

According to Husain (2003), the demand projections for various food items based on the estimated income elasticities shows that a declining growth rate is required for different food items until 2020. The annual rate of growth required is relatively low for cereals varying from 2.0% during 2010–2020. The growth rates required for fruits and vegetables is a little higher than cereals. Higher growth rates are estimated to be required for fish, fruits, meat, and milk. This is because demands for these items have been expected to be higher with rising income levels.

8.4.2 Future Scenario and Challenges

The vision BRRI was prepared to be materialized through a set of plans. But there are lot of challenges like decreasing rice coverage at the rate of 0.4% year, population pressure, increasing climatic adversaries, decreasing soil fertility, insufficient mechanization, labour crisis, rice market crisis, the crisis of water, etc.

If the trend of rice coverage continues to decrease at the rate mentioned above and the current national rice yield remains unchanged (average clean rice yield 3.17t per ha), the country would have to suffer from 16.1 MT production deficit depending on the remaining rice area of 9.8 MHa. The requirement (excluding surplus) would be 13.5 MT by 2050 (Kabir et al., 2015).

It is hard to address all these challenges individually because they are interlinked to each other. BRRI visionary team has planned to address these challenges through improving the genetic gain, reducing the yield gap, and reducing the adoption lag period (Kabir et al., 2015). Let us look at the challenges further listed by Kabir et al., (2015).

8.4.2.1 Improving Genetic Gain

It is possible to attain 2.7 MT of surplus rice production by 2050, provided the genetic yield potential could be maintained 0.044 ton per ha per year. It means that the current level of clean rice yield is to be elevated from 3.17 tonnes per hectare to 4.82 tonnes per hectare.

8.4.2.2 Yield Gap

If the existing 20% yield gap could be reduced by 1.135% per year, there would be 4.8 MT surplus in 2050. To reduce the yield, gap the scientists have a prescription to follow the recommended location-specific cultural practices such use of quality seeds, appropriate cultural management, timely pest management practices, adoption of appropriate mechanization, and maintenance of soil health.

8.4.2.3 Adoption Lag

The most popular BRRI varieties have taken 15–16 years to reach the adoption peak. By this time, there is every possibility of a variety to lose its potentiality yield with respect to the changing environment. However, Kabir et al., (2015) showed that the shortening (if possible) the lag period from 16 years to 5 years or 10 years might result in 2.1 MT and 4.3 MT, surplus, respectively, in 2050. Therefore, faster dissemination is desirable by any means to achieve the goal. BRRI is in progress with SMART technology towards food security through SMART dissemination, where SMART stands for Specific, Measurable, Achievable, Relevant, and Time-bound.

As per the study by Kabir et al. (2015), BRRI visionary teams have some more recommendations to overcome the challenges as:

- a Net cropped area to be guaranteed minimum 6.29 M ha in 2050, given the expected national clean rice yield of 5.0 t ha.
- b Crop policy planning must be done keeping the limitation that cropping intensity cannot be increased beyond 221%.
- c Gradual shifting of 15% irrigated culture to upland culture of rice.
- d Monitoring and forecasting of any kind of climatic adversaries must be available to the farmers.
- e Efficient planning to utilize sweet water (when and where available) in the southwestern belt of the country.
- f Establishment of efficient rice marketing system.
- g Hundred per cent mechanization should be targeted from planting to seed processing and storage.
- h Develop rice varieties caring the nutraceutical aspects of rice and rice products.
- i Establish a protocol to maintain rice grain quality.

8.4.2.4 Investment in Rice Research

Agricultural GDP was US$23,512 million in total in 2018 and national allocation in agriculture was 6.84% of the value of agricultural output. Although the trend of investment in agricultural research has been increasing compared to agricultural GDP and in real value terms, the increase has been on a small scale. In 2001, the government allocated about 66% of its agricultural expenditures in research in 2008, which declined to 1.6% in 2009 (BBS various year). Similarly, the share of public research expenditures in Agricultural GDP of 0.23% in 2000–01 slightly increased to 0.26% in 2009. This current share of public research expenditures is very low relative to the investment of 0.6% on average in developing countries and 2.35% in developed countries. During the last decade, one of the principal reasons for fluctuation in agricultural research expenditure was that it depended on its current (sectoral) demand in the country.

The budget for rice research depends on the total amount of institutional demand received annually from the government budget and quality of the research proposals submitted by researchers within the organization. The current budget allocated to rice research is comparatively low, which has also been varied to a large extent in value terms over the years. During 2001–2009, the range of budget for rice sector was about 1–2% of agricultural research budget despite the vital share of rice output (17%) in national agricultural GDP. Rice research receives about 17% of the total food crop research budget despite its share of 95% of the cereal crop output and about 10% of the agricultural GDP (Planning Commission, 2020).

More recent achievements in agriculture have been on development through prioritized agricultural research and force extension of new technologies that are economically viable as well as ecologically sound. Many challenges are remaining: to develop technology choices, face agro-ecological conditions and market demand, soil health management, enhancement of water conservation, quality and affordability of inputs, credit and insurance (seventh five-year plan, 2016).

In other words, agricultural research has not been provided adequate allocation of budget. This largely resulted in the "brain-drain" of trained professionals who migrated to research centres overseas. This trend might be dropped by increasing substantial allocation in research and extension as a percentage of agricultural GDP from its present allocation level of around 1.5%. Research investment needs to increase to a considerable level to facilitate lab, infrastructure, higher studies, and training opportunities. Incentives to agricultural scientists need to be considered to protect the brain drain and to attract bright students to agriculture education. To generate the demand-led agricultural technologies and scaling up the developed technologies, possible priorities for higher investment and modernized research should be categorized to achieve sustainable productivity (seventh five-year plan, 2016).

8.4.3 Agriculture in the Era of High Growth

It is now clear that Bangladesh, like almost all developing countries, has introduced modern technology into agricultural production during the era of high growth. There are two reasons for this: first, to attain food self-sufficiency for the growing population and second, to increase the supply of raw materials for the newly established industrial sector. The countries representing South Asia, Indonesia, and the Philippines are commonly identified as the cases for the former, and South Korea, Taiwan, Thailand, and Malaysia are regarded as the cases for the latter.

According to a famous Japanese agricultural economist, Professor Hayami, agricultural technology in the era of high growth has been classified into two categories: mechanical technology and biological (or biological-chemical) technology. In general, mechanical technology involves lumpy machinery capital that has labour-saving effects. In contrast, biological technology depends on divisible inputs, such as HYV seeds and chemical fertilizer, and usually geared to increase output per unit of land. As a result, nations have achieved high growth over the last three/four decades in this part of the world via so-called 'green revolution' (Hossain M, 1983).

Bangladesh is not an exception. For example, over the last four decades, the population has doubled; similarly, the rice and cereal production over these years surpassed the population growth and increased by threefold. In other words, overall, agricultural productivity in value-added terms (per worker), out of South Asian four countries (Bangladesh, India, Pakistan, and Sri Lanka), Bangladesh enjoyed the highest productivity.

Productivity increase has contributed mainly to agricultural growth and brought transformation in Bangladesh's agriculture. There exists more room for this. The question remains, however, is high productivity limitless? What are the economic shocks one needs to be careful about to keep growing sustainably? In this respect, one needs to ensure the effective management of agriculture over the transition period between self-sufficiency and high-growth era. Most importantly, it needs to be understood clearly that managing labour market, product/commodity market, and money market for agricultural investment during the transition period to high growth is a different ball game and crucial.

Very briefly, these are illustrated below, taking the South Korean experience in such a transition period. Remember, Korean agriculture in the 1950s and 1960s was experiencing low growth. In retrospect, Sri Lanka was considerably richer than Korea in terms of GDP in PPP terms. Korea had only $150 per capita income in those days. Korea is now an OECD nation. Bangladesh entered the era of moderate to high growth two decades or so back and over the last decade certainly the growth rate has been sustained over 6.5%, which can be regarded as a high trend, given some non-economic shocks to the economy such as political, climate, etc., which affected agriculture adversely since early 2000.

One cannot deny the fact that an information revolution has been compensating all the non-economic shocks to a great extent. The digital Bangladesh is a reality now and has been supporting the economy to sustain a high-growth trend, of course with on again, off again digital disruption. Soon, growth will reach the magic number again in the post-COVID-19 period, 7%. It is now recognized internationally that recent success in Bangladesh economy was due more to poverty reduction, infrastructure development, and high primary school enrolment. Thanks to the effective policy intervention by the incumbent in social safety net, for example, according to WB in 1991, 57% of Bangladesh's population was living below the poverty lines. By 2015, this number came down to below 24%. The nation has achieved MDGs top goal, halving poverty by 2015. As far as the hard-core poor goes, this figure in pre-COVID-19 period hit below 10%. Bangladesh's ascendancy not only restricted within poverty reduction, in sanitation, health, and education, the nation has surpassed the records of all other South Asian nations.

All of these have certainly made a huge contribution to the vast rural economy of Bangladesh. In addition, a huge amount of remittance has been pumping into the rural economy. With all of these, agriculture has come to a stage of high growth. As mentioned earlier, there are some challenges too, keeping high growth sustainable in the future. Most importantly effectively managing three markets: labour, commodity, and money comes to mind. In the transition period, labour supply and demand get imbalanced in the first place due to push and pull factors in the rural economy. New industrial and transportation boom make labour movement from rural to urban centres steady and eventually making a major vacuum in the rural economy. The results can be disastrous for the growers in terms of facing a hike in real agricultural wages. It is already evident now in several regions of Bangladesh.

In the areas of commodity market, generally the price volatility becomes severe in a high-growth economy. Suddenly, middlemen or roadside (mainly highway) traders flourish and this culture eventually turns out to be damaging for the growers due to the unscrupulous behaviour of the middlemen, particularly at the time of harvest. In the transition period, the growers need support from the authority so that no syndicate culture can manipulate commodity prices at the farmgate and market, too. There is an urgent need for taking effective measures for organizing marketing groups for the agricultural producers.

Last, but not least, is the money market. The money market directly and indirectly plays major role in agriculture in terms of making investments in the sector steady. In particular, the investment loan must be available to the growers at the right time and right place without too much red-taps to modernize agriculture; for example, investing in machineries, seed-water-fertilizer technology, etc. In the era of high growth, these are the bread and butter of agriculture. It is important to understand by the relevant authorities without delay, the timing and movement of interest rates at the macro level. While the interest rate subsidy together with other agricultural subsidies currently in place is costly for an economy, a transparent and accountable regime should be established so that an unnecessary drain of the taxpayers' resources can be restricted.

The time has come to understand the difference between protection and liberalization in agriculture in the era of high growth. There is a huge difference between managing a high growth and the growth of a self-sufficiency-led economy. The lessons can be learnt from Korea, Malaysia, and Thailand as those economies in the 1970s and 1980s went through a similar transition that is now being experienced by Bangladesh. To attain sustainable growth, there is no short cut, and the rural economy must be prepared for ripping benefits from rural non-farm areas too (see chapter 7).

8.5 Strategies and Policy Issues for the Future

Section 8.4 above has made some effort to predict agricultural growth and development to 2030, given its performnce over the last 50 years. In commensurate with the growth, expansion, and changes in the agricultural sector, public policies and development strategies have been reformulated substantially and revised effectively to achieve the development goals of Bangladesh agriculture in order to achieving 2030 agenda of UN Sustainable Development Goals (SDGs). Some of the issues are briefly discussed below.

Until recently, the primary goal of the development plans in the agriculture sector was to attain self-sufficiency in food production with special reference to cereal production.

With this aim in mind, HYV rice production was emphasized which led to almost a rice monoculture-based development program at the neglect of other crops. This led to displacement of land under crops like pulses and oilseeds, which had some adverse effect on the nutritional status of food intake.

With growing cereal production to a self-sufficiency level, the question of improving the quality of food deserves attention. Thus, the Fifth Five-Year Plan envisaged the goals of increasing production of more nutritious food crops (Planning Commission, 2000). The new goal thus needs emphasizing both crop and non-crop agricultural diversification. Production of more non-cereal crops has been promoted and more importance to raising the growth rate in the non-crop sectors was given in the Sixth Five-Year Plan. Subsequently, Perspective Plan of 2011 to 2021 emphasized diversification, too. With rising income levels, the need for stimulating growth in the non-crop sector deserves priority to improve the quality of food intake, which was emphasized by the Seventh Five-Year Plan, too. Thus, the goals were focused on the promotion of the fisheries, livestock, and forestry sub-sectors. Considering the questions of equity and poverty eradication, thus the provision of food security also becomes a vital issue. To achieve the goals of agricultural development, several policy measures were taken in recent years:

- Adoption of a national land use policy to rationalize its use with speed. Land area under cultivation is steadily shrinking due to population increase and growing demand in the non-agricultural sectors. A more judicious distribution of land for different purposes can be made to derive optimum returns from land resources. Currently, the government has some strategies on how not to use agricultural land indiscriminately and more strong regulation must be in place. (In this connection, it is unfortunate that an act was passed about a decade ago to stop using certain types of cultivated area for non-agricultural purposes; but it could not be implemented due to lack of enacting its necessary by-laws and other rules and regulations. This should be expedited.)
- Another policy measure relates to land tenure reform to check absentee ownership that adversely affects efficient land use and productivity. *Khas* land distribution should be implemented using a local participatory approach to prevent malpractices in the allocation of these lands.

- To preserve soil fertility and prevent land degradation, appropriate policy measures are needed to ensure judicious use of both organic and chemical fertilizers by proper soil testing, better extension methods, and crop rotation, etc.
- The procurement and distribution of fertilizer has been privatized to ensure competition in their markets. However, policy measures must be taken by the government to ensure quality control of these production inputs.
- Policy measures are needed to improve irrigation practices to economize water use and preserve and sustain water resources.
- In spite of expansion in agricultural credit facilities, the small and marginal farmers are largely bypassed. More effective measures should be taken to provide credit facilities targeted to these groups. In this connection, collaborative programs with NGOs may be undertaken for efficient operation of such programs.
- Further measures should be taken to facilitate crop diversification, improvement in market infrastructure, and promotion of exports.
- Strengthening the public sector R&D in agriculture is extremely important to realize development goals for 2041. In this, connection, GO-NGO, and GO-private sector collaboration may be strengthened further for providing active support and incentives to the NGO/private sector. Investment on R&D has always been found to show high positive returns.
- To sustain a high growth rate, allocations in the development budget should be increased and facilitating measures need to be taken for promoting both the crop and the non-crop sub-sectors of agriculture. Agricultural productivity and efficiency of production must also be improved further in view of increasing competition to be faced by Bangladesh agriculture from the globalization effect.
- To support and stimulate growth in the agriculture sector, the agro-processing industry should also be promoted. The process of mechanization in the sector should be supported. However, in the initial stage, small-scale mechanized equipment should be used to avoid possible adverse effects on farm employment. Necessary infrastructure should be developed within the country to reduce import dependence and to promote employment. The increased capital investment in agriculture would also increase labour productivity.

8.6 Conclusion

In spite of natural, technological, and socio-economic constraints, Bangladesh agriculture has been making good progress. The pace of progress has been quite impressive since the mid-1990s. In this development process, the farmers are playing a vital role. In both the crop and non-crop sub-sectors, they are showing a high degree of resilience and innovation. They have started responding to market forces and the technological changes. They have also learnt to respond to natural calamities by shifting cropping patterns. A process of transformation has started away from purely subsistence agriculture to increasing diversification leading to specialization. The private and the NGO sectors have recently started participating and the scope and volume of their participation are also growing. At this stage, what is needed most for sustaining a healthy growth of the sector is continued, effective, and judicious public support to remove existing constraints for farmers. NGOs and the private sector need to play their due roles in developing the different sub-sectors of the agricultural economy.

Farmers are the key players directly moving the agricultural sector forward. Recognition to their vital role is necessary. Their interests must be protected.

With growing involvement of the private commercial sector and the NGOs in agricultural development activities, necessary regulatory measures are needed to keep their activities on the right track, especially with respect to quality control, removal of market distortions, and other market behavioural practices. The question of maintaining equity must be taken care of. Agricultural policies should be congenial to reduction in rural poverty. Finally, keeping in view the dynamic setting of the Bangladesh agriculture due to the growing globalization process, agricultural development policies in the country should be tuned in such a way as to give priority to areas of comparative advantage. Especially significant agricultural diversification will have to be initiated with an emphasis on high-value crops and non-crop sectors, including increased exports of specialized agricultural products. If these and other necessary conditions can be satisfied, the growth of agriculture in Bangladesh can not only be sustained, but would contribute even higher growth in fulfilling the development agendas of Vision 2041.

References

Abdullah, A. and Q. Shahabuddin (1997), 'Recent Developments in Bangladesh Agriculture', in Sobhan, R. (ed.) *Bangladesh Agriculture in Growth Stagnation? A review of Bangladesh's Development 1996*, Dhaka: Centre for Policy Dialogue and The University Press Limited.

Agricultural Extension Department Reports (2020), (several issues).

Alam S and Planning Commission (2021), Eighth FYP: Crop, Livestock, Fisheries, Forest, Water Resource Management, Safe Food and Nutrition Security, presentation at BAEA virtual seminar, 3 July, Dhaka.

BBS (2019), *Report on Agriculture and Rural Statistics – 2018*, Dhaka: Bangladesh Bureau of Statistics. Statistical Division, Ministry of Planning.

BBS (1999), *Census of Agriculture 1996*. vols 1 and 2, Dhaka: Bangladesh Bureau of Statistics. Statistical Division, Ministry of Planning.

Biswas J., Salam M., and S. Kabir (2020), 'Rice Research Revisited - The Bangladesh Case', in Islam M.M. and H. Moazzem (eds.), *Science and Technology Innovation for a Sustainable Economy*, Switzerland: Springer Nature.

BRRI (2020), BRRI Reports, (several issues)

Diaz, C., M. Hossain. M.L. Rose, S. Marea, and T. Mew (2000), Paper presented in 'Review and Planning Meeting of Seed Health Project', BIDS, Dhaka. Bangladesh.

Hossain. M. and M.L. Bose (2000), 'Growth and Structural Changes in Bangladesh Agriculture: Implications for Strategies and Policies for Sustainable Development', in Mandal, M.A.S. (ed.), *Changing Rural Economy of Bangladesh*, Dhaka: Bangladesh Economic Association.

Husain, A.M.M., M. Hossain, and A. Janaiah (2001), *Hybrid Rice Adoption in Bangladesh: A Socioeconomic Assessment of Farmers' Experiences*, Research Monograph Series 18, Dhaka: BRAC and IRRI.

Hossain, M., Nabi, N., & Iyanatul, I. (2003). *Bangladeshas Vision 2021: Rhetoric or Reality?* Dhaka: University Press Limited (UPL).

Husain, A.M.M. (2003), Bangladesh Agriculture in 2020: Review of Trends and Potentials for Growth, in Hossain M. and others (eds), *Bangladesh's Development Agenda and Vision 2021: Rhetoric or Reality?* Dhaka, Bangladesh: The University Press Limited, pp. 77–90.

Hossain M. (1983), "Quantitative Analysis of Policy Alternatives for Bangladesh's Future Agrarian Development", unpublished doctoral dissertation submitted to University of Western Australia, Perth.

Kabir M.S. and Others (2015), Rice Vision for Bangladesh – 2050 and beyond, Bangladesh *Rice J.* 19(2); 1–18.

Pal, S., R. Tripp, and A. Janaiah (2000), 'Public-Private Interface and Information Flow in the Rice Seed System of Andhra Pradesh, India', Policy Paper 12 (NCAP-DRR- ODI Project) New Delhi: National Centre for Agricultural Economics and Policy Research.

Palmer-Jones, R.W. (1999) 'Slowdown in agricultural growth in Bangladesh: Neither A good description nor a description to give', in Rogly, B. (ed.), *Sonar Bangla'?* Dhaka: The University Press Limited.

Planning Commission (1998), *The Fifth Five Year Plan 1997–2002*, Dhaka: Ministry of Planning, GOB.

Planning Commission (2000), *Mid-term Review of the Fifth Five Year Plan 1997–2002*, Dhaka: Ministry of Planning, GOB

Planning Commission (2020), *Growth Performance of Agriculture Sub-Sector during the 7th FYP (2015–2019)*, Planning Commission, GOB.

Sarkar N.R. and S.M.R. Rahman (2020), 'Red Meat Intake and Nutritional Security - The Bangladesh Case', in Islam M.M. and H. Moazzem (eds.), *Science and Technology Innovation for a Sustainable Economy*, Switzerland: Springer Nature.

9 Green Development in the Era of the Fourth Industrial Revolution: Lessons from the Developed World

Mazharul M Islam

9.1 Introduction

An industrial revolution can be defined as a disruptive leap in the industrial process, a development that produces fundamental changes in the society and the economy (Lasi, 2014). Industrial revolutions over the past three centuries have helped continue the climb in human development that has resulted in dramatic increases in quality of life for billions of people. In each revolution, the technologies, the political systems, and the social institutions, have co-evolved. These have not only changed our lives and economy (dominated by industry and machine manufacturing), but also the outlook of human beings, related to one another, and interacting with the natural world (Schwab, 2018).

The First Industrial Revolution, which started in the mid-18th century, used water and steam power to mechanize production. The Second Industrial Revolution happened in a period between 1870 and 1930, which used electric power to create mass production. The Third used electronics and information technology to automate production. The Fourth Industrial Revolution (I4.0) is building on the digital revolution that has been occurring since the middle of the last century. It is characterized by a fusion of technologies e.g. digital innovations, neurotechnology, biotechnologies, materials science, energy technologies, and so on (Schwab, 2018). Compared to previous industrial revolutions, the Fourth is evolving at an exponential rather than a linear pace.

The impact of the Fourth Industrial Revolution is highly evident during the global pandemic of COVID-19, where we can see a combination of aforementioned technologies. Since the detection of the first patient infected by the novel coronavirus on the 17th November 2019, it has been causing an unprecedented havoc in the entire world. Millions of people all over the world have been infected and died, and all kinds of activities and business had to be postponed for a long period in the name of lockdown. At the beginning, no one had any clue how to face this problem. But with time, people all over the world have learnt how to deal with this devastating issue, thanks to technology. Daily activities have been based on online and virtual technologies. The genetic material of the coronavirus is ribonucleic acid (RNA). The most accurate and widely accepted laboratory method for detecting,

DOI: 10.4324/9781003231912-13

tracking, and studying the coronavirus is the real-time reverse transcription-polymerase chain reaction (RT-PCR). The successful vaccines are based on recombinant deoxyribonucleic acid (DNA) and DNA/RNA technologies.

It is hard to blame the environment or climate change for the emergence of the coronavirus. But it is easy to say that human activities performed for ensuring the development works all over the world (either in developed countries or least developed ones) are not performed in sustainable ways. These play devastating roles in destroying our environment, atmosphere, and ecosystem, and thereby aggravating climate change. These in fact create a lot of known and unknown diseases. The electricity and heat generation processes all over the world remain the major sources of greenhouse gas (GHG) emissions, while the other major sectors that contribute large amounts of CO_2 emissions are transport, manufacturing industry, buildings, and other industrial sectors (Islam, 2020a). Therefore, reducing the carbon emissions from the industrial sectors is an essential element of any low-carbon transformation strategy. In other words, in the era of Fourth Industrial Revolution, the development activities must be performed, considering the green aspects of the environment.

The focus of this chapter is to shed light on the prime sectors in Fourth Industrial Revolution. Here, categorically, the fusion of various technologies and the green development aspects are discussed.

9.2 Innovations in Industrial Revolutions and Benefits

Each Industrial Revolution is often considered as a separate event. But they can be better understood as a series of events building upon innovations of the previous revolution and leading to more advanced forms of production. In Figure 9.1, the

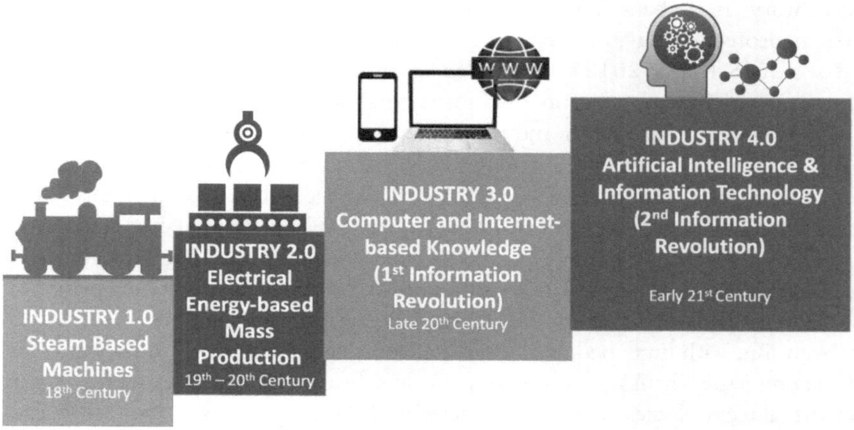

Figure 9.1 Innovations in All Industrial Revolutions.

evolution of Industrial Revolutions is depicted. The First Industrial Revolution started in 1760 with the invention of the steam engine, which allowed the transition from farming and feudal society to a new manufacturing-based civilization. Over the subsequent 100 years, it gave birth to many industries, e.g. the steam engine and railways, mechanization of spinning and weaving, machine tools, and steel manufacturing. During this transition, coal was used as the main energy while trains were the main means of transportation. Textile and steel were the dominant industries in terms of employment and new systems of value production, exchange, and distribution. Although it contributed to the spread of environmental degradation, the First Industrial Revolution succeeded in making the world wealthier. The per capita incomes of the richest countries were rising steadily, and the annual growth rates had risen to 2–3% by 1850 (Crafts, 1987).

In the backdrop of the First Industrial Revolution, there was a new wave of interrelated technologies in the period between 1870 and 1930 that gave rise to the Second Industrial Revolution. In 1900, the invention of the internal combustion engine led to an era of rapid industrialization using oil and electricity to power mass production. The internal combustion engine enabled the automobile and the airplane. This has ultimately motivated the human beings to create the roads and highway infrastructure, air-land-sea port facilities, and manufactured huge numbers of jobs. There were breakthroughs in chemistry and materials science research such as the production of new materials e.g. thermoset plastics, and synthesis of ammonia through the Haber-Bosch process, which paved the way for cheap nitrogen fertilizer (Smil, 2005). The invention and utilization of radio, telephone, television, roads and highway facilities, international air travel, home appliances, and electric lighting demonstrated that the Second Industrial Revolution has ushered in the modern world.

The Third Industrial Revolution started in around 1950 through the revolutionary breakthroughs in electronics, information technology, and digital computing. It was not due to the existence of digital technologies only, but also to the ways in which it changed the structure of our economic and social systems by the implementation of electronics and information technology to automate production. The ability to automate productions (by storing, processing, and transmitting information in digital form) has reformatted almost every industry, and dramatically changed the working and social lives of people. The aggregate impact of these three industrial revolutions has been an incredible increase in wealth and opportunity: today's Organisation for Economic Co-operation and Development (OECD) countries have per capita incomes around 30 to 100 times higher than their equivalents in 1800 (McCloskey, 2016).

Now the Fourth Industrial Revolution is building on the Third, the digital revolution that has been occurring since the middle of the last century. It has diminished the borders among the physical, digital, and biological spheres, and has connected people and technology (Petrillo, 2018). The possibilities of connecting people by mobile devices and online platforms are unlimited and unprecedented. These possibilities have been multiplied by emerging technology breakthroughs in fields including big data, artificial intelligence, machine learning and robotics, quantum computing, the Internet of Things, cyber security, virtual and augmented reality, integration, simulation, cloud computing, additive manufacturing, autonomous vehicles, and 3-D printing (Petrillo, 2018). Industry 4.0 covers three fundamental aspects (Petrillo, 2018): 1. Digitization and increased integration of vertical and horizontal value chains, 2. Digitization of product and service offerings, and 3. Introduction of innovative digital business models (Petrillo, 2018). We are now confronted with a future where digital agents and actors will cross the boundary between software and artifact, inspire new functional capabilities, and even move independently among us (Schwab, 2018). The main nine technologies that drive the digital innovation within the I 4.0 are depicted in Figure 9.2. Details of these can be found elsewhere (Schwab, 2018, Petrillo, 2018, OECD, 2016, Gillath, 2021, Boden, 2017).

Other technologies that have made the Fourth Industrial Revolution a reality are additive manufacturing, neurotechnology, biotechnologies, materials science, and energy technologies (Schwab, 2018). With a fusion of all these technologies, the Fourth Industrial Revolution has been the most powerful driver of wealth and increased wellbeing for human kinds. People around the world have the opportunity to enjoy more freedom, better health and longer life span, higher levels of education, more economic security, and more opportunities to live lives. Since the First Industrial Revolution, the average real income per person in OECD economies has increased around 2,900% (McCloskey, 2016).

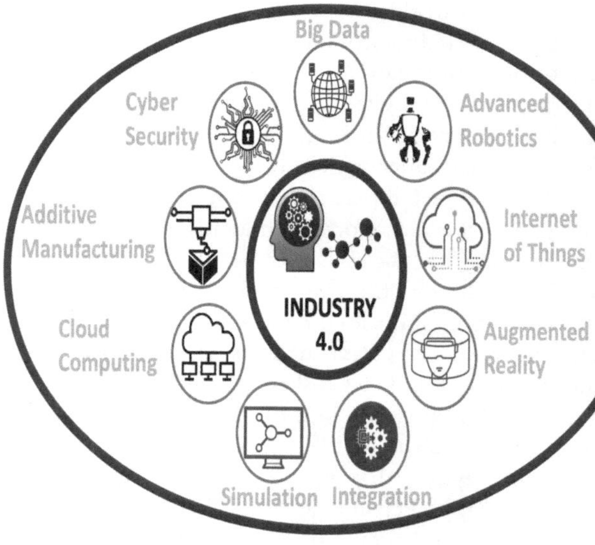

Figure 9.2 Nine Innovative Technologies within the Fourth IR.

9.3 Fourth Industrial Revolution in the Post-COVID Era

During the global pandemic of COVID-19, we have observed a combination of digital technologies with biotechnology. The invention of practical method for DNA sequencing by Frederick Sanger in 1977 has revolutionized biotechnology (Sanger, 1977). Currently, the modern biotechnology is boosted by the combination of DNA sequencing, DNA synthesis, and DNA editing technologies (Marma, 2020), as depicted in Figure 9.3. A fusion of these technologies with other digital innovations such as artificial intelligence, machine learning, robotics, IoT, etc. has enabled people to solve any known or unknown problem. Biotechnology plays key roles in medicine, agriculture, and industry. Biotechnology contributes to the progress and success of medicine in the following areas (Ma, 2021): (a) providing new reagents, new methods and new drugs for the prevention, diagnosis and treatment of disease; (b) providing new materials for medical research that advance our understanding of physiology, immunology, pathology of diseases, and pharmacology of drugs, which in turn help in the development of new drugs, new vaccines, and new treatments; (c) making it possible to personalize medicine and to cure by gene therapy those diseases that are caused by defective or mutated genes; and (d) making it possible to produce new biomaterials for treatment and transplantation that replace dysfunctional tissues and organs in the body. In agriculture, biotechnology is generating crops that produce high yields and need fewer inputs, crops that need fewer applications of pesticides, and crops with enhanced nutrition profiles (Ma, 2021). The biotech industry is now widely distributed into sectors that include biopharma, industrial biotechnology, agricultural biotechnology, food biotechnology, environmental biotechnology, and bioinformatics (Martin, 2021).

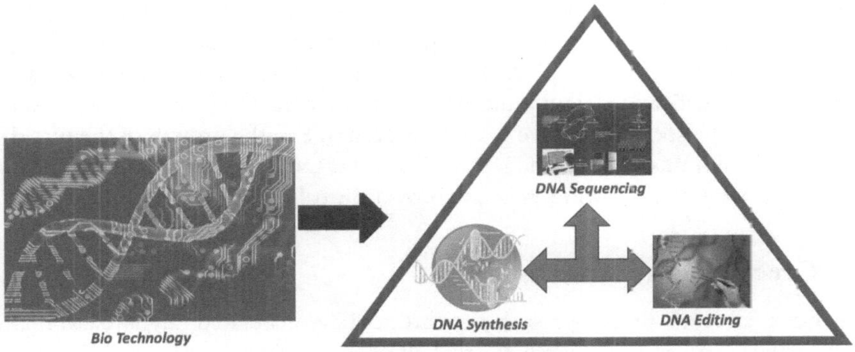

Figure 9.3 Modern Biotechnology (Parts of the figure are adapted from NIH homepage).

In 2019, the market size, number of businesses, and number of employment of worldwide biotechnology was 295 billion USD,; 11,343; and 886,386, respectively (IBISWorld, 2021). Due to the development of treatment and vaccinations for COVID-19 (coronavirus), the demand for the biotech industry has increased and the revenue of this industry has skyrocketed. RT-PCR method is the most widely accepted test globally to detect the COVID-19 virus in the human body. The presence of the virus is detected by identifying its RNA, which is the genetic material of this virus. In the RT-PCR method, the RNA is first converted to DNA. This is a process called "reverse transcription". The resultant DNA is copied/replicated millions of times and measured in real time, which is the key part of the real-time RT-PCR process for detecting the virus. The method is highly sensitive and specific and can deliver a reliable diagnosis.

Recombinant DNA technology plays a vital role in vaccine research, development, and manufacturing (Islam, 2020b). Using this technology, a specific gene of the germ can be combined with other organisms, allowing production of the gene's product. The production of various successful COVID-19 vaccines is based on this technology. For example, the vaccine mRNA-1273 by Moderna – a Boston, USA–based biopharmaceutical company is an RNA-based vaccine. The vaccine BNT162b1/b2, developed by Pfizer and BioNtech, is a chemically modified mRNA vaccine. BNT162b1 encodes an optimized COVID-19 receptor-binding domain (RBD) antigen while BNT161b2 encodes an optimized full-length spike protein antigen. The vaccine AZD1222, jointly developed by Oxford University and AstraZeneca, is a genetically engineered adenovirus. This virus is related to the virus that can cause colds and fevers. This germ carries the gene coding of the spike glycoprotein of the COVID-19 virus. Spike glycoprotein is usually found on the surface of COVID-19 virus and plays an essential role in the infection pathway. The vaccine Ad5-nCoV – by CanSino Biologics, China – is also a recombinant adenovirus.

It is expected that the biotechnology sector will achieve a steady increase in the next five years due to increases in research and development (R&D) expenditures in addition to broader macroeconomic and demographic trends, such as an aging population and the almost universally growing global economy (IBISWorld, 2021). Demographic changes, increase in life expectancy, changes in disease patterns, social globalization, significant increase in the access to health services, and emergence of the social state have played a crucial role in the growth of the world pharmaceutical industry (Martin, 2021). The total trade volume of the pharmaceutical industry in the world has been above 1.35 trillion USD (Martin, 2021).

9.4 Green Energy Development

The industrial revolutions for last three centuries have generated huge wealth that is unevenly spread among people: nearly half of the world's wealth is held by just 1.1% of the world's population (Deshmukh, 2021). This has come at a significant cost to Earth's natural systems. Today, more than 50% of the world's 7.4 billion inhabitants live in urban areas (Hanberry, 2022). Rapid and unplanned industrialization, rapid growth of urbanization, unplanned construction activities, and uncontrolled population growth have created mismanagement of urban services and general environmental quality deterioration. There is huge emission of a range of toxic effluents directly into the soil, air, and water. The enormous demands on urban utility services, waste disposal, transports, social services, etc. have generated tremendous pressure on the geo-environment. The water, air, biodiversity, forests, and oceans are all under increasing stress and the climate has been in severe torture. The observed increased concentration of certain trace gases, especially carbon dioxide, methane, chlorofluorocarbons (CFCs), and nitrous oxide, known as greenhouse gases (GHGs), in the atmosphere and their capability of affecting the surface climate of the earth, have drawn the global concern. The emission of these trace gases is widely believed to be of human activities or anthropogenic causes. One of the major causes of global warming is the excessive accumulation of CO_2 into the atmosphere, as CO_2 is the source of 76% emission globally in 2019 (Yoro, 2020). The emission of CO_2 (and other GHGs) is closely correlated with the development activities in the areas of energy, transportation, building, and other industrial sectors (Islam, 2020a). It is observed that the global CO_2 emissions have risen 165-fold since the start of the Second Industrial Revolution (IEA, 2020). As of 2019 (see Figure 9.4), the electricity and heat generation processes all over the world remain the major sources of CO_2 emissions (38.8%), followed by transport (26.56%), industrial sectors (24.76%), and buildings 98.07%). Agricultural sectors contribute only 1.81% of the global total (Yoro, 2020). If the emission occurs at the current rate, there is a great risk that the world will be between 4°C and 6°C warmer by 2100.

If total CO_2 emissions are to fall to net zero in 2050, the Intergovernmental Panel on Climate Change (IPCC) Special Report on Global Warming of 1.5°C (IPCC, 2018) indicates that energy sector and industrial process CO_2 emissions would need to fall to around 16.8–22.1 Gt in 2030, with a median value of 20.1 Gt (IPCC, 2018). The IPCC indicates that this would provide a pathway towards a 50% chance of limiting the global average surface temperature rise to

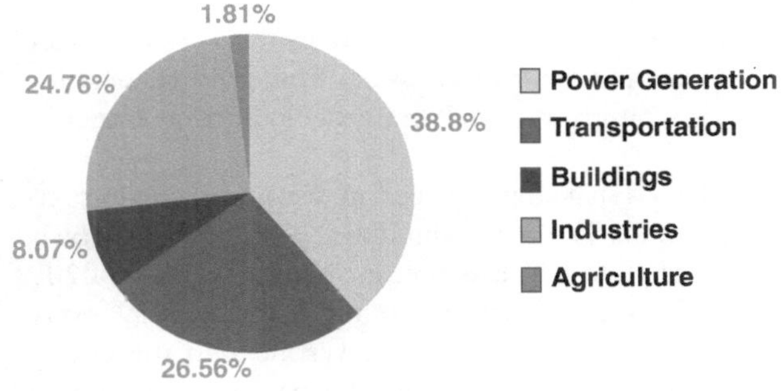

Figure 9.4 Updated Global CO_2 Emissions by Sector in 2019 (data obtained from Ref (Yoro, 2020)).

1.5°C without a large level of net negative emissions globally. This can be performed in two ways:

a It is observed that the current global CO_2 emissions from the combustion of fossil fuel alone is about 58.7 billion tonnes in 2019, which is estimated as about 80% of the global energy demand. Therefore, the first approach should be replacing all the fossil fuel-based energy production by renewable green energy sources.
b An important way for mitigating the excessive amount of CO_2 is to carbon capture, storage, and utilization (CCSU) (Yoro, 2020). CO_2 can be captured from large stationary point sources (e.g. coal or gas-fired power plants) and can be deposited in a safe storage location where it will not gain access back to the atmosphere (Nocito, 2020). Most importantly, the stored CO_2 can be transformed into valuable chemicals, such as hydrocarbon fuels for utilization.

9.4.1 Energy Mix

The energy mix is defined as the mixed sources of energy such as coal, gas, oil, nuclear, and renewables. Green energy represents all the clean sources of power that are generated using the natural source of energy available on the planet, mainly including biomass, solar power, wind power, hydropower, and geothermal energy (Bhowmik, 2017). The data on the global energy demand and power sectors for the last 20 years and the next 20 years based on the International Energy Agency (IEA) Sustainable Recovery Plan and the Sustainable Development Scenario (SDS) are provided in Table 9.1 and Table 9.2, respectively (IEA, 2020). Currently, fossil fuels still dominate the global energy system, accounting for more than 80% of the total energy supply (IEA, 2020). Global primary energy demand grew by 2.3% in 2018, its largest annual increase since 2010. It showed a similar picture for the year 2019. Despite the fact that growth in renewables has outpaced growth in all other forms of energy since 2010, the share of fossil fuels in global primary energy demand remained above 80% until 2019. The power sector was responsible for around 13.7 Gt CO_2 emissions in 2019 (Table 9.2) and is the largest single CO_2-emitting sector worldwide today (IEA, 2020). Electricity demand is set to increase substantially over the next ten years and reducing emissions from power generation is a central component of most countries' overall emissions reduction strategies (IEA, 2020).

After that period, COVID-19 has shaken up the energy sector, leaving impacts that will be felt for years to come. The most significant disruption has been observed for the most emissions-intensive fuels, i.e. coal and oil (IEA, 2020). The global energy demand in 2020 has fallen by around 5% from 2019 levels; CO_2 emissions have fallen by around 7%; and total investment in the energy sector has dropped by 18% (IEA, 2020). The demand for passenger aviation in 2020 has fallen by about 40%, and oil use for cars was down by 8%. Global energy demand may rebound to its pre-crisis level in early 2023, but this may delay until

Table 9.1 Global total energy demand (Mtoe) by fuel and scenario for past 20 years and for the next 20 years based on the International Energy Agency (IEA) Sustainable Recovery Plan, the Sustainable Development Scenario (SDS) (IEA, 2020)

	2000	*2010*	*2018*	*2019*	*2025*	*2030*	*2040*
Coal	2317	3650	3839	3775	2939	2243	1295
Oil	3665	4117	4496	4525	4253	3963	3006
Natural Gas	2083	2755	3284	3340	3450	3312	2943
Nuclear	675	719	707	727	764	895	1126
Hydro	225	296	362	370	416	475	575
Bioenergy	374	1205	1327	1354	1341	1283	1682
Other Renewables	60	110	286	314	691	1207	2393
Total	10,037	12,852	14,300	14,406	13,853	13,378	13,020
Fossil Fuel Share	80%	82%	81.25%	80.80%	76.80%	71.15%	55.64%
CO_2 Emission (Gt)	23.1	30.42	33.28	33.29	29	24.26	14.7

Table 9.2 Global energy demand (Mtoe) by fuel and scenario for power sectors (IEA, 2020)

	2010	*2018*	*2019*	*2025*	*2030*	*2040*
Coal	2171	2459	2414	1713	1180	494
Oil	265	203	203	134	92	59
Natural Gas	1114	1304	1332	1367	1233	884
Nuclear	719	707	727	764	895	1126
Hydro	296	362	370	416	475	575
Bioenergy	121	213	221	310	400	641
Other Renewables	89	237	263	590	1052	2128
Total	4775	5486	5532	5293	5326	5907
Fossil Fuel Share	74.35%	72.29%	71.14%	60.72%	47.03%	24.33%
CO_2 Emission (Gt)	12.39	13.82	13.7	10.66	7.79	3.19

2025 in the event of a prolonged pandemic and deeper slump. The worst effects are felt among the most vulnerable parts of the world. The energy mix over the next few years will be shaped by the impact of the pandemic.

Due to the uncertainty over the duration of the pandemic and its economic and social impacts, the IEA World Energy Outlook (WEO) examines various policy responses to open up a wide range of possible energy futures (IEA, 2020). By considering different assumptions about these key unknowns, along with the latest energy market data and a dynamic representation of energy technologies, this Outlook examines and explores different pathways out of the COVID-19 crisis. Within the Sustainable Recovery Plan, there was an increased annual investment in clean energy infrastructure by $1 trillion above historic levels in the three years from 2021 to 2023. It takes account of the circumstances of individual countries as well as existing energy project pipelines and current market conditions. In the Sustainable Development Scenario (SDS), a surge in clean energy policies and investment puts the energy system on track to achieve sustainable energy objectives in full, including the Paris Agreement, energy access, and air quality goals (IEA, 2020). Full implementation of the Sustainable Recovery Plan would kick-start an accelerated programme of spending on clean energy technologies in the SDS that extends beyond the Plan's initial three-year period (IEA, 2020).

The new Net Zero Emissions by 2050 case (NZE2050) extends the SDS analysis. The SDS sees many advanced economies reaching net zero emissions by 2050 at the latest, and puts the world on track for net zero emissions by 2070. The economic damage brought about by the pandemic has created an opportunity to support economic growth and jobs while boosting investment in clean energy technologies. Renewables will grow rapidly in the next 20 years and, therefore, the dependence on fossil fuels will drop drastically (see Tables 9.1 and 9.2).

Although there is a huge development in the renewable sectors, the fossil fuels remain the major sources of total generated electricity in 2019, with a staggering 63% (Table 9.3). Within the Sustainable Development Scenario (SDS), from 2025 onwards, the renewables account for a greater share of generation than coal, with hydropower remaining the largest low-carbon source of electricity. By 2040, wind gets close to equalling its share on the back of a rapidly expanding offshore wind market. By the early 2030s, the installed capacity of solar PV overtakes coal and by 2040 its share of generation rises above 10%. The global electricity generation grows by around 30% (11,832 terawatt-hours [TWh]) between 2019 and 2040 (Table 9.3). In 2040, the renewables constitute the major portion (72%) of the total generation by 2040 due to the sharp increase in hydro, wind, and solar photovoltaics (PV). The fossil fuels, such as coal, oil, and gas provide only 5%, 0.4%, and 11.7% of total generated electricity indicating a drastic reduction of CO_2 emission by 2040. In general, the advance of renewable sources of generation as well as the contribution of nuclear power are strong in the SDS and NZE2050.

The global pandemic has opened another avenue: a combination of digital innovations and energy generation. As most renewable energy sources can be remotely controlled and digitally intelligent, there is a possibility to combine the Internet of Things (IoT) with renewable energy generation. It allows technicians to use cloud-based controllers to deploy distributed generation based on different stages of electricity demand (Panda, 2021). Besides, based on sensors' perception of ambient environment information such as light intensity and wind speed, power generation equipment can also be started and stopped automatically, greatly improving energy efficiency and equipment life (Aman, 2021).

The pace of change in the electricity sector puts an additional premium on a robust grid and its flexibility to generate, transmit, distribute, and consume electricity to the end users. Energy storage systems play an increasingly vital role in ensuring the flexible operation of power systems both for fossil fuel-based and renewable energy sectors.

9.4.2 Energy Storage

Energy storage is an essential unit that stores electric energy. Energy storage devices are charged when they adsorb energy, either directly from energy sources or indirectly from the electricity grid. They discharge as they deliver the stored energy back into the grid. The charge and discharge processes normally require power conversion devices to transform electrical energy (AC or DC) into different forms of chemical, mechanical, thermal, or electrochemical energy. Accordingly, the energy storage systems are divided into four different classes (Olabi, 2021), as depicted in Figure 9.5.

The **chemical storage systems** include hydrogen, biofuels, and saturated natural gas (SNG) systems. These systems are integral parts of green energy technology. The SNG is the product of a very recent technology called power to

Table 9.3 Global electricity generation (TWh) within Sustainable Development Scenario (SDS) (IEA, 2020)

	2000	*2010*	*2018*	*2019*	*2025*	*2030*	*2040*
Coal	5995	8662	10,160	9849	7101	4864	1951
Oil	1207	970	786	785	502	326	187
Natural Gas	2760	4842	6150	6317	7007	6465	4550
Nuclear	2591	2756	2710	2789	2930	3435	4320
Renewables	2862	4260	6778	7167	11,305	16,345	27,737
Hydro		3448	4214	4305	4839	5521	6690
Bioenergy		367	635	667	991	1282	2155
Wind		342	1273	1423	2952	4770	8680
Geothermal		68	89	92	158	293	553
Solar PV		32	554	665	2316	4315	8799
CSP		2	11	15	44	149	788
Marine		1	1	1	4	14	70
Total	15,436	21,524	26,619	26,942	28,874	31,465	38,774

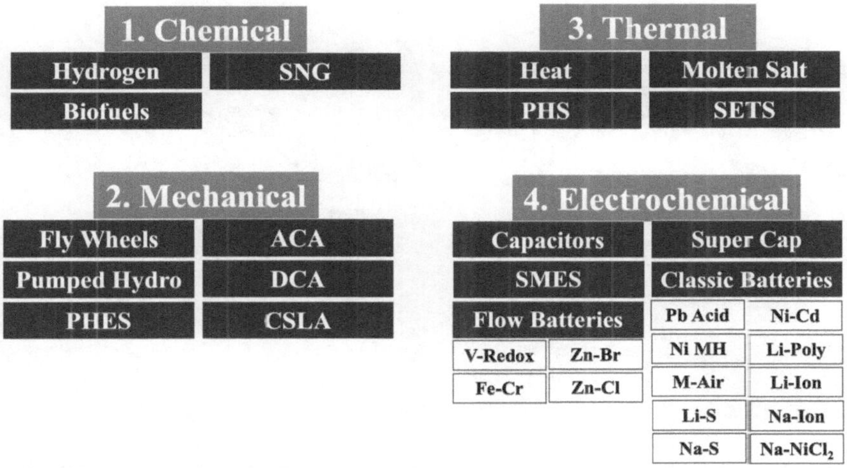

Figure 9.5 Classification of the Energy Storage Systems.

gas (PtG) (Islam, 2020a). The SNG storage system is termed one of the largest energy storage systems. Storage of energy using **mechanical energy storage** systems is conducted by transforming the energy into both mechanical and electrical energy. During off-peak when demand is low, the electrical energy is converted to mechanical energy via the principle of potential, kinetic, or even pressurized gas (Olabi, 2021). The common types of **mechanical energy storage** systems are flywheels, pumped hydro storage (PHS), pumped heat electrical storage (PHES), adiabatic compressed air (ACA), diabatic compressed air (DCA), compressed storage of liquid air (CSLA), and gravity energy storage systems (GES). **Thermal energy storage** application is utilized by storing heat or cold storage medium using different conditions, namely temperature, place, and power (Cabeza, 2015). Hot water can hold about 3.5 times as much energy by volume as natural gas at atmospheric pressure and temperature. There are numerous mechanisms for producing heat, including direct capture of solar energy, biomass combustion, the trapping of geothermal energy, and, if all else fails, burning fossil fuels. The existing thermal energy storage systems are hot water, phase change materials (PCM), molten salt, thermal oil, and smart electrical thermal storage (SETS). The **electrochemical storage systems** consist of purely electrical systems, including capacitors, supercapacitors, superconducting magnetic energy storage (SMES), and batteries, including the classical batteries and flow batteries, as shown in Figure 9.5. Some technologies (such as pumped hydro storage, SNGs, compressed air energy storage, hydrogen, and thermal storage) are characterized by their ability to store energy over time (several hours/days). Others, e.g. batteries and flywheels, are characterized by their ability to deliver power very fast.

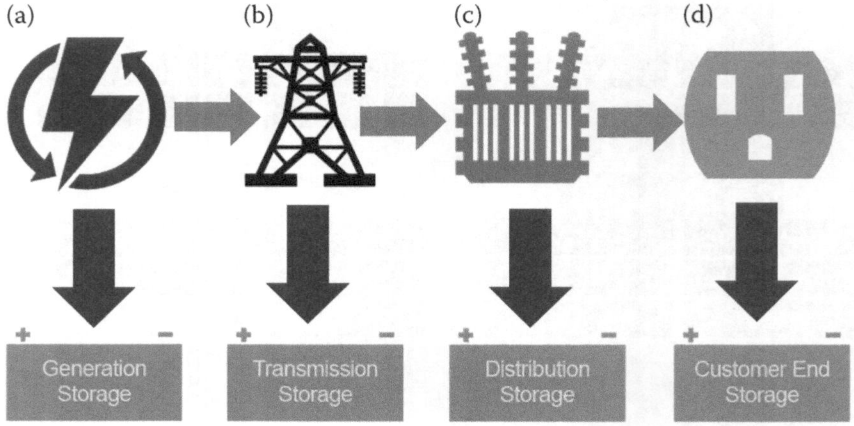

Figure 9.6 Utilization of Energy Storage at Electricity Grid. (a) Electricity Generation, (b) Transmission, (c) Distribution, and (d) Consumption (This figure is adapted from the presentation slides of "Energy Storage for Federal Installations by John Schaaf, August, 2015 at Energy Exchange: Federal Sustainability for the Next Decade": https://slideplayer.com/slide/6840134/).

Energy storage systems are designed to sustain unforeseen occurrences during peak and off-peak times. The grid is inefficient and is being used differently. As shown in Figure 9.6, a grid is a combination of energy generation (Figure 9.6(a)), transmission (Figure 9.6(b)), distribution (Figure 9.6(c)), and consumption (Figure 9.6(d)). The energy is generated at high voltage (~ 20 kV) and it must be stored. The generated energy is transmitted at very high voltage (70 kV–350 kV); therefore, it requires transmission storage. Energy is distributed at step-down voltage through a distribution line below 7 kV, where distribution storage is required. Finally, the energy is consumed at domestic or industrial levels at very lower voltage. As all electricity generated is utilized, storing the excess energy during off-peak times will significantly improve the system efficiency, as well as sustain varying power demands at different times of the day.

Storage systems are essential for the proper utilization of energy generated by renewable sources such as off-shore and on-shore wind and solar power. Subject to the time and season of the year, these sources are intermittent. It is therefore important to store the excess energy when demand is low and then the stored energy can be released when demand is high. Designing any distribution grid will require the integration of energy storage technologies. Another great advantage of the energy storage system is the decarbonization of gas sectors, such as saturated natural gas (SNG) which is the integral part of Power to Gas (PtG) sector (Islam, 2020a). More detail about decarbonization of energy sectors is provided in the next section.

9.4.3 Carbon Capture, Storage, and Utilization/Decarbonization

CO_2 is the major source of global warming. As discussed previously, the most effective option to mitigate CO_2 emission is the switching from fossil fuel-based energy to renewable energy sources. Other options are capturing and storing CO_2 (CCS) and capturing and utilization of generated CO_2 (CCU) to produce valuable products (Ravanchi, 2021, Garba, 2021, Alcasabas, 2021).

In Figure 9.7, various routes within the CCS and CCU options are presented. CO_2 capture is at the heart of both CCS and CCU strategies. The emitted CO_2 can be captured from various sources e.g. energy sectors and industrial processes, by different capturing methods depending on the source of emission. Common CO_2 capture technologies are known as pre-combustion capture, post-combustion capture, and oxy-fuel combustion (Cuéllar-Franca, 2015). The captured CO_2 is separated by various methods such as physical or chemical absorption, membrane separation, adsorption, and cryogenic distillation (Ravanchi, 2020). CCS technologies typically involve large water consumption during their energy-intensive capture process. CO_2 can be stored in geological formations without any practical use, such as deep saline aquifers, un-mineable coal beds, deep basalt rock formations, or in depleted oil and gas reservoirs (Leung, 2014). A good geological storage site can hold tens of millions of tonnes of CO_2, trapped for hundreds of years by physical and chemical means. Deep-ocean storage is another option of CCS, but one has to be very careful about potential impacts on ocean acidification and eutrophication (Bisinella, 2021). Industrial carbon capture and storage (CCS) allows for the removal of 90–99% of CO_2 emissions from an industrial plant and, thereby, if deployed, it could have a high potential to make deep reductions in industrial GHG emissions.

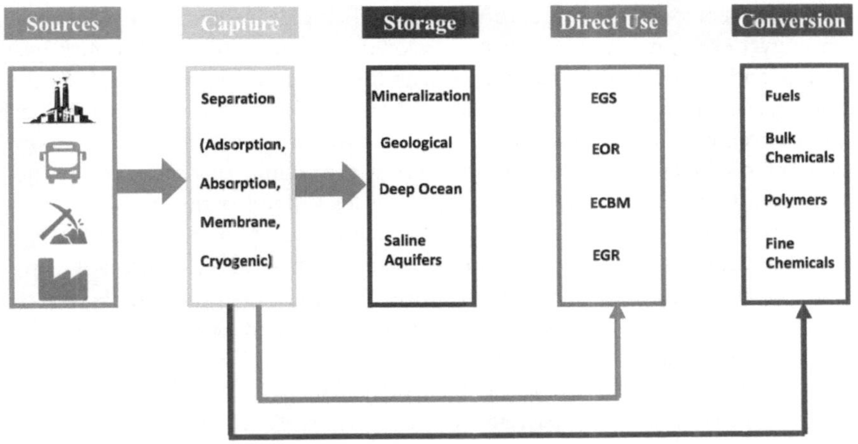

Figure 9.7 Different Routes for CCS and CCU (adapted from Ravanchi, 2021).

There are two possibilities within a CO_2 capture and utilization (CCU) strategy: direct (unconverted) use of CO_2 and conversion of CO_2 into important chemicals, as shown in Figure 9.7. The most notable direct utilizations of CO_2 are for carbonated drinks, fire extinguisher, refrigerant, dry ice, solvent, process fluid, and welding medium (Ravanchi, 2021). The large-scale industrial examples for direct utilization of CO_2 are enhanced geothermal systems (EGS), enhanced gas recovery (EGR), enhanced coal-bed methane recovery (ECBM), and enhanced oil recovery (EOR) (Muradov, 2014).

Carbon dioxide is an abundant C_1 building block that can be used as a renewable and non-toxic feedstock for the synthesis of different categories of chemicals (Ravanchi, 2020). CO_2 can be converted into important materials such as fuels, chemicals, and building materials (Alcasabas, 2021a, Alcasabas, 2021b). The list of products is huge, and it varies due to route of conversion processes. Here, only the names of various routes for CO_2 conversion to valuable products are mentioned. These are biological routes, catalytic conversion, electrocatalytic conversion, photochemical conversion, photoelectrochemical conversion, plasma technology, and microbial electro-synthetic routes (Alcasabas, 2021a, Alcasabas, 2021b). The main difference between CCS and CCU is the destination of the captured CO_2: in CCS it is sent to a suitable place for long-term storage while in CCU it is changed into different products. The main advantage of CCU is the production of many important fuels and chemicals, which makes CCU an integral part of future sustainable strategy within the circular economy.

9.5 Sustainable Strategy for Development: Lessons for Bangladesh

The invention, commercialization, widespread adoption, and use of technological innovations during all these industrial revolutions have been the most powerful drivers of wealth and increased wellbeing. However, the focus on technology development and industrial growth has increased greenhouse gas emissions and further diminished the availability of natural resources. The new technologies and practices should be used in line with two following objectives: (i) the full value of used products should be recovered for reaching a maximum of economic efficiency, and (ii) by recovering this value, the pressure on the nature should be lowered. These two objectives lead together to the rising trend of conversion from the linear economy approach to the circular economy (CE). The linear economy is based on the so-called "take-make-use-disposal" approach, as shown in Figure 9.8(a). In terms of consumer products, the waste materials after use are discarded into the environment and thereby polluting it. This is the root cause of global issues, like waste disposal in natural areas, resource scarcity, and climate change. On the other hand, CE is based on a "make-use-reuse-repair-recycle" approach in a circular way, as shown in Figure 9.8(b). A circular economy designs out waste and pollution by reusing and repurposing products and materials that would normally be discarded into the environment.

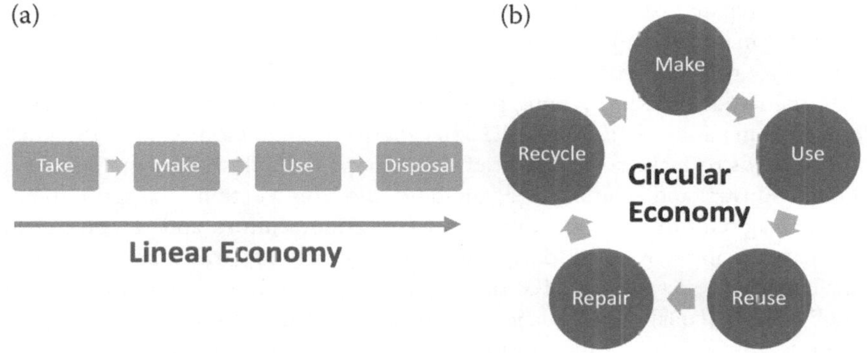

Figure 9.8 Schematic Representation of Linear Economy (a) and Circular Economy (b).

By this way, CE contributes to meet the requirements of the social, economic, and environmental sustainable development (de Souza Junior, 2020, Kirchherr, 2019, Dantas, 2021).

The convergence and combination between the Fourth Industrial Revolution and the Circular Economy would promote the minimization of resource consumption, waste generation, and emissions, while still ensuring socioeconomic development. It will link the groundbreaking technologies to system-wide shifts in our economic and industrial models (Dantas, 2021). This kind of combination could be a proper strategy for the ongoing development policies for a fast-developing country like Bangladesh.

Through two major programs, namely Millennium Development Goals (MDGs: 2000–15) and Sustainable Development Goals (SDGs: 2016–2030), the United Nations has been attempting to address the problems of climate change and building sustainable economies involving its member nations. Bangladesh has met all the goals within MDGs in time and has made laudable progress on many aspects of SDGs. Due to extraordinary achievements in the economic and social fronts, according to the World Bank's definition of prosperity, Bangladesh has shifted from being a "low-income" to a "middle-income" country (United Nations Committee for Development Policy announced in March, 2018) (Islam, 2020c). This nation is recognized now as a "Role Model of Development" all over the world. Bangladesh has stepped into a new journey as it qualified to graduate into a developing nation from a Least Developed Country (LDC) in 2021, after 45 years. The United Nations Committee for Development Policy (UN CDP) recommended the graduation in its final evaluation. It gave five years to prepare for the graduation to a developing country. Hence, the decision will come into effect on November 24, 2026. The policymakers of the country now have now an optimistic vision for transforming Bangladesh into a "developed" nation by 2041. To achieve this goal, the country needs to make a sustainable development strategy in a combination of I4.0 and

CE. Taking lessons from the developed nations, the development paradigm should be prepared based on green technologies. The particular focus should be to use the materials and resources more efficiently to reduce the pressure on natural resources and to create sustainable growth and jobs. The country must utilize the large number of young populations. The target should be to achieve Net Zero Emissions by 2050 (NZE2050) and to halt the biodiversity loss. The country needs to make sustainable development in the following major sectors: energy, industry and manufacture, building and construction, transportation, food and agriculture, public health, and education, culture and design. The important driving forces for developing these sectors are waste and resource management, reduction of GHG, development of hi-tech for being able to accomplish I4.0, collaborations and cooperation in various cross sectors, new economic growth, and creation of jobs. The government has the decisive role as it possesses the unique capacities to act and to guide the actions for the country. It can lead the way by providing the strategic vision, the stimulation to innovation, the incentives for inhabitants, the policy signals, and the public finance that catalyzes action by private sectors, and the support for communities where livelihoods are affected by rapid change. It has the responsibility to avoid unintended consequences for the reliability or affordability of supply. Therefore, good governance, democratic practice, and curbing corruption would be also keys for the future success. Our secured and sustainable future is a choice – for us, the people, and for the government.

9.6 Conclusions

The emerging technologies in I4.0 are not merely incremental advances or a prolongation of the Third Industrial Revolution, but they represent entirely new and distinct ways of creating value for organizations and citizens. These technologies provide a huge boost to the intelligence level of machines through continuous data accumulation and analysis. Today, people can continuously produce new information and generate new knowledge, can improve the productivity, and be able to transform modes of production and the relationships between elements of production processes. It has positively influenced our processes of production and transportation of goods and services, ways of communication and collaboration, and the mechanisms of experiencing the world around us. I4.0 has created a new economic form of the "sharing economy", which is not only limited to "online ride-hailing services", but also includes the shared space service (Sun, 2018). Very popular examples are Uber and Airbnb, respectively (Sun, 2018).

There are a variety of challenges originating from the I4.0 to overcome, such as (a) distributing benefits, (b) managing externalities, and (c) ensuring a human-centred future (Schwab, 2018). The technologies are truly disruptive: they could yield greater inequality in labour markets. With the growth of automation, robots, and computers, low-skilled jobs will disappear, and the poor will face tougher challenges. We must overcome the issues regarding cyber security and ethical dilemmas and manage the externalities in terms of the risks and harm that it causes. It must be ensured that the Fourth Industrial Revolution is human-led and human-centred, the emerging technologies empower, rather than determine, all of us as human beings. Human values must be respected in themselves, rather than weighed only in financial terms. To harness the benefits of the Fourth Industrial Revolution, all stakeholders must be part of global technology innovations that are changing the systems and creating extraordinary values in everyone's life.

Over a hundred years ago, Albert Einstein mentioned in a letter that "Technological progress is like an axe in the hands of a pathological criminal". Therefore, we must be more vigilant than ever and bear the huge responsibility to shape new technologies in ways that promote the common good, enhance human dignity, and protect the environment. There is a good chance that the challenges we experience today will only be aggravated, as narrow interests and biased systems further entrench inequalities and compromise the rights of people in every country.

References

Alcasabas, A., Ellis, P.R., Malone, I., Williams, G., and Zalitis, C. (2021), A comparison of different approaches to the conversion of carbon dioxide into useful products: Part I: CO_2 reduction by electrocatalytic, thermocatalytic and biological routes. *Johnson Matthey Technology Review*, 65(2), pp. 180–196.

Alcasabas, A., Ellis, P.R., Malone, I., Williams, G., and Zalitis, C. (2021), A Comparison of different approaches to the conversion of carbon dioxide into useful products: Part II: More routes to CO_2 reduction. *Johnson Matthey Technology Review*, 65(2), pp. 197–206.

Aman, A.H.M., Shaari, N., and Ibrahim, R. (2021), Internet of things energy system: Smart applications, technology advancement, and open issues. *International Journal of Energy Research*, 45(6), pp. 8389–8419.

Bhowmik, C., Bhowmik, S., Ray, A., and Pandey, K.M. (2017), Optimal green energy planning for sustainable development: A review. *Renewable and Sustainable Energy Reviews*, 71, pp. 796–813.

Biotechnological Equipment, 35(sup1), pp. S5–S14.

Bisinella, V., Hulgaard, T., Riber, C., Damgaard, A., and Christensen, T.H. (2021), Environmental assessment of carbon capture and storage (CCS) as a post-treatment technology in waste incineration. *Waste Management*, 128, pp. 99–113

Boden, M., Bryson, J., Caldwell, D., Dautenhahn, K., Edwards, L., Kember, S., Newman, P., Parry, V., Pegman, G., Rodden, T., and Sorrell, T. (2017), Principles of robotics: Regulating robots in the real world. *Connection Science*, 29(2), pp. 124–129.

Cabeza, L.F., Martorell, I., Miró, L., Fernández, A.I., and Barreneche, C. (2015), Introduction to thermal energy storage (TES) systems. *Advances in Thermal Energy Storage Systems*, pp. 1–28. Woodhead Publishing.

Crafts, N.F.R. (1987), Long-term unemployment in Britain in the 1930s. *The Economic History Review*, 40, pp. 418–432.

Cuéllar-Franca, R.M. and Azapagic, A. (2015), Carbon capture, storage and utilisation technologies: A critical analysis and comparison of their life cycle environmental impacts. *Journal of CO_2 Utilization*, 9, pp. 82–102.

Deshmukh, A. (2021), This Simple Chart Reveals the Distribution Of Global Wealth, Visual Capitalist. https://www.visualcapitalist.com/distribution-of-global-wealth-chart/

de Souza Junior, H.R.A., Dantas, T.E.T., Zanghelini, G.M., Cherubini, E., and Soares, S.R. (2020), Measuring the environmental performance of a circular system: Emergy and LCA approach on a recycle polystyrene system. *Science of The Total Environment*, 726, p. 138111.

Dantas, T.E., De-Souza, E.D., Destro, I.R., Hammes, G., Rodriguez, C.M.T., and Soares, S.R., (2021), How the combination of Circular Economy and Industry 4.0 can contribute towards achieving the Sustainable Development Goals. *Sustainable Production and Consumption*, 26, pp. 213–227.

Earth League joining forces." Global Challenges Foundation.

Garba, M.D., Usman, M., Khan, S., Shehzad, F., Galadima, A., Ehsan, M.F., Ghanem, A.S., and Humayun, M., (2021), CO_2 towards fuels: A review of catalytic conversion of carbon dioxide to hydrocarbons. *Journal of Environmental Chemical Engineering*, 9(2), p.104756.

Gillath, O., Ai, T., Branicky, M.S., Keshmiri, S., Davison, R.B., and Spaulding, R., (2021), Attachment and trust in artificial intelligence. *Computers in Human Behavior*, 115, p. 106607.

Hanberry, B.B. (2022), Global population densities, climate change, and the maximum monthly temperature threshold as a potential tipping point for high urban densities. *Ecological Indicators*, 135, p. 108512.

IBISWorld. (2021), World biotechnology industry. Available from: https://www.ibisworld.com/global/market-research-reports/global-biotechnology-industry/.

IEA. (2020), The IEA World Energy Outlook (WEO) 2020. Available from: https://www.iea.org/reports/world-energy-outlook-2020

IPCC. (2018), Special Report on 1.5 degrees: Summary for Policymakers. https://www.ipcc.ch/site/assets/uploads/sites/2/2019/05/SR15_SPM_version_report_LR.pdf.

Islam, M.M., and Hossain, M. (2020c), *Conclusion. In Science and technology Innovation for a Sustainable Economy* (pp. 191–197). Cham: Springer.

Islam, M.M., and Marma, M.S. (2020b), Evolution of vaccinology and vaccines for Covid-19: Where do we stand now? https://www.dhakatribune.com/feature/2020/07/27/evolution-of-vaccinology-and-vaccines-for-covid-19-where-do-we-stand-now

Islam, M.M. (2020a), Power to gas: A green technology for decarbonization of energy sector. In Hossain, M.M., Ahmad, Q.K. and Islam, M., 2020. *Climate Adaptation for a Sustainable Economy: Lessons from Bangladesh, an Emerging Tiger of Asia* (pp. 1–312). Nova Science Publishers. ISBN: 978-1-53616-927-0

Kirchherr, J. and Piscicelli, L. (2019), Towards an education for the circular economy (ECE): five teaching principles and a case study. *Resources, Conservation and Recycling*, 150, p. 104406.

Lasi, H., Fettke, P., Kemper, H.G., Feld, T., and Hoffmann, M., (2014), Industry 4.0. *Business & Information Systems Engineering*, 6(4), pp. 239–242.

Leung, D.Y., Caramanna, G., and Maroto-Valer, M.M. (2014), An overview of current status of carbon dioxide capture and storage technologies. *Renewable and Sustainable Energy Reviews*, 39, pp. 426–443.

Marma, M.S. (2020), Terminator to reversible terminator: Generational shift in DNA sequencing technologies. In *Science and Technology Innovation for a Sustainable Economy* (pp. 43–58). Cham: Springer.

Ma, Q.P. (2021), Biotechnology: Recent Developments, Emerging Trends, and Implications for Business. *Technological Breakthroughs and Future Business Opportunities in Education, Health, and Outer Space*, pp. 112–132.

Martin, D.K., Vicente, O., Beccari, T., Kellermayer, M., Koller, M., Lal, R., Marks, R.S., Marova, I., Mechler, A., Tapaloaga, D., and Žnidaršič-Plazl, P. (2021), A brief overview of global biotechnology. *Biotechnology & Biotechnological Equipment, 35*(sup1), pp. S5-S14.

McCloskey, D. (2016), *Bourgeois Equality*. Chicago: University of Chicago Press.

Muradov, N. (2014), Industrial utilization of CO_2: a win–win solution. In *Liberating Energy from Carbon: Introduction to Decarbonization* (pp. 325–383). New York, NY: Springer.

Nocito, F. and Dibenedetto, A. (2020), Atmospheric CO2 mitigation technologies: carbon capture utilization and storage. *Current Opinion in Green and Sustainable Chemistry*, 21, pp. 34–43.

OECD (Organisation for Economic Co-operation and Development) (2016), Big data: Bringing competition policy to the digital era. In Background note by the OECD Secretariat for Meeting of the Competition Committee, November 29–30. Paris: OECD.

Olabi, A.G., Onumaegbu, C., Wilberforce, T., Ramadan, M., Abdelkareem, M.A., and Al-Alami, A.H. (2021), Critical review of energy storage systems. *Energy*, 214, p. 118987.

Panda, D.K. and Das, S. (2021), Smart grid architecture model for control, optimization and data analytics of future power networks with more renewable energy. *Journal of Cleaner Production*, 301, p. 126877.

Petrillo, A., De Felice, F., Cioffi, R. and Zomparelli, F. (2018), Fourth industrial revolution: Current practices, challenges, and opportunities. *Digital transformation in smart manufacturing*, pp. 1–20.

Ravanchi, M.T. and Sahebdelfar, S. (2021), Catalytic conversions of CO_2 to help mitigate climate change: Recent process developments. *Process Safety and Environmental Protection*, 145, pp. 172–194.

Ravanchi, M.T. and Soleimani, M. (2020), Porous materials for CO_2 fixation: Activated carbon, MOFs, nanomaterials. *Chemo-Biological Systems for* CO_2 *Utilization*, pp. 161–188.

Rogelj, J., Shindell, D., Jiang, K., Fifita, S., Forster, P., Ginzburg, V., Handa, C., Kheshgi, H., Kobayashi, S., Kriegler, E., and Mundaca, L. (2018), Global Warming of 1.5° C. An IPCC Special Report on the impacts of global warming of 1.5° C above pre-industrial levels and related global greenhouse gas emission pathways, in the context of strengthening the global response to the threat of climate change, sustainable development, and efforts to eradicate poverty. *Sustainable Development, and Efforts to Eradicate Poverty, V. Masson-Delmotte et al., Eds.(Cambridge University Press, Cambridge, UK, 2018).*

Schwab, K. and Davis, N. (2018), *Shaping the Future of the Fourth Industrial Revolution*. Currency.

Sanger, F., Nicklen, S., and Coulsen, A.R. (1977), Sequencing by chain termination with dideoxynucleotides. *Proceedings of the National Academy of Sciences of the United States of America*, 74(12), pp. 5463–5467.

Smil, V. (2005), *Creating the twentieth century: Technical innovations of 1867-1914 and their lasting impact*. Oxford University Press.

Sun, M. (2018), *The Impacts of the Fourth Industrial Revolution on Jobs and the Future of the Third Sector Impact.* Oxford University Press.

Yoro, K.O. and Daramola, M.O. (2020), CO_2 emission sources, greenhouse gases, and the global warming effect. In *Advances in Carbon Capture* (pp. 3–28). Woodhead Publishing.

Part IV
Challenges to 2030

This part identifies Bangladesh's challenges to prosperity due to the impact of the sudden global catastrophe of the COVID-19 pandemic.

DOI: 10.4324/9781003231912-14

10 Poverty and Inequality Reduction in Bangladesh: Making Growth Inclusive and Adopting Transformative Social Policy

Mustafa K Mujeri

10.1 Introduction

The ultimate aim of development in Bangladesh is the improvement in the living conditions and the quality of life of all populations, especially the poor and deprived sections in society. One of the fundamental principles of state policy as laid out in the Constitution of the People's Republic of Bangladesh states that: 'It shall be a fundamental responsibility of the State to emancipate the toiling masses the peasants and workers and backward sections of the people from all forms of exploitation' (14. Part II; Fundamental Principles of State Policy). Thus, development in Bangladesh should lead to sustained reductions in poverty in its multidimensional forms and inequality in all aspects of human lives.

In the context of a dynamic and rapidly changing economy such as Bangladesh, the interactions of economic, sociocultural, political, and other structural factors shape the institutions and the rules in society which in turn shape the nature of poverty and inequality. More importantly, the way these institutions function affects the people's opportunities and their ability to invest and improve their wellbeing. Unequal economic opportunities lead to unequal outcomes and reinforce unequal political power (World Bank, 2006). On its part, unequal power structure shapes the institutions and policies that favour the persistence of unjust initial conditions.

Similarly, unequal distribution of power and voice between the rich and the poor allows the rich to maintain control over resources; and unequal distribution of assets, opportunities, and political power gives rise to a vicious cycle of mutually reinforcing patterns of poverty and inequality.[1]

10.2 Economic Growth and Structural Changes

The growth of gross domestic product (GDP) – the value of all the goods and services a country produces in a given year – is an important indicator of development. In Bangladesh, the rate of GDP growth slightly increased from 3.77 per cent during 1961–1970 (pre-independence period), to 3.99 per cent during 1976–1980, and decreased to 3.62 per cent during 1986–1990; but the next

DOI: 10.4324/9781003231912-15

Table 10.1 Bangladesh's GDP Growth Rate at Constant Prices

Period	*Average yearly growth rate, % (constant 2006 prices)*	*Annual per capita GDP growth rate, constant 2006 prices, %*	*GDP per capita, constant 2006 BDT*	*GDP per capita Index, 2006 prices (2006 = 100)*
1961–1970 (Pre-independence period)	3.77	1.01	22,700	68.41
1976–1980	3.99	1.40	18,293	55.13
1986–1990	3.62	1.07	20,490	61.75
1996–2000	4.61	2.62	25,346	76.39
2006–2010	5.52	4.60	36,637	110.42
2014–2018	6.63	5.54	54,485	164.21

Source: World Bank. 2018.

three decades saw average GDP growth rate rising by about one percentage point in each decade. The five-year average rose to 4.61 per cent during 1996–2000, to 5.52 per cent in 2006–2010, and accelerated further to 6.63 per cent during 2014–2018 (Table 10.1).

The per capita level of GDP provides a rough summary indicator of the average living standard in a country. The annual per capita GDP growth rate, which was only around 1 per cent till the 1990s, accelerated in the later years, and reached 5.54 per cent during 2014–2018. As Table 10.1 shows, Bangladesh's GDP per capita increased by nearly threefold in absolute terms from BDT 18,293 to BDT 54,485 (at constant 2006 prices) since the second half of the 1970s.

In 2017, real GDP per capita for Bangladesh was USD 1,093. Real GDP per capita of Bangladesh increased from USD 401 in 1968 to USD 1,093 in 2017 growing at an average annual rate of 2.14 per cent. Bangladesh's GDP per capita, based on purchasing-power parity (PPP) dollars, is estimated at $4,200 in 2017, which was $510 in 1980 (MOF, 2019). Over the years, changes in the strategy and the rate of growth of GDP also affected the structure of the economy.

As is well known, the process of economic development does not merely involve increases in the levels of economic growth and productivity, but also entails changes in the distribution of inputs and outputs across different economic sectors and population groups. Over the years, structural changes in terms of key economic parameters have occurred in the Bangladesh economy as economic growth has proceeded. More generally, in terms of percentage share of GDP, saving rates have increased as income has grown; government revenue (and expenditure) has increased; growth in food consumption has decelerated; relative output of services – and, of industry as well – has increased, while that of agriculture has fallen (Table 10.2).

Table 10.2 Sectoral Composition of GDP and Growth Rates (at 1995–96 constant prices), 1976–2018

	Agriculture		*Industry*		*Services*		*GDP*
	Share (%)	*Annual average growth rate (%)*	*Share (%)*	*Annual average growth rate (%)*	*Share (%)*	*Annual average growth rate (%)*	*Annual average growth rate (%)*
1976–1980	43.75	19.83	10.88	39.35	43.64	43.13	36.24
1981–1985	31.60	2.68	11.59	5.47	49.20	4.27	3.81
1986–1990	28.99	2.18	12.80	5.24	50.31	3.64	3.56
1991–1995	26.92	1.73	14.33	8.17	49.63	4.68	4.65
1996–2000	24.52	4.89	15.91	5.67	49.99	5.59	5.34
2001–2005	22.66	2.86	16.44	7.64	51.19	6.13	5.71
2006–2010	20.37	5.05	18.20	7.92	51.78	5.82	6.07
2011–2015	16.45	3.30	27.87	9.06	53.59	5.86	6.32
2016–2018	14.08	2.94	27.31	11.10	53.62	6.42	7.43

Sources: Calculated from Statistical Annex [The Sixth Five Year Plan (2011–2015) and Bangladesh Bureau of Statistics (2016)].

It is seen that the tertiary, i.e. the services (non-commodity) sector, has been growing at a stable and faster rate than the primary and secondary sectors in the country. This means that income generated in the process of circulation grows faster than that in the directly productive process; resulting in an increase in the share of the services sector.

The expansion in the services sector has wider implications for population, employment, and trade prospects of the Bangladesh economy. The growing share of the services sector points to the need for policy initiatives towards introducing greater competition and efficiency in this sector so as to ensure its sustained contribution to exports and to higher long-term growth.

10.2.1 GDP Growth and Occupational Structure

In a developing economy like Bangladesh, it is generally expected that the percentage of the labour force dependent on agriculture should decline over time, while the share of industry should increase. There may be an increase in the percentage of labour dependent on services. But, for a country in the early stages of industrialization, this increase should be less than the increase in manufacturing. At a later stage of development, a faster increase in the services sector may be expected.

The classical reasons for such a change are twofold. With rise in incomes, the demand for agricultural goods does not rise proportionately. On the other hand, rise in incomes brings about a large increase in the demand for manufacturing goods and services, resulting in increasing demand for labour in the manufacturing and services sectors. With economic development, modern technologies and better techniques become available with agriculture, so that the productivity of land and labour rises. As a result, there is less need for labour in agriculture. On the contrary, in the industrial sector, although an increase in capital and modern techniques makes it possible to bring about increases in productivity, demand increases at a faster rate than the rise in per head productivity, resulting in increasing demand for labour in the industrial and the services sectors.

Table 10.3 gives the occupational structure of Bangladesh's labour force since the mid-1990s. The data show that the occupational structure of the Bangladesh economy is somewhat lopsided. There is a heavy dependence on agriculture; about 41 per cent of the working population derives its subsistence from agriculture, although its contribution of GDP is only 15 per cent. The changes in the occupational structure largely correspond to the celebrated Kuznets-Clark-Kaldorian path in the aggregate (see, Kongsamut et. al., 2001).

Within the changed structure, the government's dominant strategy is to promote a more sustainable growth supported by broad-based political and social policies that provides equality of opportunity, especially in education and employment. It also envisions expanded social protection systems and social safety nets to protect the poor and the vulnerable. The overall emphasis is on reducing poverty and inequality (see, PC, 2015).

Table 10.3 Changes in Occupational Structure and Sectoral Contribution to GDP, 1996 to 2017

	Agriculture		*Industry*		*Services*		*Total employed labour (In million)*
	Employed labour, %	*Share in GDP, %*	*Employed labour, %*	*Share in GDP, %*	*Employed labour, %*	*Share in GDP, %*	
1995–96	48.85	21.44	13.22	21.79	37.92	56.76	
1999–00	50.77	21.34	13.08	22.89	36.16	55.77	39.00
2002–03	51.69	19.77	13.56	24.08	34.75	56.15	44.30
2005–06	48.10	19.01	14.55	25.40	37.35	55.59	47.40
2010	47.33	18.38	17.49	26.78	35.18	54.83	54.10
2013	45.10	16.78	20.80	29.00	34.10	54.22	58.10
2016–17	40.60	14.74	20.40	32.42	39.00	52.85	60.80

Sources: BBS, *Labour Force Survey* (LFS), 1995–96, 1999–00, 2002–03, 2005–06,2010, 2016–2017; BBS, *Labour Force Surveys* 1992 to 2010; and Ministry of Finance, *Bangladesh Economic Review 2019.*

10.3 Trends in Poverty and Inequality in Bangladesh

It is now well-recognized that poverty is not only a lack of material resources; it is correlated closely with deprivations in all aspects of human life (UN, 2015). The poor in Bangladesh are malnourished; they have less access to services like education, electricity, sanitation, and healthcare; they are more vulnerable to risks and disasters and to adverse impact of climate change. Understanding the causes of poverty is fundamental to reducing poverty.

Reducing poverty and inequality forms the key objectives of Bangladesh's development agenda and is central to the Sustainable Development Goals (SDGs). National statistical systems, household surveys, and poverty measurement methodologies are at the heart of tracking important poverty goals.

10.3.1 Conceptualizing Poverty in Bangladesh

Poverty is an important element of disparity in Bangladesh. The official poverty measure in the country uses money-metric poverty or poverty measured on the basis of a money value of expenditure, adopting the more commonly used headcount ratio (the number of the poor as a proportion of the population), which are derived from a poverty line approach that we are more familiar with. Bangladesh's poverty line is anchored in a 'nutritional norm'; it is based on notions of what is a basic minimum of nutrition an individual must obtain every day in order not to be considered undernourished.

However, when we speak of income poverty per se, there seems to be a case for viewing income not to an end, but as an end in itself; that is, to see the attainment of command over some satisfactory level of income as a desired human functioning. If we wish to speak of poverty lines, then we must see income as a means (for achieving the end of some level of satisfactory human functioning), and this will entail avoiding the logical lapse of seeking invariance of the poverty line in the space of resources rather than functionings. This, in turn, raises the question of why we should not, instead, measure poverty directly in the space of human functionings with the help of multidimensional measures of deprivation. The problem would not arise if we thought of money-metric poverty as a matter of avoiding low incomes, as such. The measurement of deprivation requires a more human engagement with poverty.

Poverty and economic wellbeing is multidimensional, although in practice this multidimensional character is summarized into a single monetary measure by employing money metric approaches to measure wellbeing, favouring in particular income and expenditure measures, seen as an adequate proxy for poverty. These measures are cardinal, allowing one to make direct comparisons and quantitative analysis and are straightforward to interpret. However, there is a clear difference between definitions of poverty that are restricted to income (or consumption) and those that incorporate such factors as autonomy, self-esteem, or participation.

Only by understanding the causes can the designing, implementing, and evaluating interventions for attacking poverty begin. In designing poverty programmes, it is important to incorporate the perception of poverty as articulated by the poor people themselves. This may need to begin by implementing income generation measures in some cases; but in the case of others, this may need to begin by reducing the variability of income, or strengthening women's autonomy, or improving the quality of services the poor receive at the health centres. In practice, it is multidimensional poverty that matters for policy.

The macro perspective on poverty provides information on macro indicators of growth, income, employment, education, and others. Similarly, information on several micro indicators such as access to water and sanitation, structure of houses, and many more can also be gleaned from these statistics. Taken together, the picture gives useful information on the socioeconomic situation of the larger sections of the country's people. But what we miss in these statistics are the ground realities experienced by the people themselves. We also miss the insights of local people who have a clear understanding of their developmental problems and the way out.

Moreover, the micro perspectives on poverty can provide the elements of a sustainable graduation approach which needs to blend together elements of livelihoods, social protection, financial inclusion, and social integration. For the extreme poor, the multidimensional support approach should address both immediate needs of participants using grants, interest-free loans, and asset transfers, as well as long-term investments in life skills and technical skills training, enterprise development, positive behaviour change, savings, and financial planning.

10.3.2 Changes in Poverty

In Bangladesh, the national poverty line is typically a monetary threshold below which a person's minimum basic needs cannot be met, taking into account the country's economic and social circumstances. The poverty line is also revised as the country develops. The government tracks how many people are living on less than the national poverty line so that it can monitor its development progress.

The official statistics on poverty and inequality are provided by the Bangladesh Bureau of Statistics (BBS), the government statistical agency, using data from the Household Income and Expenditure Survey (HIES) series. These surveys are designed by BBS to make them comparable over time (e.g. in terms of methodology, questionnaire content, interviewing procedures, and others) and are carried out usually at five-year intervals. The BBS uses the Cost-of-Basic-Needs (CBN) method to derive poverty lines and poverty measures, which entails three main steps.

First, a food bundle yielding 2,122 kcal per day per person is chosen, comprising rice, wheat, pulses, milk, mustard oil, beef, fresh water fish, potato, other vegetables, sugar, and bananas. The prices of various food items in this bundle are estimated for 16 different geographic regions to ascertain the total cost of consuming the bundle in different parts of the country. The second step is to estimate the cost of basic non-food needs. For the purpose, two non-food allowance components are calculated: the first is obtained by taking the amount spent on non-food items by those households whose total consumption is equal to their regional food poverty line (corresponding to the lower poverty line), while the second is obtained by taking the amount spent on non-food items by those households whose food consumption is equal to the regional food poverty line, corresponding to the upper poverty line. The third step in calculating the lower and upper poverty lines for each region entails simply adding up the cost of purchasing the food bundle in each region to the respective non-food allowance components. The lower poverty lines thus incorporate a minimal allowance for non-food goods (the typical non-food spending of those who could just afford the food requirement) while the upper poverty lines made a more generous allowance (the typical non-food spending of those who just attain their food requirement).

The poverty measures used in Bangladesh are drawn from the Foster-Greer-Thorbecke class of functions, written as:

$$P_\alpha = \Sigma_{yi<z}[(z - y_i)/z]^\alpha / \qquad (10.1)$$

where yi is the consumption of the Ith household or the jth class of household, z is the poverty line, n is the population size, and α is a non-negative parameter (Foster, Greer and Thorbecke, 1984). The headcount ratio, H, given by the percentage of the population who are poor, is obtained when $\alpha = 0$. The poverty gap index (PG), given by the aggregate income shortfall of the poor as a proportion of the poverty line and normalized by the population size, is given by $\alpha = 1$, and the squared poverty gap index (SPG) is obtained when $\alpha = 2$.

The available poverty estimates are based on poverty lines developed by the Bangladesh Bureau of Statistics (BBS) using Household Income and Expenditure Survey (HIES) data and employing a Cost of Basic Needs (CBN) approach (see, for instance, World Bank, 2006). The CBN poverty lines represent the level of per capita expenditure at which a household can be expected to meet its basic needs (food and non-food). This is measured by (i) estimating a food poverty line as the cost of a fixed food bundle (consisting of 11 key items), providing minimal nutritional requirements corresponding to 2,122 kcal/day/person; and (ii) adding an allowance for non-food consumption to the food poverty line.

For the lower poverty line, the non-food allowance is the average non-food expenditure of households whose total consumption is equal to the food poverty line; whereas for the upper poverty line, the non-food allowance is the average nonfood expenditure of households whose food consumption equals the food poverty line.

As prices and consumption patterns vary across different geographical areas, poverty lines are estimated for 16 different geographical areas separately. For obtaining poverty estimates for previous years, the current poverty lines are deflated by price indices to represent identical purchasing power for all years. Estimates using alternative methodologies, which serve as important sensitivity checks for poverty trends, reveal similar trends for a wide range of methods for estimating and updating poverty lines.

10.3.2.1 Trends in Poverty

Poverty in Bangladesh has declined remarkably since the early-2000s, as a result of decades of accelerated economic growth. It is widely recognized that, after independence in 1971, Bangladesh's poverty rate was extremely high estimated at more than 80 per cent in 1972. According to the HIES data, national poverty headcount rate has declined to 24.3 per cent in 2016 (Table 10.4). Based on the current rate of poverty reduction, Bangladesh is projected to eliminate extreme poverty by 2021, the first nation in South Asia to do so.

The national poverty headcount rate declined by more than 57 per cent (32 percentage points) between 1992 and 2016. In 1991–92, nearly 57 per cent of Bangladesh's population was poor (per capita consumption below the upper poverty line) as compared with 24 per cent in 2016. The percentage decline in poverty rate was almost similar in urban areas (nearly 56 per cent) and rural areas (55 per cent).

A notable feature of recent poverty reduction is a sizeable decline in the incidence of extreme poverty. The percentage of population under the lower poverty line--the threshold for extreme poverty--fell by nearly 69 per cent (or 28 percentage points) between 1992 and 2016. A fall of 68 per cent (or 16 percentage points) occurred in urban areas and 66 per cent (29 percentage points) in the rural areas (see Table 10.4). The percentage decline in extreme poverty rate is thus more than that in the poverty rate, which shows higher growth in per capita consumption for the bottom two deciles.

During the period, the fall in poverty headcount rates was large enough to significantly reduce the number of people in poverty or extreme poverty. The size of the population below the upper poverty and the lower poverty lines declined by 23.3 million and 22.9 million, respectively, between 2000 and 2016. However, it must also be remembered that an estimated 39.6 million Bangladeshis are still below the (upper) poverty line in 2016, and 24 million among whom are below the lower or extreme poverty line.

The depth (poverty gap) and the severity (squared poverty gap) of poverty have shown significant improvements as well, falling by 61 per cent and 67 per cent, respectively. The rates of decline are similar for urban and rural areas – the poverty gap declined by 57 per cent and 61 per cent and squared poverty gap by 64 per cent and 65 per cent for urban and rural areas, respectively. These trends suggest significant improvement among those below the poverty line. A fall in poverty gap indicates that the average consumption of the poor has improved, while a decline in squared poverty gap implies more equitable distribution of consumption among the poor. These improvements have also taken place at similar rates for the urban and rural poor. (Figure 10.1)

Table 10.4 Poverty Headcount Rates in Bangladesh

	% of population below upper poverty lines					*% of population below lower poverty lines*				
	1991–92	*2000*	*2005*	*2010*	*2016*	*1991–92*	*2000*	*2005*	*2010*	*2016*
National	56.7	48.9	40.0	31.5	24.3	41.1	34.3	25.1	17.6	12.9
Urban	42.8	35.2	28.4	21.3	18.9	24.0	19.9	14.6	7.7	7.6
Rural	58.8	52.3	43.8	35.2	26.4	43.8	37.9	28.6	21.1	14.9

Source: HIES reports, various years.

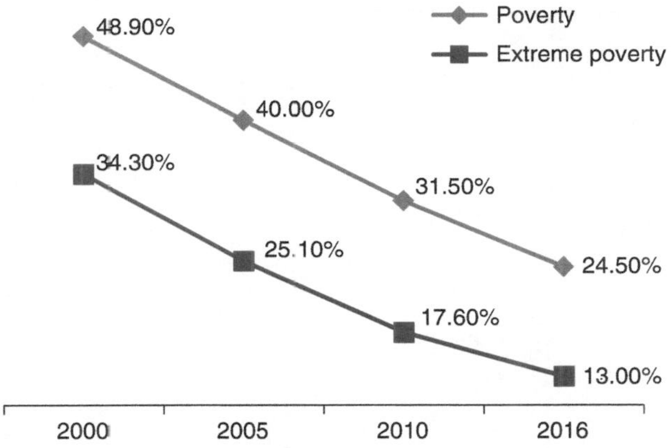

Figure 10.1 Poverty and Extreme Poverty Headcount in the 2000s.
Source: HIES, various years.

It may, however, be noted that, while the rural-urban gap in poverty rate is narrowing down, the gap still remains considerable. The rural poverty rate in 2016 was 26.4 per cent compared with the urban poverty rate of 18.9 per cent. Thus, although the rural areas account for about 64 per cent of the total population of Bangladesh, they are home to more than 71 per cent of the poor people in the country.

The above shows that Bangladesh has experienced a substantial poverty reduction over the last 24 years (between 1991–92 and 2016), with the pace accelerating during the 2000s. Since poverty is measured by consumption-based indicators in Bangladesh, rapid growth in consumption is the primary contributing factor. However, since there exist a large disparity in the initial distribution of consumption between the poor and the non-poor, even similar growth rates for all consumption groups would necessarily imply an increase in the average size of the gap in consumption between the poor and the non-poor (Figure 10.2).

The HIES data show that absolute inequality or the size of the gap in consumption between different groups has expanded for the country as a whole (World Bank, 2008). For rural areas, consumption growth has been the dominant force in reducing poverty, whereas in urban areas, a marginal reduction in inequality has also had a sizeable poverty reducing impact.

At the international level, poverty measured at the international poverty line of $1.90 a day is used to track progress towards meeting the target of reducing the share of people living in extreme poverty to zero by 2030 as measured by the international poverty line and set by the SDG1 (see, Ravallion, Chen and Sangraula, 2008). Using the international poverty line of $1.90, the poverty headcount ratio was estimated at 44.2 per cent in 1991 in Bangladesh, which has

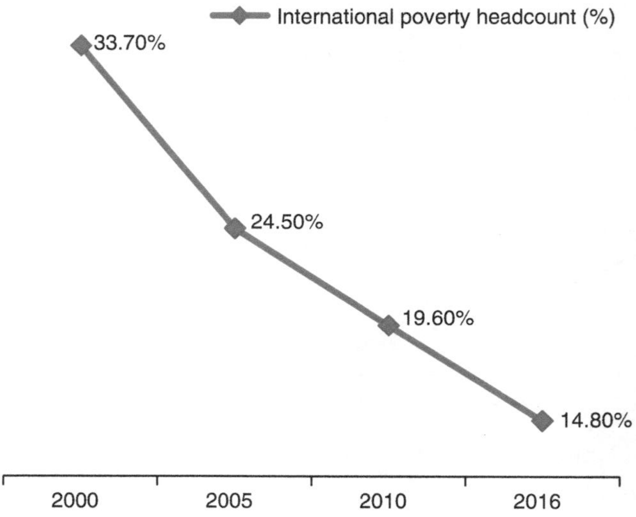

Figure 10.2 International Poverty Headcount (2011 $1.90 PPP).

come down to 14.8 per cent in 2016 (World Bank's Poverty and Equity DataBank).

On the other hand, the multidimensional poverty index (MPI) provides a comprehensive view of the various ways in which people worldwide experience poverty in their daily life. The traditional poverty measures – such as those calculated by numbers of people who earn less than $1.90 a day – shed light on how little people earn but not on whether or how they experience poverty on a day-to-day basis.

More specifically, MPI looks at the multifaceted nature of poverty. It identifies people's deprivations across three key dimensions – health, education, and living standards; lacking amenities such as clean water and sanitation; adequate nutrition or primary education. Those who are left behind in at least a third of the MPI's components are defined as multidimensionally poor. The global MPI can be used to create a comprehensive picture of people living in poverty, and permits comparisons both across countries and world regions, and within countries by ethnic group, urban/rural area, and age group, as well as other key household and community characteristics. For each group and for countries as a whole, the composition of MPI by each of the ten indicators shows how people are poor.

This makes the MPI and its linked information platform invaluable as an analytical tool to identify the most vulnerable people – the poorest among the poor, revealing poverty patterns within countries and over time, enabling policymakers to target resources and design policies more effectively. The global MPI was developed by Oxford Poverty and Human Development Initiative (OPHI) with the United Nations Development Programme (UNDP).

The 2019 global MPI shows that the population in multidimensional poverty in Bangladesh has dropped to 74.4 million in 2014 from 93.7 million in 2004. Thus Bangladesh got about 19.3 million people out of poverty between 2004 and 2014, which is the fastest reduction in MPI during the period across 101 countries of the world (see, OPHI/UNDP, 2019).

The survey data for Bangladesh from 2014 shows that 21.5 per cent of the population is vulnerable to multidimensional poverty and 16.2 per cent is vulnerable to severe multidimensional poverty. The data also reveal that a clear majority of the multidimensional poor live in the rural areas, where poverty rates are four times higher than that of urban areas. Further, nearly half of the people living in multidimensional poverty are 18 years or younger. The data also show that a large majority of the people in countries like Bangladesh are at risk of sliding into multidimensional poverty, which can be hastened by conflicts, sickness, unemployment, and climatic impacts.

10.3.3 Inequality in Bangladesh

As we have seen in earlier sections, Bangladesh, along with rapid economic performance, has shown a significant reduction in poverty incidence over the last few decades. However, inequality in Bangladesh is rising. Inequality is not a new phenomenon in Bangladesh. But the real concern is: If left unchecked, it can undermine the very foundation of development and the country's social fabric.

Since independence, Bangladesh has witnessed impressive average gains against multiple indicators of material prosperity. The country's GDP per capita has more than tripled in real terms; average life expectancy has risen to nearly 73 years. However, this is only part of the picture. Although Bangladesh is richer than ever before today, more than 30 million people still live in poverty. The richest 5 per cent of the households receives nearly 28 per cent of the total income, while the bottom 5 per cent gets only 0.23 per cent.

Despite overall declines in maternal mortality, women in rural areas are still up to three times more likely to die while giving birth than women living in urban centres. Social protection has been extended, yet persons with disabilities are up to five times more likely than average to incur catastrophic health expenditures. Women are participating more in the workforce, but continue to be disproportionately represented in vulnerable employment.

Over the last few decades, income inequality has been rising in Bangladesh. The Gini coefficient of income distribution stands at 0.483 nationally in 2016; which is 0.498 in rural areas and 0.454 in urban areas.[2] Figure 10.3 shows the trend of income inequality since 1963. Over the entire period of 1963–2016, national Gini has risen from 0.36 to 0.483 – an increase by more than 34 per cent – while rural Gini increased by nearly 38 per cent and urban Gini by 21 per cent over the same period. These figures suggest that Bangladesh has experienced increases in the Gini coefficient over the period of last half century but the rate has accelerated especially since the 1990s.

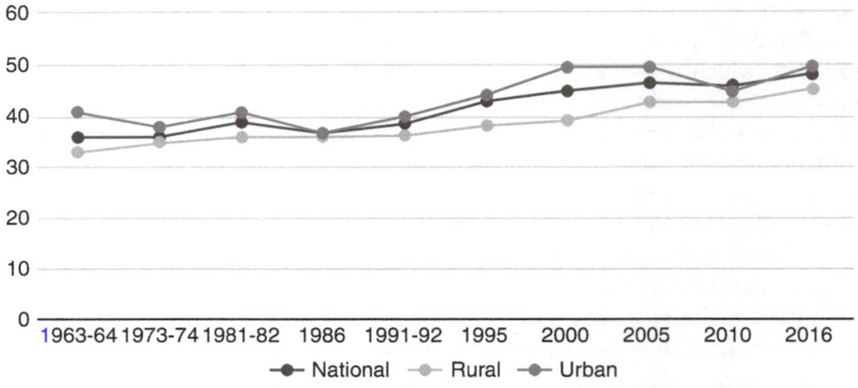

Figure 10.3 Gini Coefficient of Income Distribution in Bangladesh, 1963–2016.
Source: HIES, different years.

It is seen that inequality increased rather sharply in the rural areas while urban areas experienced a somewhat moderate rise in income inequality. As a result, the country's population lives in a society that is more unequal today than after independence. The income gap has deepened – and, with it, the difference in quality of life between the rich and the poor – despite the immense progress made through impressive growth performance. Economic progress in the country has not alleviated disparities. Overall, the Bangladesh society is more unequal today than at any point in time after independence!

Broadly, inequality in the Bangladesh society has many dimensions, such as economic (income and wealth) inequality, gender inequality, educational inequality, ethnic inequality, health and nutrition inequality, demographic inequality, political inequality, and so on. There exist complex interactions among these different forms of inequality; and there are multidimensional drivers of inequality. As such, a holistic approach is needed to mitigate and overcome the challenges (LSE and Oxfam, 2018).

As a measure of inequality, the Palma ratio focuses on extremes of inequality. It is a widely used indicator for looking at the worst form of income inequality. The Palma ratio is the ratio of the richest 10 per cent of the population's share of gross national income (GNI), divided by the poorest 40 per cent of the population's share and is considered to be a more policy-relevant indicator than the Gini, especially when it comes to poverty reduction.

Palma suggests that 'middle classes' – more accurately the middle income groups between the 'rich' and the 'poor' (defined as the five 'middle' deciles, 5 to 9) – tend to capture around half of GNI almost universally. The other half of national income is shared between the richest 10 per cent and the poorest 40 per cent but the share of those two groups varies considerably across countries. He therefore holds

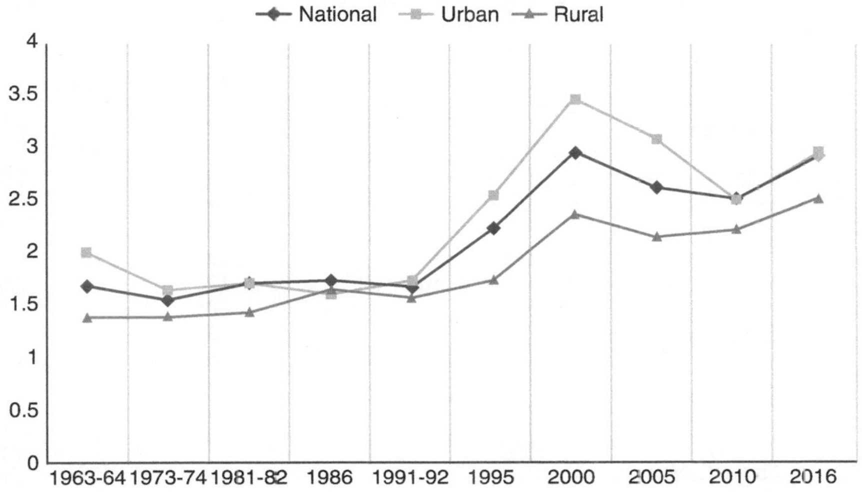

Figure 10.4 Palma Ratio in Bangladesh, 1963–2016.

Source: Authors' calculation using HIES data.

Note: Due to data limitations, the Palma ratio has been constructed using total household income rather than gross national income (GNI).

that distributional politics is largely about the battle between the rich and poor for the other half of national income, and who the middle classes side with.

For a given high Palma value, it is clear what needs to change: to narrow the gap, by raising the share of national income of the poorest 40 per cent and/or reducing the share of the top 10 per cent (see, Palma, 2011; Cobham and Sumner, 2013). In Bangladesh, it is changes in these extremes that are most noticeable; while the share of income in the middle is relatively stable (Appendix A, Table 10.A1). As can be seen from Figure 10.4, the Palma ratio at the national level has consistently increased from 1.68 in 1963–64 to 2.93 in 2016; in urban areas, it rose from 2.00 to 2.96 while, in rural areas, it grew from 1.38 to 2.51 over the same period.

In Appendix A, Figure 10.A1 shows the changes in the income shares of the poorest 40 per cent, middle 50 per cent, and the richest 10 per cent in the income distribution at the national level; and Figures 10.A1a and 10.A1b show separately for urban and rural areas, respectively. These show that the share of the middle 50 per cent is relatively stable, while the poorest 40 per cent generally loses in terms of income share while the richest 10 per cent gains. The policy implication is that Bangladesh should focus on its 'extreme' inequalities, that is, inequalities that do most harm to inclusive and sustainable economic growth and undermine social and political stability.

Table 10.5 Selected Social Indicators for Poorest and Richest Quintiles in Bangladesh

Indicator	*Quintile*	
	Poorest	*Richest*
Child malnutrition rate, per cent	50	21
Child (12–23 months) immunization rate, per cent	77	94
Infant mortality rate, per 1,000 live births	62	30
Child (under 5 years) mortality rate, per 1,000 live births	78	38
Total fertility rate	3.1	1.9
Teenage mothers (% of women 15–19 years)	42	19
Per cent births attended by skilled health attendant	12	64
Per cent women receiving prenatal care	30	87
Primary school completion rate, per cent	65	97

Source: WDI 2014.

10.3.3.1 Social Inequalities

The HIES data show that income inequality is much higher than consumption inequality; and the ratio of income inequality to consumption inequality is rising over time. This means that given similar poverty thresholds for income and consumption, income poverty reduction would be slower than the reduction in consumption poverty. It is well known that social indicators vary significantly across countries depending on their level of development; but these may vary widely across different income groups as well in the same country. Table 10.5 shows the glaring social inequalities that exist between the poorest and richest quintiles of Bangladesh population.

The table shows that inequalities in education, health, and other basic services are significantly related to income and wealth. It shows that the percentage of malnourished children under 5 is about 50 per cent in the poorest quintile, whereas it is 21 per cent for the richest quintile in 2011; whereas only about 12 per cent of women in the poorest quintile in 2014 are lucky enough to have the opportunity to be attended by skilled health staff while giving birth, it is around 64 per cent for the richest quintile.

Bangladesh has already achieved gender parity in primary and secondary education at the national level. This positive development has occurred due to some specific public interventions focusing on female students, such as stipends and exemption of tuition fees for girls in rural areas, and the stipend scheme for girls at the secondary level. This has contributed to promoting the objectives of ensuring gender equality and empowerment of women.

There has also been steady improvement in the social and political empowerment scenario of women in Bangladesh. The government has adopted the National Policy for Women's Development 2011 and a series of programmes for empowerment of women. Women participating in the decision-making process has also marked a significant improvement in the country. There has been a sharp increase in the number of women parliamentarians elected in 2014 (20 per cent) compared with 1991 (about 13 per cent). However, women employment is still low; around 30 per cent of women aged 15–24 are engaged in employment against 52 per cent of men (Gender Statistics, World Bank 2017).

The issue of inequality is thus multidimensional. An equal society can only be ensured if all individuals and social groups can use their productive abilities to the maximum extent for enjoying greater social welfare and inclusive development. In reality, while much progress has been made towards reducing gender inequality, inequality in income, wealth, and employment still remains high. To achieve universal realization of equality and empowerment, it is critical to address key areas of inequality, in particular inequalities in opportunities; discrimination in law and in practice; women's and men's unequal opportunities in the labour market; unequal division of unpaid care and domestic work; the poor's limited control over assets and property; and their unequal participation in private and public decision making and businesses.

10.4 Quality of Growth in Bangladesh

It is now widely recognized that, for a country like Bangladesh, high growth alone does not necessarily lead to better social outcomes, including significant declines in poverty, inequality, and unemployment (see, Commission on Growth and Development, 2008; Dollar and Kraay, 2002; Dollar et al., 2013). Growth has to be inclusive, broad-based, and pro-poor (Anand et al., 2013). It matters whether the 'quality' of growth is good or not.

As we have seen earlier, Bangladesh has made steady progress in GDP growth since its independence and the country's per capita income has also grown rapidly.[3] While one important challenge for Bangladesh is to sustain and achieve a growth rate of 10 per cent by FY2023–24, it is necessary to make economic growth more inclusive for eradicating extreme poverty before 2030. Further, rapid and sustained poverty reduction requires pro-poor growth that allows the poor people to contribute to and benefit from economic growth. While a rapid pace of growth is necessary for Bangladesh, for this growth to be sustainable, this has to be broad-based across sectors and inclusive, especially of the disadvantaged population.

With respect to the above challenges, one key question is: how pro-poor has Bangladesh's economic growth been in the last decade? Although there does not exist consensus regarding specific interpretation of pro-poor growth, we consider two alternatives of pro-poor growth (Ravallion, 2004). The first treats growth as pro-poor if income of the poor people grows faster than that of the population as a whole, which means that income inequality should decline. The alternative is to treat growth as pro-poor as long as poor people benefit in absolute terms, as measured by standard poverty measures.

We illustrate the difference between the two concepts using Figure 10.5. The figure shows the share of income of the richest 20 per cent of the population on the vertical axis and that of the poorest 20 per cent on the horizontal axis. We have used 20 per cent as the cut-off point since the share of the poor in total

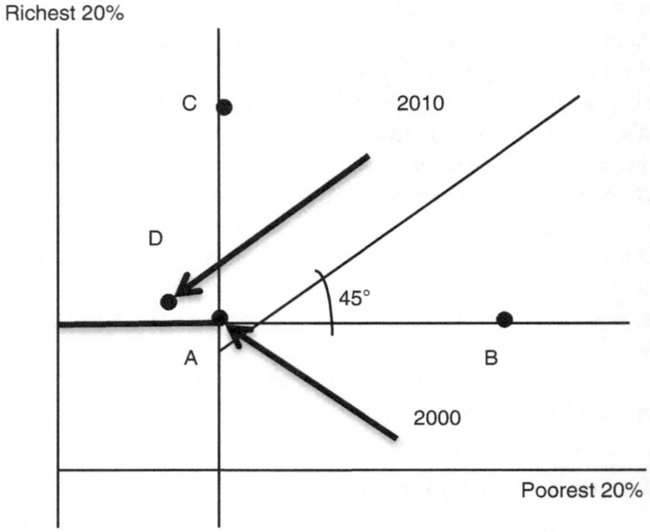

Figure 10.5 Quality of Growth in Bangladesh.

population in Bangladesh is around that number. For our purposes, we consider the shares in 2000 as the base case scenario, depicted by point A.

The growth strategy followed by Bangladesh has resulted in changes in the distribution of income between these groups. This has altered their shares in total income as well. We can term such changes as Pareto optimal if the outcomes fall at any point within the space bounded by BAC. This is due to the fact that any movement from point A to a point say B represents a situation in which economic growth raises the income share of the 20 per cent of the poorest without making the rich any worse off (as their share does not fall). On the other hand, movement from point A to a point like C represents a case where the income benefit of additional growth accrues to the rich without making the poor any worse off in terms of shares in total income.

Similarly, any point located on the 45-degree line divides the income in a manner such that the income distribution does not change; while any point between the horizontal line containing B and the 45-degree line indicates that a larger share of income accrues to the poor relative to the rich and the opposite happens in the case when the point lies between the 45-degree line and the vertical line containing C.

In terms of the two alternative definitions of pro-poor growth mentioned above, the first requires that the changed income shares should be located within the area covered by the 45-degree line and the above-mentioned horizontal line such that the poor benefit more from economic growth. On the other hand, the alternative interpretation suggests that growth will be pro-poor as long as the poor also benefit from growth indicating that the changed situation should lie at any point to the northeast of point A, irrespective of any specific location around the 45-degree line.

The question is: how has the income share changed between the rich and the poor over the last decade in Bangladesh? According to the Household Income and Expenditure Survey (HIES) data of the Bangladesh Bureau of Statistics (BBS), the share in total income of the richest 20 per cent was 55.02 per cent in 2000, which declined to 41.44 per cent in 2016. On the other hand, a similar share of the poorest 20 per cent rose from 4.97 per cent to 8.64 per cent over the same period. This shows that, in 2016, we have moved to the right of the vertical line containing C (say, to a point like D) such that the share of the poorest 20 per cent has increased between 2000 and 2016 while the share of the richest 20 per cent has declined. This shows that, relatively speaking, the poorest 20 per cent have gained and the richest 20 per cent have not benefited from the economic growth during the period. On the other hand, the middle 60 per cent have raised their share in total income from 40.01 per cent in 2000 to 49.92 per cent in 2010, showing their relative gain in terms of accessing the growth benefits.

In this respect, changes in rural and urban areas show similar movements. Again, using the HIES data, one observes that the income share of the poorest 20 per cent have declined from 5.63 per cent in 2000 to 4.06 per cent in 2016 in the rural areas while the share of the richest 20 per cent also declined over the same period from 51.12 per cent to 50.33 per cent of the total. The middle 60 per cent in the rural areas are the gainers in terms of income share since their share rose from 43.25 per cent in 2000 to 45.61 per cent in 2016.

In the urban areas, the poorest 20 per cent lost as their income share fell from 4.51 per cent to 4.15 per cent over the 2000–2016 period. On the other hand, the income share of the richest 20 per cent declined from 57.66 per cent in 2000 to 54.75 per cent in 2016. The middle 60 per cent turned out to be the gainers who could raise their share from 37.83 per cent to 41.10 per cent over the same period.

The above results indicate that the pattern of economic growth in Bangladesh during the first 16 years of this century has not been much inclusive, resulting in loss of income share by the bottom 20 per cent of the population. On the other hand, the middle 60 per cent have gained the most in both rural and urban areas. This shows that adopted policies and structural features of the growth process during the period had similar impacts on rural and urban growth in terms of changing the income shares of various population deciles.

The empirical evidence on inclusive growth in different countries suggests that no specific growth strategy is uniquely appropriate and the outcome with respect to growth inclusiveness depends on individual country characteristics and its structural features. The general conclusions, however, show that inclusive growth is facilitated by rapid growth in agriculture and the rural economy especially at the initial stages, emphasis on adequate and efficient delivery of essential public services especially health and education, development of infrastructure, and good governance, all of which are vital for the poor to access socioeconomic opportunities.

10.5 Policies for Poverty and Inequality Reduction

Since both poverty and inequality are multidimensional, the poverty and inequality reduction policies have to be comprehensive, covering not only inequalities in income but also social, political, and economic exclusion and discrimination, and inequalities in opportunities and outcomes.

In Bangladesh, changes in the structure of output and income are one of the major sources of changes in inequality (World Bank, 2008). Among different components of personal income, wage is the most equalizing component; but its share is declining steadily in both rural and urban areas. For reversing the trend, policies for broad-based nonfarm growth and expanding employment-intensive growth are needed. Over the medium term, this can be a powerful tool of reducing inequality in Bangladesh, for which investments in both physical infrastructure and human capital are necessary.

According to the HIES data, there exist several sources of income inequality in Bangladesh: income from nonfarm enterprises, land and non-land assets, and remittances from abroad (Khan and Sen, 2001). Income from nonfarm enterprises largely represents return to enterprise ownership and is the return to wealth. International remittances are also concentrated to relatively better-off households as overseas migration entails high costs beyond the reach of most poor households. Thus, the increase in the relative importance of incomes from nonfarm enterprises and remittances are both highly inequalizing as the incomes accrue mostly to higher-income groups.

Obviously, curbing growth in these components is not a desirable policy, as it could lead to reduced income growth. There are two options. First, to tax these income components in a way that does not reduce incentives. Second, introduce public transfer to the poor. However, the prospect for large transfers which can make a difference is somewhat limited due to inadequate availability of public resources and inevitable leakages in the distribution system. Table 10.B provides a list of specific policies that may be considered for ensuring a more equitable development in Bangladesh.

The current status of inequality suggests that Bangladesh should focus on 'extreme' inequalities; that is, inequalities that do most harm to inclusive and sustainable economic growth and undermine social and political stability. For achieving inclusive and sustained development, Bangladesh cannot ignore extreme inequalities. The World Bank study on *Voices of the Poor* highlights that the poor suffer not just from a lack of income but from insecurity and a lack of voice.[4]

Since most of Bangladesh's poor live in rural areas and are engaged in farming, agricultural development is essential to directly increase the incomes of the poor who farm; but also for releasing labour and capital that can be used in non-agricultural enterprises and for stimulating the demand for non-agricultural goods. This emphasizes the positive linkages between agricultural development and non-farm activity growth – local 'trickle-down' from improving farm productivity. Thus, policies that encourage investment in the rural, non-farm sector may be the best means of reducing rural poverty and inequality.

But even in rural areas, rural non-farm activity ranges from household and village production on a very small scale producing simple, low-quality products on the one hand; to micro, small, and medium enterprises (MSMEs) on the other, sometimes using imported technology and producing modern high-quality products. The high-quality products sector that plays a central role in this framework combines two separate elements: production of exportable goods that can be traded on a larger market and production of non-tradable goods and services.

Bangladesh's Seventh Five-Year Plan (2016–2020) recognizes that, since the existing distribution of assets and human capabilities are unequal, the benefit of growth favours the better endowed with these assets. The long-term income inequality reduction strategy must therefore focus on reducing this initial gap. A human development strategy with an emphasis on alleviating the access gap for the poor is one powerful instrument for this purpose. Similarly, facilitating asset accumulation through better access to credit for the poor, social inclusion of the poor, and disadvantaged by eliminating physical and social barriers are important instruments for reducing income inequality in Bangladesh.

The Seventh Plan identifies two major areas for a specific focus to ensure better income distribution – asset (land) redistribution and fiscal policy. In the case of land, the aim is to strengthen the land administration regime and related land market through a range of institutional, regulatory, and fiscal policy reforms. A proper capital gains tax on land transactions can provide an important way to reduce windfall capital gains; it will also help to stabilize land prices by discouraging land speculation and providing additional revenues for spending on social services.

Clearly, a major way through which the government can help improve income distribution is by making faster progress in building up the human capital of the poor. Along with better health and education, a strong social protection system can be used as instruments for improving income distribution. One area where public spending should be increased is rural infrastructure – rural roads, rural electricity, irrigation, and flood control. In addition, availability of rural credit is an important instrument for helping the poor to build up assets and also protect their consumption. Another area where public spending should be scaled up concerns social protection.

10.6 Concluding Remarks

No doubt, despite rapid reduction in poverty, rising inequality is a big issue for policy in Bangladesh. This has serious implications for ensuring secure, sustainable lives and livelihoods for all. Obviously, *'when inequality creates discriminatory outcomes, it becomes a human rights issue'* too. In Bangladesh, rising vertical inequality that concentrates greater amounts of wealth among a small group of elites along with horizontal inequalities that marginalize specific groups and communities undoubtedly creates discriminatory outcomes.

Despite resource constraints, many tools are available with the government for reducing poverty and inequality. Universal social protection policy, including healthcare and microinsurance, can ensure that all people have access to basic services and social protections. Similarly, an effective and progressive tax system can help produce a more equal distribution of wealth. The critical challenge is to address social and cultural inequalities that are deeply rooted and woven into the fabric of the society.

For the medium term, Bangladesh needs to create effective economic institutions and proper policy incentives, while also pursuing sound macroeconomic policies and efficiency-enhancing reforms over time. The key for Bangladesh is to build a robust middle class and reduce extreme poverty and social marginalization for creating a more equitable society.

Notes

1 For a discussion on these links, see Gaventa and Martorano, 2016; Moncrieffe, 2004.
2 Gini coefficient is an inequality index that has value starting from 0 to 1. The higher the value, the greater the inequality. Thus, a value of 1 means highest unequal situation in a society and a value of 0 means there is perfect equality.
3 The per capita gross national income (GNI) jumped more than 9 per cent to \$1,909 in FY2018–19 from \$1,751 a year ago; and per capita gross domestic product (GDP) rose to \$1,827 in FY2018–19 from \$1,675 in the previous year. The economy grew by 8.13 per cent in FY2018–19 which is projected to grow at 8.20 per cent in FY2019–20. See, MOF, 2019.
4 See also World Bank's World Development Report on Poverty in 2000. The International Commission on the Measurement of Economic Performance and Social Well-Being (2010) emphasizes that metrics of performance (including output and inequality) should be expanded beyond just conventional measures of GDP and/or income. The OECD has carried on this work in their Better Living Initiative, including the construction of the Better Life Index. An important part of the agenda of OECD High Level Expert Group on Measurement of Economic Performance and Social Well-Being is the construction/evaluation of alternative measures of inequality.

References

Ahluwalia, M. S. (1976), 'Inequality, Poverty and Development', *Journal of Development Economics*, 3: 307–342.

Anand, R., S. Mishra, and J. S. Peiris (2013), *Inclusive Growth: Measurement and Determinants*, IMF Working Paper No. 13/135, International Monetary Fund, Washington D.C.

Barro, A. (2000), 'Inequality and Growth in a Panel of Countries', *Journal of Economic Growth*, 5: 5–32.

Bourguignon, F. (2003), 'The Growth Elasticity of Poverty Reduction: Explaining Heterogeneity across Countries and Time Periods'. In T. S. Eicher and S. J. Turnovsky (eds.), *Inequality and Growth: Theory and Policy Implications*, MIT Press, Cambridge, MA

Cobham, A. and A. Sumner (2013), *Putting the Gini Back in the Bottle? 'The Palma' as a Policy-Relevant Measure of Inequality*, King's College, London.

Commission on Growth and Development (2008), *Growth Report: Strategies for Sustained Growth and Inclusive Development*, World Bank, Washington D.C.

Deininger, K. and L. Squire (1998), 'New Ways of Looking at Old Issues: Inequality and Growth', *Journal of Development Economics*, 57: 259–287.

Dollar, D., T. Kleineberg, and A. Kraay (2013), *Growth is Still Good for the Poor*, World Bank Policy Research Working Paper No. 6568, World Bank, Washington D.C.

Dollar, D. and A. Kraay (2002), 'Growth is Good for the Poor', *Journal of Economic Growth*, 7(3): 195–225.

Fields, G. S. (1980), *Poverty, Inequality, and Development*, Cambridge University Press, New York

Forbes, K. (2000), 'A Reassessment of the Relationship between Inequality and Growth', *American Economic Review*, 90: 869–897.

Foster, J., J. Greer, and E. Thorbecke (1984), 'A Class of Decomposable Poverty Measures', *Econometrica*. 3. 52(3): 761–766.

Gaventa, J. and B. Martorano (2016), 'Inequality, Power and Participation – Revisiting the Links', *IDS Bulletin*, 47, (5).

Khan, A. R. and B. Sen (2001), 'Inequality and Its Sources in Bangladesh, 1991/92 to 1995/96: An Analysis Based on Household Expenditure Surveys', *Bangladesh Development Studies*, 27(1): 1–49.

Kongsamut, P., S. Rebelo, and D. Xie. (2001), 'Beyond Balanced Growth', Review *of Economic Studies*, 68(4): 869–882.

LSE and Oxfam (2018), *Multidimensional Inequality Framework*, Atlantic Fellows in Social and Economic Equity Programme, International Inequalities Institute of the London School of Economics and Political Science and Oxfam, London.

MOF, (2019) *Bangladesh Economic Review 2019*, Finance Division, Ministry of Finance, Government of the People's Republic of Bangladesh, Dhaka.

Moncrieffe, J. M. (2004). *Power Relations, Inequality and Poverty*, A Concept Paper for Empowerment Team, Poverty Reduction Group, World Bank, Overseas Development Institute, London.

Mujeri, M. K., S. Azam, F. Nargis, N. Akhter, and F. Muneer, (2018), *SDG10 Reduced Inequalities: Sharpening People's Voice in Bangladesh*, People's Voice and Institute for Inclusive Finance and Development, Dhaka.

OPHI/UNDP (2019), *Global Multidimensional Poverty Index 2019: Illuminating Inequalities*, United Nations Development Programme and Oxford Poverty and Human Development Initiative, New York and London.

Palma, J. G. (2011), *Homogenous Middles vs. Heterogeneous Tails, and the End of the 'Inverted-U': The Share of the Rich is What It's All About*, Cambridge Working Papers in Economics (CWPE) 1111, Cambridge University, Cambridge.

PC (2015), *7th Five Year Plan FY2016-FY2020: Accelerating Growth, Empowering Citizens*, General Economics Division (GED), Planning Commission, Government of the People's Republic of Bangladesh, Dhaka.

Ravallion, M. (2001), 'Growth, Inequality and Poverty: Looking Beyond Averages', *World Development*, 29(11): 1803–1815.

Ravallion, M. (2004), *Pro-Poor Growth: A Primer*, World Bank Policy Research Working Paper No. 3242, World Bank, Washington D.C.

Ravallion, M., S. Chen and P. Sangraula (2008), *Dollar a Day Revisited*, Policy Research Working Paper 4620, Development Research Group, World Bank, Washington DC.

Sen, A. K. (1973), *On Economic Inequality*. Clarendon Press, Oxford.
UN (2015), *Multidimensional Poverty*, Development Issues No. 3, Development Strategy and Policy Analysis Unit, Development Policy and Analysis Division, Department of Economic and Social Affairs, United Nations, New York.
UNDP (2014), *Humanity Divided: Confronting Inequality in Developing Countries*, United Nations Development Programme, New York.
World Bank (2006), *Equity and Development, World Development Report 2006*, Oxford University Press, New York.
World Bank (2008), *Poverty Assessment for Bangladesh: Creating Opportunities and Bridging the East-West Divide*. Bangladesh Development Series Paper No. 26. Poverty Reduction, Economic Management, Finance & Private Sector Development Sector Unit, South Asia Region, The World Bank Office, Dhaka.

Appendix

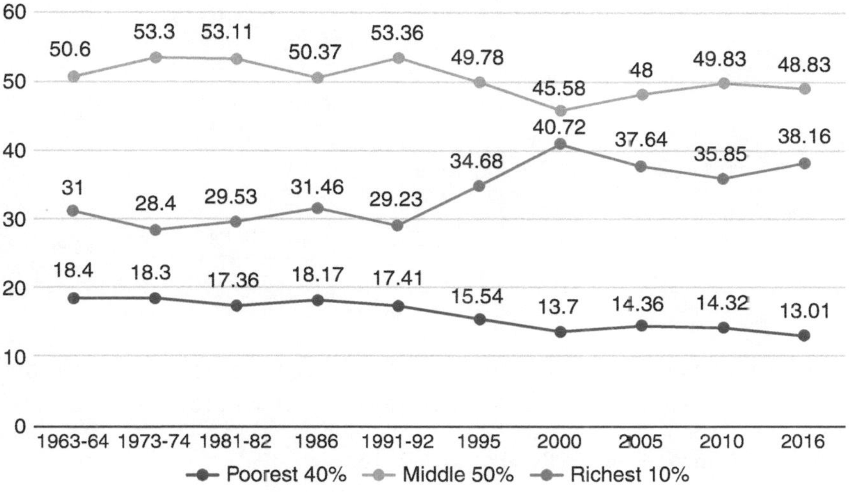

Figure 10.A1 Share of Deciles in Total Household Income at National Level, 1963–2016.

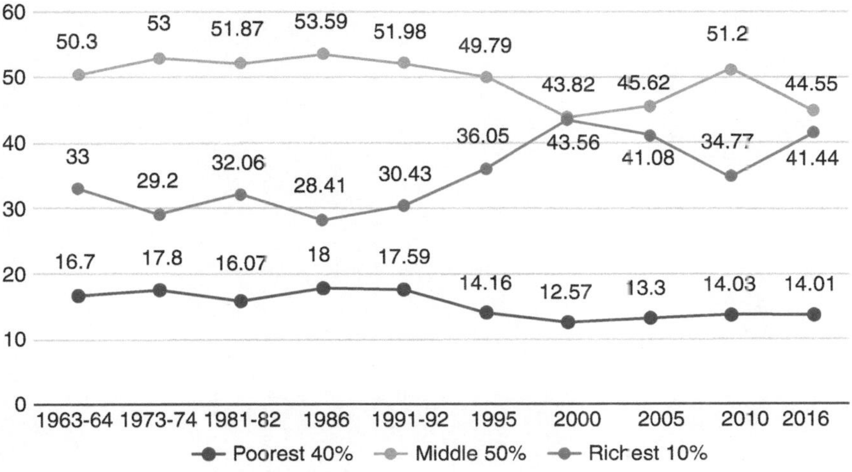

Figure 10.A1a Income Share (Urban), 1963–2016.

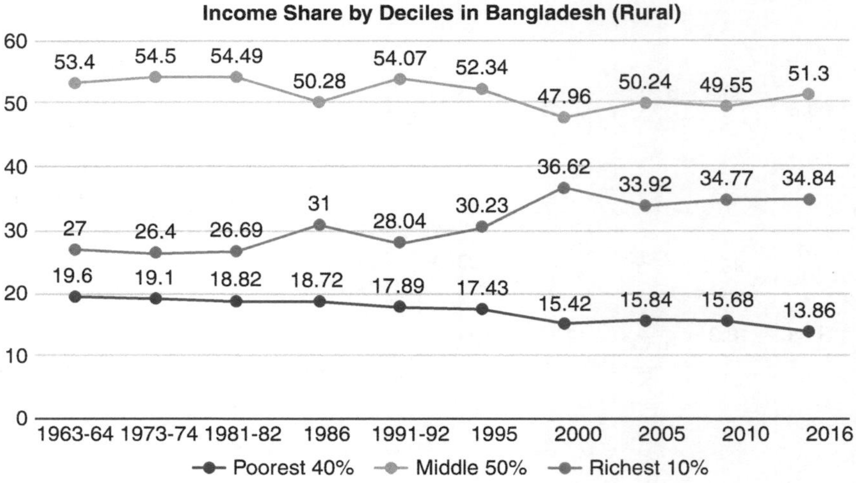

Figure 10.A1b Income Share (Rural), 1963–2016.

Table 10.A1 Income Share by Deciles and Palma Ratio in Bangladesh

Income Share	*1963–64*	*1973–74*	*1981–82*	*1986*	*1991–92*	*1995*	*2000*	*2005*	*2010*	*2016*
National										
Poorest 40%	18.4	18.3	17.36	18.17	17.41	15.54	13.70	14.36	14.32	13.01
Middle 50%	50.6	53.3	53.11	50.37	53.36	49.78	45.58	48.00	49.83	48.83
Richest 10%	31.0	28.4	29.53	31.46	29.23	34.68	40.72	37.64	35.85	38.16
Palma Ratio	1.68	1.55	1.70	1.73	1.68	2.23	2.97	2.62	2.50	2.93
Urban										
Poorest 40%	16.7	17.8	16.07	18.00	17.59	14.16	12.57	13.30	14.03	14.01
Middle 50%	50.3	53.0	51.87	53.59	51.98	49.79	43.82	45.62	51.20	44.55
Richest 10%	33.0	29.2	32.06	28.41	30.43	36.05	43.56	41.08	34.77	41.44
Palma Ratio	2.00	1.64	1.68	1.58	1.73	2.55	3.47	3.09	2.48	2.96
Rural										
Poorest 40%	19.6	19.1	18.82	18.72	17.89	17.43	15.42	15.84	15.68	13.86
Middle 50%	53.4	54.5	54.49	50.28	54.07	52.34	47.96	50.24	49.55	51.30
Richest 10%	27.0	26.4	26.69	31.00	28.01	30.23	36.62	33.92	34.77	34.84
Palma ratio	1.38	1.38	1.42	1.66	1.57	1.73	2.37	2.14	2.22	2.51

Source: Authors' calculation from HIES data.

Table 10.A2 Growth in Real Per Capita Household Income (Average and Bottom 40 Percent)

	National		*Urban*		*Rural*	
	Average	*Bottom 40%*	*Average*	*Bottom 40%*	*Average*	*Bottom 40%*
1986–1995	0.94	- 0.40	4.34	0.91	- 0.49	- 1.61
1995–2005	1.93	- 0.72	2.61	- 0.89	0.52	- 1.14
2005–2016	3.99	1.09	4.45	2.48	2.28	0.37
1986–2016	1.43	0.28	2.28	0.68	4.41	-0.24

Source: Authors' calculation using HIES data.

Table 10.B1 Specific Policies for More Equitable Development in Bangladesh

Broad agenda	*Policy measures*
Policy 1: Moderate income inequality	
Induce changes in the pattern of growth such that incomes of low-income population grow faster than average	**Decent employment creation and labour market reforms**: Create sufficient employment (quantity); that gives adequate income, security and stability (quality); and accessible to all groups (equal access); target MSMEs by providing access to finance (both start-up and for expanding operations) and markets, assist in adopting new technologies and identifying strategically important sectors; provide information on improved production methods, technical support services, vocational training, establishing/ strengthening business links and subcontracting; adopt strategies to ensure that MSMEs are integrated with the industrial sector as providers of inputs and raw materials to bigger firms. **Employment guarantee schemes:** Implement government-sponsored employment guarantee schemes to absorb low-skilled poor workers and allow them to earn a basic income which act as a safety net to guarantee a certain level of income for those otherwise unemployed, while putting in place much needed economic and social infrastructure. Scaling up of employment guarantee schemes can be effective in reducing inequality,

(*Continued*)

Table 10.B1 (Continued)

Broad agenda	*Policy measures*
	including horizontal inequalities. Moreover, the infrastructure built will increase labour productivity; cost per net job created could be much lower than for alternative policies, and the programme wage may emerge as the de facto minimum wage, reducing minimum wage enforcement costs.
	Labour market policies: Create stronger labour market institutions along with effective minimum wage legislation, collective bargaining to reduce wage inequality; manage drivers of inequality associated with financial and trade globalization.
	Macroeconomic strategy to promote inclusive growth: This will prioritize three elements--economic growth, employment creation and macroeconomic stability.
Adopt effective redistributive measures to improve income inequalities	**Social protection providing minimum income security**: Social insurance (e.g. microinsurance) and social assistance programmes to cope with contingencies and adverse events.
	Consumer subsidies: For reducing the costs of household goods for which low-income households spend a disproportionate share of their incomes which can have an immediate impact on nutrition and consumption as well as general well-being of low-income households.
	Progressivity of tax system: Strengthen direct taxation including income and property taxes and adopting well-designed tax brackets and rationalizing personal exemptions and deductions; make VAT progressive by taxing goods and services consumed by the rich and poor at different rates, such as basic food items.
Promote income opportunities for the low income population groups	**Administrative reforms to improve access to employment and income:** Address all discriminatory provisions and discriminatory practices including statutory or customary barriers to access or ownership of assets; use affirmative

(*Continued*)

Table 10.B1 (Continued)

Broad agenda	*Policy measures*
	action policies for improving income-generating opportunities of specific groups, allocate jobs, public contracts, credit, access to higher education and legislative seats on the basis of belonging to a disadvantaged group; barriers to participating in productive employment.
	Access to labour markets: Remove barriers to skill sets, information gaps or mobility constraints of individuals and groups; design policies to promote higher employability of the poor and disadvantaged groups involving a package of instruments that address different barriers to access employment and income generation opportunities; improve access of women to labour market by addressing gender-based discrimination and specific barriers that women face when entering productive employment; ensure on-site child care centres and other worksite facilities (e.g. medical aid, drinking water, toilet facilities and shade) in informal employment locations.
	Access to finance: Ensure financial inclusion for all by removing both price and non-price barriers in both demand and supply sides.
Policy 2: Reduce gaps in health, nutrition and education	
Ensure better targeting and pro-poor composition of public expenditures	**Increase level of public expenditures in education, health and nutrition sectors:** Ensure that these basic social services are available in sufficient quantity; physically and economically accessible; affordable without being a disproportionate burden for the poorest; and of good quality in terms of relevance and cultural acceptability; ensure greater flow of public expenditures to social services with the biggest gaps (e.g. expenditures on health sector in rural areas need to grow faster than expenditures in urban areas; as secondary school enrolment rates lag behind primary completion rates, more

(*Continued*)

Table 10.B1 (Continued)

Broad agenda	*Policy measures*
	resources should be directed towards secondary education, large gaps in nutrition outcomes across wealth quintiles imply that expenditures should target those at the tail end of the distribution etc.); increase investments in early childhood development having strong redistributive power while being highly cost-effective; direct public investments in infrastructure, especially in rural and geographically isolated areas, with strong positive growth and inequality-reducing benefits.
	Create better access for poor, excluded and disadvantaged groups: Focus on sectors, geographic locations and groups that are more isolated and disadvantaged by increasing availability and quality of social services and programmes for the poorest and most excluded groups; investments in infrastructure like basic water and energy reduce the time women spend in household unpaid labour, allowing them to spend more time in paid labour to reduce income inequality across genders and improve mothers' health, which benefits children's well-being.
Improve delivery channels of quality services	**Focus on (i) multi-sector early childhood development programmes, (ii) integrated local service delivery systems, and (iii) community-based programmes:**
	Early childhood development: Early childhood development programmes work across sectors to achieve a series of mutually reinforcing objectives to improve the well-being of children, directly providing health and nutrition services to participating low-income and disadvantaged children while also providing the stimulation, support and attention to improve their school readiness and chances to earn higher future incomes.
	Integrated service delivery systems: Integrated delivery systems that group relevant services under one scheme and

(*Continued*)

Table 10.B1 (Continued)

Broad agenda	*Policy measures*
	overcome issues of fragmentation can improve access to services and avoid dropout of beneficiaries. Integrated delivery systems are networks of providers and organizations that aim to deliver a coordinated continuum of services to a defined population and are accountable for the outcomes of the population served. **Community-based programmes:** Interventions that support participatory, community-based programmes focused on improving outcomes in education, health and nutrition can have an important impact in closing gaps in well-being. By involving beneficiaries in programme design, implementation and evaluation, participatory programmes help empower communities, create a sense of ownership and foster accountability to poor clients. Community outreach and community-based services are also useful strategies for reaching isolated groups or those who would not otherwise seek services.
Strengthen institutions and improve capacity for provision of quality services	Focus on three important tools to build institutional capacity: (i) improving the quantity and quality of human resources to deliver services, (ii) strengthening local governments so that services reach the most marginalized communities, and (iii) enabling inter-sectoral coordination so that services are comprehensive.
Implement governance reforms for installing greater responsiveness to disadvantaged groups	Ensure that institutions operate not only efficiently, but also responsively to the needs and aspirations of those who are lagging behind. Effective accountability mechanisms are needed to ensure full implementation of inequality-reducing measures, particularly those based on public expenditures. A variety of instruments within the broad realm of social accountability, such as social audits, citizen report cards and public expenditure tracking surveys, can be used for the purpose.

(*Continued*)

Table 10.B1 (Continued)

Broad agenda	*Policy measures*
Expand access to un/underserved population and regions	Disadvantaged groups need to be reached through specific reforms that address the particular access barriers that they face, including social norms that allow for exclusion and discrimination. Social norms are significant in explaining inequality in education, health and nutrition outcomes across gender and place of residence.
Policy 3: Remove social and gender exclusion and discrimination	
Expand civic/political/economic engagement for socially excluded/ marginalized population groups including women	**Broaden participation in political and public life:** Create civic and political space for inequality reduction such as involvement of civil society in policy debates on national development plans and budget priority setting; resolve specific economic, social and cultural barriers that prevent the poor and marginalized from participating in public life; CSOs must themselves be inclusive, accountable and transparent if they are to effectively promote greater social justice; work towards a truly inclusive democracy—in which nobody is left out of the public dialogue based on income or other grounds—which is critical to distributional outcomes; new technologies hold great potential to create inclusive citizen networks e.g. platforms based on simple SMS capacity for collecting and mapping inputs from citizens can enable initiatives of mapping community needs.
Adopt affirmative action and anti-discriminatory laws/policies	**Promote conditions that are conducive to inequality reduction:** Prejudice and discrimination are based not only on gender, racial, ethnic or cultural grounds, but also on economic grounds; use the space for specific interventions to revise the norms underpinning inter-generational transmission of inequalities using effective enactment of anti-discriminatory legislation; improving access to justice for the poor, marginalized and disadvantaged; introduction of affirmative action

(*Continued*)

Table 10.B1 (Continued)

Broad agenda	*Policy measures*
	policies; and engagement with the media and other public opinion makers. Affirmative action interventions that aim at directly promoting the socioeconomic status of specific groups in the areas of education, employment and business creation can improve the opportunities for disadvantaged groups; these policies can use quota system for racial and ethnic groups, women and persons with disabilities.

Source: Mujeri et al. (2018).

11 Bangladesh's Rohingya Conundrum

Moazzem Hossain

11.1 Introduction: Bangladesh Economy, 1983–2015

Table 11.1 compares the major economic indicators between 1983 and 2015. Bangladesh had more than 90 million people with a density of population over 590 per square kilometre in 1983. The annual rate of population growth was 2.7 per cent. The GDP per capita was very low at USD150 in 1983 prices. The growth rate in 1982 was only 0.1 per cent. The ready-made garment (RMG) and shrimp exports had been nil or negligible. The remittance from abroad was only USD300 million in 1983. The population under the poverty line (head count ratio) was 60 per cent in the same year. The production of rice was only 13 million tonnes and inflation was at 19 per cent. The literacy rate was dismal, below 50 per cent. Longevity was less than 50 years in the early 1970s. The picture has changed dramatically over the last three decades to 2015 (see Table 11.1). The population increased by 80 per cent as a result of a drop of growth by 60 per cent. Population density per square kilometre increased has been 70 per cent. The GDP per capita advanced to almost ninefold as a result of sustained growth in GDP between 5.0 and 6.5 per cent in recent decades. The difference of population growth and GDP growth in 2015 suggests that GDP has been growing by more than four times. In 1983, the population growth was more than 27 times the GDP rate. The garment exports reached more than USD25 billion and shrimp exports worth USD650 million in 2015. The remittance hit USD15 billion and foreign reserve was at its peak at USD27 billion in 2015. Foreign reserves in 1983 were negligible while it climbed to USD43 billion in early 2022, well above the required minimum three months' imports for LDCs. On the rice production front (staple food), the nation was having a surplus of 2 million tonnes in 2015 as against a deficit of the same amount a few years back. The production has hit 33 million tonnes in recent years. The inflation rate has been brought down to a single digit, at 6.5 per cent in 2015. The inflation has been running at double digits over a long period of time since 1983. The literacy rate has improved with a strong pace, which is at 75 per cent or more at present and the longevity has crossed 72 years. Poverty reduction in terms of reducing extreme poverty in Asia; certainly the East Asian nations have been ahead of South Asia. The Head Count Ratio (HCR)

DOI: 10.4324/9781003231912-16

Table 11.1 Bangladesh's Achievements Over 1983–2015

Items	*1983*	*2015*	*Folds*
Population (in million)	90	160	1.80
Population growth rate (%)	2.7	1.7	1.60
Population per sq kilometre	590	1,030	1.70
GDP (in billion US$)	NA	205	–
GDP per capita (in US$)	150	1,300	8.67
Growth rate (%)	0.1	6.5	65.00
Garments Exports (in billion US$)	Nil	26	–
Shrimp Exports (in billion US$)	Neg	0.64	–
Remittance (in billion US$)	0.3	15.50	51.67
Foreign Reserve (in billion US$)	NA	27	–
Under Poverty Line (in %)	60	23	–2.60
Rice Production (in million tonne)	13	33	2.54
Inflation Rate (%)	19	6.5	–3.00
Literacy Rate (%)	25	65	2.60
Longevity (years)	45	70	1.60

Source: Several studies by this author and others.

Note: NA = Not available; Neg = Negligible.

Table 11.2 Poverty Reduction in Bangladesh, 2002–2015 (%)

Year	*People under Poverty**	*Hard-Core Poor***	*People above Poverty Level*
2002	44.6	–	55.4
2006	38.4	–	61.6
2009	33.4	–	66.6
2013	26.2	–	73.8
2015	24.3	10.6	75.5
2020	21.0	10.0	79.0

Source: The Planning Commission (PC) defines poverty in terms of calories a person requires per day. In Bangladesh this is about 2122Kcal. To purchase required calories the income of a person per month has been considered to determine who are poor or people under poverty and hard core poor. It has been estimated that Taka 3000 per capita per month is needed to buy 2122 Kcal per day. The following estimates have been provided by the PC for these groups:
*People under poverty: Having income below Taka 3000 per month per person is a poor
**Hard core poor: Having income below Taka 1600 per month per person is hard core poor.

suggests that almost half of the population in Bangladesh and 41 per cent in India lived under Purchasing Power Parity (PPP) $1.25 a day. Recently, the Bangladesh Planning Commission (PC) published a report on the country's achievements and non-achievements in poverty reduction until 2014. The PC's assessment was based on data collected by the Bangladesh Bureau of Statistics (BBS).

Table 11.2 presents a picture of poverty reduction over 2002 and 2014. Figures for 2014 are very encouraging. The national poverty level went down to one-fourth of the population compared to almost one-half in early 2000. More interestingly, hard core poor in 2015 makes 10.6 per cent out of the 24.3 per cent of total poor. This suggests that if this momentum can be continued; the prediction is by 2021, the 50th anniversary of the nation's independence, it would be in a position to push another 15 per cent out of poverty and the entire hard-core poor eliminated with only 10 per cent of the total population would remain poor. In absolute terms, this would be below 20 million under the poverty line as against the present-day 40 million. In absolute terms, indeed poverty will remain a challenge for the nation in the years to come due to the pandemic, COVID–19.

With all these achievements in the economic and social fronts, according to the World Bank's definition of prosperity, Bangladesh has now on the path to become a lower-middle-income nation, progressing from least developed. The next step on the ladder is achieving middle income and it appears that with current development in economic activities, it is indeed likely to be achieved by 2030, providing the country maintains political stability. In view of the above, the incumbent government has a major agenda in place called Vision 2041. The aim of this vision is to make the nation catch up with more developed nations, at least in economic and social terms. In other words, it would like to achieve a GDP per capita in PPP terms equivalent to developed nations and reach literacy rate, longevity, sanitation, maternal and child mortality, nutrition intake, and so on at par developed nations. Of course, these are tall orders to achieve by another quarter of a century. However, if Bangladesh continues to grow at the present pace for another 25 to 30 years, there is a possibility of reaching the targets before it celebrates 100 years of its birth in 2071. The major obstacles that appear on the horizon at this moment are the impacts of global warming induced climate change to 2100. It is predicted that the sea level will rise by 2100; if unabated, almost 40 per cent of the farmland would be inundated by saline water and more than half of its population would become climate refugees.

Education has a relative prosperity on the economic front; in recent years, education and its importance in Bangladesh have been effectively and sustainably gaining recognition over the last three decades. The country has now a literacy rate of 70 per cent; this was only 20 per cent in 1981 and 17 per cent in 1961. Education beyond the primary level has been within the reach of only the well-off. Some of the major problems and difficulties in improving education in Bangladesh have been inadequate implementation mechanisms in introducing education programmes, social inhibitions discouraging the education of girls, poverty, shortage of trained teachers, and lack of or poor quality of physical facilities. These are typical problems of developing countries in the 1960s and 1970s (Hossain and NOOSR, 1992). However, in Bangladesh, two forces, the GOs (public) and the NGOs (private), have worked together to improve education since the 1980s. Major efforts have been made to change the century-old education system, to make it more effective and universal and less elitist.

The Second Five-Year Plan (SFYP) of 1980–85, for the first time made a provision for a national primary education and mass literacy program. The government was willing to develop a skilled labour force base instead of expanding liberal education. The Third Five-Year Plan (TFYP) for 1986–1990 aimed at increasing primary age enrolments to 70 per cent and improve retention rate to the end of the primary school cycle. It also aimed to reduce the rural-urban gap in educational facilities, reduce the gap in educational opportunities between the sexes, continue the efforts to reduce illiteracy among adults, and provide more in-service training for teachers. To improve the degree of participation of the people in education development, efforts are being made to decentralize basic education at the Upazila (sub-district) level. However, there exist some issues that need immediate attention: unsatisfactory participation rate in post-primary education; high drop-out rates in all stages; access to education is unequal. The imbalance is twofold: a rural-urban imbalance and a gender imbalance; the availability of trained and committed teachers at the primary level. This has caused a major problem in terms of teacher-student ratio at the primary level, where a participation rate has jumped in recent years; the physical infrastructure still remains inadequate given the increase in participation rate; and absenteeism by primary teachers is a major cause of concern too. Given the above social issues and their impact on development, the Rohingya refugee crisis is a matter of great concern for Bangladesh. The next section presents how Bangladesh has been coping with more than a million refugees sheltered here.

11.2 Rohingya Conundrum

It is now recognized by both foreign and multilateral development partners and agencies that Bangladesh at last has momentum towards achieving prosperity; for example, a study by Kaushik Basu, the former chief economist of the World Bank, recently published an essay, *why is Bangladesh booming?* While domestically, the nation has been enjoying political stability, in a land of non-stop political unrest between military and quasi military regimes over 1975 and 1990, democratic regimes at work since 1991, the two political alliances are at loggerhead over the last quarter of a century. On top of these, there is always a threat of terrorism exists since many incidents have occurred in the nation since 1996. All these made great loss in GDP over the last two decades.

The Rohingya refugee crisis has been making the political stability and security of the nation from bad to worse. Myanmar's atrocities towards Rohingya people in the Arakan province pushed hundreds and thousands of refugees to Bangladesh. This is now recognized by the United Nations as ethnic cleansing on the part of Myanmar's military junta along with the support of religious monks. This operation pushed more than 1.1 million Rohingyas across the Bangladesh border in the space of 12 months. This refugee crisis created by Myanmar at a scale was unexpected and took the Bangladesh government entirely off-guard. The government had no option than open the border for Rohingya refugees as a safe haven. Now, Bangladesh is stuck with the problem. A few years back, the UN secretary general and the president of the World Bank visited refugee camps in Cox's Bazar together. Of course, this was not a pleasure trip for them, but wanted to show the world the seriousness of the crisis and that the poor Bangladesh cannot live like this alone for an indefinite period.

Also, recently the Bangladesh Diaspora in Brisbane Australia sent a petition with more than 2000 signatures to the parliament via the Hon. Graham Paratt, MP and Dr Jim Chalmers MP on 23 October 2017. Hon. Chambers said, "Labor expressed our deep concerns through the Shadow Foreign Minister, Senator Wong. What is happening there is horrific and inexcusable." In his speech Hon. Parett has forcefully said, "The atrocities committed against the Rohingya community in Rakhine State are almost beyond our comprehension ... It is crucial that there is unimpeded humanitarian access to the camps in Bangladesh and that regional partners, including Australia, work together in response to this crisis to ensure that the Rohingya population has a safe and secure place to live in peace." At this stage, repatriation of 1.1 million Rohingya refugees is the priority of the Bangladesh government. In one count, it has confirmed that the Rohingya refugees are staying in 12 cramped camps spread across 5,000 acres of land (Photo 11.1 and 11.2).

To get firsthand knowledge about the crisis, UN Secretary-General António Guterres and World Bank President Jim Yong Kim visited the camps together, accompanied by Bangladesh's former Foreign Minister AHM Mahmood Ali in the month of July. It is unprecedented that such a visit took place to see

Photo 11.1 "Rohingya Support Group" Leaders in Brisbane, Australia with Honourable Graham Perret, MP.

Photo 11.2 "Rohingya Support Group" Leaders in Brisbane, Australia with Honourable James Chalmers, MP and Treasurer of Australian Government.

conditions of the camps firsthand in the monsoon season. They have watched by moving freely in the camps the worst conditions refugees have been dealing with in a foreign land, in one hand. On the other, the locals seem to now realize, enough is enough, and asking what on earth made these people suffer from untold conditions for no reason. The Bangladesh government is getting nervous about this huge crowd of locals and refugees who could be in conflict at any time over the entitlement of aid money and inadequate resources for the refugees. This is not new. Many such incidents took place in South Pacific nations in recent times when Australia sent the boat people in the offshore camps to several South Pacific nations (Photo 11.3 and 11.4).

11.3 Conclusion

One must emphasize that, in the era of uncertainty and looming trade wars between US-China, war between Russia and Ukraine, and the pandemic, the bed of politics is warming up again in several parts of the world and taking a turn to create more uncertainty in both economic and security fronts of the Asia Pacific and other parts of the world. Opening a new front in a strategic region, crowded by interest groups of two large Asian giants, India and China, is certainly a matter

Photo 11.3 Refugees Participated in a Peaceful Protest in the Camps.

Photo 11.4 The UN Secretary General and World Bank President, Together with Bangladesh's Former Foreign Minister with Refugee Leaders in the Camp.

of great concern for this part of the world. Australia, a middle power nation in the region, needs to recognize this new threat of uncertainty close to its doorstep involving its trading partners and political allies. The Rohingya issue must be addressed soon before it gets out of hand, to say the least. Repatriation of 1.1 million Rohingya refugees within a short period of time indeed remains a priority.

References

Aga Khan Development Network (AKDN) (2017).

Haider, A (2016), 'Bangladesh Out of the Basket' *The Daily Star*, 23 January, Dhaka.

Hossain M and Hoque S (2016), Rhetorical Bottomless Basket Case versus Bangladesh's Success with the MDGs, *Outlook 2016*, World Association for Sustainable Development (WASD), Emerald Press, London.

Hossain M and Howard P (2014), 'The Sanitation Access to Developing Asia: India's Performance Over 2001 and 2011', *World Journal of Science, Technology and Sustainable Development*, vol 11, no 2, pp. 93–101.

Hossain M and Noosr (1992), *Country Education Profiles – Bangladesh – A comparative Study*, National Office of Overseas Skills Recognition, Department of Employment, Education and Training, Australian Government Publishing Service (AGPS), Canberra.

Hossain M and Selvanathan E eds (2011), *Climate Change and Growth in Asia*, Edward Elgar Publishing, Cheltenham and Mas.

Prothom Alo (2018) Bengali Daily, 4 June.

'Rohingya Support Group' (2017), Interview with Leaders, Brisbane, Australia.

Sen A and Dreze J (2013), *An Uncertain Glory: India and Its Contradiction*, Princeton University Press, Princeton.

Shah, J (2015), 'Four Crore (40 million Out of 160) People are under Poverty', *Prothom Alo* (Bengali Daily), 12 February, Dhaka, http://southasiajournal.net/bangladeshs-rohingya-conundrum/

12 Sanitation Development in Asia: India, Bangladesh, and Cambodia Compared

Paul Howard

12.1 Introduction

12.1.1 India

Let us look at first the case of India. Sanitation development became a major focus of the government in India when Narendra Modi and his BJP party swept to power in a landslide election in 2014. Indeed, the goal of providing universal access to sanitation with a nationalist fervour formed part of Modi's explicit election platform during the campaign. Given the relatively undeveloped status of sanitation development, particularly in rural and peri-urban India at the time (Sen, 2013; Hossain and Howard, 2014), the recent claims by Modi of success in attaining universal sanitation access would seem remarkable. There is no denying the fact that sanitation infrastructure development has been given focus within the government and there were successes too on the ground in many areas.

However, the reality can be contested, and it could be argued that claims of success may be premature. One of the difficulties in obtaining a meaningful picture of the current state of sanitation access in India (and in other places too) is the lack of substantive data. This is not a criticism, as governmental focus was largely on fighting the COVID-19 pandemic and, of course, the very nature of the pandemic and the lockdowns have put much data gathering on hold or at least delayed. This extends to the national census, which has now been targeted for completion and release in 2024. Prior censuses provided a rich source of data for prior research (see Hossain and Howard, 2014).

With that in mind, one may argue that the current situation is certainly complex. On the one hand, it seems that despite lack of political focus on the issue and claims of success, there are any challenges remaining in terms of providing universal access to sanitation. This though does not negate the fact that India is now farther down the road to the goal of achieving universal access to sanitation and that should be celebrated. Having said that, truly resolving the issue of fragmented sanitation will ultimately be achieved by a continued focus and cooperation at all levels of government. In other words, the relative successes can be applauded but the focus must remain on the still elusive goal of sanitation for all, regardless of geographical location, local context, gender, or socioeconomic circumstances.

DOI: 10.4324/9781003231912-17

12.1.2 COVID-19 Pandemic Impact on Sanitation Development in India

Whilst this chapter builds on previous research, there was not the broad-scale data available for this study as there had been previously i.e. there was a fairly comprehensive suite of relevant data from the 2000 and 2010 censuses (Hossain and Howard, 2014). As a result, a variety of secondary sources have also been utilized to build on the more comprehensive statistical picture obtained from the earlier analyses. Given this, a definitive assessment of the situation is impossible and it is hoped that the ultimate completion of the national census will allow a substantial longitudinal analysis at some point.

The COVID-19 pandemic led to numerous problems for India's improve sanitation rollout. For example, with supply chain issues and problems with access to fresh water in many places, the construction of unsanitary and illegal toilet facilities boomed. Akhilesh (2021) summarizes some of the pandemic-related issues:

> Newly-built 'dry latrines' and 'hanging toilets' in rural India are the result of the lockdowns of 2020–21 despite the Prohibition of Employment of Manual Scavengers and their Rehabilitation Act, 2013, and a strict ban. Sanitary toilet usage has declined because of the COVID-19 scare as, currently, more than six lakh (six hundred thousand) toilets in rural India have acute water shortage. Around 1,20,000 toilets have no water supply and thousands of toilets are completely abandoned, with collapsing roofs, water pipes in poor shape and soggy, broken doors. This is primarily the reason for the construction of illegal toilets, as sanitary toilets have become hotbeds of disease.

12.2 Claims of India's Success with Sanitation Development

On 2nd October 2019, the Indian government essentially declared India defecation free (Swachh Barat Mission, 2021). Some claimed this was more a politically based claim rather than the actuality on the ground. It is worth pointing out that interpretation of data pertaining to the rollout of facilities may also account for discrepancies. For example, there may be in some cases a possible disconnect between installation of facilities and usage and even functioning of facilities as intended. Further to this, Behera et al. (2021) offer analysis of the progress of the 'Clean India Mission' (known in India as the Swachh Barat Mission), which includes some analysis of the overall achievements of the program along with pertinent observations about discrepancies between official data and reality on the ground.

For example, Behera et al. (2021) note that over 100 million latrines had been built by the end of phase one of the Swachh Barat Mission and that all villages in India had been officially declared 'Open Defecation Free'. However, at the same time, the authors assert that over half of the population was still engaging in open defecation. Behera et al. (2021) cite contributing factors to this discrepancy between officially recognized infrastructure development and actual usage of the facilities including 'lack of piped water supply, poor construction of toilet substructures and misconception among people about toilet use'.

While substantive hard data (such as that may be available in the delayed national census) may not be readily available, an interview-based assessment of the outcomes of India's National Sanitation Campaign by Curtis (2019) provides some pertinent insights. Curtis interviewed '17 actors in the government's 'Clean India' programme across the national capital and four states' which were analyzed utilizing 'a theory of change grounded in Behaviour Centred Design'. Curtis (2019) ultimately concludes that whilst 'many challenges remain, governments seeking to achieve the sustainable development goal of universal access to safe sanitation can emulate the success of India's Swachh Bharat Mission'.

Interestingly, Curtis (2019) provided a summary of interviewees' explanations for the 'discrepancies between individual surveys and government figures' along with their collective assessment of the actual progress made:

> that included inaccuracies in the original government baseline against which progress is reported, the omission from the SBM programme of households with old toilets which had fallen out of use, and systemic incentives to over-report results. Nevertheless, interviewees described exceptional progress in improving toilet coverage over the past 4 years, transforming India from a country where the majority defaecated in the open, to one where most people have, and use, toilets.

There are a couple of points that one can make, seeng disparity between the overall assessment by Curtis and alternate views. Firstly, it should be noted that Curtis is not simply saying that universal sanitation has been achieved. The point Curtis ultimately makes as outlined above is that great progress has been made. In other words, this does not contradict her findings but rather provides context and consideration of the situation that had persisted previously.

12.3 Parallels and Comparisons

12.3.1 Bangladesh

According to the World Bank, Bangladesh saw open defecation virtually eradicated to less than 1 per cent of the population by 2015. However, only around 61 percent of the population had access to 'improved sanitation' as of 2016 with that rate only increasing by around 1.1 percent per annum (World Bank, 2020). Further, the World Bank (2020) notes that 'Planning and service delivery are often supply driven, and government agencies have overlapping functions and pay insufficient attention to operation and maintenance issues'. This suggests that co-operation between government agencies is lacking and/or that a purely market-driven response does not guarantee a sufficient and sustainable solution.

This does reinforce the notion that whilst market-driven solutions may be effective in terms of economic incentive-driven change and adoption, non-investor oversight is crucial. To lean on a purely financial parallel, stock exchanges and associated authorities and corruption etc. must all work effectively to provide sufficient oversight for companies and exchanges to operate in a sustainable fashion. In other words, sanitation, just like financial markets, requires both robust market-driven innovation in conjunction with independent (at least in theory) oversight.

In terms of a direct comparison to the situation in India, the commonality is that the development of infrastructure must be matched with ongoing maintenance, with real usage of facilities the ultimate focus.

12.3.2 Cambodia

12.3.2.1 Market-Based Solutions

The World Bank, in partnership with the Stone Family foundation (SFF), developed a framework for a market-driven approach to addressing Cambodia's sanitation issues. The framework was incorporated into the Cambodia Improving Rural Water and Sanitation Services (CIRWSS) program that ran from 2016 until 2020 (World Bank, 2020). The CIRWSS focused on developing both institutional capacity and private-sector capacity such that government and private sectors could operate in an efficient symbiotic relationship that worked toward universal sanitation coverage in the country.

For example, under the partnerships' technical assistance program (TA), the National Action Plan for Rural Water Supply, Sanitation and Hygiene was aimed at decentralizing rural sanitation oversight to the various levels of government from provincial level to district level and ultimately commune level along with developing private-sector capacity (World Bank, 2020). One very specific initiative was the development of the Cambodia Rural Sanitation Development Impact Bond (DIB), which was developed by a partnership between SFF, IDE, and USAID. The DIB would be 'repaid with a modest return' but this is contingent on quantifiable outcomes being achieved (Hedley, 2021).

The 'community-led total sanitation' (CLTS) approach was implemented in numerous villages throughout rural Cambodia under the oversight of Plan International. Plan International claims that since its initial beginnings in 2006, CLTS has seen 750 villages eradicating the practice of open defecation (Plan International, 2021) with over 700 latrines and hand-washing facilities being constructed since its inception.

12.4 Comparison to Indian Access

Before comparing, it is useful to present data of the three nations and their status, taking rural and urban use of improved sanitation facilities. The data shown in the table below have been taken from Hossain and Howard (2014) (Table 12.1).

Table 12.1 Access to improved sanitation for India, Bangladesh, and Cambodia; Rural, urban, and combined, 2010 (in %)

Nation	*Rural*	*Urban*	*National*
India	23	56	34
Bangladesh	55	57	56
Cambodia	20	85	31

Source: Hossain M and Howard P (2014).

As could be expected, the percentages for urban sanitation access are generally far higher than rural access for all three nations. Comparing national averages, certainly Bangladesh was doing much better than India and Cambodia. More than half of the population of Bangladesh had access, whereas both India and Cambodia had one-third of the population with sanitation access in 2010.

Both Cambodia and India's levels of sanitation access have been among the lowest in the world. Indeed, on an aggregate national basis, as of 2011 Cambodia is the second worst performer in the broader Asian region (incorporating East; Northeast; Southeast; Southwest and North and Central Asia) with just 33 percent of the Cambodians having access to 'improved sanitation' (UNESCAP, 2014). Only Afghanistan ranks lower on this basis, with just 28 percent of the population having access to improved sanitation (UNESCAP, 2014). Significantly, India performed only marginally better than Cambodia, with 35 percent of Indians having access to improved sanitation.

At the urban level, Cambodia does perform better than some countries in the region. Seventy-six percent of urban Cambodians have access to improved sanitation. However, at the rural level, Cambodia has the lowest levels of sanitation access in the Asian region. Just 22 percent of rural Cambodians have access to improved sanitation (UNESCAP, 2014). This compares to the next worst performers, Afghanistan (23 percent) and India (24 percent) rural residents having sanitation access (UNESCAP, 2014).

There is as might be expected with great diversity among Southeast Asian countries in terms of sanitation access and Cambodia performing poorly at the overall national level. For example, at one end of the spectrum, Singapore has 100 percent coverage, followed by Malaysia (96 percent) and Thailand (93 percent) (UNESCAP, 2014). In contrast, Timor-Leste has the second-lowest level of sanitation coverage (39 percent) at an aggregate national level (UNESCAP, 2014) with Cambodia having the lowest aggregate national level of sanitation access at 33 percent of people having access to improved sanitation (UNESCAP, 2014). The picture is more fragmented in terms of the more specific levels of rural and urban coverage. Indeed, on an urban basis, Cambodia has 76 percent coverage. This figure is higher than the urban-level coverage for both Timor-Leste (68 percent) and Indonesia, with 73 percent of urban residents having access to improved sanitation (UNESCAP, 2014).

In 1990, Cambodia's levels of sanitation access were around 19 percent in urban areas, but only around 2 percent nationally (WHO/UNICEF, 2015). Like India, Cambodia's population was predominantly agrarian, but sanitation access in India was far higher with nearly 50 percent of urban residents and a national figure of around 17 percent. By the year 2000, the percentage of Cambodians with access to sanitation on a national basis had risen to 16 percent, with the percentage of urban residents with sanitation access more than doubling to 43 percent in the ten-year period from 1990. In the year 2000, Cambodia's sanitation access levels were still significantly lower than India's on a comparative basis in both rural and urban areas.

By 2015 though, Cambodia's levels of sanitation access had surpassed India's. For example, the 2015 data shows that 88 percent of urban Cambodians have sanitation access compared to around 63 percent of urban residents in India (WHO/UNICEF, 2015). In rural areas, the percentage of Cambodians with sanitation access had trebled between 2000 and 2015 to reach 30 percent of the population as opposed to rural India, where access levels had doubled in the same period to stand with to arrive at around 28 percent. On a national basis, by 2015, just over 42 percent of Cambodians had access to improved sanitation, slightly more than the approximately 40 percent of Indians with access to improved sanitation (WHO/UNICEF, 2015).

12.5 Sanitation Nationalism

There are several parallels that can be drawn between India's and Cambodia's sanitation development from low access during pre-2015 period. Both have comparatively low levels of sanitation development in global and regional terms. Both countries have large rural-urban disparities in terms of levels of sanitation access. Both places also have in common the need for education about the need for improved sanitation and hygiene practices among the broader population, particularly in rural areas. In recent times though, India has been making significant progress in achieving its goals in relation to these issues. Indeed, India has seemingly embraced a form of 'sanitation nationalism' where sanitation is not merely seen as a developmental issue that needs to be addressed but is actually a national priority that has resonated among the public and political leaders.

Cambodia's relatively strong performance in recent years does not in itself dismiss the need for clearer political focus as irrelevant. It could be equally argued, for example, that a more decisive and coordinated approach by government may have seen Cambodia with even better levels of sanitation access. The political focus aside, the question remains as to why Cambodia's sanitation levels have increased so substantially in recent years. NGOs have been very active in Cambodia and the UN and WHO have focused on addressing the country's low levels of sanitation access and the World Bank has worked directly with the Cambodian government.

As far back as 2007, Cambodia's Prime Minister Hun Sen did explicitly note the need for Cambodia to improve its levels of sanitation development, but the message seems to have been one of prescription about what should be done by ordinary Cambodians. For example, Kimsong (2007) asserted at that time that 'improvement in the health situation does not require complicated modern technology and a lot of money ... It should start with what people already have and understand to change their living habits'. What was not so clear was the government's commitment to a sustainable integrated programme of sanitation development to get people onto the 'sanitation ladder'.

In India, it was difficult to really discern a complete integrated approach toward achieving universal nationwide sanitation development. In recent times, that has changed, and it is fair to say that it was driven by the imperative of the election process. The BJP under Modi's leadership designated sanitation development as an explicit priority policy area during the 2014 general election. For example, the BJP's 2014 'election manifesto' designated that in urban areas 'cleanliness and sanitation' be 'prioritized' and under the geographically broader health initiatives, it was explicitly stated that 'integrated infrastructure' would be 'rolled out in Model towns' and that in pursuit of the goal of having an 'open defecation free India', there will be sanitation rankings of 'cities and towns' with rewards for the 'best performers' (BJP, 2014). In May 2014, the BJP with Modi as prime minister won the election. In the period following the election though, India's sanitation fervour increased and in October, PM Modi launched the 'Clean India' campaign, which has sanitation as a national priority.

12.6 Women and the Young

In early 2014, UNICEF India launched 'Mr Poo', an animated character serving as India's 'mascot' for sanitation awareness. Mr Poo even came with a 'techno' song, 'take the poo to the loo' (UNICEF India, 2014), in a clear effort to appeal to younger Indians. This focus on the young potentially mobilizes action that will create a sanitation mentality among subsequent generations. At the policy level, the Indian prime minister had stipulated a deadline of August 15, 2015, for all schools to have separate toilets for boys and girls (Joshua, 2014). In conjunction with this, The Union Human Resource Development Ministry issued a handbook as part of the 'Clean Schools' campaign outlining how sanitation facilities should be maintained (Joshua, 2014).

In Cambodia, actions appear to be more fragmented with some NGOs trying to develop awareness. For example, in Kampong Cham, Plan International has had children marching in the village areas with signs about the need for sanitation. Similarly, IDE Cambodia is engaging villagers in sanitation development and using what they describe as an 'edgy' campaign to get the message across. The common thread amongst all these campaigns is that they primarily are aimed at school-aged children.

Chakrabati et al. (2020) conducted a 'cross-sectional analysis of 134 882 children and adolescents aged 0 to 18 years in India' utilizing data collected from an India-wide District Level Household and Facilities Survey (2012 to 2014). The conclusion of that study was that 'poor sanitation (ie, open defecation and lack of access to boiled or filtered drinking water) was associated with lower height-for-age scores across all ages in childhood and adolescence' (Chakrabati et al., 2020). Based on their findings, the authors' suggested that 'a reduction in open defecation and improved access to clean drinking water may benefit growth across multiple periods in childhood and adolescence'.

The study (Chakrabati et al., 2020) also pointed to a differentiation of outcomes between genders and in terms of the rural-urban divide. For example, women face more difficulties accessed proper sanitation facilities. This also has an effect with girls suffering a greater incidence of absenteeism during school years due to both difficulties with menstruation and/or lack of sufficiently private sanitation facilities in some schools.

This disparity of sanitation outcomes based on gender and location is consistent with the outcomes observed previously. Whilst the disparity of access and outcomes remains, there is now a clear will for this to be addressed via the Swach Barat Mission. For example, a report entitled 'Access to toilets and the safety, convenience and self-respect of women in rural India' was the result of co-operation between Department of Drinking Water and Sanitation, Ministry of Jal Shakti, UNICEF, the Bill & Melinda Gates Foundation, and the WASH Institute (2021).

Ironically, whilst women in many developing countries are more likely to suffer negative education and health impacts from poor sanitation facilities and practices, they generally have far less input into meaningful sanitation development and reform processes. Livani et al. (2021) assert that even if women are technically part of the consultative and decision-making processes, they in actuality of relatively minimal input. This gender disparity of input is largely driven by social and cultural norms i.e. the women represented in working groups to address sanitation issues 'either do not attend meetings, and when they do, they tend to sit in the back and speak less than men, because they don't think their opinion matters, they are afraid to make mistakes and they don't want to undermine male family members' (Livani et al., 2021).

It is particularly difficult to make any definitive assessment of the current situation about outcomes for children and women given the lack of specific data. What is certain though is that the continued development and operation of adequate sanitation facilities must incorporate education for children to ensure complete generational change. In regard to sanitation development and women, it would seem that there remains some challenges with regard to the ability of women to have input into the decision-making process. This is not a criticism but rather simply underscoring the notion that women must not be peripheral to the process. Indeed, an argument could certainly be made those women are more affected by many of the issues surrounding inadequate sanitation facilities or the ability to access them safely.

12.7 Conclusion

In the absence of more specific recent data, there is evidence of a disconnect between some proclamations of success and reality on the ground. There may be a roll-out of infrastructure development, but emphasis needs too to be on the ultimate levels of usage of facilities. This may in part depend in some cases on education but, more critically, there needs to be checks and balances down to the local level where installations have occurred to ensure ongoing maintenance.

There is also some evidence of women perhaps not have the level of input into the decision-making process that may be needed. This may be driven in part by sociocultural factors, which is problematic but not insurmountable. The solution to those very sensitive and complex issues are beyond the scope of this chapter to address but it is important to at least underscore the need for the consultative process to fully incorporate the voice of women. This is not a criticism but rather is simply to point out the tremendous potential to overcoming many challenges in sanitation development by addressing any gender divide regarding decision making.

India has inarguably made great strides toward universal access to sanitation. A declaration of total victory in delivering sanitation to all seems though to be premature. In the coming years, ultimate success in truly providing quality sanitation access may be achieved with infrastructural practicalities such as facility management and maintenance in conjunction with building social capital including a stronger voice in the decision-making process for women.

As noted at the beginning of this chapter, the response to the pandemic led to the postponement of the Indian census. Consequently, there is limited real data to form a meaningful picture of the true state of sanitation development in India. It is hoped that a further longitudinal analysis (building on prior research) can be developed when more data becomes available.

References

Akhilesh, P. (2021), 'The pandemic has exposed India's dirty truth: a broken sanitation system' in *The Indian Express*. Available at https://indianexpress.com/article/opinion/columns/the-pandemic-has-exposed-indias-dirty-truth-a-broken-sanitation-system-7292937/

Behera, M.R., Pradhan, H.S., Behera, D.J., and Satpathy, S.K (2021), 'Achievements and challenges of India's sanitation campaign under clean India mission: A Commentary', *Journal of Education and Health Promotion*, 10 September, Vol. 10, pp 1–7.

BJP (2014), 'BJP Election Manifesto 2014', accessed 10 December, available at http://www.narendramodi.in/wp-content/uploads/2014/04/Manifesto2014highlights.pdf

Chakrabati, S., Singh, P., and Bruckner T., 'Association of Poor Sanitation With Growth Measurements Among Children in India'. JAMA Netw Open. 2020 Apr 1;3(4):e202791. doi: 10.1001/jamanetworkopen.2020.2791

Curtis, V. (2019), 'Explaining the outcomes of the 'Clean India' campaign: institutional behaviour and sanitation transformation in India', *BMJ Global Health*, 4

Hedley, S. 'Why we invested in the Cambodia Rural Sanitation Development Impact Bond' Stone Family Foundation, November 22 2019, https://www.thesff.com/why-we-invested-inthe-cambodia-sanitation-dib/

Hossain, M. and Howard, P. (2014), 'The sanitation access to developing Asia: India's performance over 2001 and 2011' *World Journal of Science, Technology and Sustainable Development*, 11(2), 93–101.

IDE Cambodia, 'Sanitation Marketing' accessed 17 December, available at http://www.ide-cambodia.org/index.php?option=com_content&view=article&id=57:projects&catid=34:about-us&Itemid=2&lang=en

Joshua, A. (2014), 'Ministers give a head start for 'Clean India' campaign', *The Hindu*, October 2, accessed 16 December, available at http://www.thehindu.com/todays-paper/tp-national/ministers-give-a-head-start-for-clean-india-campaign/article6467366.ece

Kimsong, K., (2007), 'PM Urges for Increase of Sanitation Coverage', *Cambodia Daily*, November 14, available at https://www.cambodiadaily.com/archives/pm-urges-for-increase-of-sanitation-coverage-56066/

Livani, T., Ahmed R., and Ahmed, S.O. (2021), July 27, 'Enhancing women's access to water, sanitation, and hygiene in Bangladesh' *World Bank Blogs* https://blogs.worldbank.org/endpovertyinsouthasia/enhancing-womens-access-water-sanitation-and-hygiene-bangladesh

Plan International (2021), 'Cambodia Sanitation Project' accessed 17 December, available at http://plan-international.org/pictures/slideshows/cambodia-sanitation-project/

Plan International (2021), 'Water, Sanitation and Hygiene in Cambodia'. https://plan-international.org/water-sanitation-and-hygiene-cambodia

Sen, A. (2013), 'India: a defence and a critique' GL Mehta Memorial Lecture, Indian Institute of Technology, Bombay, January 5

Swach Barat Mission – Grameen (Department of Drinking Water and Sanitation, Ministry of Jal Shakti (2021), 'About SBM' https://swachhbharatmission.gov.in/sbmcms/index.htm

UNESCAP (2014), 'Statistical Yearbook for Asia and the Pacific 2013', accessed 5 December available at http://www.unescap.org/stat/data/syb2013/D.2-Access-to-water-and-sanitation.asp

UNICEF, Bill and Melinda Gates Foundation and Sambodhi Research, 'Access to toilets and the safety, convenience and self-respect of women in rural India' Available at https://swachhbharatmission.gov.in/sbmcms/writereaddata/Portal/Images/pdf/Safety-security-and-dignity-of-women.pdf

UNICEF India (2014), 'Take the Poo to the Loo', animated video, available at https://www.youtube.com/watch?v=_peUxE_BKcU

World Bank (2016), 'Bangladesh: Improving Water Supply and Sanitation' https://www.worldbank.org/en/results/2016/10/07/bangladesh-improving-water-supply-and-sanitation

World Bank (2020), *Partnering for Impact – Strengthening Institutions to Bring Water and Sanitation Services to Cambodia's Rural Areas*, Results Briefs July 22, https://www.worldbank.org/en/results/2020/07/22/partnering-for-impact---strengthening-institutions-to-bring-water-and-sanitation-services-to-cambodias-rural-areas

WHO/UNICEF (2015), JMP (Joint Monitoring Program for Water Supply and Sanitation), Data Tables, accessed 30 November 2015, available at http://www.wssinfo.org/data-estimates/tables/

Part V
Conclusions

The final part provides concluding remarks.

DOI: 10.4324/9781003231912-18

13 Sustainable Growth and Bangladesh's Prospects of Long-Term Prosperity

Moazzem Hossain

13.1 Introduction

The overall aim of this volume was to make a medium- to long-term assessment of the ascendancy of Bangladesh. Why Bangladesh? This is the only nation in South Asia, since the declaration of the pandemic, that has been posting positive economic growth. According to the IMF, this nation has achieved a GDP growth of 4.3 per cent in fiscal 2020. Of course, Bangladesh has suffered a decline, too. For example, the GDP declined by almost 3.9 percent in fiscal 2020 from a strong growth of 8.2 per cent in fiscal 2019 (PC 2021).

It is now confirmed from various sources like the International Monetary Fund (IMF) and the World Bank (WB) that, due to the 2020 pandemic, the South Asia region has taken a deep downturn economically, except for Bangladesh. It occurs to the editors of this volume that the pandemic has thrown the region into an alarming position economically and health-wise. Moreover, the future remains uncertain in the short to medium term. Despite being one of the most populous nations in the region, and while reporting a reduction of almost half the prior year's economic growth in fiscal 2020 (8.2 in 2019, 4.3 in 2020), Bangladesh is the only nation in South Asia that is reporting positive growth in fiscal 2020.

Indeed, Bangladesh achieved significant economic progress in terms of GDP growth and per capita income during the decade since 2009. The GDP growth was continuously at over 6 per cent per annum up to fiscal 2015, over 7 per cent in the following three years, and over 8 per cent in fiscal 2019. Per capita income increased from USD 781 in 2010 to USD 1,909 in 2019 and hit USD 2,036 in 2020 and has been growing. Significant improvements have been made in key social indicators, including in poverty and extreme poverty ratios; infant, child, and maternal mortality rates; life expectancy at birth; and literacy rate.

The pandemic, however, has impacted the nation strongly. It would be interesting to assess the recovery and the growth trajectory in the short to medium term in years to come. Given that Bangladesh's growth has ranged from 6 to more than 8 per cent between 2009 and 2019, it certainly warrants a close look at the nation's hidden capacities to grow further in the post-pandemic period. The editors are of the view that, given Bangladesh's ascendancy over the last one and a half decades, this country certainly provides a developmental role model for South Asia.

DOI: 10.4324/9781003231912-19

Bangladesh's developmental capability has recently been noted by its long-term political arch-rival Pakistan, which recently referred to Bangladesh using the following words "Fifty Years of Bangladesh: The Rising Sun!"

"An inspiration and a challenge for policy makers, the story of Bangladesh is an unmatched development. The country's economic performance all around achievements are unprecedented in the region and worth emulating" (South Asia, March 2021).

It is indeed a prime time now to investigate the secrets of Bangladesh's miracle and lessons learned by other South Asian economies and beyond. Most recently, in the middle of a pandemic, Bangladesh celebrated its 50th year of independence (1971–2021). It appears that over the last 50 years the nation attracted friends and foreign investors from all over the world. More than 27 nations, including leaders from the United States, Canada, United Kingdom, Japan, South Korea, EU, Russia, and China made commitments in their messages to the leader of Bangladesh that they will keep investing for Bangladesh's prosperity to the next 50 years. Moreover, leaders of India, Sri Lanka, Nepal, Maldives, and Bhutan have visited Bangladesh as state guests over 17–26 March 2021 in the middle of the COVID-19 pandemic and made commitments to become part of Bangladesh's ascendancy. There were 54 big businesses and foreign investors joined with their respective nations and committed with their counterparts in Bangladesh in international business collaboration in the future. Bangladesh has established 100 industrial development parks all over the nation and invited the foreign businesses to take part with Bangladeshi counterparts engaged in international trade. This nation also is in the middle of building infrastructure with mega projects like the six-kilometre-long Padma Bridge, Karnafuli river tunnel, deep seaport, and metro rail projects in Dhaka. All these mega projects are scheduled to open for business by June 2022 and end of 2025. In fact, Padma Bridge is ready to open for the public on 23 June 2022. Hon PM Sheikh Hasina will open the bridge on this day. This 6.5 km bridge will add to the GDP from 2022 to the tune of 1.35 to 2 per cent gradually. This will also connect the west and southern parts of Bangladesh to the capital, Dhaka, within six hours. Earlier, the return trip between these regions took a day or two. It is a two-storey bridge. The top storey is used for road and communications and the bottom storey will be used for modern railway service. Most importantly, this huge investment was born by domestic sources (see more in the web) (Image 13.1).

13.2 An Overview of Bangladesh's Growth and Development

13.2.1 Growth Between 1990 and 2005

South Asia consists of a number of countries of very disparate size and complexity. For example, the region consists of a vast economy like India, a population with more than 1.3 billion, which ranks number five in the world in

Image 13.1 Newly Built Padma Bridge of Bangladesh.

Source: Prothom Alo (2022).

terms of industrial production, to the tiny Maldives, with a population about a little over 300,000 and an economy primarily based on fishing and tourism. Since this volume is about Bangladesh, this nation has a population of more than 170 million and an economy of garment and remittance sectors, witnessing meteoric rise since 1990. Table 13.1 presents Bangladesh's socio-economic development in the 1990s, covering the pre-MDGs initiative of the United Nations. It is clear from this table that Bangladesh was at the bottom of the ladder to 1995.

Table 13.1 Bangladesh's Conditions: Per Capita GDP and Human Development Indicators Against Other South Asian Nations and Korea

Country	*GDP per capita ($PPP)*		*Adult literacy*		*Life expectancy (yrs)*	
	1960	*1995*	*1970*	*1995*	*1960*	*1995*
Bangladesh	621	1,380	24	37	39.6	56
India	617	1,400	34	51	44	61
Pakistan	820	2,230	21	36	43.1	62
Sri Lanka	1,389	3,250	77	90	62	72
Korea	690	11,450	88	95+	53.9	72

Source: Hossain et al. (2010).

13.2.2 MDGs: A Tale of Two Asias (2000–2015)

One would remember this author made a brief presentation in the introduction of this volume in order to introduce what one expects out of the volume. It was clear in the intro that the eight goals of MDGs is the first of the two UN plans for developing countries to make a start in the very beginning of the millennium, engaging in the development process more seriously. Now the MDGs period well and truly is over. In this section, we tried to analyze the Bangladesh case and would like to make it clear how Bangladesh performed over 2000 and 2015.

It must be clear that the first goal of the MDGs was to reduce poverty by half by 2015 from the 1990 level. Bangladesh has its share of achievements in meeting all these goals. The nation reduced poverty by half well before 2015. In achieving the sanitation target, Bangladesh made a breakthrough in providing access to both rural and urban people (see chapter 12 of this volume, including India and Cambodia). Table 13.2 provides results for three developing countries in Asia on MDGs in the early period in 2005. Of course, this table suggests that Bangladesh was sitting at the bottom of these countries with respect to poverty, headcount ratio (35 per cent), and also in terms of child mortality, maternal mortality rate, and primary education completion.

Table 13.3 investigates poverty in terms of extreme poverty eradication with a higher cost of daily requirements in 2008 in the middle of the MDGs period, including five countries from South and Southeast Asia. Once again, Bangladesh ranks bottom among these nations with almost half of the population suffering from extreme poverty.

To make the issue of poverty eradication from Bangladesh clearer, the Planning Commission took an alternative method than the HCR method, as shown in Table 13.3. Table 13.4 explains the method used for more accurate estimation with satisfying minimum kilocalories (Kcal) per day. In the literature of poverty eradication, the Kcal method was certainly found to be more acceptable to the experts and professionals. Table 13.4 covered MDGs almost the whole period from 2002 to 2014 for Bangladesh. In other words, Bangladesh reduced poverty by half in 2014, a year ahead of the deadline.

Table 13.2 Eradication of Extreme Poverty and Condition on Other Social Indicators

Country	*Poverty US$1 a day*	*Child mortality (under five maternal mortality ratio primary ed*		
	headcount ratio (%)	*mortality rate per 1,000)*	*per 100,000 live birth)*	*comp. %*
	2005	*2005*	*2005*	*2005*
Bangladesh	35	73	380	77
India	33.6	74	540	89
Philippines	10.5	33	200	98

Source: Hossain et al. (2010).

Table 13.3 Eradication of Extreme Poverty

Country *Year*	*Poverty (PPP$1.25) a day HCR (%)* *2008*	*National poverty line (%)* *2008*	*Share of consumption to poorest quantile* *2005*
Bangladesh	49.6	40.0	9.0
India	41.6	28.6	8.9
Pakistan	22.6	–	9.3
Indonesia	29.4	16.7	8.4
Vietnam	21.5	28.9	9.0

Source: Hossain and Hoque (2016).

Table 13.4 Poverty Reduction in Bangladesh During MDGs Period (2000–2015)

Year	*People under poverty**	*Hard-core poor***	*People above poverty level*
2002	44.6	–	55.4
2006	38.4	–	61.6
2009	33.4	–	66.6
2013	26.2	–	73.8
2014	24.3	10.6	75.5

Source: Shah (2015).

Notes: The Planning Commission defines poverty in terms of the calories a person requires per day. In Bangladesh, this is about 2,122 Kcal. To purchase required calories, the income of a person per month has been considered to determine who are poor or people under poverty and hard-core poor. It has been worked out that Taka 3000 per capita per month is needed to buy 2,122 Kcal per day. The following estimates have been provided by the PC for these groups.

* People under poverty: Having income below Taka 3000 per month per person is poor.

** Hard core poor having income below Taka 1600 per month per person is a hard-core poor.

13.2.3 Remittance in the Era of MDGs

Remittances, one of the most significant outcomes of international migration, are now estimated more than USD600 billion globally. Remittances sent home by international migrants from developing countries in 2015 stood at around USD432 billion in 20015, a figure that exceeded that of International Development Assistance. Among the top ten remittance-receiving countries in the world in 2015, five were in Asia, a pattern that is likely to be sustained into the future even though COVID-19 hit Asia badly too. Table 13.5 presents a clear picture of the volume of remittance inflows to the top five Asian receiving

Table 13.5 Remittance Over Last Four of the MDGs Years Among Top Ten Receiving Countries of the World: (2012–2015), USD billion

Country	*2012*	*2013*	*2014*	*2015*
Bangladesh	14.12	13.87	14.99	15.39
India	68.82	69.97	70.39	68.91
Pakistan	14.01	14.63	17.24	19.39
China	57.99	59.49	62.33	63.94
Philippines	23.35	25.37	27.27	28.48

Source: Hossain et al. (2017, p. 3).

countries. Bangladesh in particular gained rapid access to the international migrating countries and now in 2015 is one of the top ten remittance senders of the world. Even in the middle of COVID-19, this nation sustained sending remittances mainly from Gulf Cooperation Countries (GCC) and ASEAN member nations.

13.2.4 Ready-Made Garment Exports in the Era of MDGs

The RMG sector of Bangladesh started slowly, with a low rate of growth during the 1980s. However, it proliferated between 1991 and 2013, with factories rising from 834 to 5876. After 2013, a sharp decline was noticed in 2014, though an immediate recovery was observed from 2015. This is evidence of the substantial depth of the sector. In terms of employment, the industry employed 0.12 million people in 1985, and that number climbed to 4.00 million, nearly without interruption until 2018. Among these 4 million workers, the majority are female. Thus, the RMG industry plays a vital role in women's empowerment in Bangladesh (see Chapter 4 for details). The table below provides how the RMG exports are performing between 2000 and 2015, during the period of MDGs.

Between 2000 and 2015 the RMG exports increased by sixfold, while the total exports increased by almost the same. The RMG exports in 2000 was 75.61 per cent of the total exports while this was 81.68 per cent in 2015, the last year of the MDGs program (Table 13.6).

Table 13.6 Exports of RMG Over MDGs Period, 2000–2015 (in USD billion)

Year	*Export of RMGs*	*Total Exports of Bangladesh*	*% of RMG Exports*
2000	4.35	5.75	75.61
2015	25.49	31.30	81.68
Folds	6.00	5.50	–

Source: Chapter 4 of this volume.

Table 13.7 Apparel Exports Growth of Bangladesh as Against Other Asian Nations (%): 2000–2015

Bangladesh	*India*	*Pakistan*	*Vietnam*	*China*
25	15	7	20	15

Source: Selvanathan (2018).

Table 13.7 suggests that in Bangladesh, apparel exports growth over 2000 and 2015 was 25 per cent compared to India at 15 per cent, Pakistan at 7 per cent, Vietnam at 20 per cent, and China 15 per cent. Again, Bangladesh was ahead of its competitors by miles in the MDGs period.

13.2.5 Bangladesh's Vision 2021: What Lessons?

Hon Prime Minister Sheikh Hasina, MP, and her first government (1996–2001) made major contributions to transform the image of the nation at home and abroad. This five-year term was a time of significant changes and developments in Bangladesh, due in part to her government's development agenda and vision for the nation to 2021, known as Vision 2021. The 2021 vision is inspired by the optimism implicit in the dream of the Father of the Nation, Bangabandhu Sheikh Mujibur Rahman, to make Bangladesh a 'Golden Bengal'. Vision 2021 addresses the following issues, which Sheikh Hasina outlined in 2000:

- Is Bangladesh likely to be free from poverty by 2021, its golden jubilee of independence?
- Is Bangladesh likely to become a middle-level industrialized nation by 2021?
- Will Bangladesh continue to be a democracy in 2021? What changes need to occur and what institutions need to be in place to achieve the goals of the 2021 vision? [As the author of this chapter was a former Sheikh Mujibur Rahman (SMR) Professorial Fellow at the University of Hull, UK, he studied the Vision 2021 at Hull in 2001 and at Griffith University, Australia with his permanent position there and published a conference proceeding in 2003 out of an international conference held in Dhaka, Bangladesh] (Hossain et al 2003).

It was indeed a pleasure to write this piece and revisit Vision 2021, standing in year 2022. Certainly, the time has arrived to examine the reality of this vision when the nation has already reached the concluding year. Due to lack of space, this section investigates only the overall economic development between 2000 and 2015, covering the MDGs years.

Chapter 8 of this volume presents the phenomenal advancement enjoyed by the agriculture sector since 2000. The rice production has hit 33 million tonnes in 2015. The inflation rate has been brought down to a single digit, to 6.5 per cent in 2015, while the inflation has been running at double digits over a long period of time. The literacy rate has improved with a strong pace, which is at 90 per cent or more at present and the longevity has crossed 70 years.

Professor Amartya Sen and Jean Dreze have published a volume in 2014 called *An Uncertain Glory: India and its Contradictions*, in which authors have strongly criticized India's non-achievement in sanitation access even after this nation's recent success in economic prosperity. When compared with India's neighbors, they were disappointed that India placed well behind. Compared to its immediate neighbors, on an aggregate nationally, Bangladesh performs quite well in terms of improved and shared sanitation access. For example, a study by the present author jointly shows India, with 53 per cent access (improved plus shared facilities) to sanitation performs about the same relative to Pakistan (54 per cent) and poorly against Bangladesh (81 per cent) in 2010. Comparing this national performance in rural and urban areas, the difference at the urban level in India (77 per cent) is lower against Bangladesh (83 per cent) and Pakistan at 78 per cent. At the rural level, the difference has been phenomenal. For example, in Pakistan, 40 per cent of the rural population has access to an improved plus shared sanitation facility, which is significantly higher than the 27 per cent of rural people in India. In stark contrast to both India and Pakistan, in Bangladesh, 80 per cent of rural people have access. This raises the question of why Bangladesh has been outperforming Pakistan and India. The main reason was availability of microfinance and increased remittance to the rural people (Hossain and Howard (2014). These achievements are also mentioned in Sen's observations in the 16 July 2014 edition of the prestigious London-based daily, *The Guardian*.

With all these achievements in the economic and social fronts, according to the World Bank's definition of prosperity, Bangladesh is now on the path of becoming a middle-income nation, progressing from least developed. The next step on the ladder is joining OECD nations (USD 40,000 per capita income in PPP terms) by 2041 and it appears that with current development and economic activities, it is indeed likely to be achieved providing the country maintains the present growth trajectory.

In view of the above, the present government of Hon. Sheikh Hasina, MP, has the next agenda in place called Vision 2041. The aim of this vision is to make the nation catch up with more developed nations, at least in economic and social terms. In other words, it would like to achieve a GDP per capita in PPP terms equivalent to developed nations and reach the literacy rate, longevity, sanitation, maternal and child mortality, nutrition intake, and so on on par with developed nations and these goals are also included in the SDGs of the United Nations to 2030.

13.2.5.1 Vision 2041

What is in it and what difference will Vision 2041 make against the backdrop of Vision 2021? The daughter of Bangabandhu, Sheikh Hasina, by following her father, will make Bangladesh a middle-income nation by 2031 and she has been working tirelessly to transform the nation into a developed one by 2041. Against this backdrop, on 16 March 2018, on Bangabandhu's 99th birth anniversary,

Table 13.8 Changes in Major Indicators for Bangladesh Over the Vision 2021 Period: 2000–2020

Indicators	*2000*	*2020*
GDP in USD (billion)	33	300
Growth rate (%)	5	7.8
Income (P/C USD)	378	2,100 2,500 (2021)
Inflation Rate (%)	10	6.5
Literacy Rate (%)	49	76
Longevity (years)	60	72

Source: Hossain et al. (2022).

Bangladesh progressed to become a developing country from a least developed nation. Bangladesh is recognized all over the world as a 'Role Model of Development' at present. Given the growth and development over last ten years (2009–2019), finally the nation found momentum and Hon Sheikh Hasina's Vision 2041 will be a reality. Bangabandhu's dream of creating a 'Golden Bengal' would be a reality too, long before Bangladesh celebrates its centenary year of birth, a nation created by its Father of the Nation Bangabandhu Sheikh Mujibur Rahman at the expense of 3 million lives and 200,000 women lost their dignity at the hands of enemy forces and their collaborators during the nine months of liberation war in 1971.

Table 13.8 presents that the Bangladesh economy was doing extraordinarily well during Vision 2021. The GDP had increased from 33 billion in 2000 to 300 billion in 2020. The growth rate reached to 7.8 per cent in 2021 from 5 per cent in 2000. Income per capita in USD increased from only 378 to 2,100 in 2020. The planning commission has recently claimed income per capita reached USD 2,500 in 2021.

The inflation rate dropped from 10 per cent in 2000 to only 6.5 per cent in 2020. The literacy rate reached 90 per cent and longevity was found to be 72 years in 2020. This is indeed phenomenal progress over a 20-year period.

13.3 Responsible Future Research

13.3.1 Rural Enterprise Development: A Pillar for Sustainable Growth and Development

The massive development in information and communication technology, together with economic reforms in the developing nations over the last two decades, have made responsible future research more urgent and it is certainly challenging. Having said this, the new opportunities for the responsible future research in Bangladesh are wide. It is now clear that almost all developing nations of Asia have been achieving high to moderate growth over the last two decades (2000–2020), thanks to economic globalization and the information revolution, which have created more opportunities for trade in these nations. The COVID-19 pandemic, however, put a break in the momentum of economic globalization. Now, the Ukraine-Russia war certainly makes the future of trade expansion of nations uncertain again. Thus, now the time is right to identify new areas of research with a view to address the development challenges of the 21st century, which is also known as the Asian century. The time has arrived to deliver constructive policy directions to sustain growth momentum under difficult and uncertain conditions not only in developing nations, but in more developed nations too.

Having said that, let us provide a brief background of the Asian prosperity or so-called Asian century in which Bangladesh's participation was not guaranteed in 2000 (Hossain et al., 2013). As one knows, the 19th century was regarded as the British century, the 20th was a North American century, and now the 21st is called the Asian century. This name calling began in 1985 by the US Senate Committee on Foreign Relations hearing of the United States, led by Senator John Kerry. In more recent years Australian PM Julia Gillard established a committee in 2011, led by former Treasury Secretary Dr Ken Henry, to produce a White Paper on the Asian century. The White Paper was released in October 2012. However, the front runner in studying this phenomenon is the Asian Development Bank, which published a report entitled, "Asia 2050-Realizing the Asian Century" in June 2011.

The ADB emphasized that Asia's rise this century would be led by seven countries: India, China, Indonesia, Japan, Korea, Malaysia, and Thailand. In 2010, these seven economies had a total population of 3.1 billion (78 per cent of Asia) and a GDP of USD14.2 trillion. But by 2050, these economies alone will account for 45 per cent of the global GDP. Thus, under the Asian century scenario, Asia's GDP would rise to USD174 trillion and account for 51 per cent of the global output compared to the present 30 per cent approximately. Based on Purchasing Power Parity (PPP), GDP per capita income of Asia would also rise to USD45,800 in 2050, compared to the global average of USD 36,000. The forecast was global economic activity would be shifting towards Asia and contribute to half of the global trade and investment. About 3 billion more Asians would enjoy a prosperous standard of living, the same as the present-day Europeans. This prediction in post–COVID-19 pandemic time has certainly been put on the back burner. This was not the first time such an optimistic view about Asia was formed by global institutions. For example, the World Bank in its East Asia Miracle book was very optimistic about the newly industrialized nations in the early 1990s. In 2002, an ADB study revisited the East Asian Miracle and concluded that, "the future is not going to be a replay of the past".

Prior to all this drama taking place on the Asian stage, a Nobel laureate in economics in 1974 (later, in dramatic fashion, refused the prize), a Swedish development economist wrote a bestseller called, "Asian Drama: An inquiry into the poverty of nations" in 1968. In the 1970s and 1980s, this was a must-read volume for the students of development studies worldwide. Professor Gunner Myrdal was also instrumental in providing policy alternatives to Scandinavian nations to adopt a social welfare led growth model for sustainable development. As a result, these nations have been enjoying a long "growth with equity" era over the last half a century. What did Myrdal have in mind for Asia? He was very pessimistic indeed and emphasized Asia was plagued by overpopulation, corrupt regimes, and poverty; and risked being failed states. It was too painful for Asian leaders. If one goes back to pre-1968 Asia, was Myrdal wrong? Absolutely not. With all the miracles and Asian century business, Asia indeed remains overpopulated, having corrupt regimes, and of course, suffers from hunger and poverty in many parts. In the future research, given COVID-19 and the Ukraine-Russia war, one should address this hypothesis, taking the achievements and non-achievements during the initial two decades of the 21st century. Unlike Myrdal's time, Asia is now enjoying an information technology revolution; it has been in two financial crises over ten years, including the Global Financial Crisis (GFC) and of course, the added burden of global warming and climate change. Indeed, this is a time to revisit the Asian drama with a view to realize or otherwise, of the Asian prosperity or so-called Asian century.

13.3.2 Bangladesh Context

To defy Myrdal, it is important that Bangladesh, like the rest of Asia, keeps growing sustainably, as analyzed by several chapters in this volume. In doing so, the nations would need new policy initiatives under changed conditions. Moreover, the present era of global warming induced extreme weather conditions that would be a major hurdle (Hossain et al., 2020). As a result, policy intervention in new areas is needed, with a view to bringing innovative and effective reforms in the present global hostile environment financially and environmentally.

First, what immediately comes to mind is identifying the responsible future issues, such as:

i Sustainable development of rural enterprise: taking extra care of the livelihoods of the coastal population and social safety net issues
ii Ensuring additional resources for the vast rural population from the public sector

Second, investing future policy reforms that matter to rural enterprise development:

iii Introduction of productive agriculture, rural industry, and micro business
iv Public health and sanitation
v No restriction on migration and movement of people from rural to urban areas
vi Decentralization of administration and speedy alleviation of all types of poverty
vii Keeping sustainable momentum in growth matters.

References

Hossain, Moazzem, Ahmed, Q. K. and Islam, M. M. (2022). Research Paper on Bangladesh's Vision 2041, presented in a Research seminar of Griffith Asia Institute, Nathan campus on 13 October.

Hossain, Moazzem, Ahmad, Q. K. and Islam, M. M., Eds. (2020). *Climate Adaptation for a Sustainable Economy: Lessons from Bangladesh, An Emerging Tiger of Asia*, Nova Science Publishers, NY.

Hossain, Moazzem and Hoque, Samsul (2016). Rhetorical bottomless basket case versus Bangladesh's success with the MDGs, in *Outlook 2016*, World Association of Sustainable Development, Brighton, Sussex.

Hossain, Moazzem and Howard, P. (2014). The sanitation access to developing Asia: India's performance over 2001 and 2011, *World Journal of Science, Technology and Sustainable*, World Association of Sustainable Development Journal, Brighton, Sussex.

Hossain, Moazzem, Sarker, T. and McIntosh, M. (eds.), (2013). *The Asian Century, Sustainable Growth and Climate Change: Responsible Futures Matter*, Edward Elgar, Cheltenham and Northampton, pp. 292.

Hossain, Moazzem, Kathuria, R. and Islam, I. (2010). *South Asian Economic Development, 2 nd Edition*, Routledge, London and New York, pp. 288.

Hossain, Moazzem, Nabi, Nurun and Islam, I. Eds. (2003). *Bangladesh's Vision 2021: Rhetoric or Reality*, University Press Limited, Dhaka.

Prothom Alo (2022). Padma Bridge Opening on 25 June, Report, Daily Newspaper published from Dhaka.

Selvanathan, E. A. (2018). Readymade Garments: Long term prospects for Bangladesh, Conference paper, Pathways to a Sustainable Economy, Vision 2041 Agenda for Bangladesh, PKSF, Dhaka, October 30–31.

Short, P., Hossain, M., and Khan, A. Eds. (2017). *South-South Migration: Emerging patterns, Opportunities and Risks*, Routledge, Singapore and London, pp. 204.

Shah, J. (2015). *Four crore people are under poverty, Prothom Alo*, Daily Newspaper, Dhaka.

Index